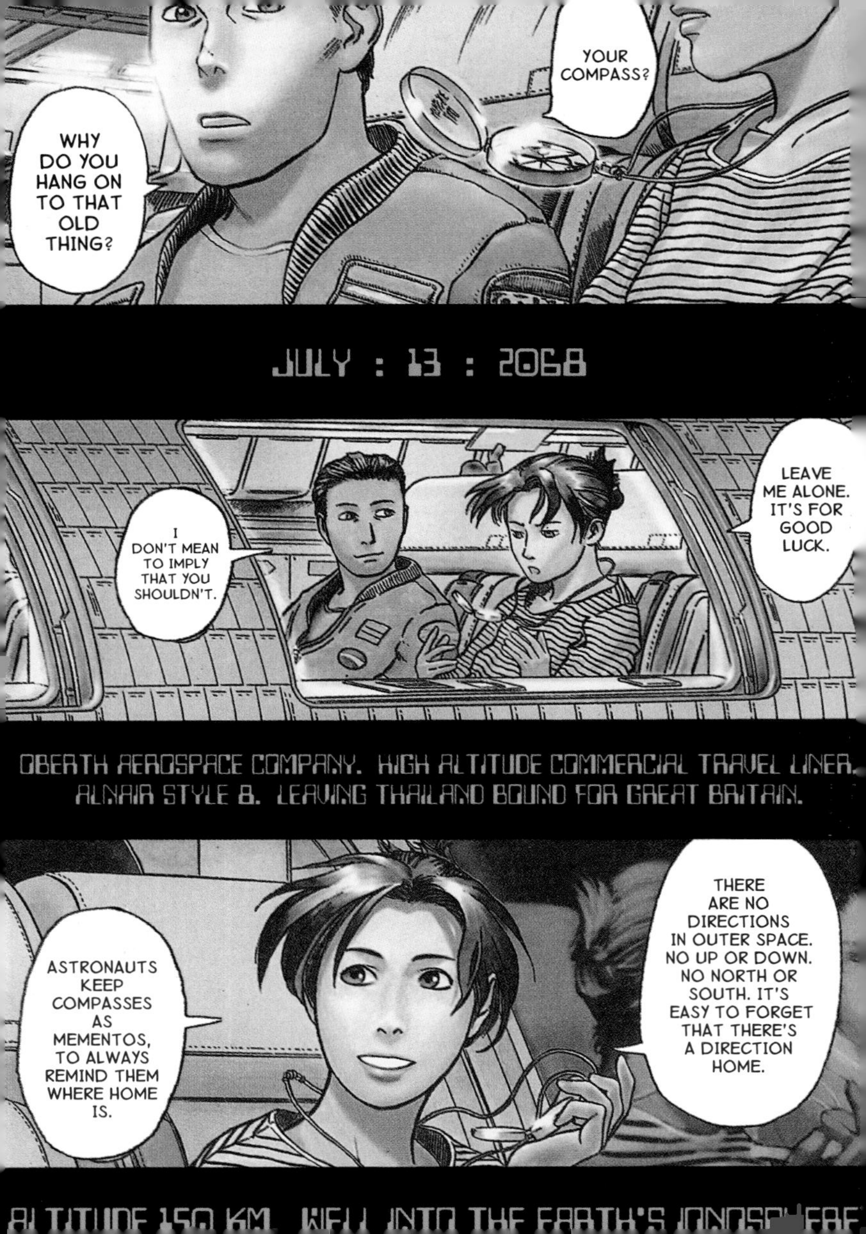
YOUR COMPASS?
WHY DO YOU HANG ON TO THAT OLD THING?
JULY : 13 : 2068
LEAVE ME ALONE. IT'S FOR GOOD LUCK.
I DON'T MEAN TO IMPLY THAT YOU SHOULDN'T.
OBERTH AEROSPACE COMPANY. HIGH ALTITUDE COMMERCIAL TRAVEL LINER. ALNAIR STYLE 8. LEAVING THAILAND BOUND FOR GREAT BRITAIN.
THERE ARE NO DIRECTIONS IN OUTER SPACE. NO UP OR DOWN. NO NORTH OR SOUTH. IT'S EASY TO FORGET THAT THERE'S A DIRECTION HOME.
ASTRONAUTS KEEP COMPASSES AS MEMENTOS, TO ALWAYS REMIND THEM WHERE HOME IS.
ALTITUDE 150 KM. WELL INTO THE EARTH'S IONOSPHERE

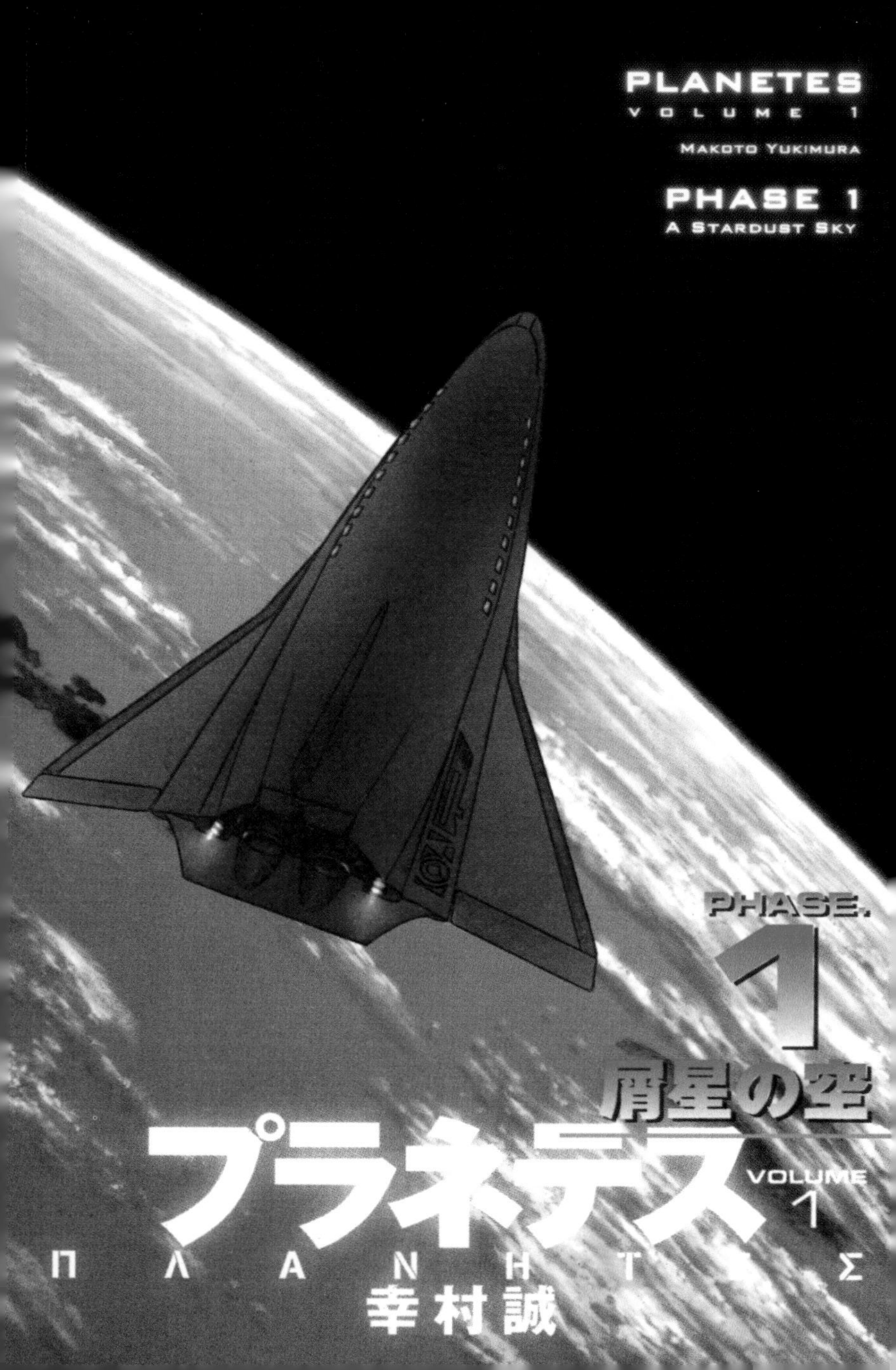
PLANETES
VOLUME 1
MAKOTO YUKIMURA
PHASE 1
A STARDUST SKY
PHASE.
1
屑星の空
プラネテス
VOLUME
1
Π Λ Α Ν Η Τ Ε Σ
幸村誠

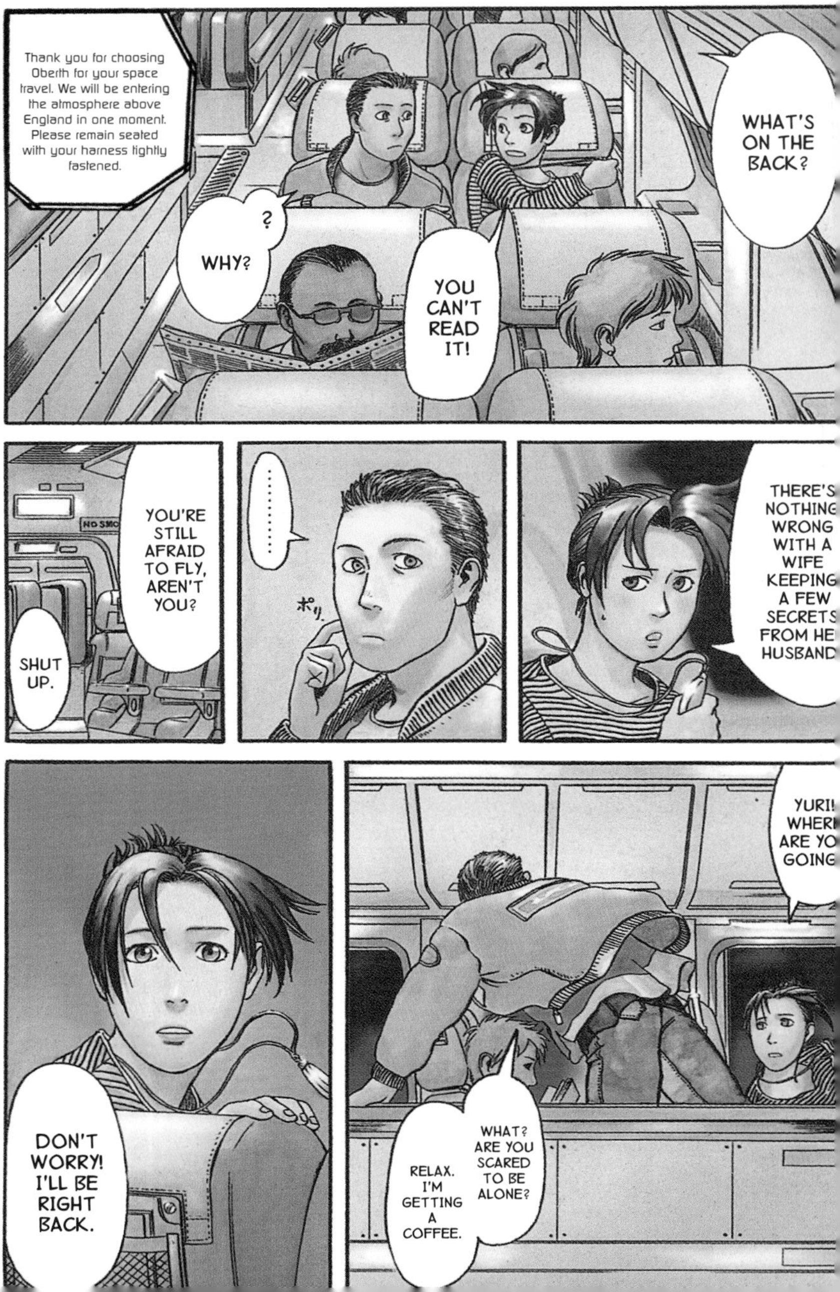
WHAT'S ON THE BACK?
Thank you for choosing Oberth for your space travel. We will be entering the atmosphere above England in one moment. Please remain seated with your harness tightly fastened.
? WHY?
YOU CAN'T READ IT!
THERE'S NOTHING WRONG WITH A WIFE KEEPING A FEW SECRETS FROM HE HUSBAND
......
ポリ
YOU'RE STILL AFRAID TO FLY, AREN'T YOU?
SHUT UP.
YURI! WHER ARE YO GOING
WHAT? ARE YOU SCARED TO BE ALONE?
RELAX. I'M GETTING A COFFEE.
DON'T WORRY! I'LL BE RIGHT BACK.

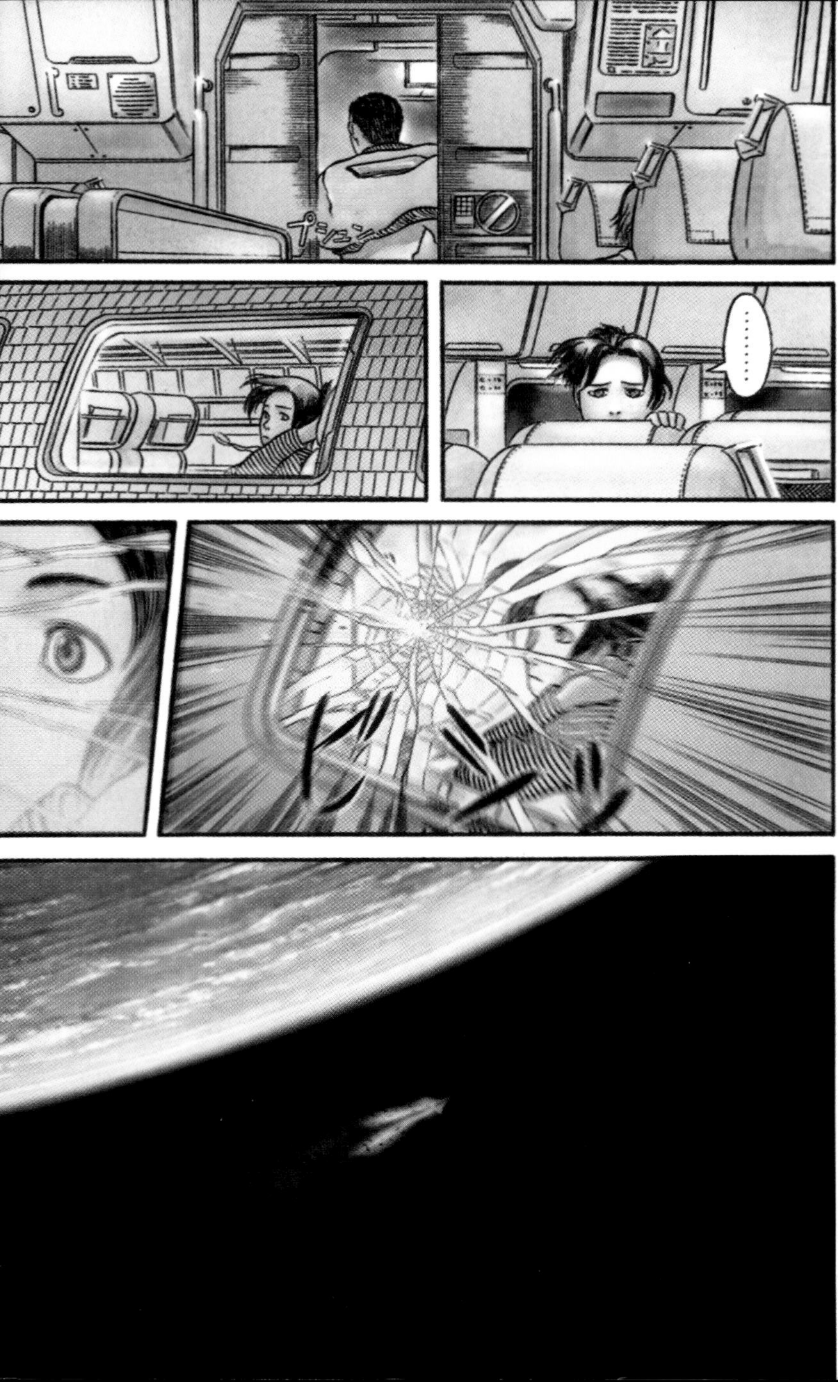

プシュン
……

PLANETES

VOL. 1

BY
MAKOTO YUKIMURA

TOKYOPOP®
LOS ANGELES • TOKYO • LONDON

ALSO AVAILABLE FROM TOKYOPOP®

MANGA

For more information visit www.TOKYOPOP.com

*INDICATES 100% AUTHENTIC MANGA (RIGHT-TO-LEFT FORMAT)

CINE-MANGA™

NOVELS

TOKYOPOP KIDS

ART BOOKS

ANIME GUIDES

080503

Translator - Yuki Nakamura
English Adaptation - Anna Wenger
Copy Editors - Aaron Sparrow & Jodi Bryson
Retouch and Lettering - Jesse Fernley
Cover Layout - Gary Shum

Editor - Luis Reyes
Managing Editor - Jill Freshney
Production Coordinator - Antonio DePietro
Production Manager - Jennifer Miller
Art Director - Matt Alford
Editorial Director - Jeremy Ross
VP of Production - Ron Klamert
President & C.O.O. - John Parker
Publisher & C.E.O. - Stuart Levy

Email: editor@TOKYOPOP.com
Come visit us online at www.TOKYOPOP.com

A 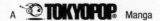 Manga

TOKYOPOP Inc.
5900 Wilshire Blvd. Suite 2000
Los Angeles, CA 90036

ISBN: 1-59182-262-9

First TOKYOPOP printing: October 2003

10 9 8 7 6 5 4 3 2 1
Printed in the USA

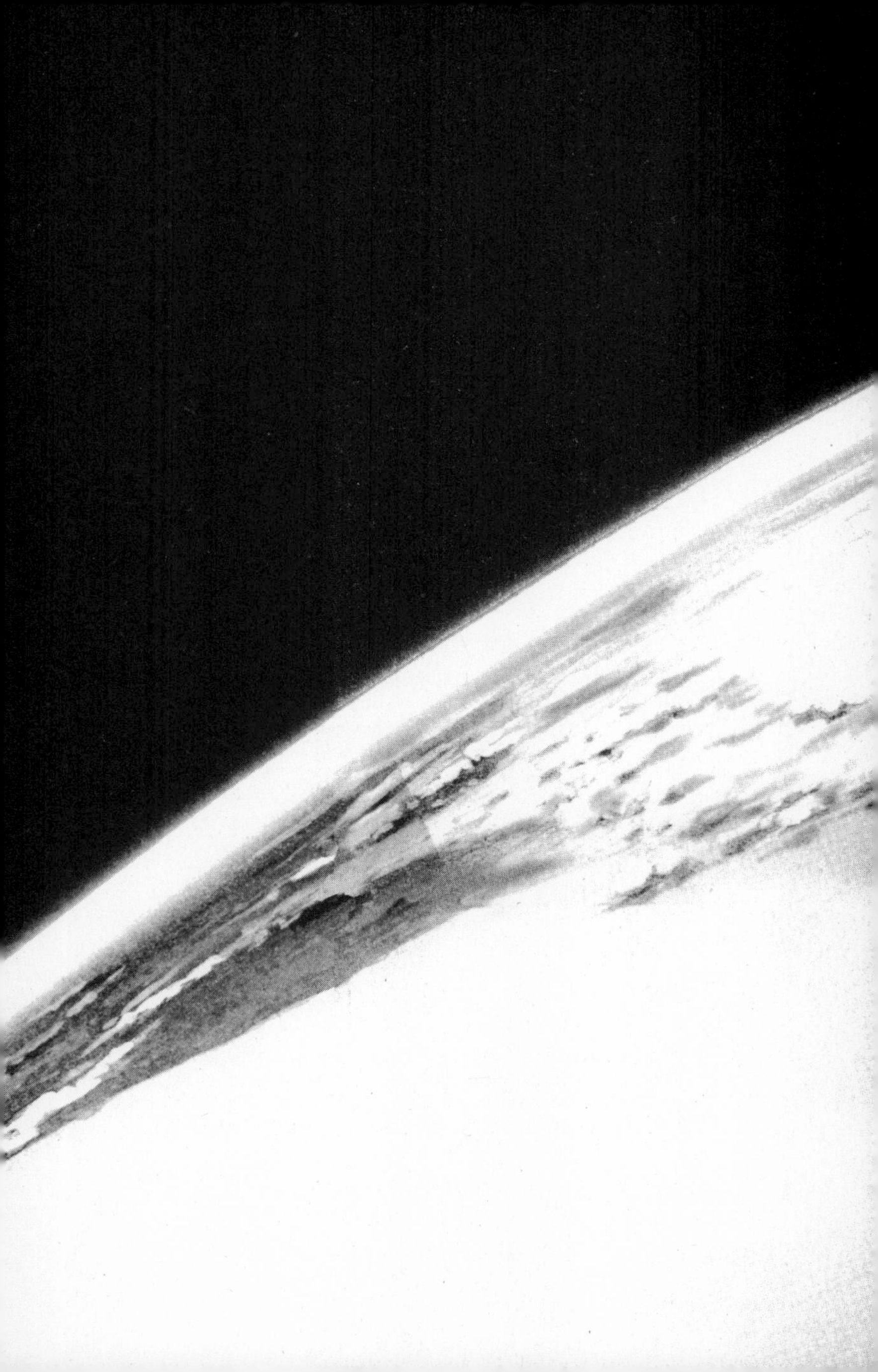

The human race has made a habit of contaminating the Earth with its refuse, and that habit hasn't waned now as mankind pushes into space. However, sanitation work on terra firma hardly compares to the task in zero gravity, where garbage includes disused satellites, discharged fuel canisters, all manner of corrosive and explosive material, and other bits of junk and debris that trickles off the glorious ships now poised to tackle the new frontier. It is dangerous, lack-luster work, but someone's got to do it.

It is the year 2074. Hachirota Hoshino serves as the rookie debris collector on a semi-dilapidated DS-12 sanitation/cargo ship. Hachimaki—as he has become known because of the headband he wears constantly—has ambitions of being a rich and famous astronaut, destined to explore Sol beyond the Asteroid Belt and to usher in a new age for humanity. For now, however, he sweeps up the terrestrial orbit along with this team-mates, Fee and Yuri.

PLANETES 1

CONTENTS

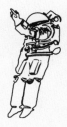

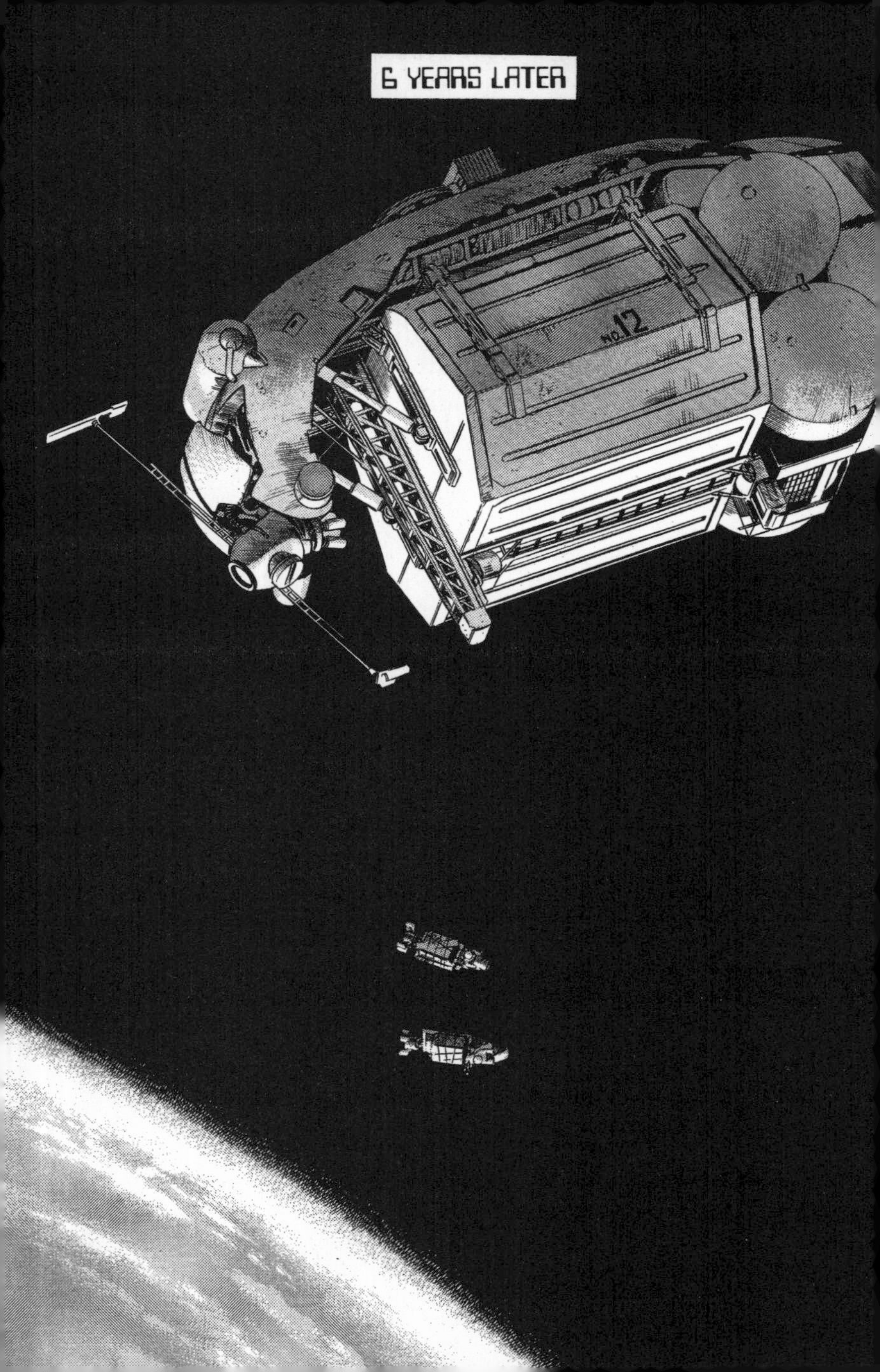
6 YEARS LATER
No. 12

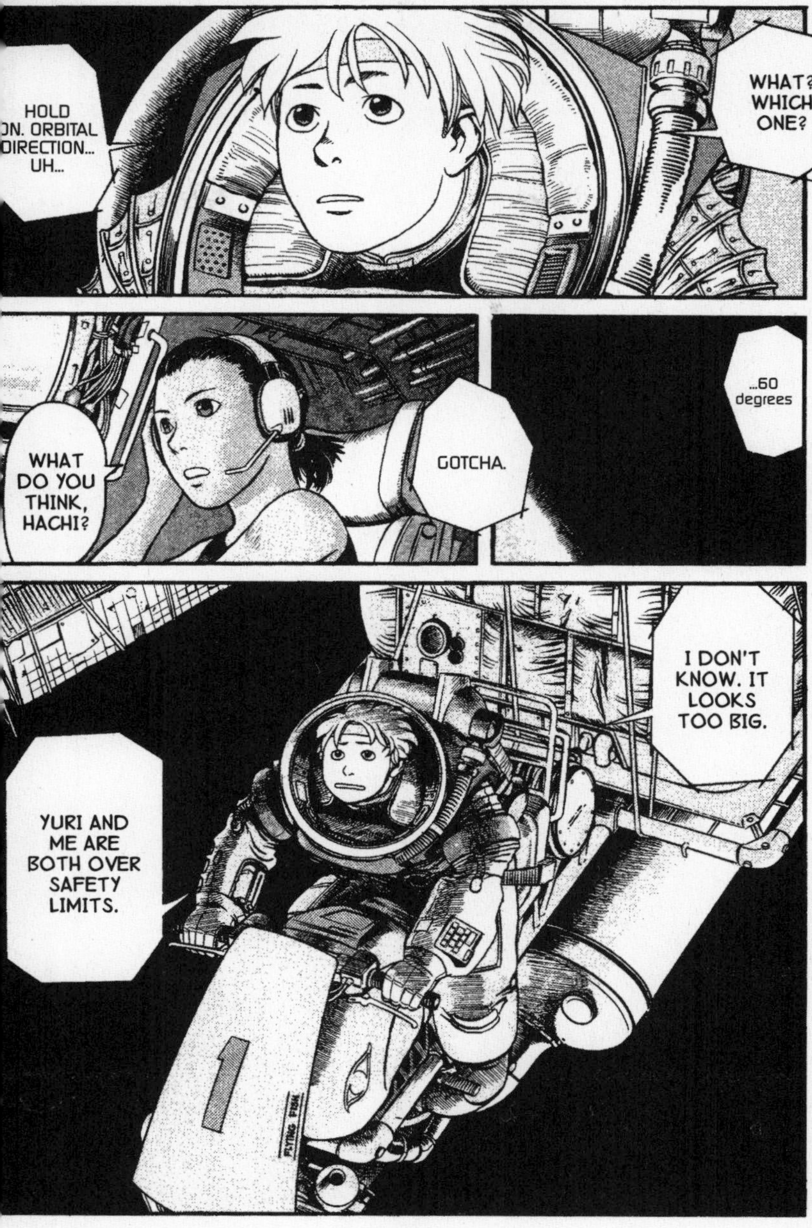

WHAT? WHICH ONE?
HOLD ON. ORBITAL DIRECTION... UH...
...60 degrees
GOTCHA.
WHAT DO YOU THINK, HACHI?
I DON'T KNOW. IT LOOKS TOO BIG.
YURI AND ME ARE BOTH OVER SAFETY LIMITS.

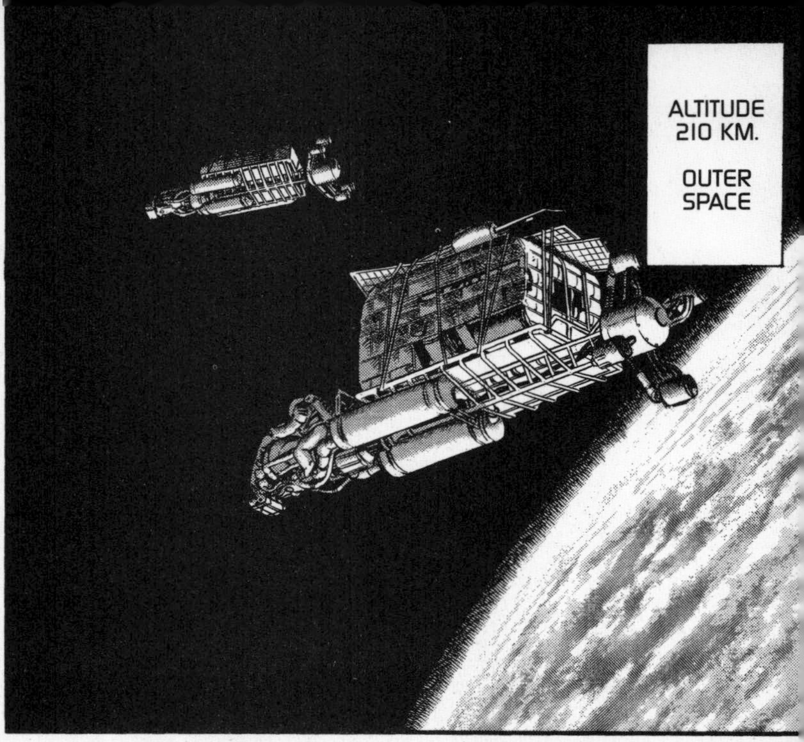
ALTITUDE 210 KM.
OUTER SPACE

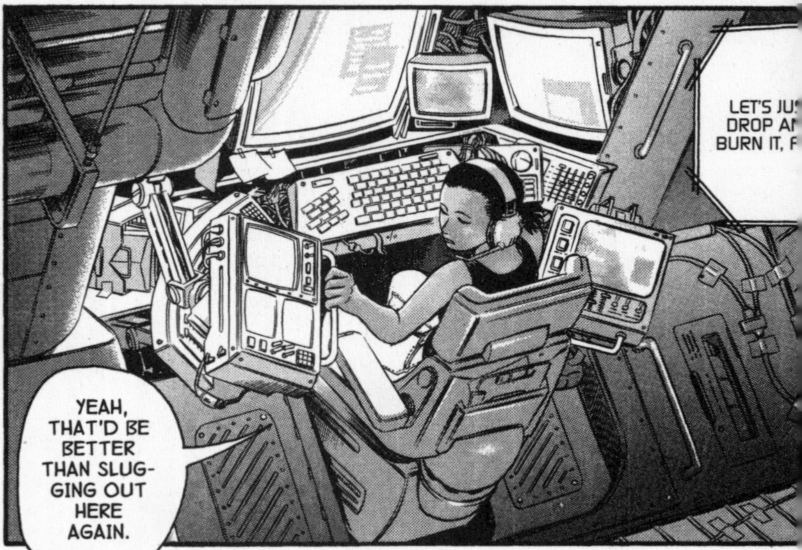
LET'S JU DROP A BURN IT, F
YEAH, THAT'D BE BETTER THAN SLUG-GING OUT HERE AGAIN.

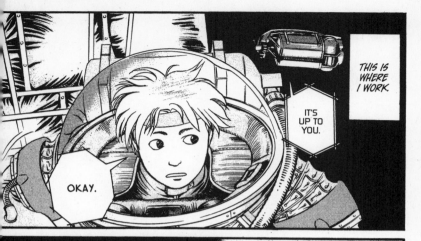

THIS IS WHERE I WORK.

IT'S UP TO YOU.

OKAY.

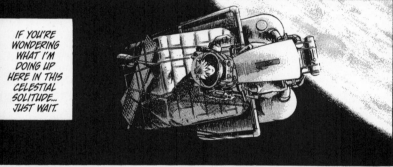

IF YOU'RE WONDERING WHAT I'M DOING UP HERE IN THIS CELESTIAL SOLITUDE... JUST WAIT.

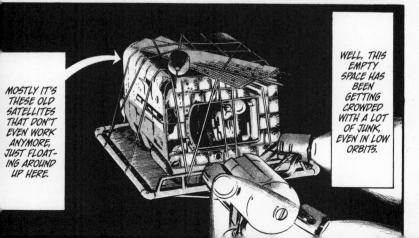

WELL, THIS EMPTY SPACE HAS BEEN GETTING CROWDED WITH A LOT OF JUNK, EVEN IN LOW ORBITS.

MOSTLY IT'S THESE OLD SATELLITES THAT DON'T EVEN WORK ANYMORE, JUST FLOATING AROUND UP HERE.

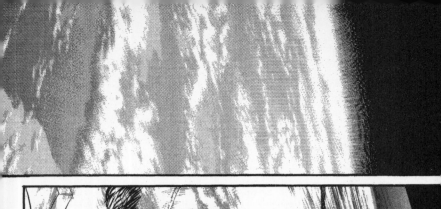

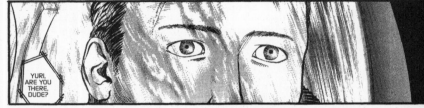

YURI,
ARE YOU
THERE,
DUDE?

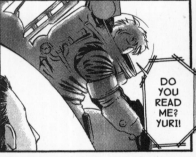

DO
YOU
READ
ME?
YURI!

HELLO?

YURI!

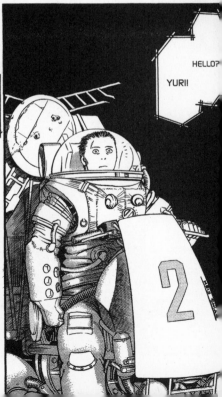

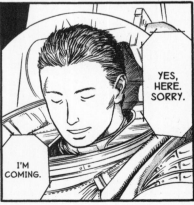

YES,
HERE.
SORRY.

I'M
COMING.

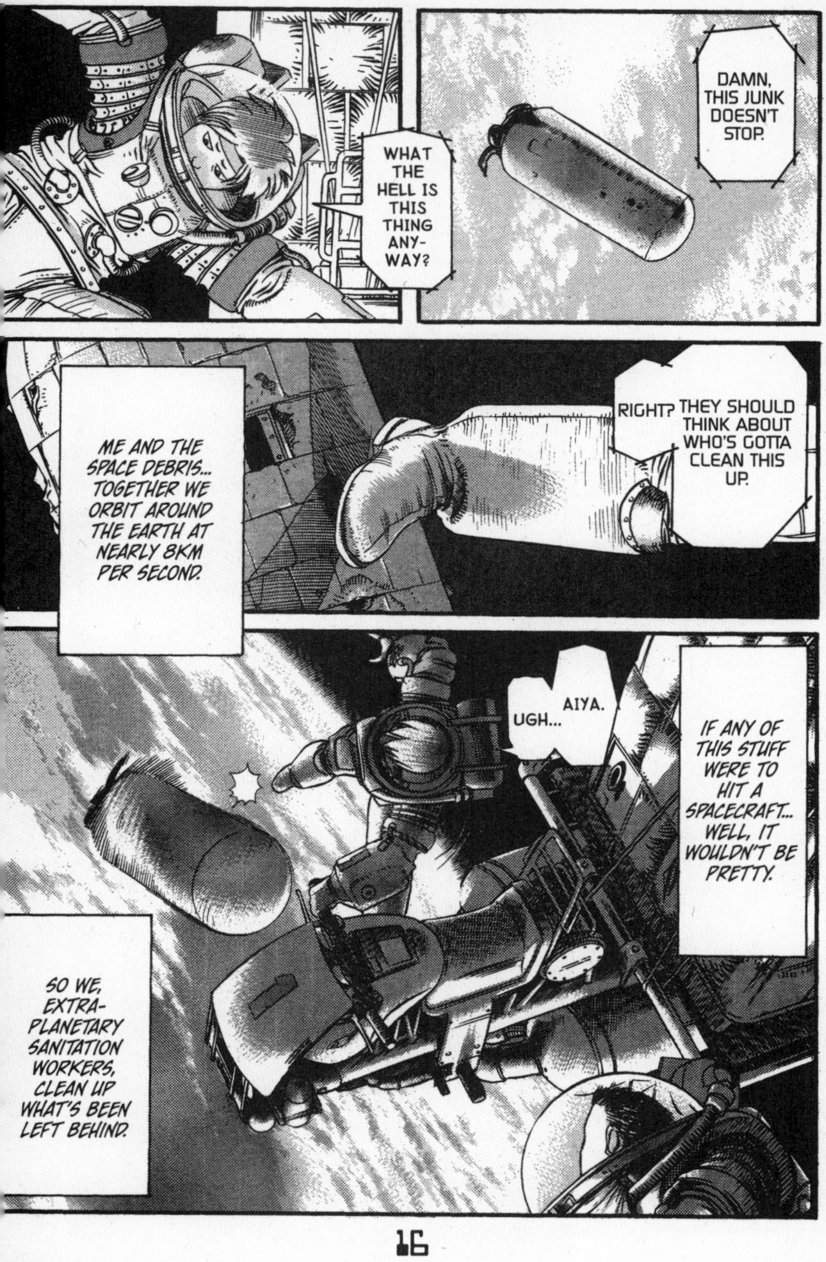
DAMN, THIS JUNK DOESN'T STOP.
WHAT THE HELL IS THIS THING ANY-WAY?
THEY SHOULD THINK ABOUT WHO'S GOTTA CLEAN THIS UP.
RIGHT?
ME AND THE SPACE DEBRIS... TOGETHER WE ORBIT AROUND THE EARTH AT NEARLY 8KM PER SECOND.
IF ANY OF THIS STUFF WERE TO HIT A SPACECRAFT... WELL, IT WOULDN'T BE PRETTY.
AIYA.
UGH...
SO WE, EXTRA-PLANETARY SANITATION WORKERS, CLEAN UP WHAT'S BEEN LEFT BEHIND.

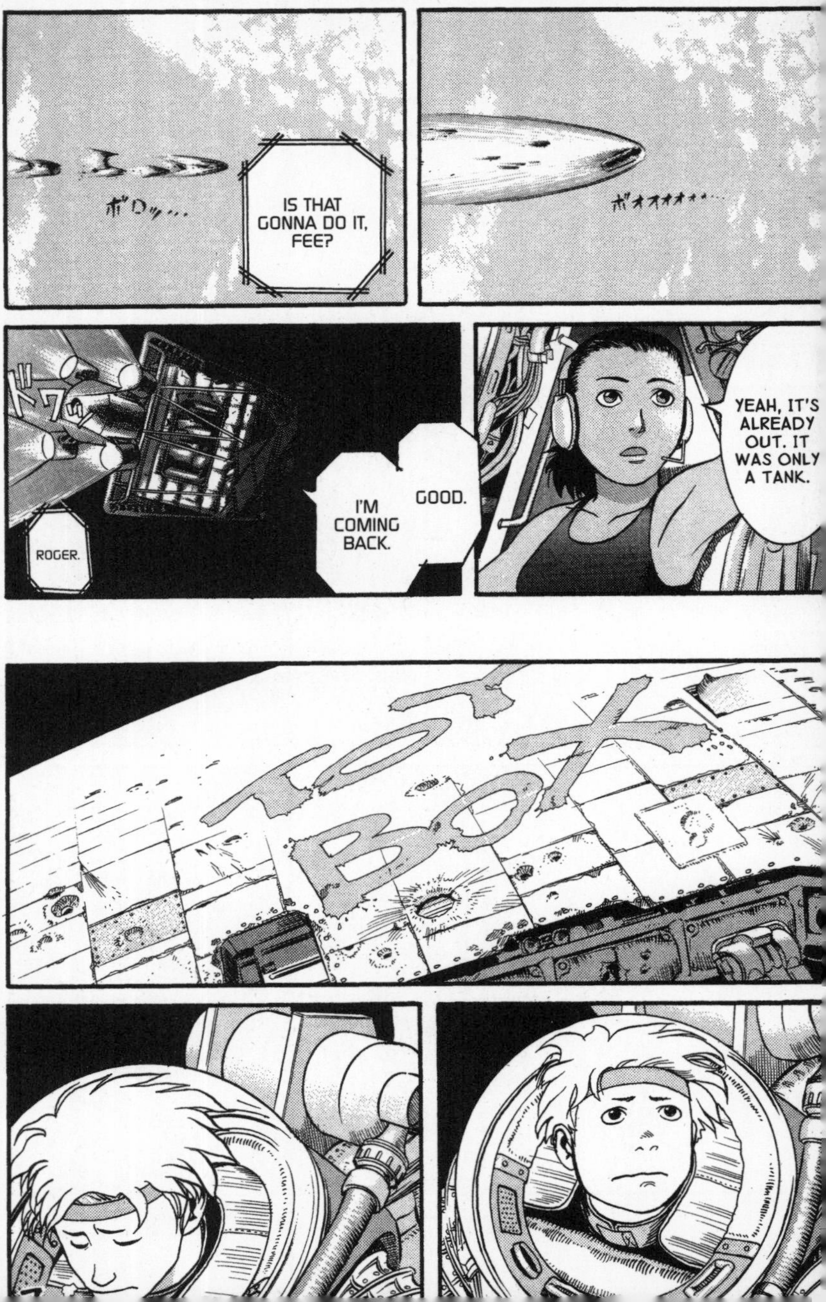
IS THAT GONNA DO IT, FEE?
YEAH, IT'S ALREADY OUT. IT WAS ONLY A TANK.
GOOD.
I'M COMING BACK.
ROGER.
TOY BOX

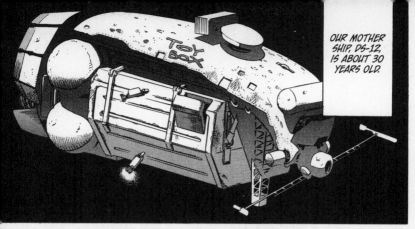

TOY BOX
OUR MOTHER SHIP, DS-12, IS ABOUT 30 YEARS OLD.
IT'S A HUNK OF JUNK. WE KNOW.
ALL THE DEBRIS HAULERS ARE.
WELCOME BACK.
ポイ。
I WARMED IT UP FOR YA.

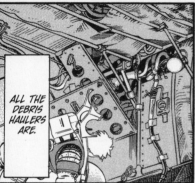

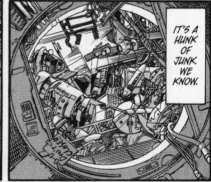

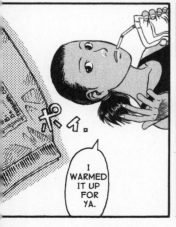

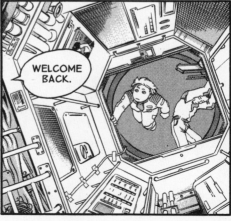

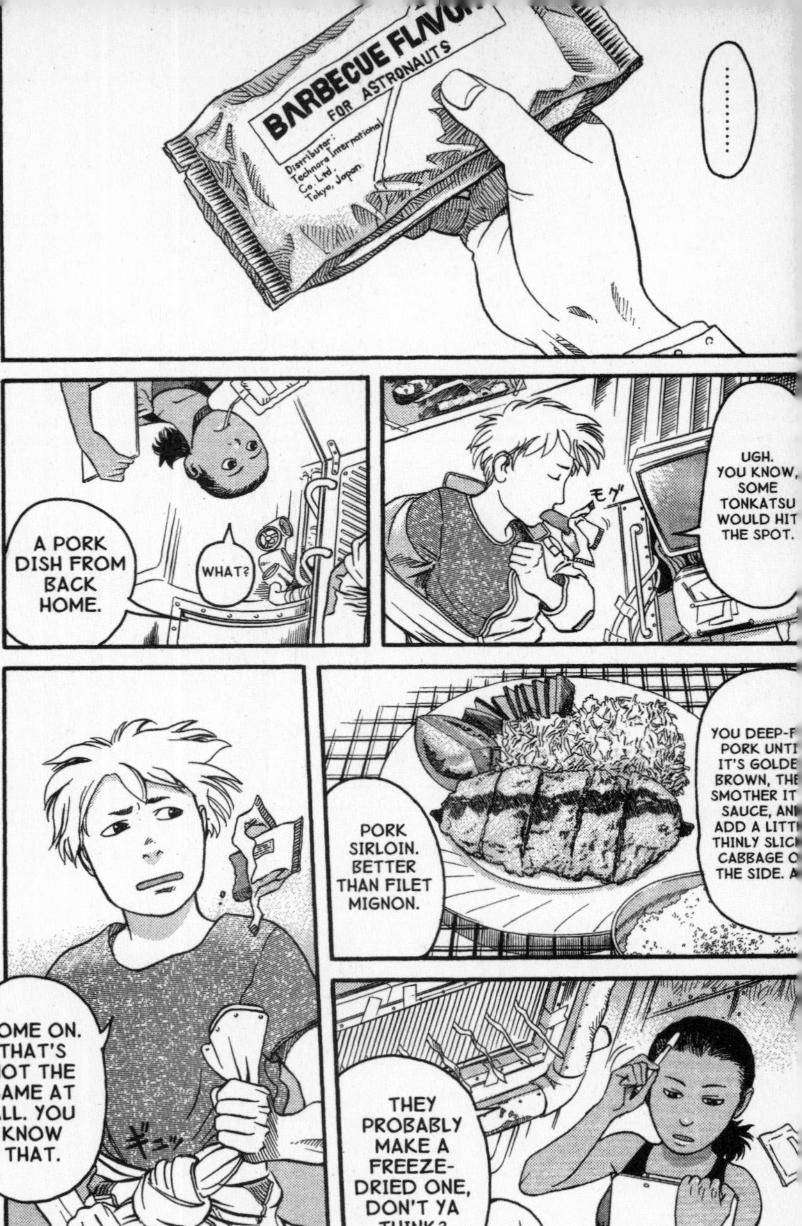
……
BARBECUE FLAVO
FOR ASTRONAUTS
Distributor: Technora International Co. Ltd. Tokyo, Japan
UGH. YOU KNOW, SOME TONKATSU WOULD HIT THE SPOT.
モグ
WHAT?
A PORK DISH FROM BACK HOME.
YOU DEEP-F PORK UNTI IT'S GOLDE BROWN, THE SMOTHER IT SAUCE, AN ADD A LITT THINLY SLIC CABBAGE O THE SIDE. A
PORK SIRLOIN. BETTER THAN FILET MIGNON.
THEY PROBABLY MAKE A FREEZE-DRIED ONE, DON'T YA THINK?
COME ON. THAT'S NOT THE SAME AT ALL. YOU KNOW THAT.
ギュッ

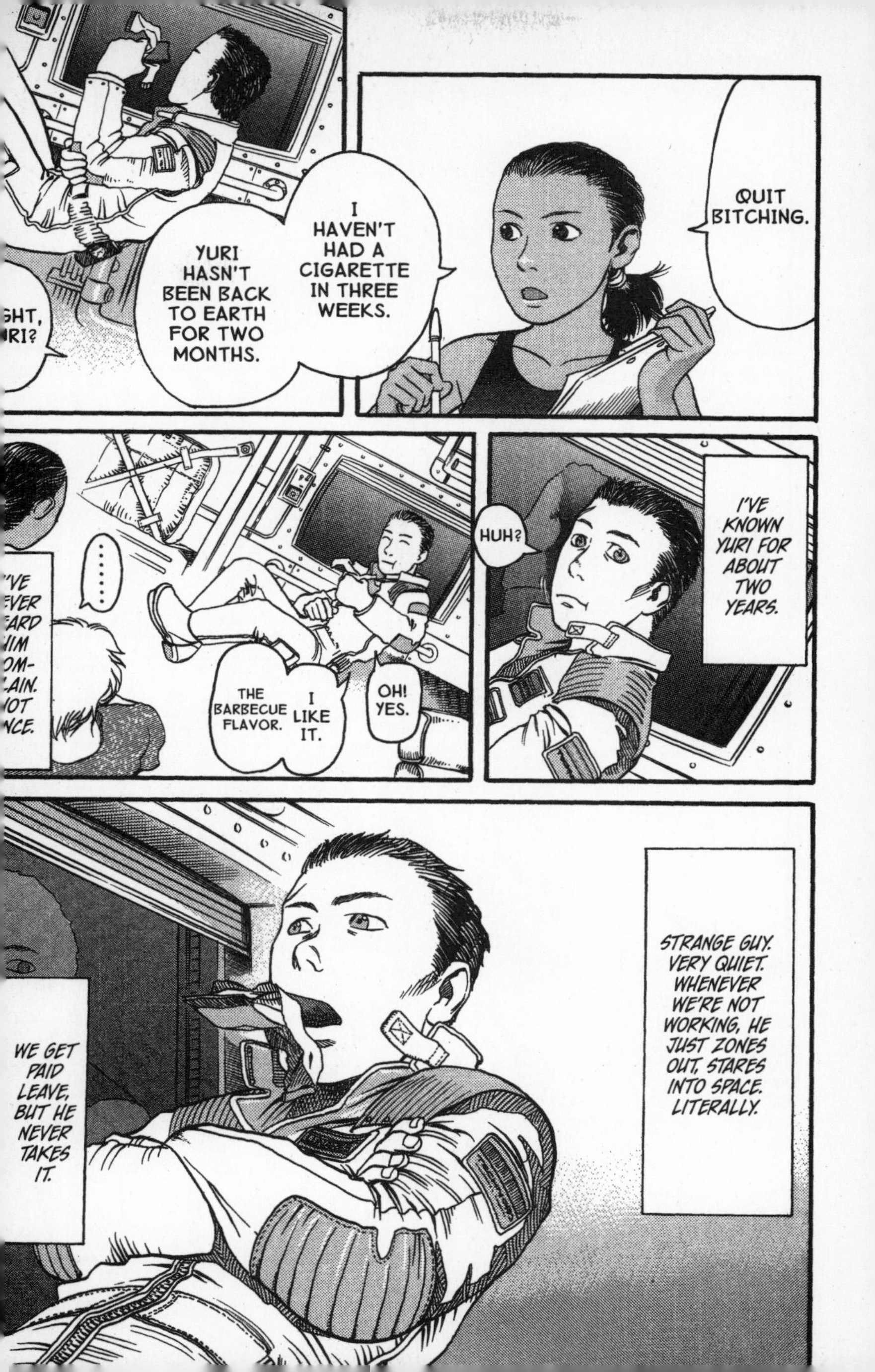
QUIT BITCHING.
I HAVEN'T HAD A CIGARETTE IN THREE WEEKS.
YURI HASN'T BEEN BACK TO EARTH FOR TWO MONTHS.
I'VE KNOWN YURI FOR ABOUT TWO YEARS.
HUH?
OH! YES.
I LIKE IT.
THE BARBECUE FLAVOR.
......
STRANGE GUY. VERY QUIET. WHENEVER WE'RE NOT WORKING, HE JUST ZONES OUT, STARES INTO SPACE. LITERALLY.
WE GET PAID LEAVE, BUT HE NEVER TAKES IT.

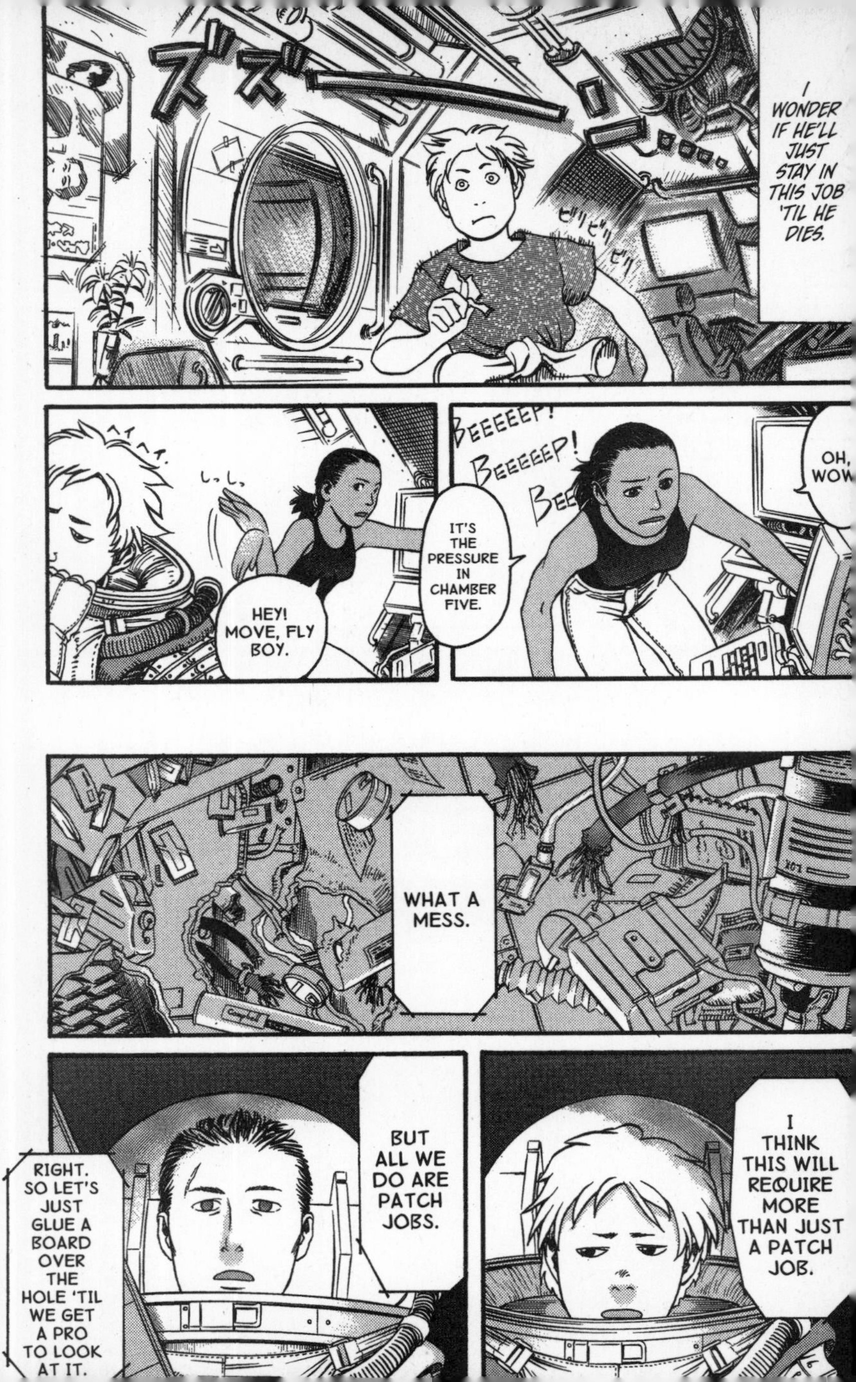
I WONDER IF HE'LL JUST STAY IN THIS JOB 'TIL HE DIES.
ズズー
ビリビリ
BEEEEEP!
BEEEEEP!
OH, WOW
IT'S THE PRESSURE IN CHAMBER FIVE.
ヘイヘイ
しっし
HEY! MOVE, FLY BOY.
WHAT A MESS.
I THINK THIS WILL REQUIRE MORE THAN JUST A PATCH JOB.
BUT ALL WE DO ARE PATCH JOBS.
RIGHT. SO LET'S JUST GLUE A BOARD OVER THE HOLE 'TIL WE GET A PRO TO LOOK AT IT.

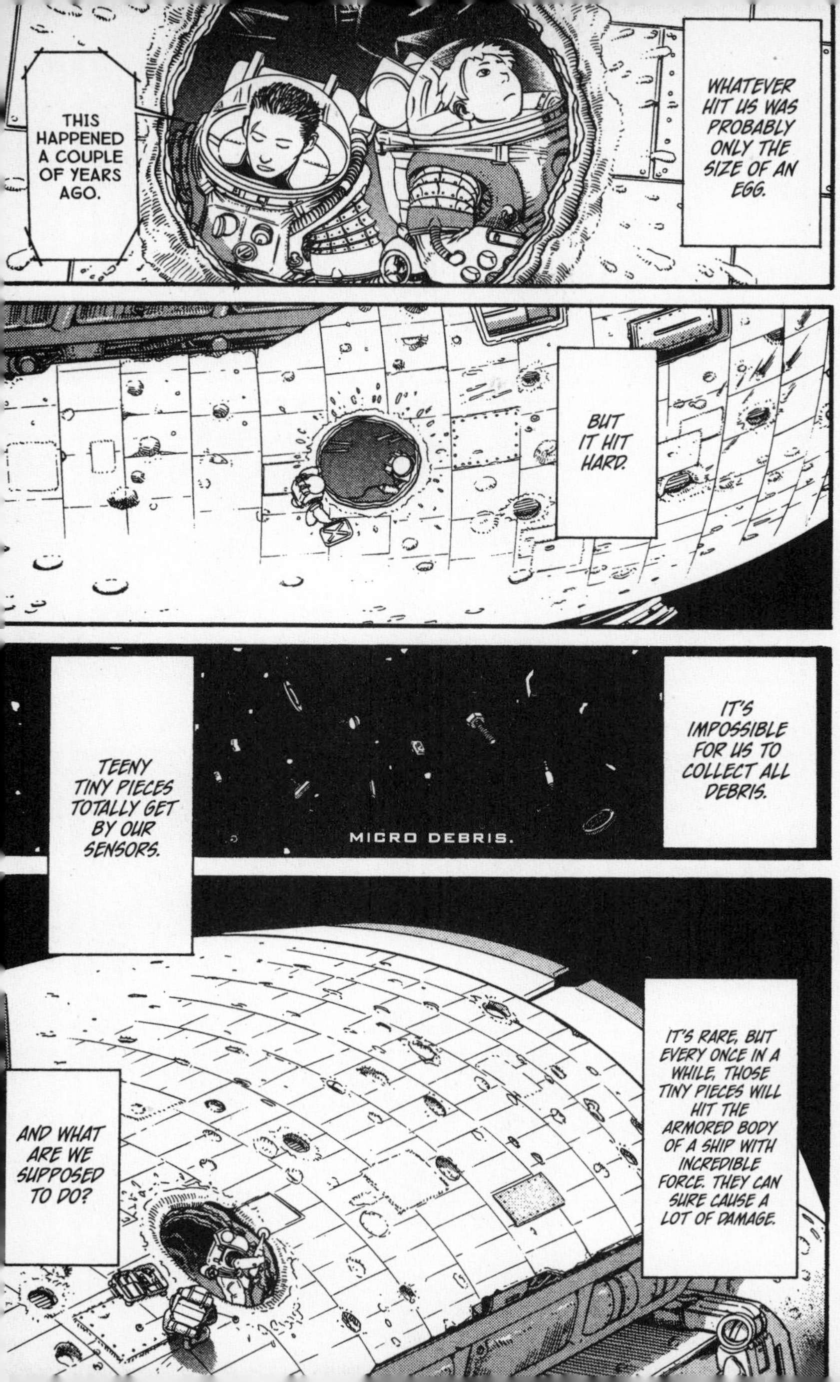
WHATEVER HIT US WAS PROBABLY ONLY THE SIZE OF AN EGG.
THIS HAPPENED A COUPLE OF YEARS AGO.
BUT IT HIT HARD.
IT'S IMPOSSIBLE FOR US TO COLLECT ALL DEBRIS.
TEENY TINY PIECES TOTALLY GET BY OUR SENSORS.
MICRO DEBRIS.
IT'S RARE, BUT EVERY ONCE IN A WHILE, THOSE TINY PIECES WILL HIT THE ARMORED BODY OF A SHIP WITH INCREDIBLE FORCE. THEY CAN SURE CAUSE A LOT OF DAMAGE.
AND WHAT ARE WE SUPPOSED TO DO?

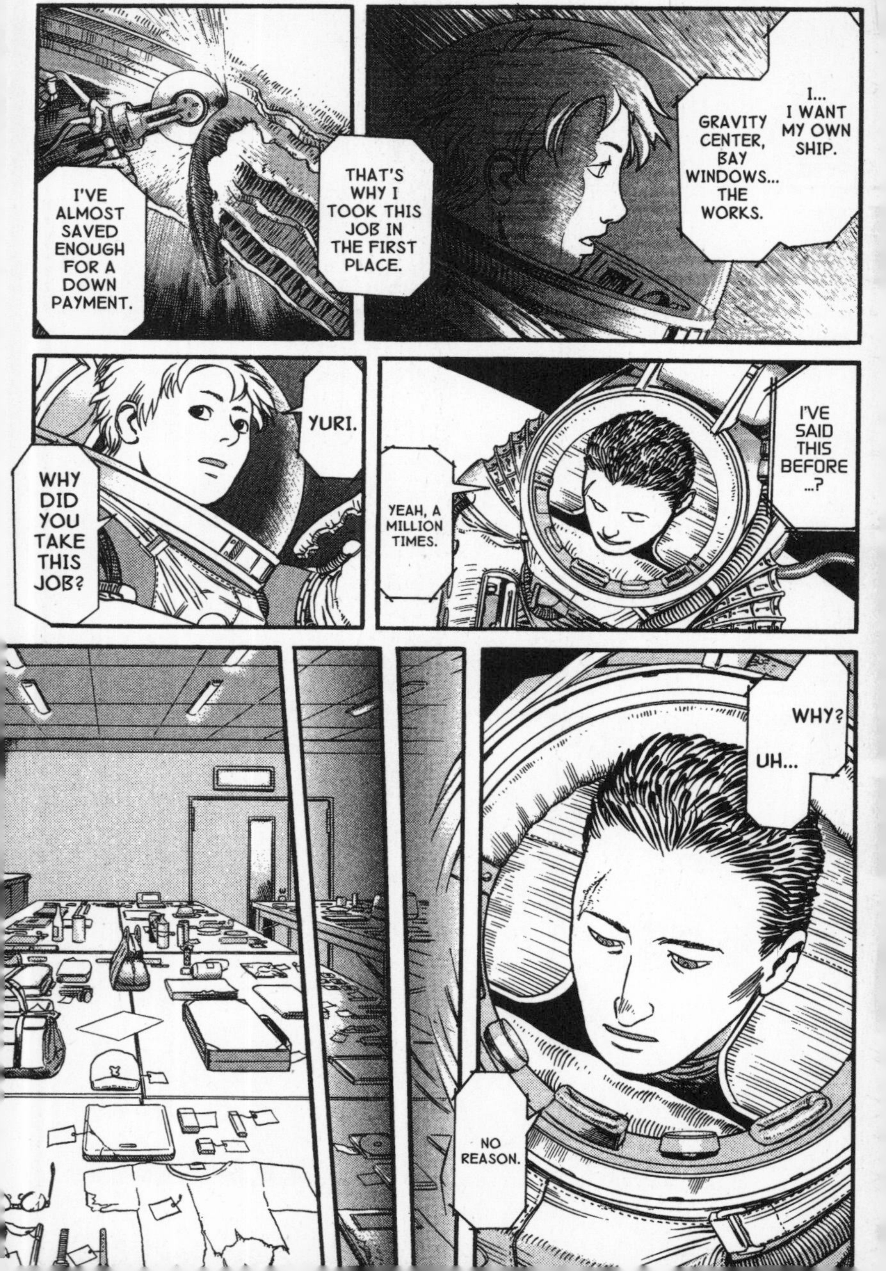
I... I WANT MY OWN SHIP.
GRAVITY CENTER, BAY WINDOWS... THE WORKS.
THAT'S WHY I TOOK THIS JOB IN THE FIRST PLACE.
I'VE ALMOST SAVED ENOUGH FOR A DOWN PAYMENT.
I'VE SAID THIS BEFORE ...?
YEAH, A MILLION TIMES.
YURI.
WHY DID YOU TAKE THIS JOB?
WHY?
UH...
NO REASON.

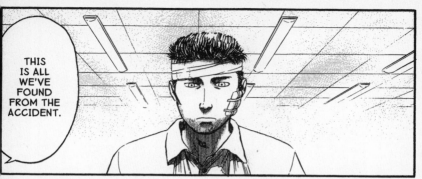

THIS IS ALL WE'VE FOUND FROM THE ACCIDENT.

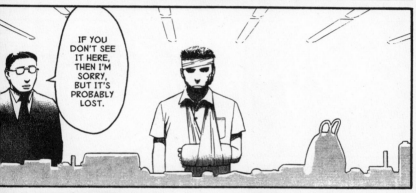

IF YOU DON'T SEE IT HERE, THEN I'M SORRY, BUT IT'S PROBABLY LOST.

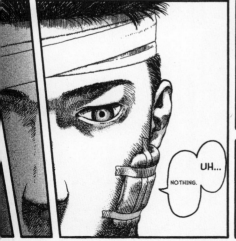

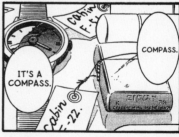

IT'S A COMPASS.

COMPASS.

UH...

NOTHING.

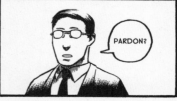

PARDON?

24

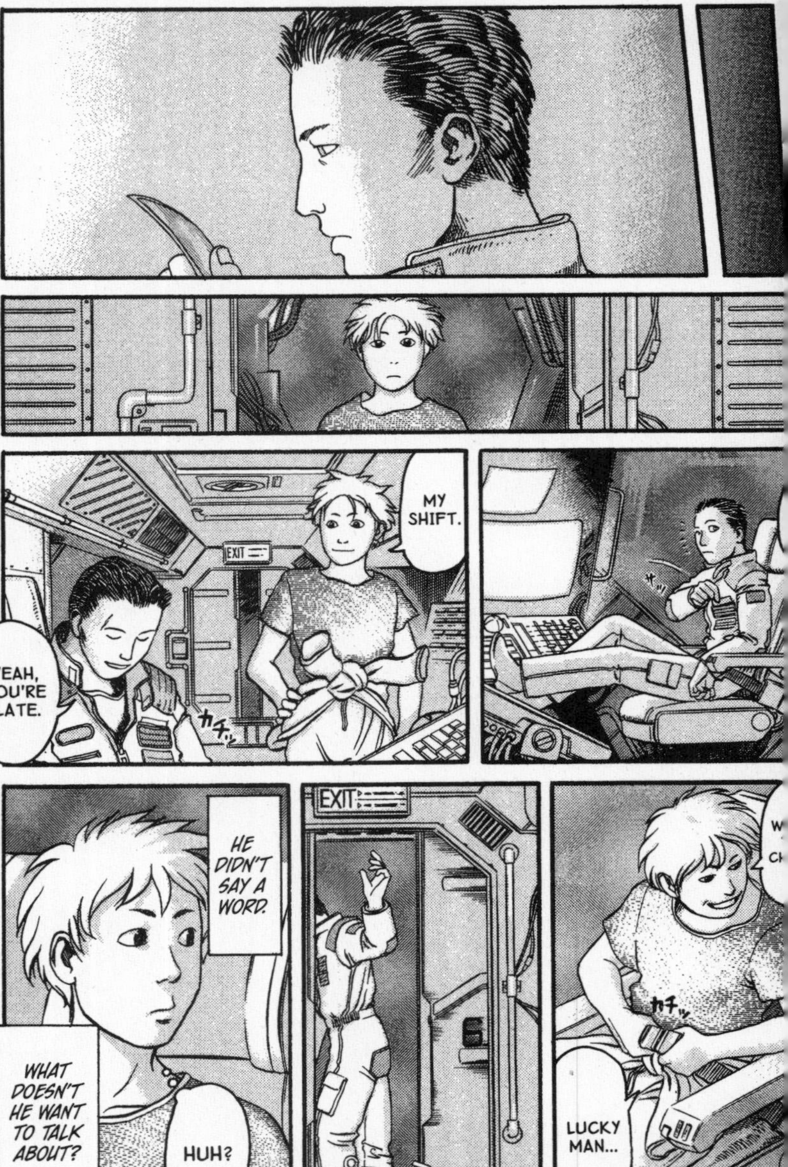
MY SHIFT.
YEAH, YOU'RE LATE.
カチッ
LUCKY MAN...
カチッ
HE DIDN'T SAY A WORD.
HUH?
WHAT DOESN'T HE WANT TO TALK ABOUT?

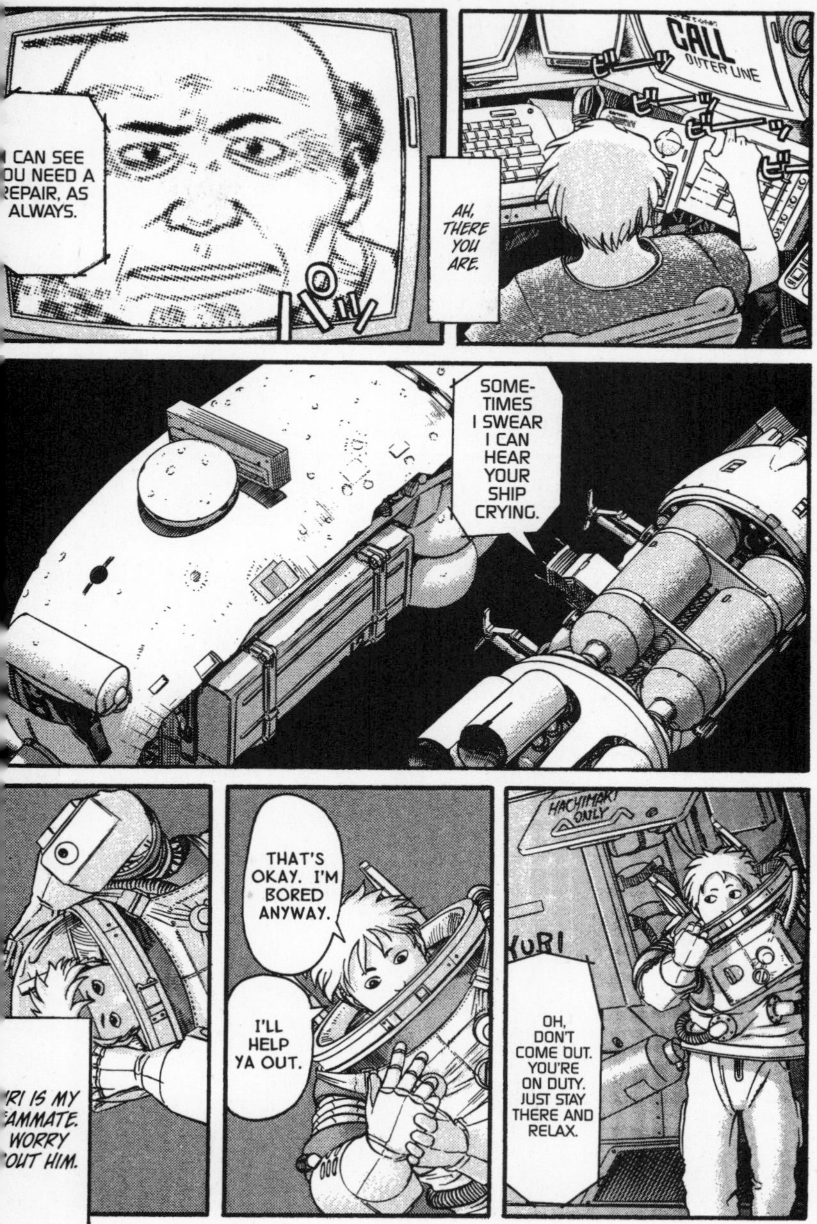
CALL
OUTER LINE
AH, THERE YOU ARE.
CAN SEE
OU NEED A
EPAIR, AS
ALWAYS.
SOMETIMES I SWEAR I CAN HEAR YOUR SHIP CRYING.
HACHIMAKI ONLY
YURI
OH, DON'T COME OUT. YOU'RE ON DUTY. JUST STAY THERE AND RELAX.
THAT'S OKAY. I'M BORED ANYWAY.
I'LL HELP YA OUT.
RI IS MY
AMMATE.
WORRY
OUT HIM.

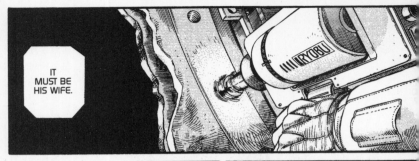

IT MUST BE HIS WIFE.
WIFE?
HE'S MARRIED?
HE WAS MARRIED. I THOUGHT YOU KNEW.
GET THE OTHER END.
WAS?
ABOUT SIX YEARS AGO.
WAY BEFORE YOU GOT HERE.

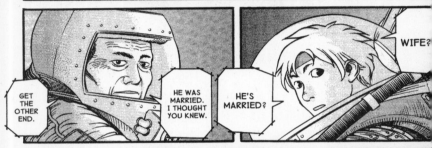

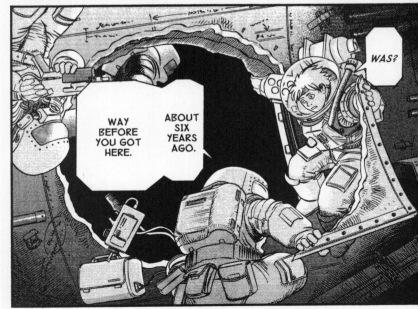

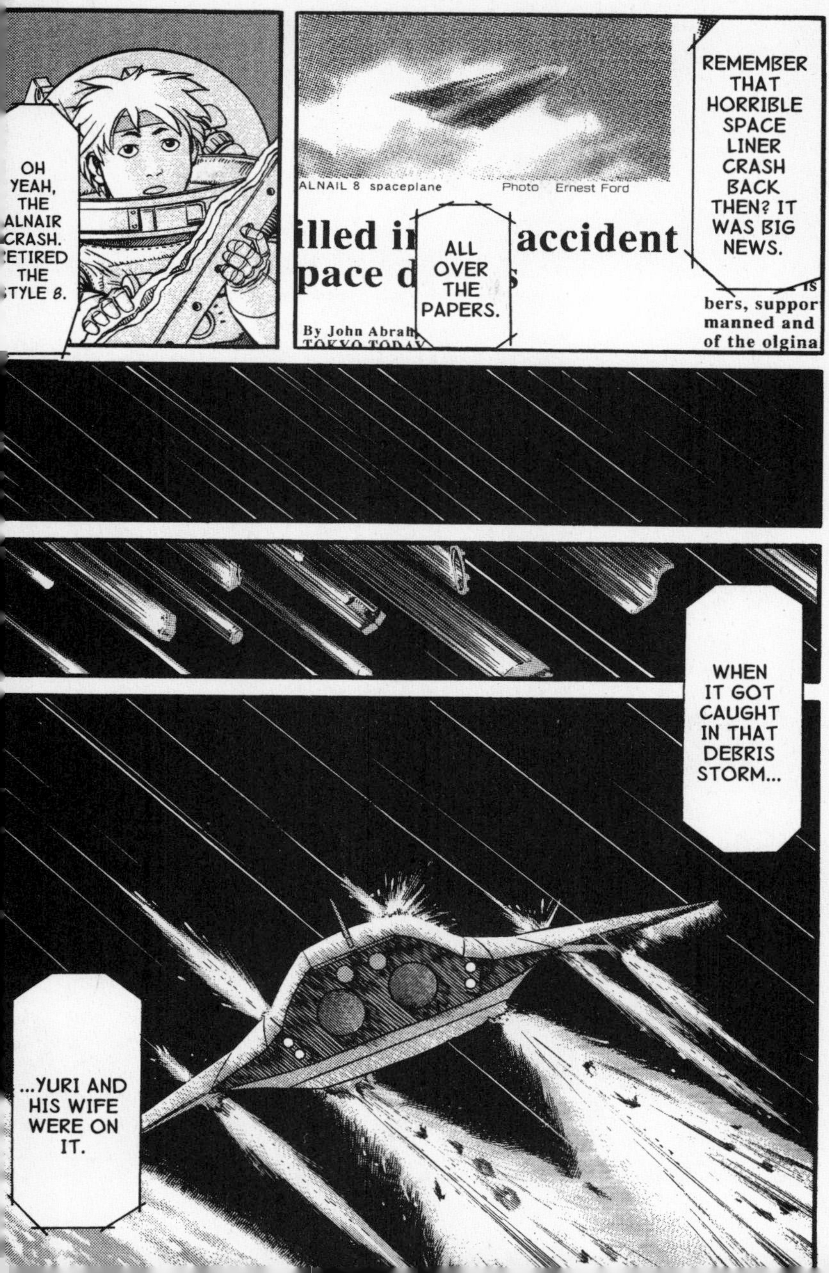
REMEMBER THAT HORRIBLE SPACE LINER CRASH BACK THEN? IT WAS BIG NEWS.
ALNAIL 8 spaceplane Photo Ernest Ford
illed in accident
pace d s
By John Abrah
TOKYO TODAY
bers, suppor
manned and
of the olgina
ALL OVER THE PAPERS.
OH YEAH, THE ALNAIR CRASH. ETIRED THE TYLE 8.
WHEN IT GOT CAUGHT IN THAT DEBRIS STORM...
...YURI AND HIS WIFE WERE ON IT.

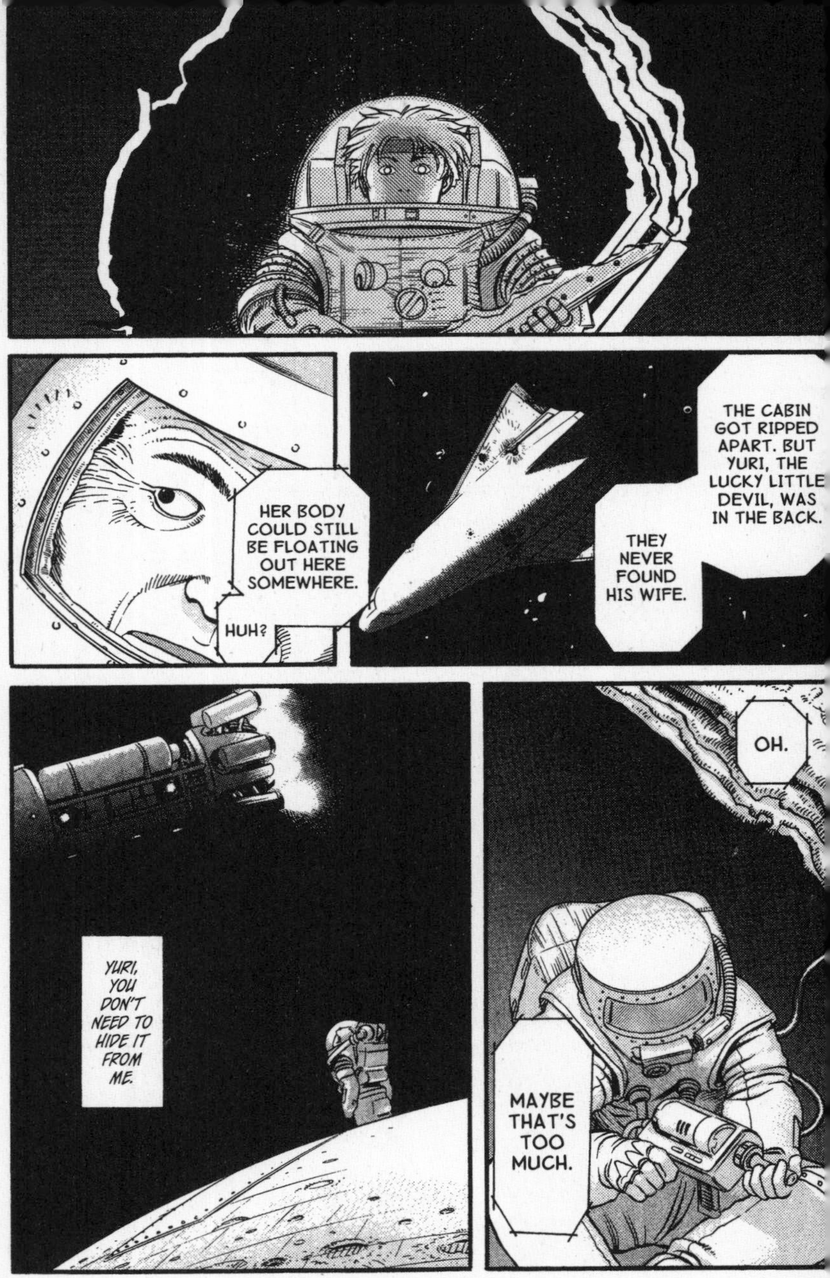
THE CABIN GOT RIPPED APART. BUT YURI, THE LUCKY LITTLE DEVIL, WAS IN THE BACK.
THEY NEVER FOUND HIS WIFE.
HER BODY COULD STILL BE FLOATING OUT HERE SOMEWHERE.
HUH?
OH.
MAYBE THAT'S TOO MUCH.
YURI, YOU DON'T NEED TO HIDE IT FROM ME.

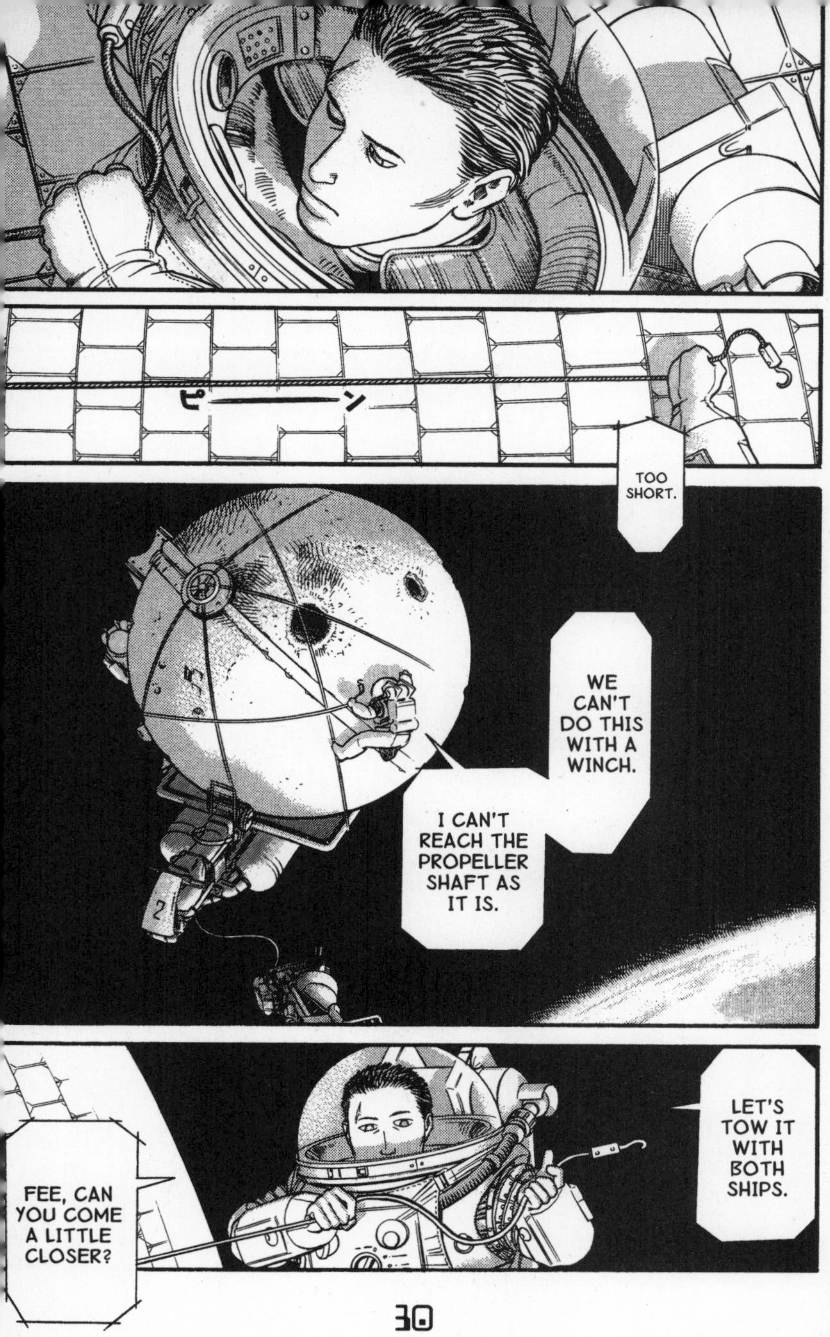
ピーーーン
TOO SHORT.
WE CAN'T DO THIS WITH A WINCH.
I CAN'T REACH THE PROPELLER SHAFT AS IT IS.
LET'S TOW IT WITH BOTH SHIPS.
FEE, CAN YOU COME A LITTLE CLOSER?

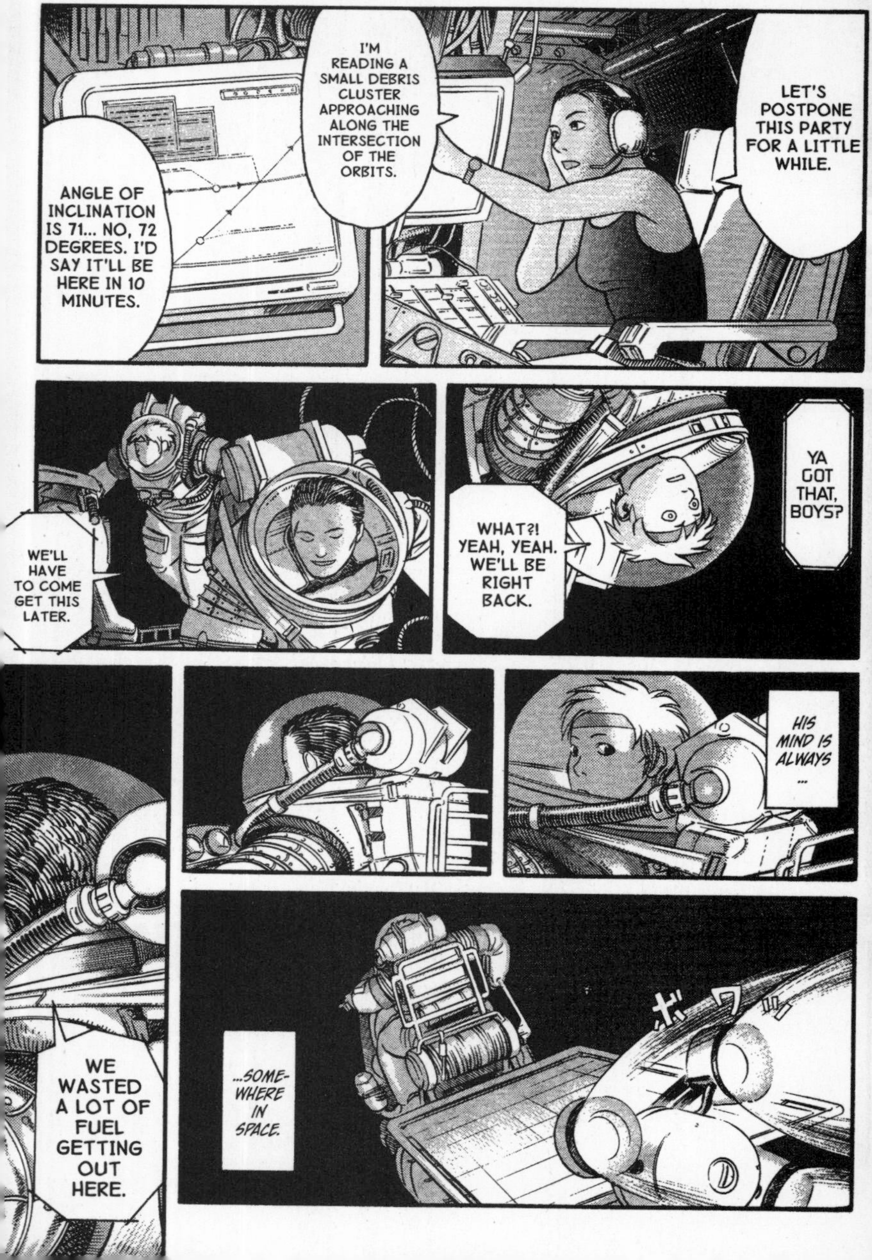
LET'S POSTPONE THIS PARTY FOR A LITTLE WHILE.
I'M READING A SMALL DEBRIS CLUSTER APPROACHING ALONG THE INTERSECTION OF THE ORBITS.
ANGLE OF INCLINATION IS 71... NO, 72 DEGREES. I'D SAY IT'LL BE HERE IN 10 MINUTES.
YA GOT THAT, BOYS? ...
WHAT?! YEAH, YEAH. WE'LL BE RIGHT BACK.
WE'LL HAVE TO COME GET THIS LATER.
HIS MIND IS ALWAYS ...
...SOME-WHERE IN SPACE.
WE WASTED A LOT OF FUEL GETTING OUT HERE.

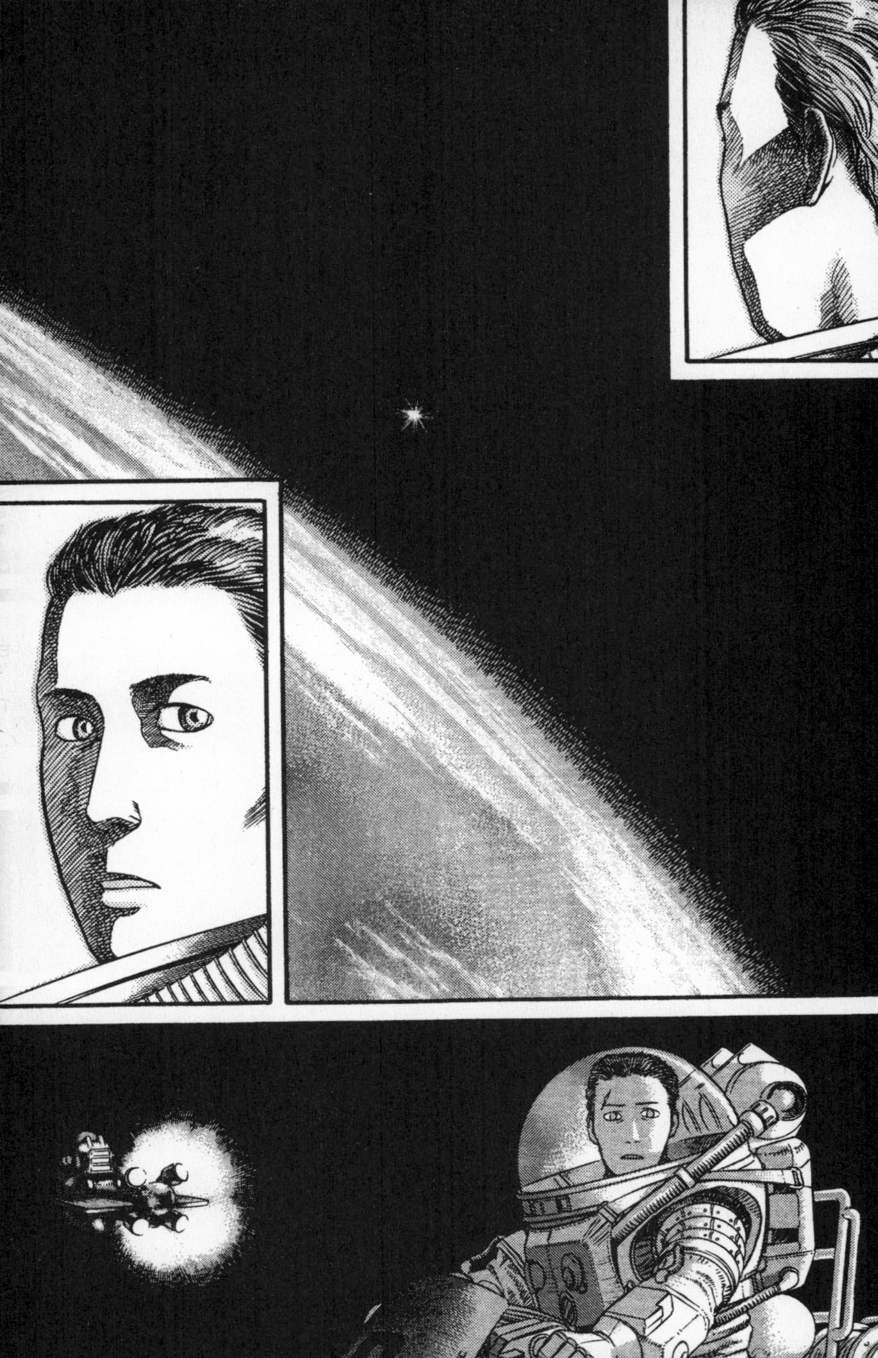

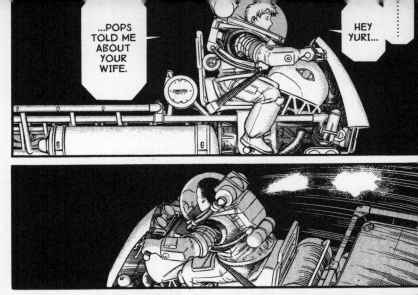

......
HEY YURI...
...POPS TOLD ME ABOUT YOUR WIFE.
I HOP THAT ALL RIGH HE JUST
...I DON'T MEAN TO BUTT IN, BUT...
...WELL, IT MADE ME THINK...
...ABOUT WHY YOU'RE DOING THIS JOB AND...
ピッ ピッ ピッ
WHOA, WAIT A SEC.
ピッ ピッ ピッ ピッ
YURI
HACHIMAKI
YURI?!

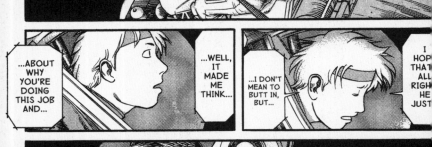

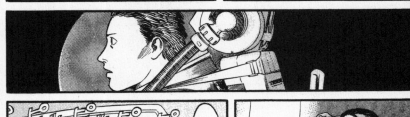

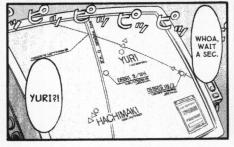

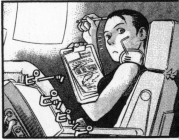

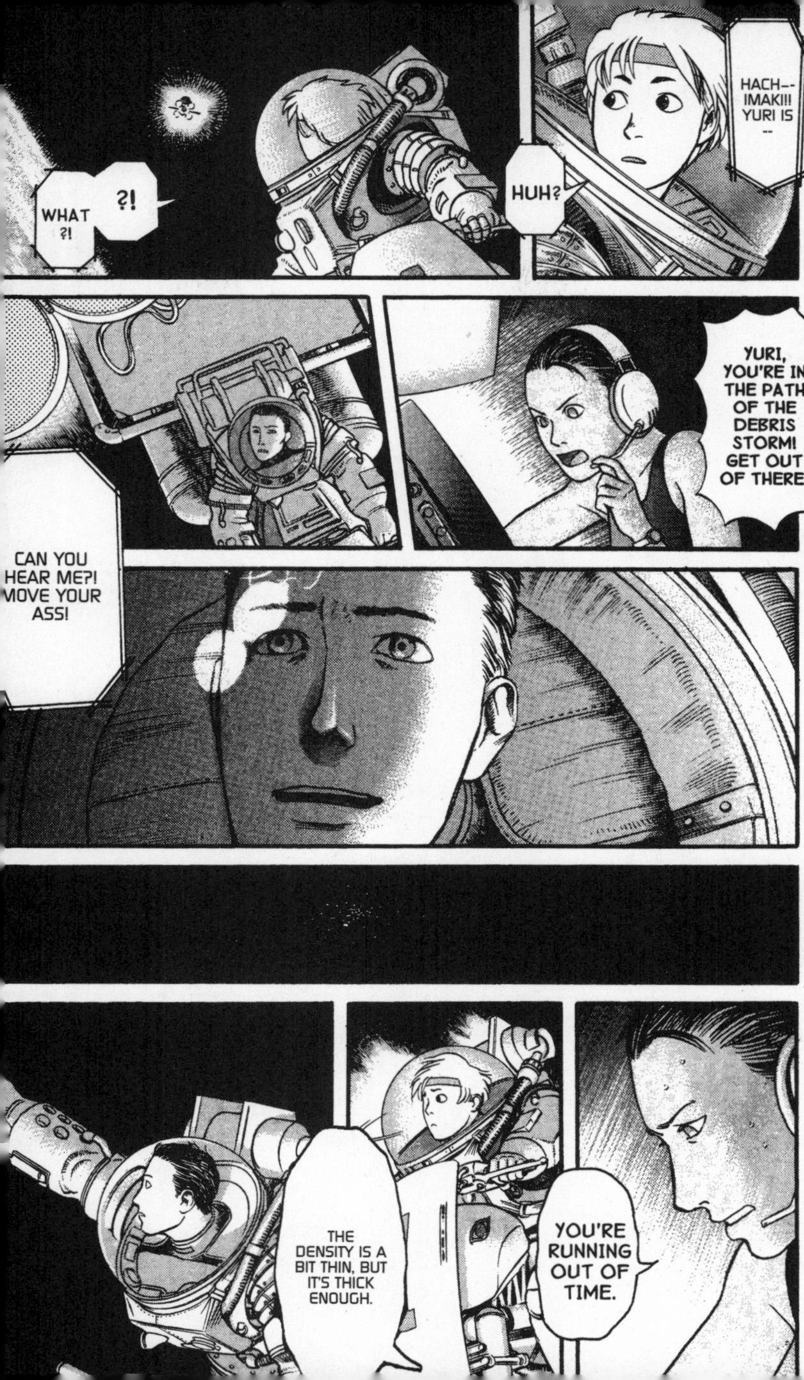
HACH-- IMAKI!! YURI IS --
HUH?
?!
WHAT ?!
YURI, YOU'RE IN THE PATH OF THE DEBRIS STORM! GET OUT OF THERE!
CAN YOU HEAR ME?! MOVE YOUR ASS!
YOU'RE RUNNING OUT OF TIME.
THE DENSITY IS A BIT THIN, BUT IT'S THICK ENOUGH.

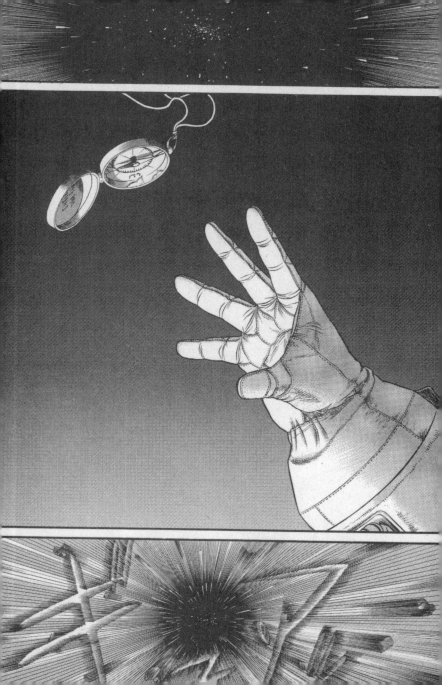

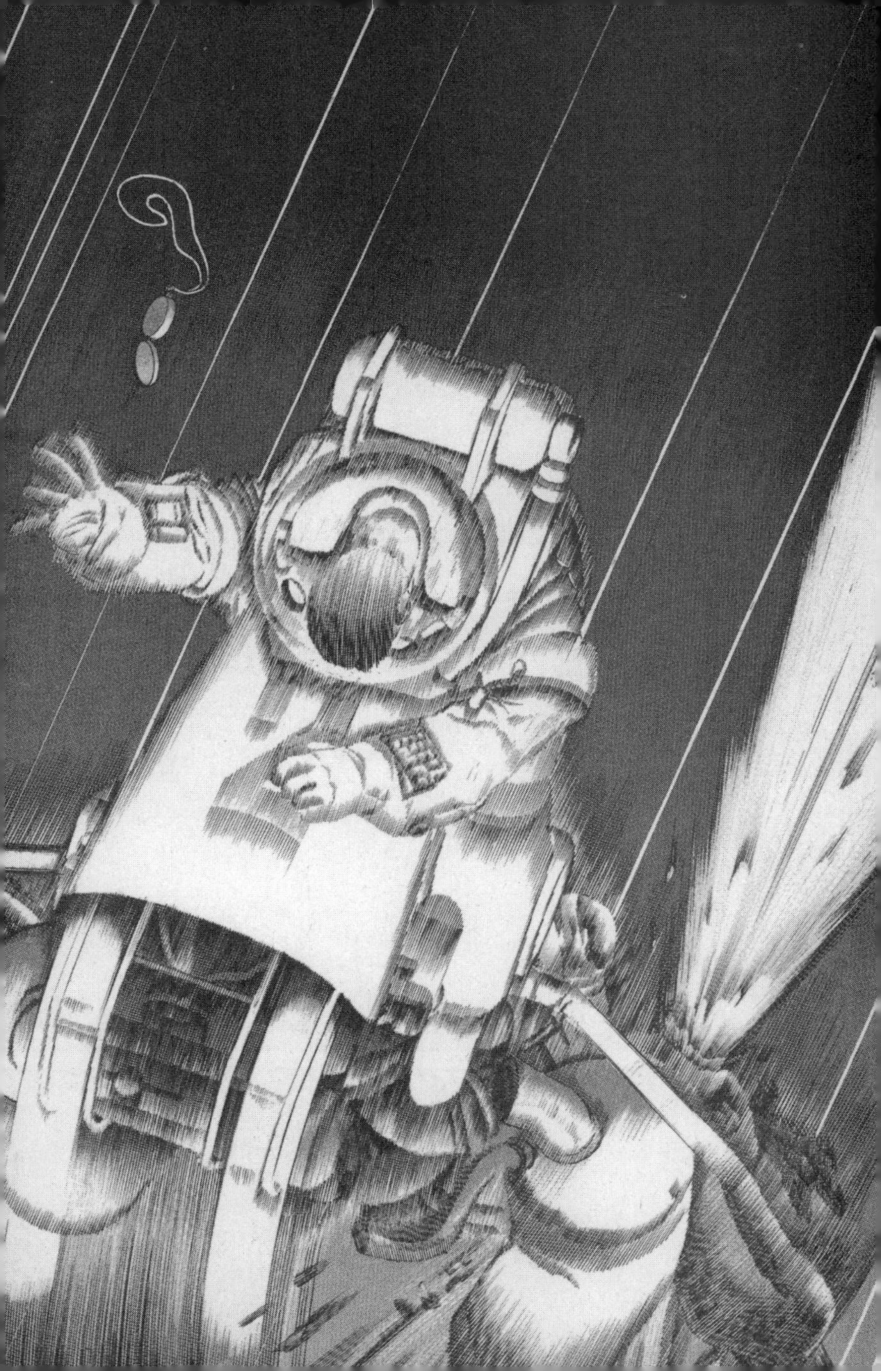

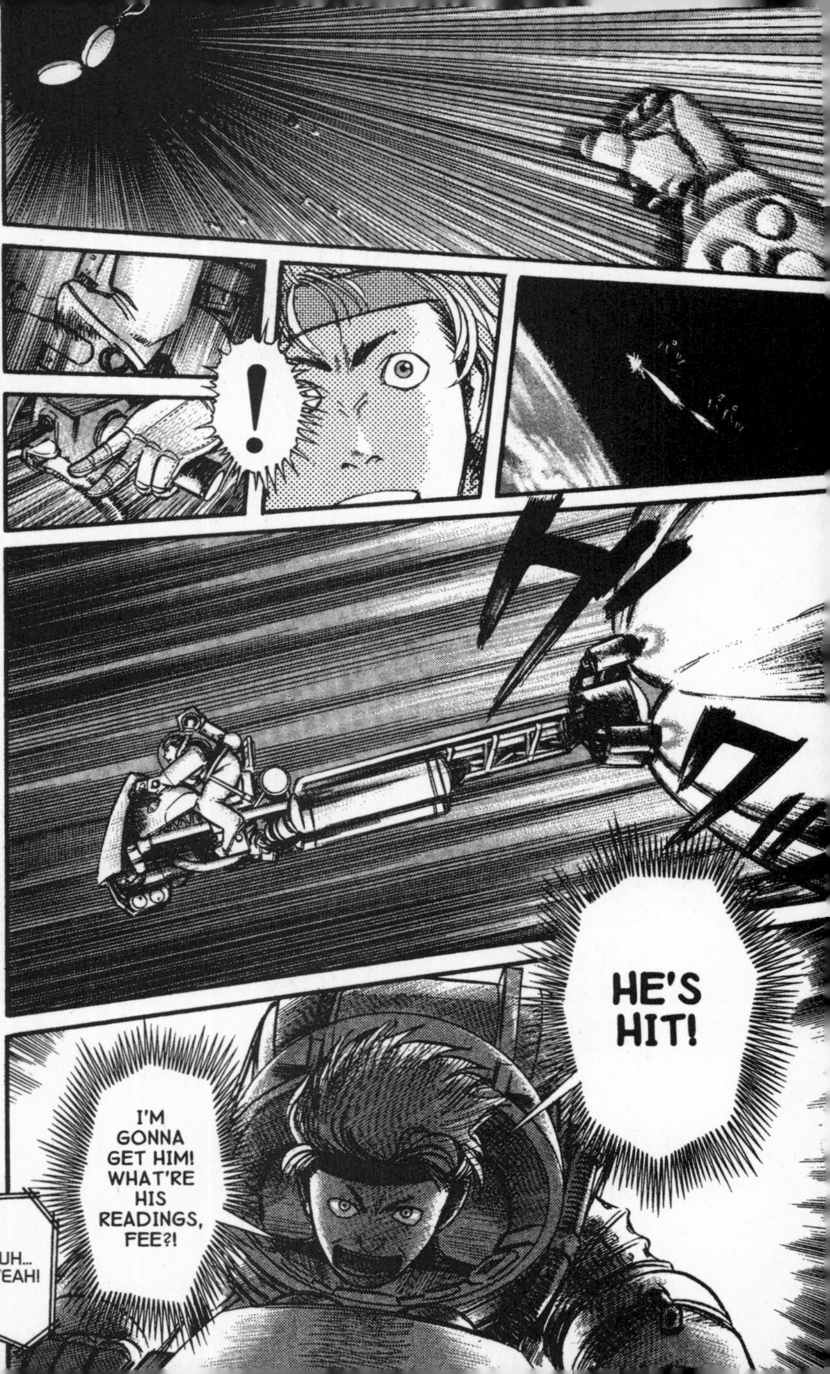
!
HE'S HIT!
I'M GONNA GET HIM! WHAT'RE HIS READINGS, FEE?!
UH... YEAH!

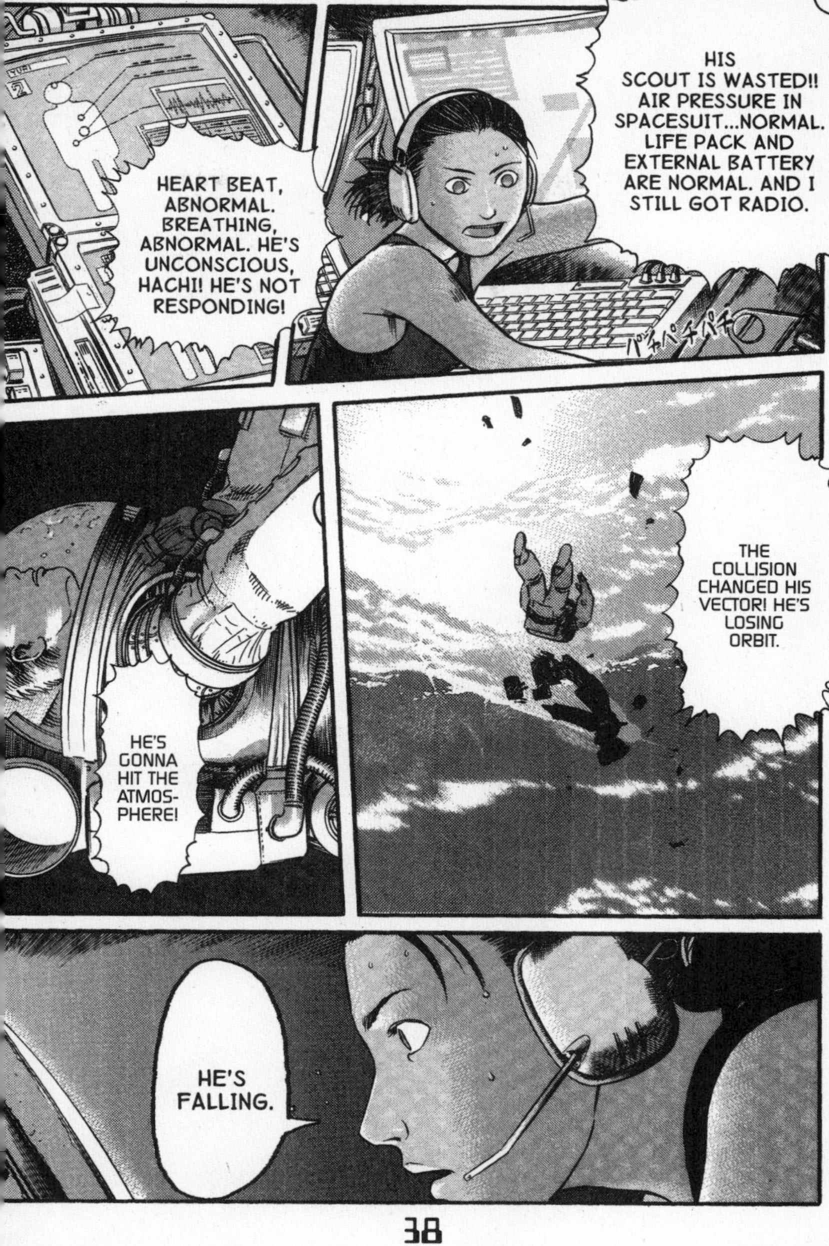
HIS SCOUT IS WASTED!! AIR PRESSURE IN SPACESUIT...NORMAL. LIFE PACK AND EXTERNAL BATTERY ARE NORMAL. AND I STILL GOT RADIO.
パャパチパチ
HEART BEAT, ABNORMAL. BREATHING, ABNORMAL. HE'S UNCONSCIOUS, HACHI! HE'S NOT RESPONDING!
THE COLLISION CHANGED HIS VECTOR! HE'S LOSING ORBIT.
HE'S GONNA HIT THE ATMOS-PHERE!
HE'S FALLING.

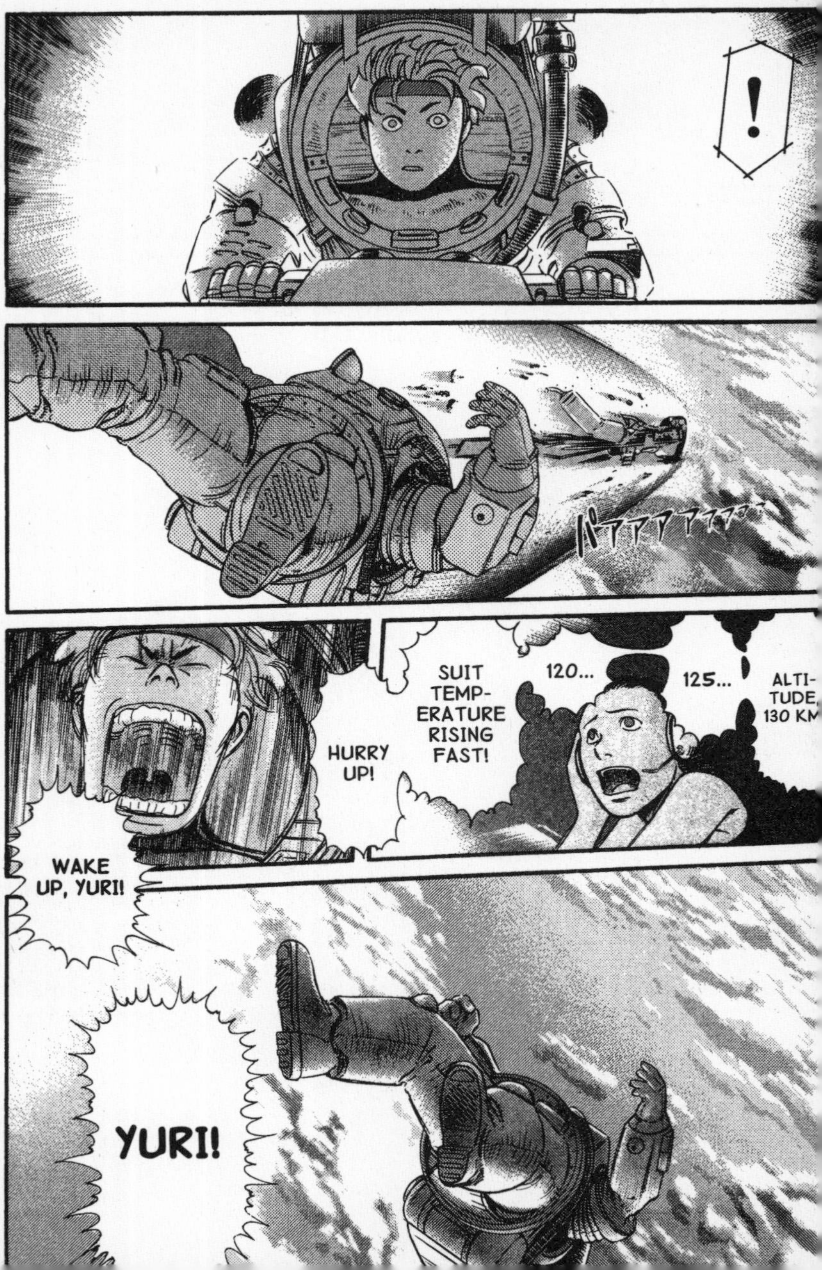
!
ALTI-TUDE, 130 KM
125...
120...
SUIT TEMP-ERATURE RISING FAST!
HURRY UP!
WAKE UP, YURI!
YURI!

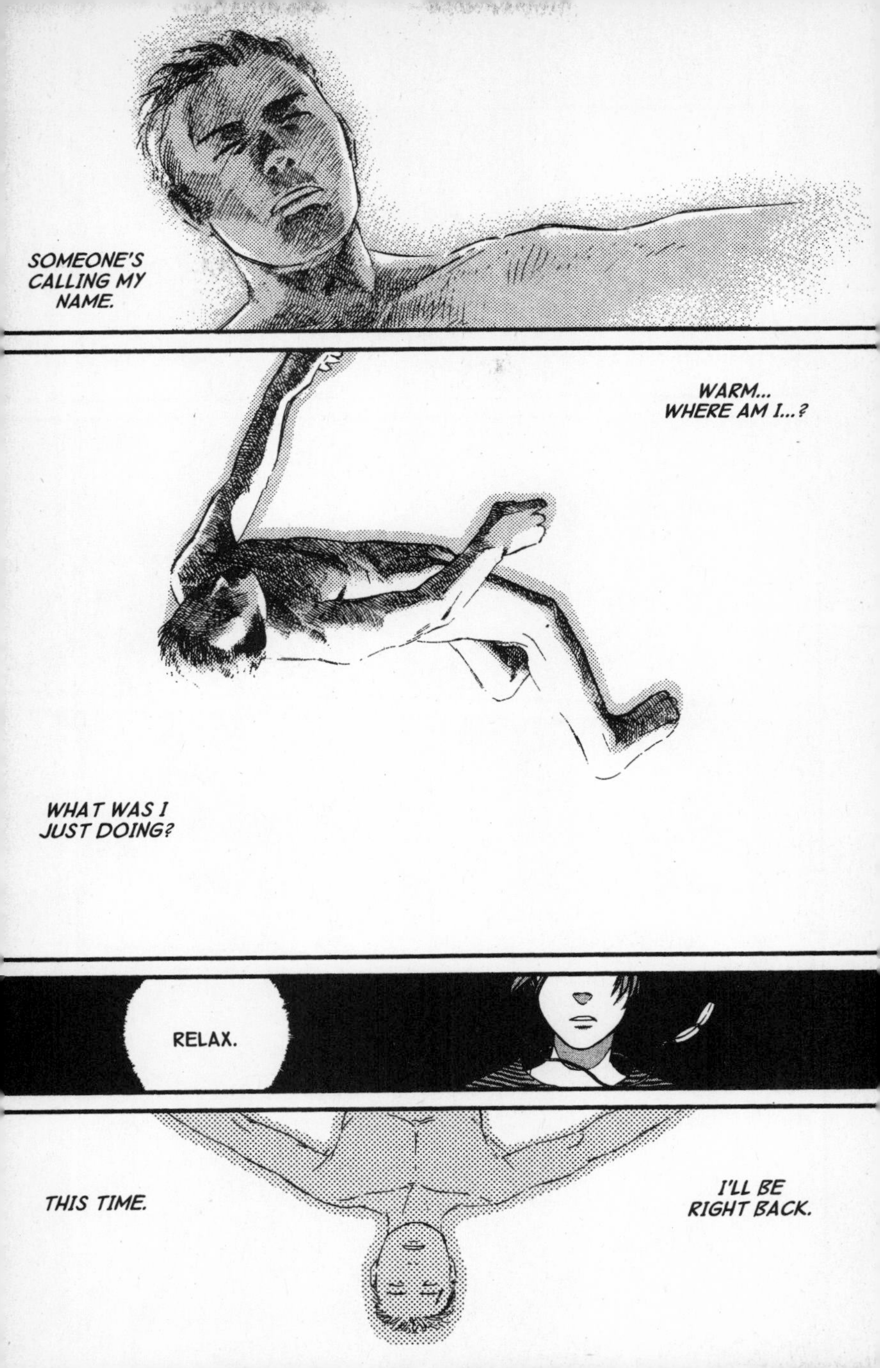
SOMEONE'S CALLING MY NAME.
WARM... WHERE AM I...?
WHAT WAS I JUST DOING?
RELAX.
I'LL BE RIGHT BACK.
THIS TIME.

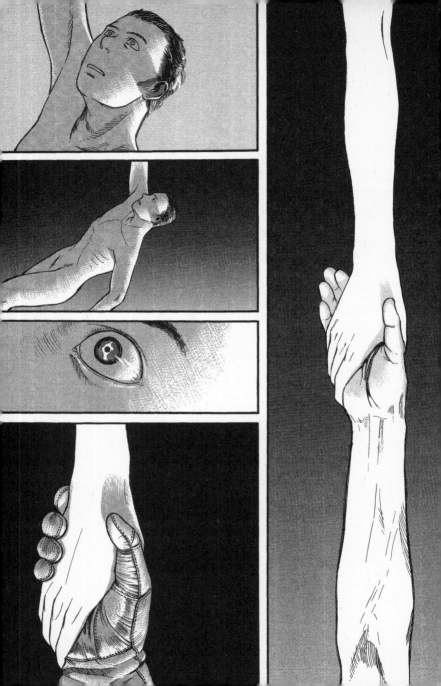

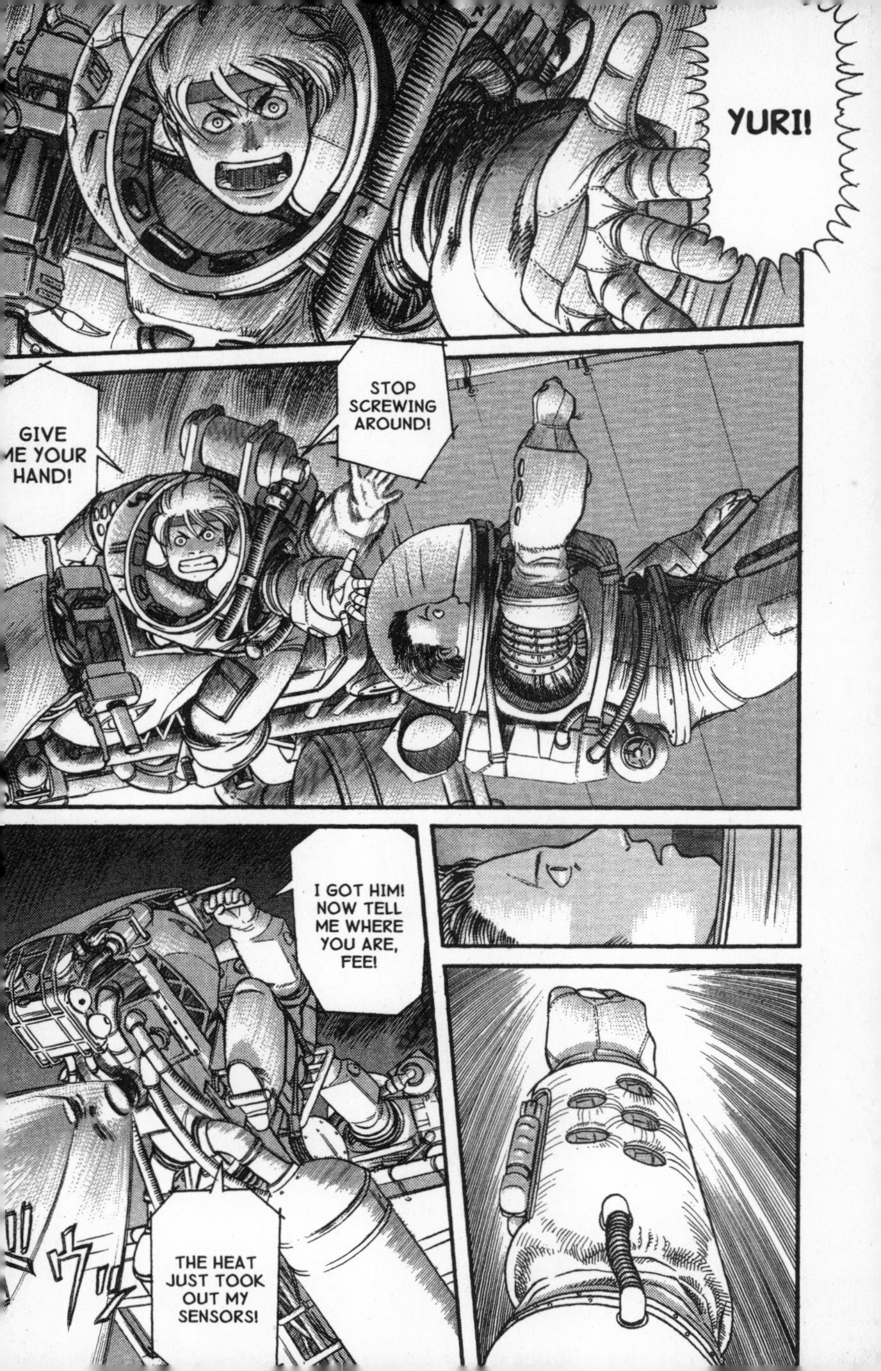
YURI!
STOP SCREWING AROUND!
GIVE ME YOUR HAND!
I GOT HIM! NOW TELL ME WHERE YOU ARE, FEE!
THE HEAT JUST TOOK OUT MY SENSORS!

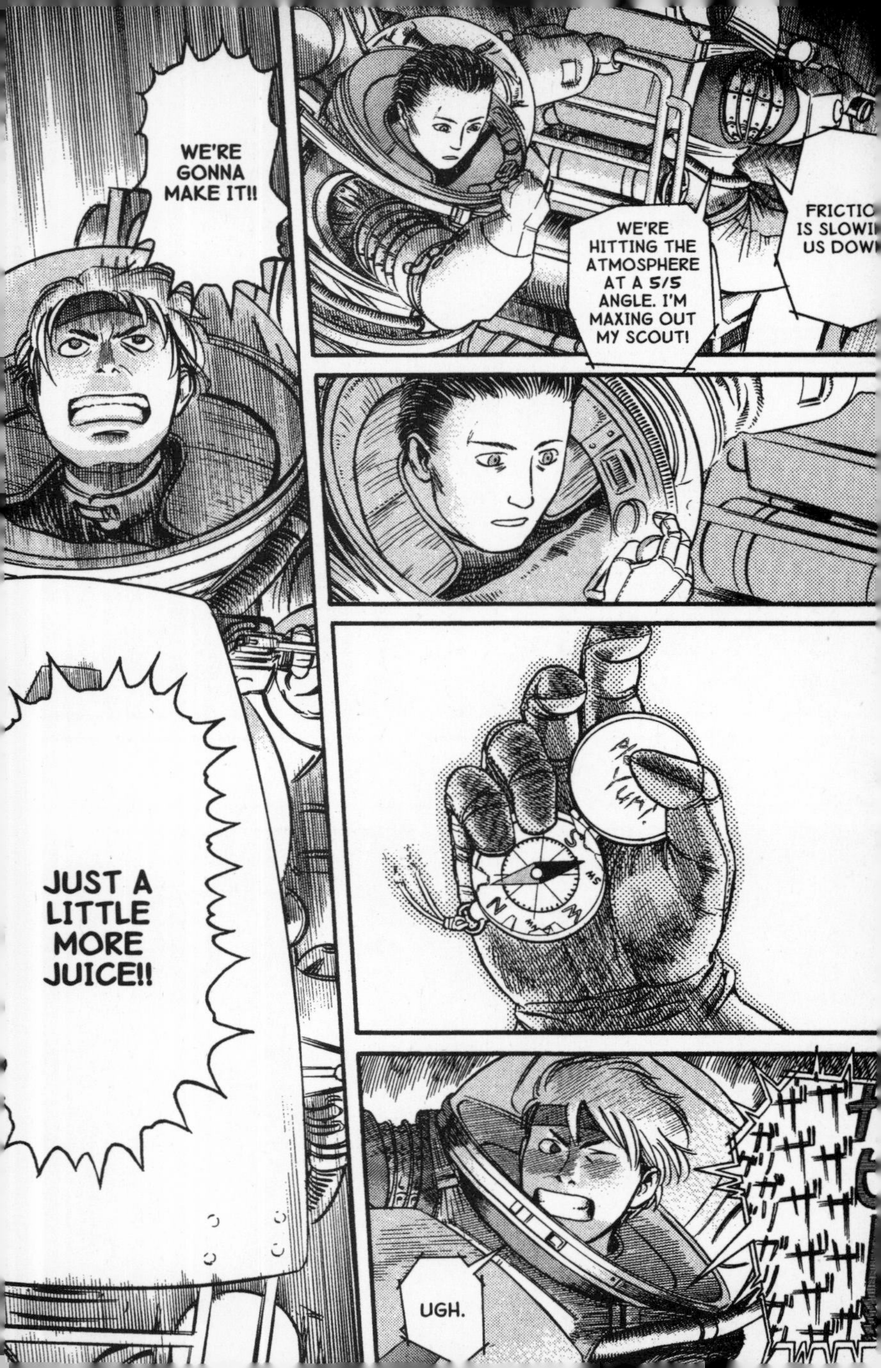
FRICTIO IS SLOWI US DOW
WE'RE HITTING THE ATMOSPHERE AT A 5/5 ANGLE. I'M MAXING OUT MY SCOUT!
UGH.
WE'RE GONNA MAKE IT!!
JUST A LITTLE MORE JUICE!!

Please save Yuri.
PLEASE SAVE YURI.

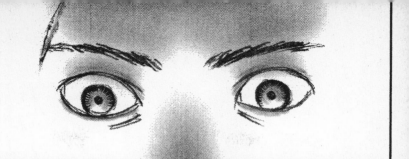

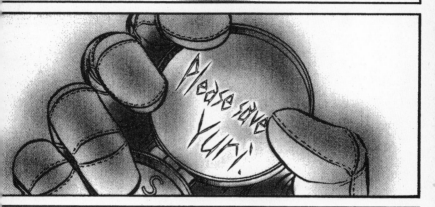

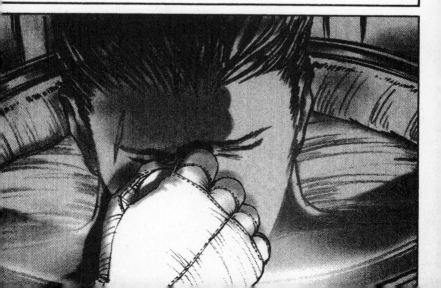

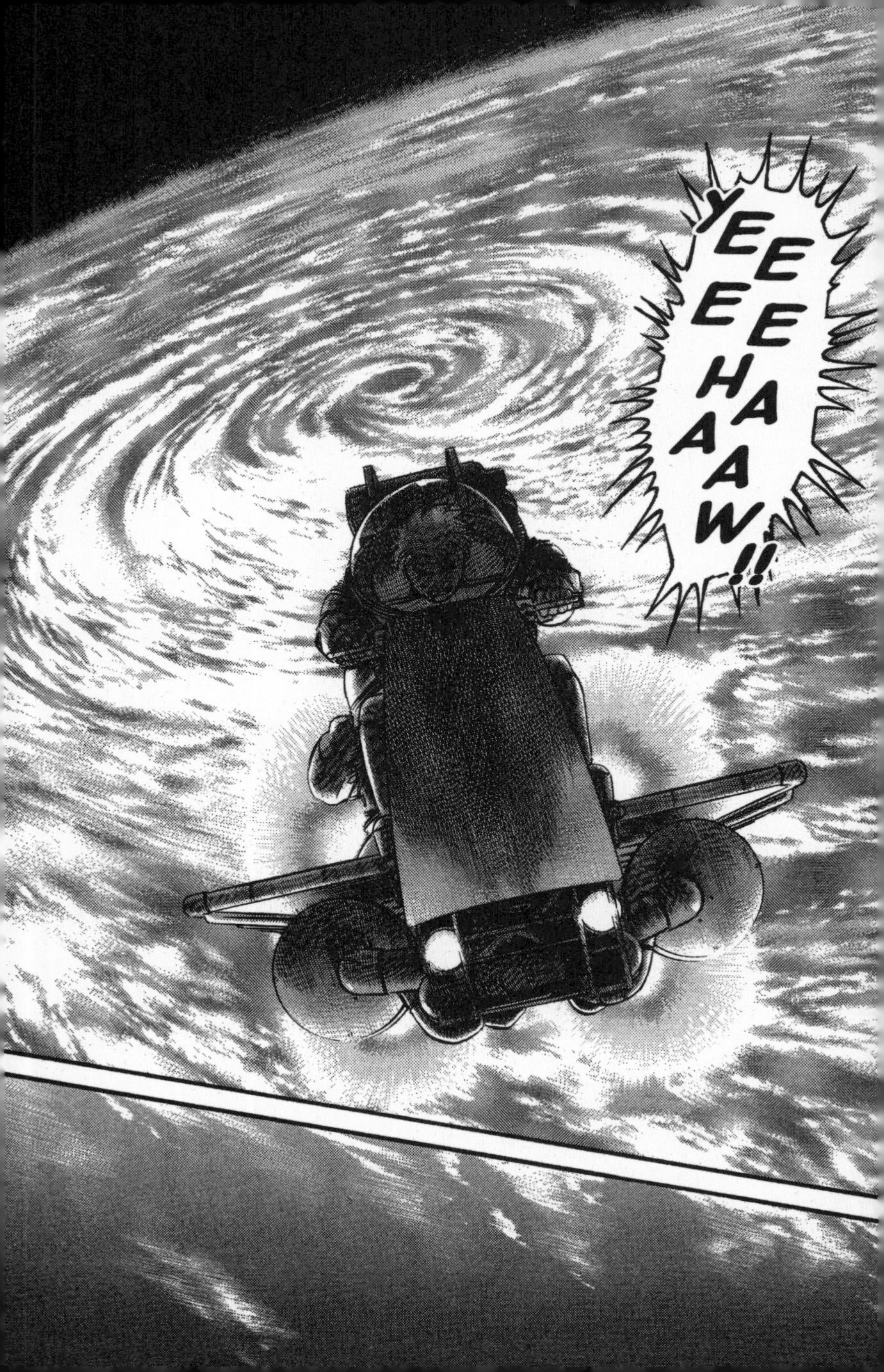
YEEEEEHAAAAAAW!!

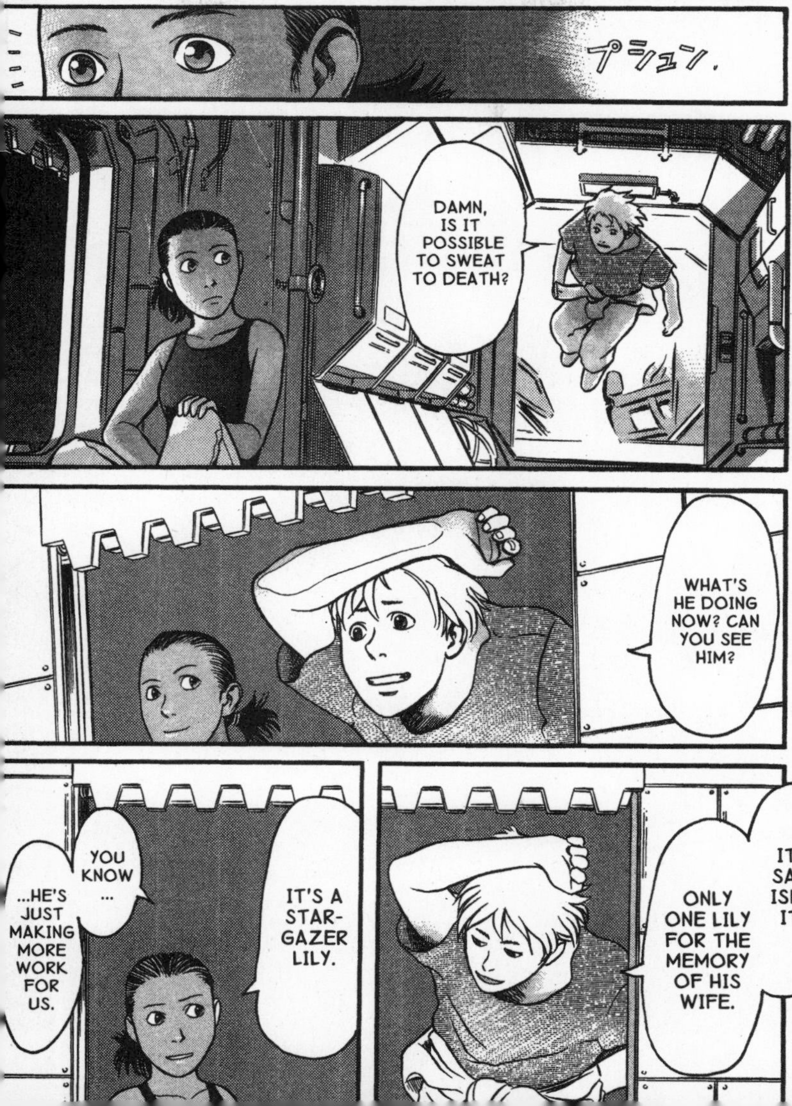
プシュン
DAMN, IS IT POSSIBLE TO SWEAT TO DEATH?
WHAT'S HE DOING NOW? CAN YOU SEE HIM?
IT'S SAD, ISN'T IT?
ONLY ONE LILY FOR THE MEMORY OF HIS WIFE.
IT'S A STAR-GAZER LILY.
YOU KNOW...
...HE'S JUST MAKING MORE WORK FOR US.

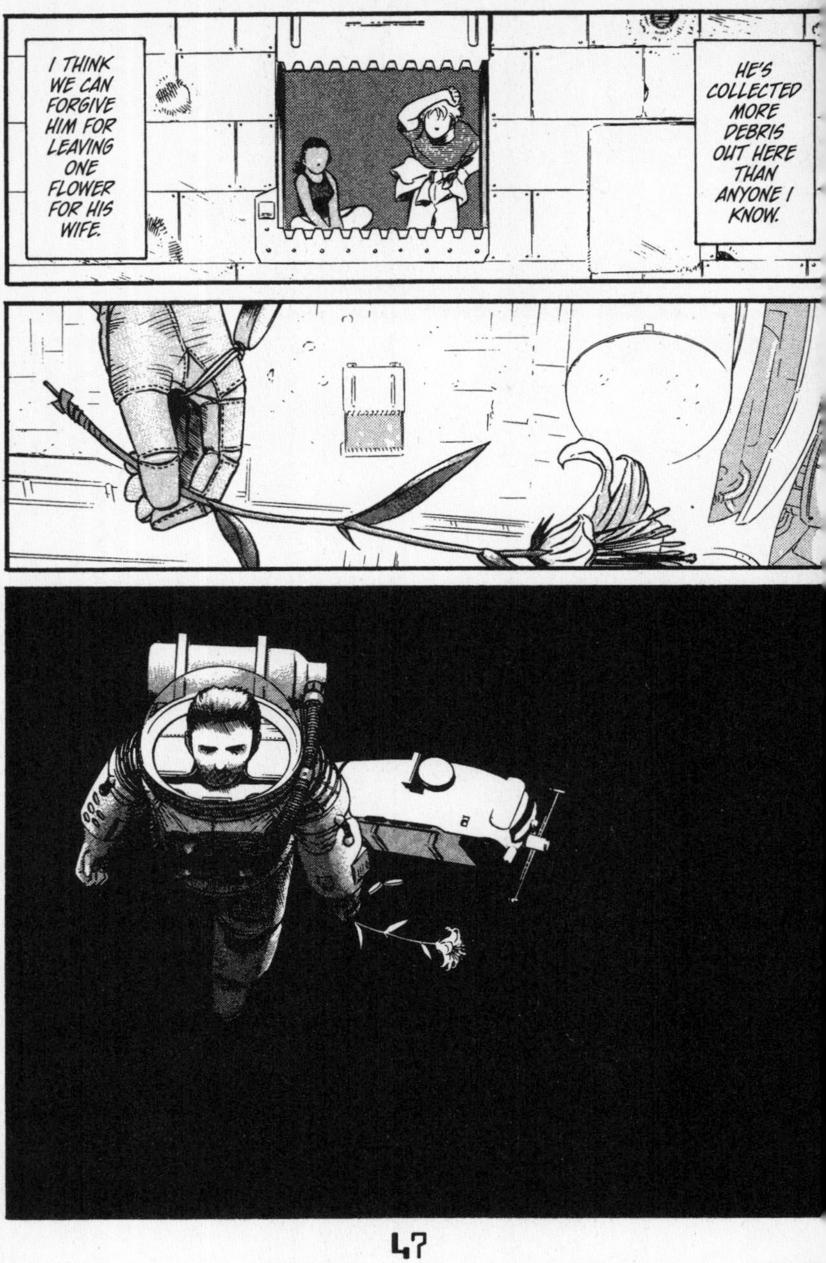
HE'S COLLECTED MORE DEBRIS OUT HERE THAN ANYONE I KNOW.
I THINK WE CAN FORGIVE HIM FOR LEAVING ONE FLOWER FOR HIS WIFE.

ジュ
ボッ

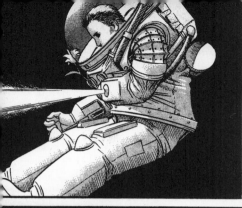

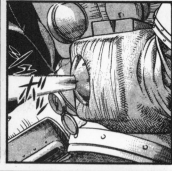

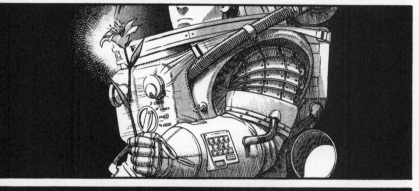

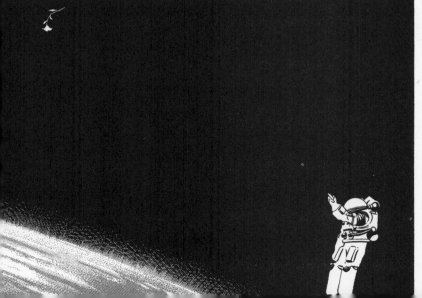

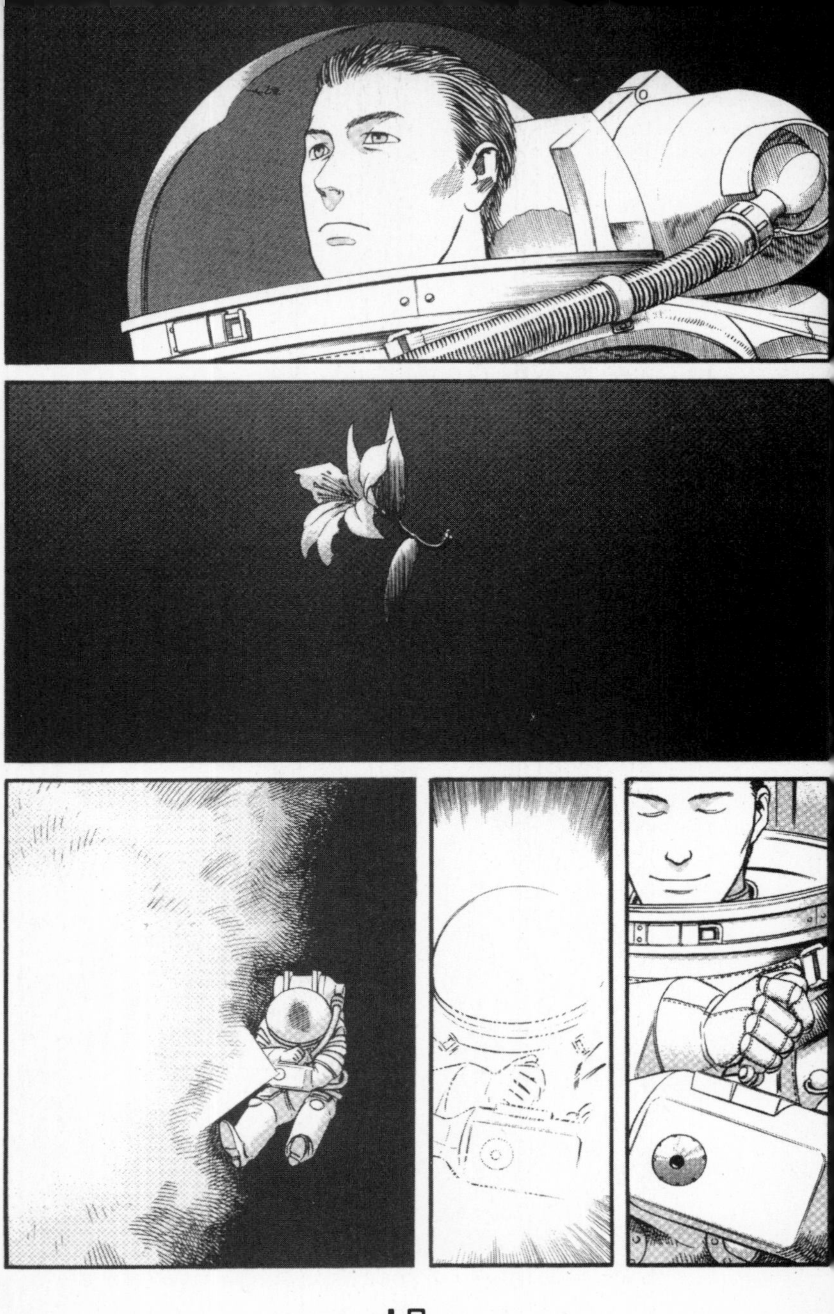

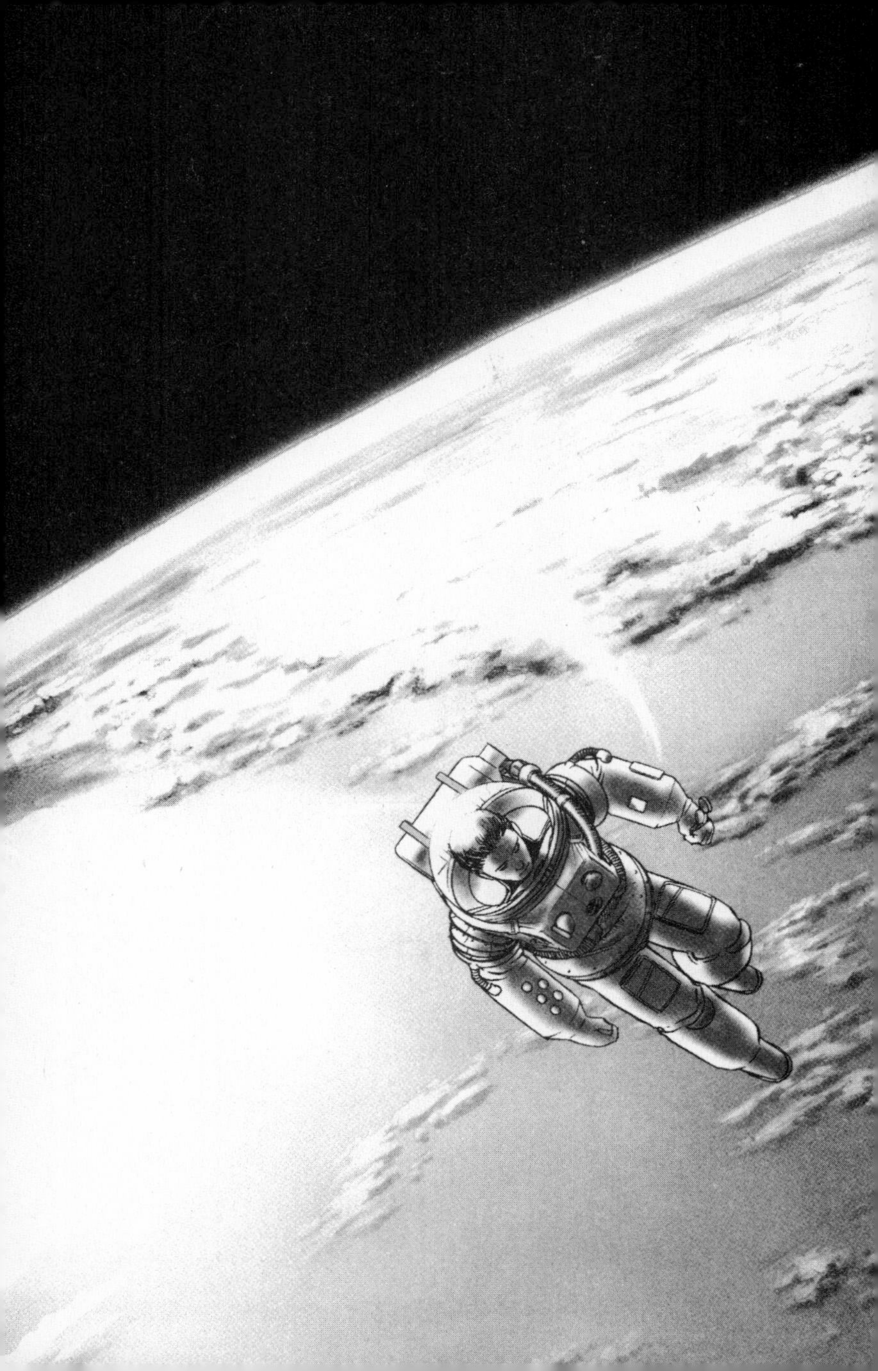

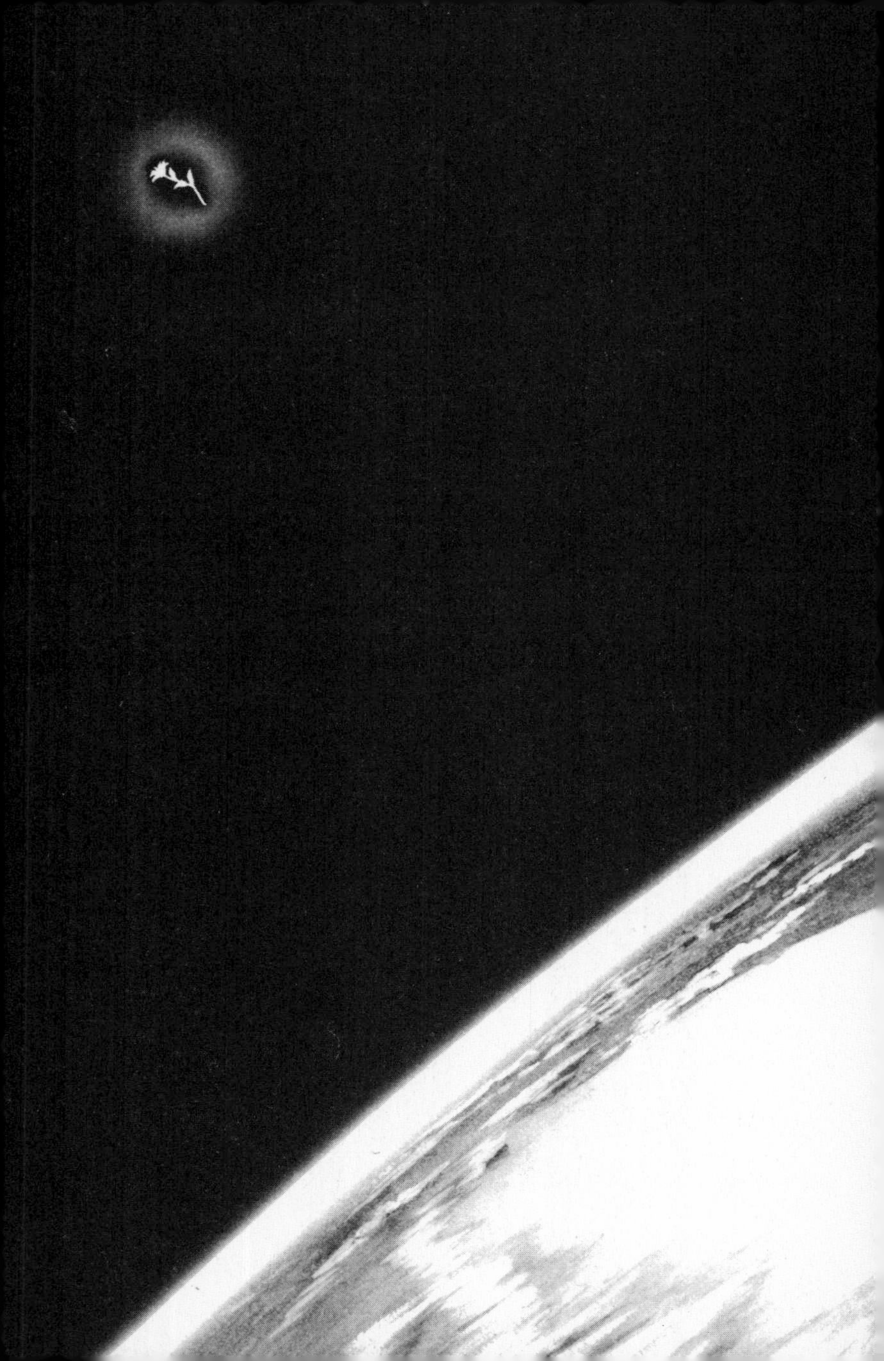

I'M ON MY WAY BACK.

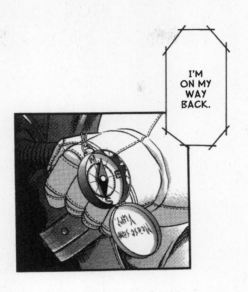

PHASE. 1
END

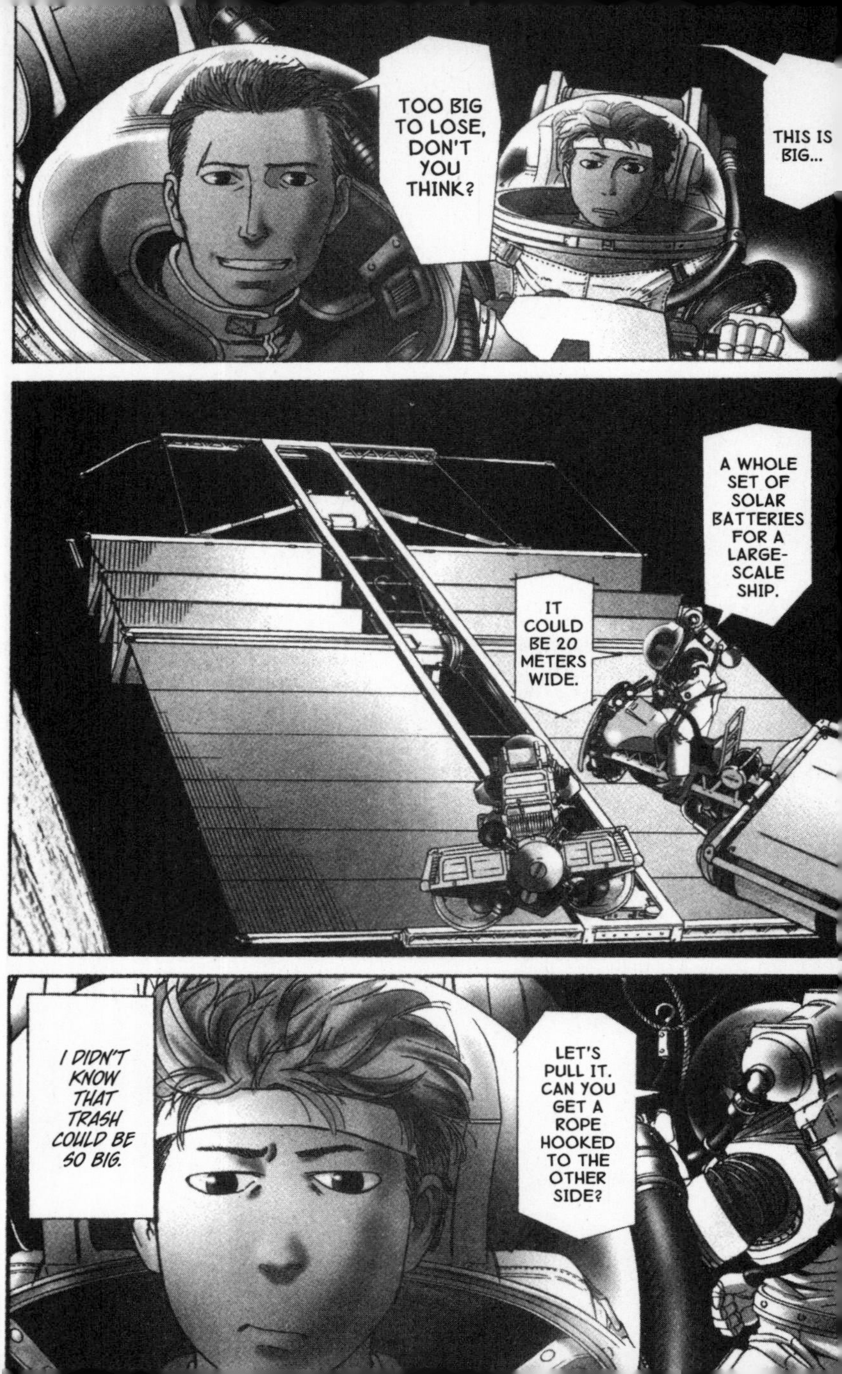
THIS IS BIG...
TOO BIG TO LOSE, DON'T YOU THINK?
A WHOLE SET OF SOLAR BATTERIES FOR A LARGE-SCALE SHIP.
IT COULD BE 20 METERS WIDE.
LET'S PULL IT. CAN YOU GET A ROPE HOOKED TO THE OTHER SIDE?
I DIDN'T KNOW THAT TRASH COULD BE SO BIG.

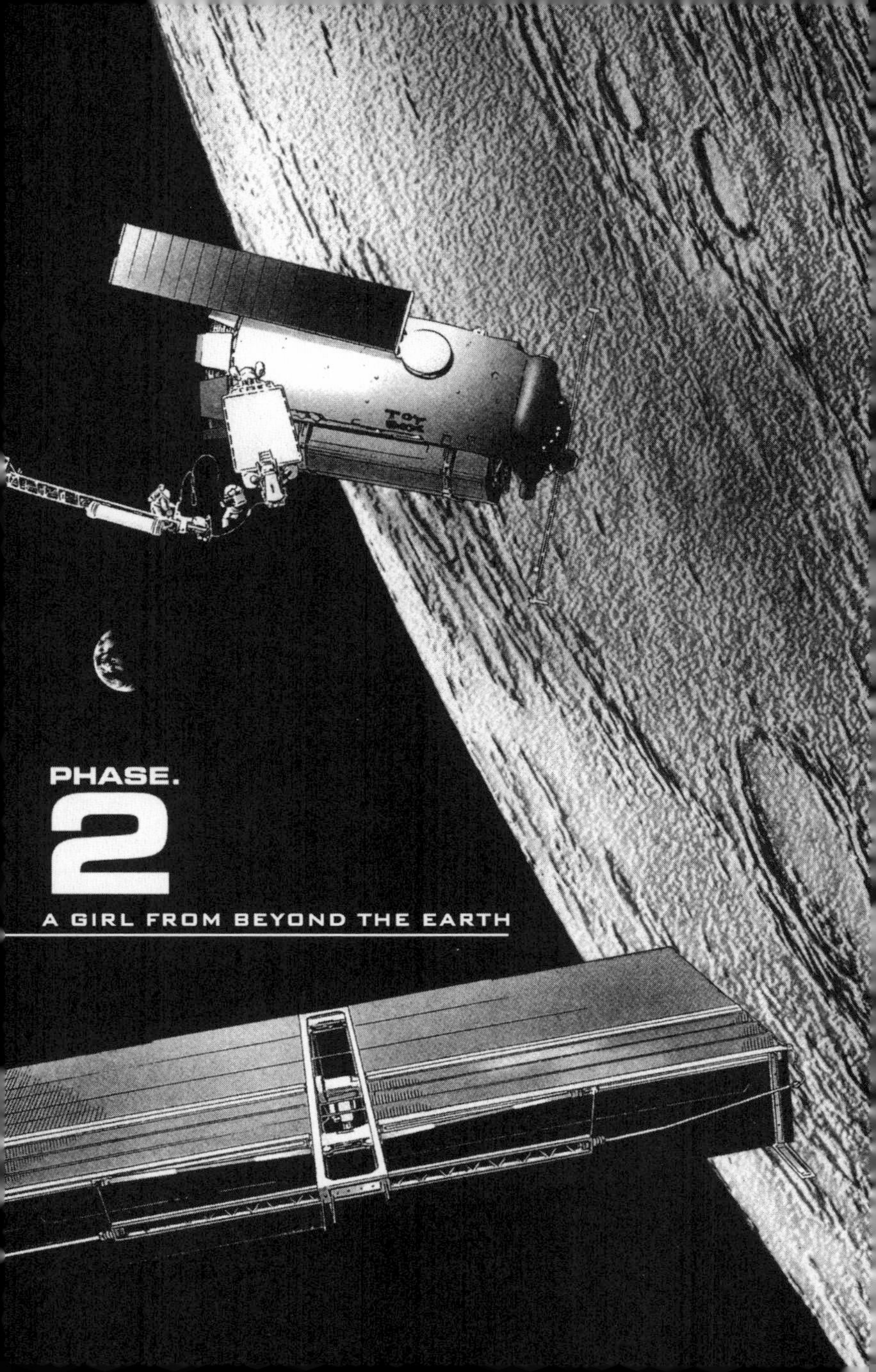
PHASE.
2
A GIRL FROM BEYOND THE EARTH

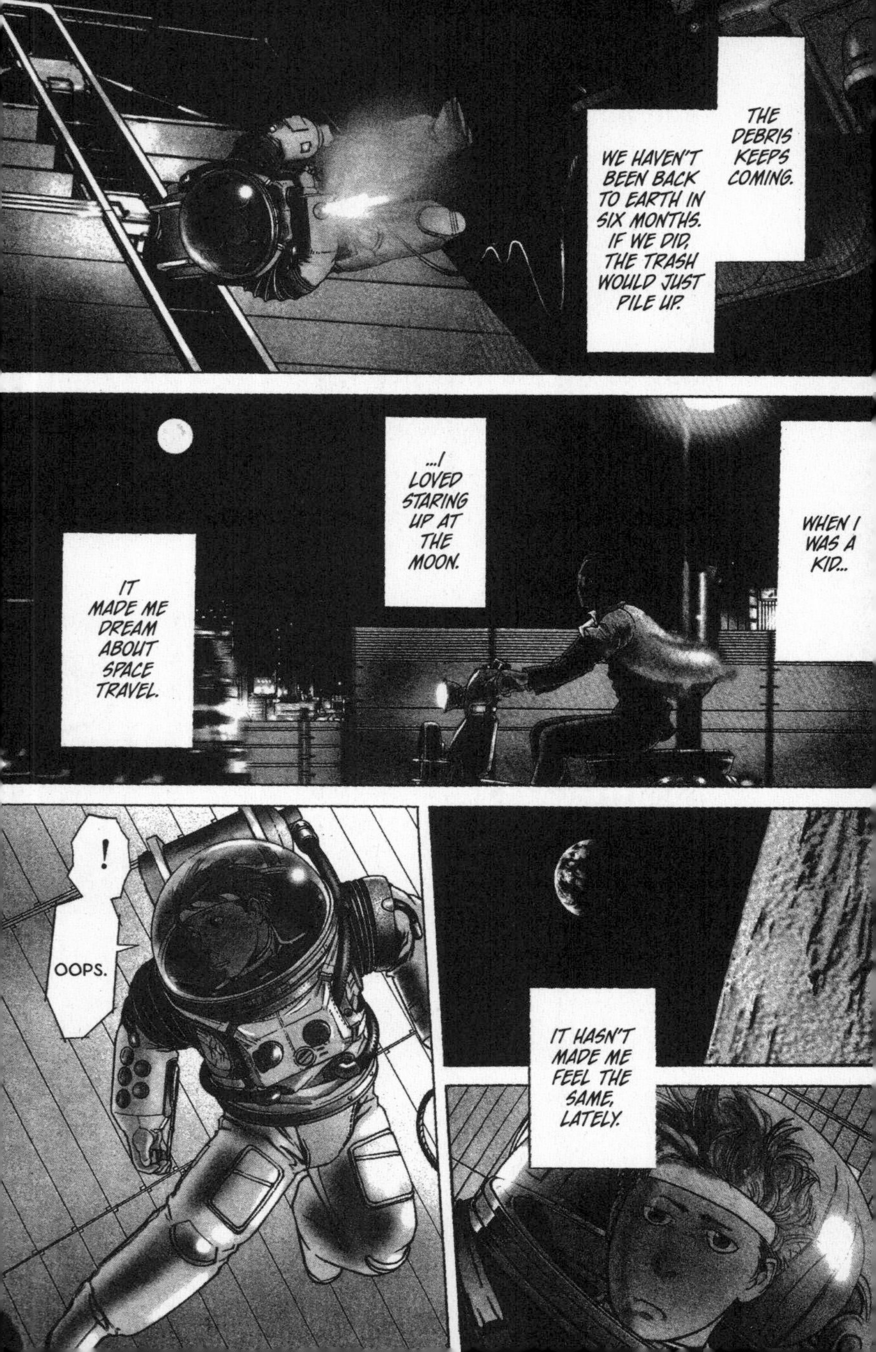
THE DEBRIS KEEPS COMING.
WE HAVEN'T BEEN BACK TO EARTH IN SIX MONTHS. IF WE DID, THE TRASH WOULD JUST PILE UP.
WHEN I WAS A KID...
...I LOVED STARING UP AT THE MOON.
IT MADE ME DREAM ABOUT SPACE TRAVEL.
IT HASN'T MADE ME FEEL THE SAME, LATELY.
!
OOPS.

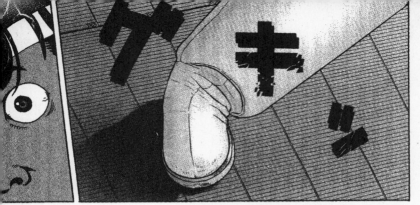

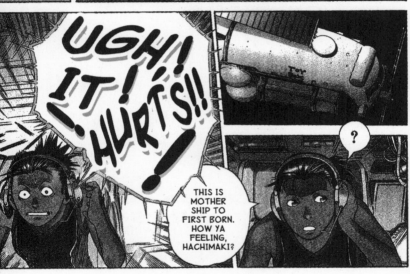

UGH! IT! HURTS!!!

THIS IS MOTHER SHIP TO FIRST BORN. HOW YA FEELING, HACHIMAKI?

?

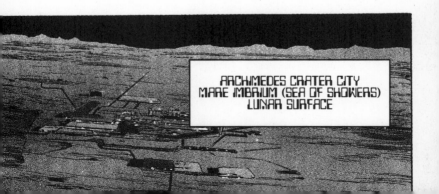

ARCHIMEDES CRATER CITY
MARE IMBRIUM (SEA OF SHOWERS)
LUNAR SURFACE

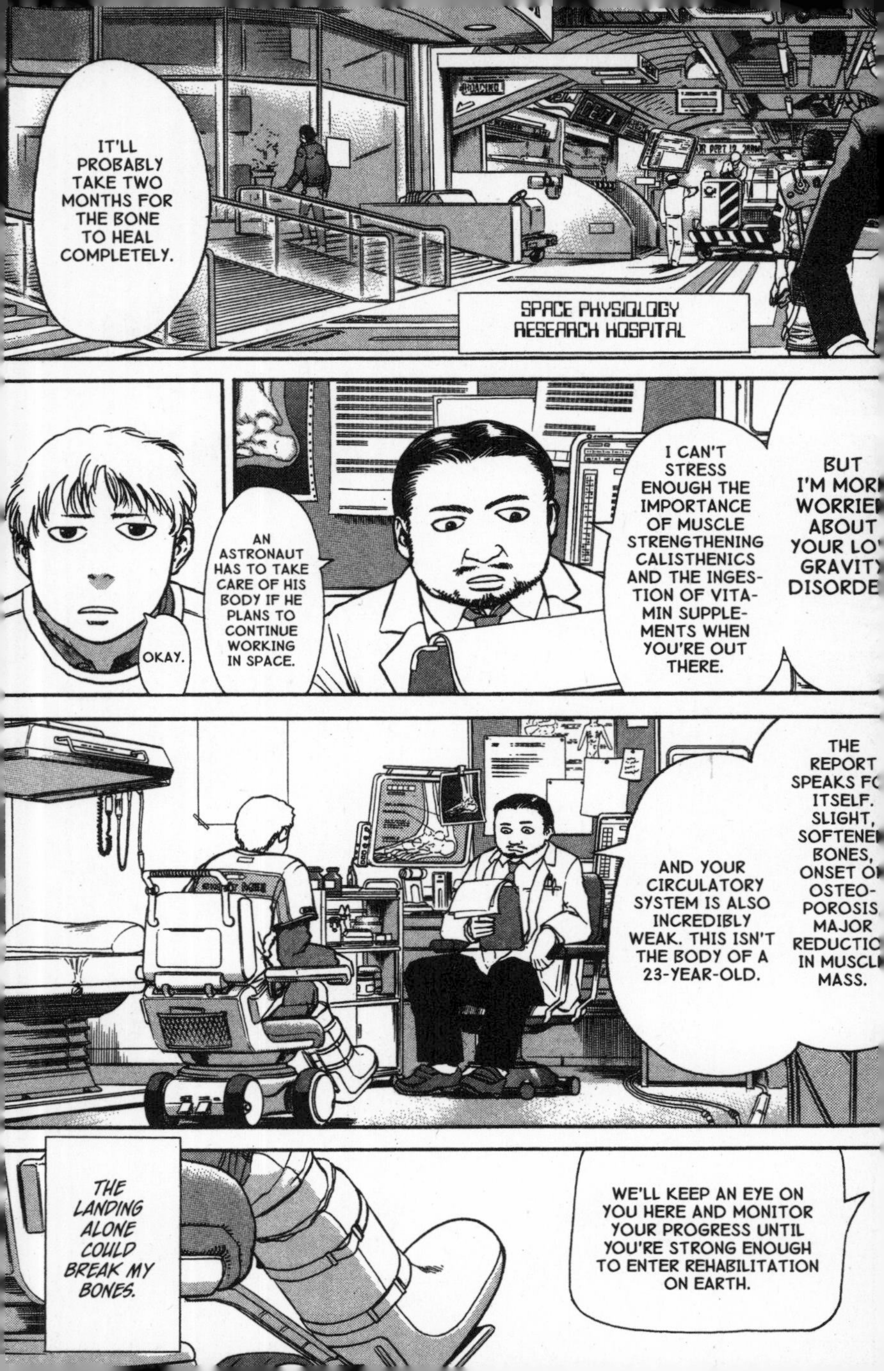
IT'LL PROBABLY TAKE TWO MONTHS FOR THE BONE TO HEAL COMPLETELY.
SPACE PHYSIOLOGY RESEARCH HOSPITAL
BUT I'M MOR WORRIE ABOUT YOUR LO GRAVITY DISORDE
I CAN'T STRESS ENOUGH THE IMPORTANCE OF MUSCLE STRENGTHENING CALISTHENICS AND THE INGESTION OF VITAMIN SUPPLEMENTS WHEN YOU'RE OUT THERE.
AN ASTRONAUT HAS TO TAKE CARE OF HIS BODY IF HE PLANS TO CONTINUE WORKING IN SPACE.
OKAY.
THE REPORT SPEAKS FO ITSELF. SLIGHT, SOFTENE BONES, ONSET O OSTEOPOROSIS MAJOR REDUCTIO IN MUSCL MASS.
AND YOUR CIRCULATORY SYSTEM IS ALSO INCREDIBLY WEAK. THIS ISN'T THE BODY OF A 23-YEAR-OLD.
WE'LL KEEP AN EYE ON YOU HERE AND MONITOR YOUR PROGRESS UNTIL YOU'RE STRONG ENOUGH TO ENTER REHABILITATION ON EARTH.
THE LANDING ALONE COULD BREAK MY BONES.

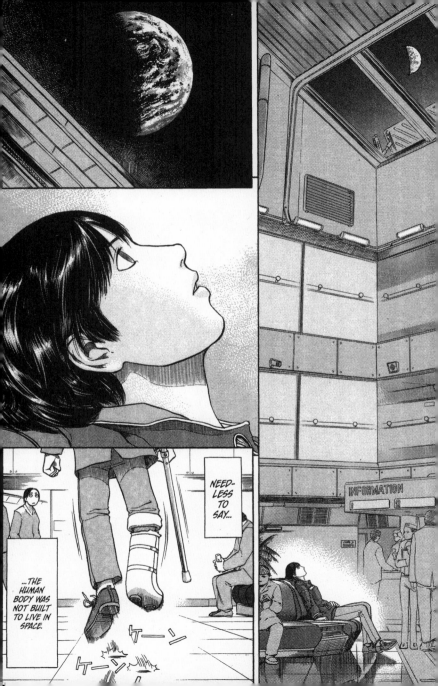

NEED-
LESS
TO
SAY...

...THE
HUMAN
BODY WAS
NOT BUILT
TO LIVE IN
SPACE.

INFORMATION

ケーン

ケーン
ケーン

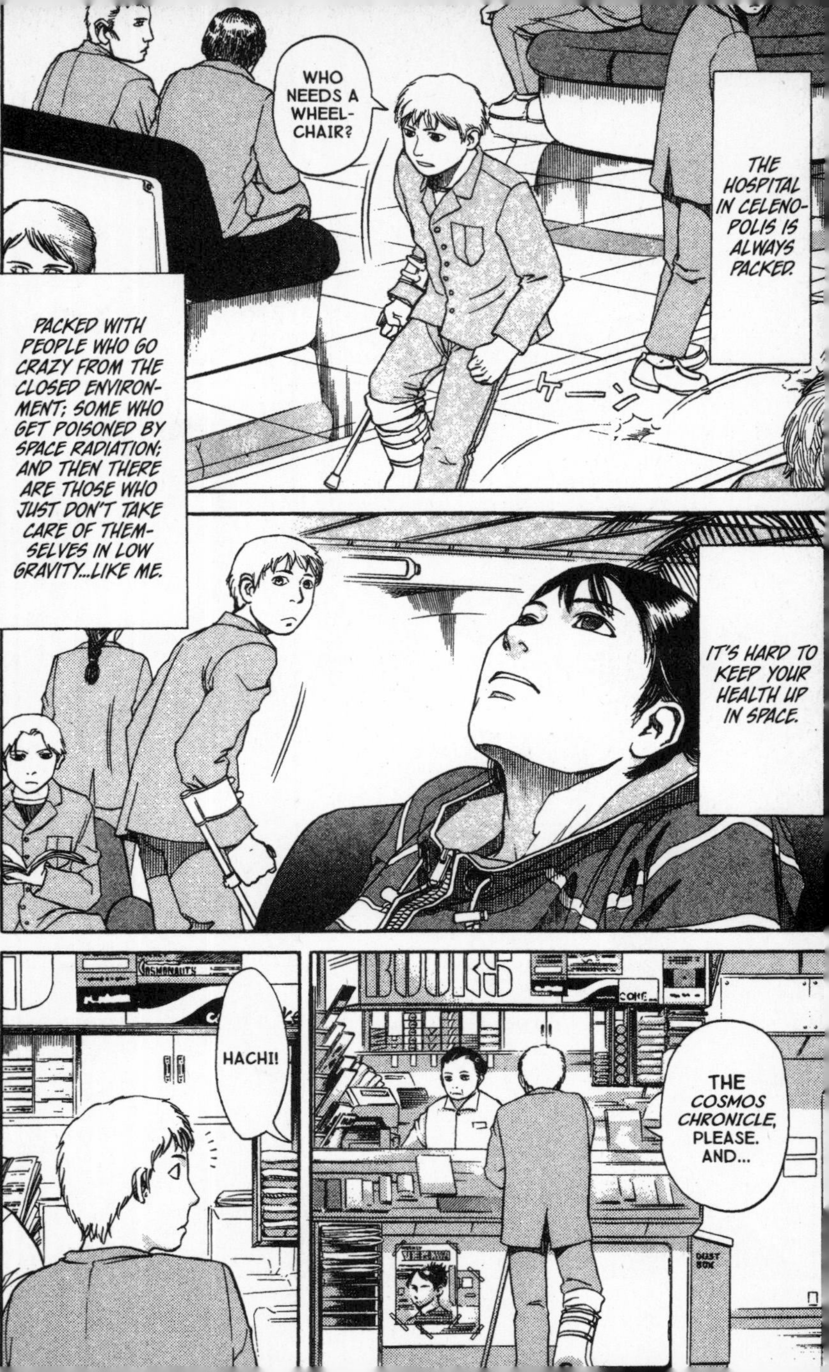
THE HOSPITAL IN CELENO-POLIS IS ALWAYS PACKED.
WHO NEEDS A WHEEL-CHAIR?
ケーン
PACKED WITH PEOPLE WHO GO CRAZY FROM THE CLOSED ENVIRON-MENT; SOME WHO GET POISONED BY SPACE RADIATION; AND THEN THERE ARE THOSE WHO JUST DON'T TAKE CARE OF THEM-SELVES IN LOW GRAVITY...LIKE ME.
IT'S HARD TO KEEP YOUR HEALTH UP IN SPACE.
BOOKS
THE COSMOS CHRONICLE, PLEASE. AND...
DUST BOX
COSMONAUTS
HACHI!

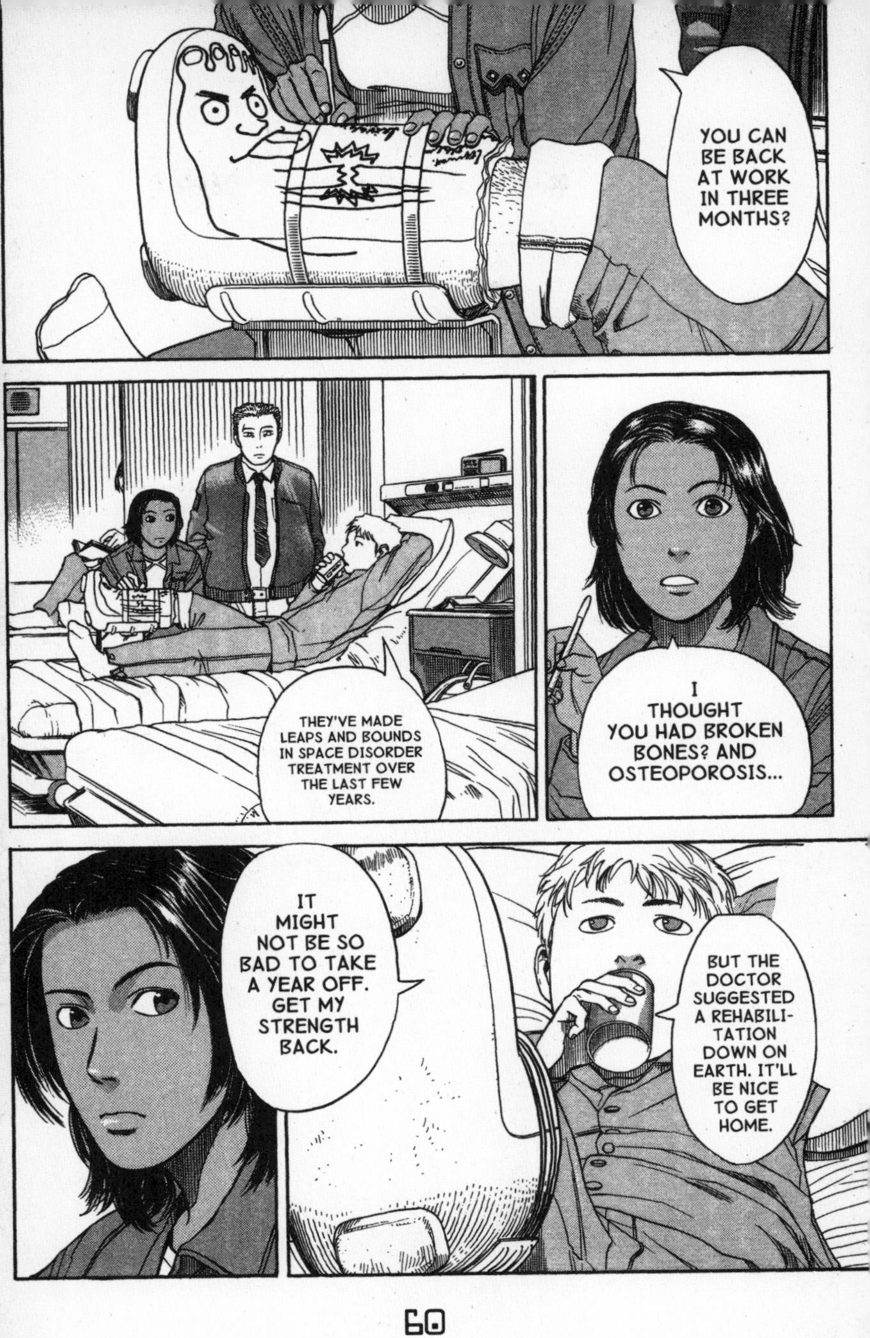
YOU CAN BE BACK AT WORK IN THREE MONTHS?
I THOUGHT YOU HAD BROKEN BONES? AND OSTEOPOROSIS...
THEY'VE MADE LEAPS AND BOUNDS IN SPACE DISORDER TREATMENT OVER THE LAST FEW YEARS.
BUT THE DOCTOR SUGGESTED A REHABILI-TATION DOWN ON EARTH. IT'LL BE NICE TO GET HOME.
IT MIGHT NOT BE SO BAD TO TAKE A YEAR OFF. GET MY STRENGTH BACK.

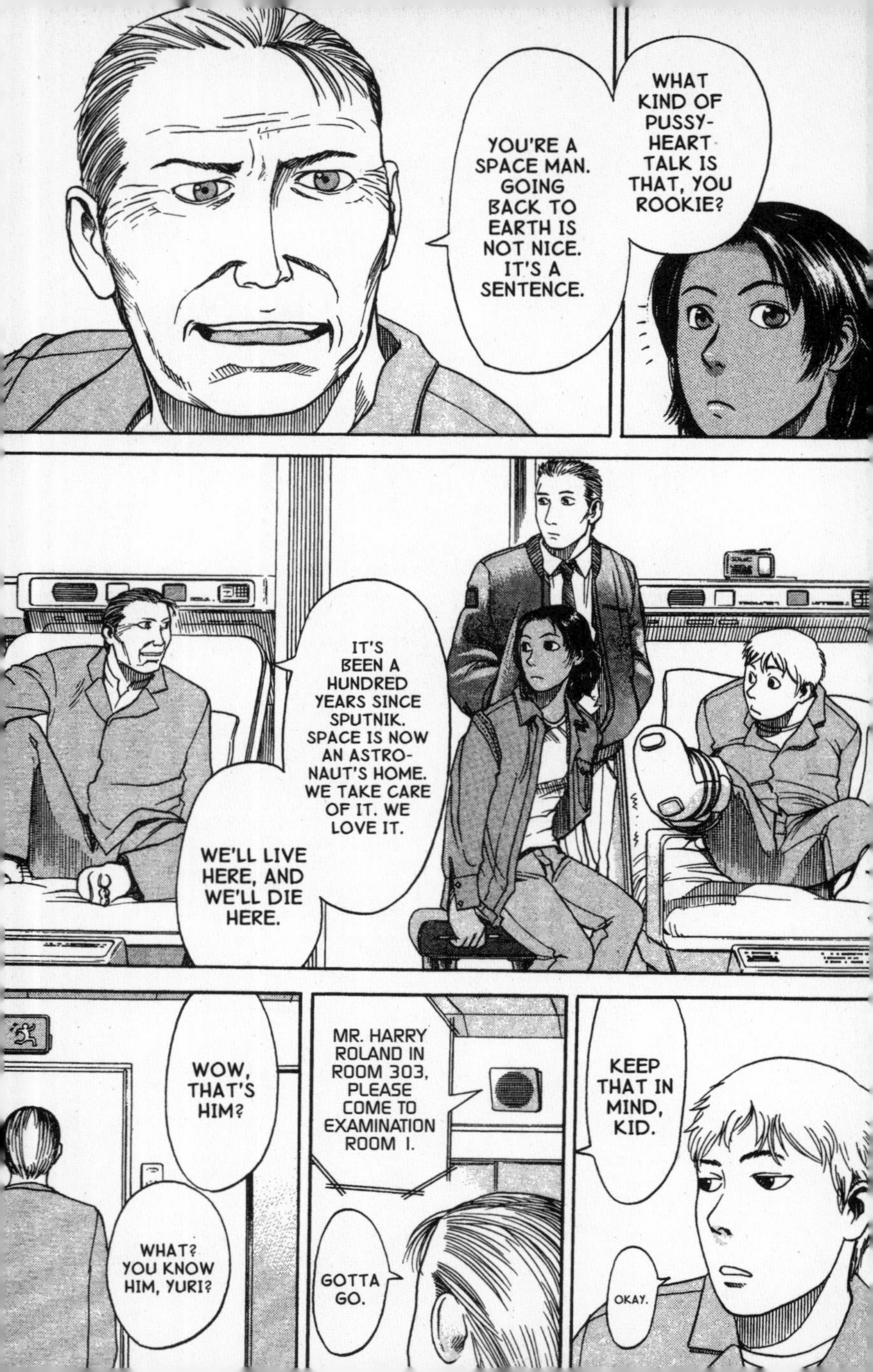
WHAT KIND OF PUSSY-HEART TALK IS THAT, YOU ROOKIE?
YOU'RE A SPACE MAN. GOING BACK TO EARTH IS NOT NICE. IT'S A SENTENCE.
IT'S BEEN A HUNDRED YEARS SINCE SPUTNIK. SPACE IS NOW AN ASTRO-NAUT'S HOME. WE TAKE CARE OF IT. WE LOVE IT.
WE'LL LIVE HERE, AND WE'LL DIE HERE.
KEEP THAT IN MIND, KID.
OKAY.
MR. HARRY ROLAND IN ROOM 303, PLEASE COME TO EXAMINATION ROOM 1.
GOTTA GO.
WOW, THAT'S HIM?
WHAT? YOU KNOW HIM, YURI?

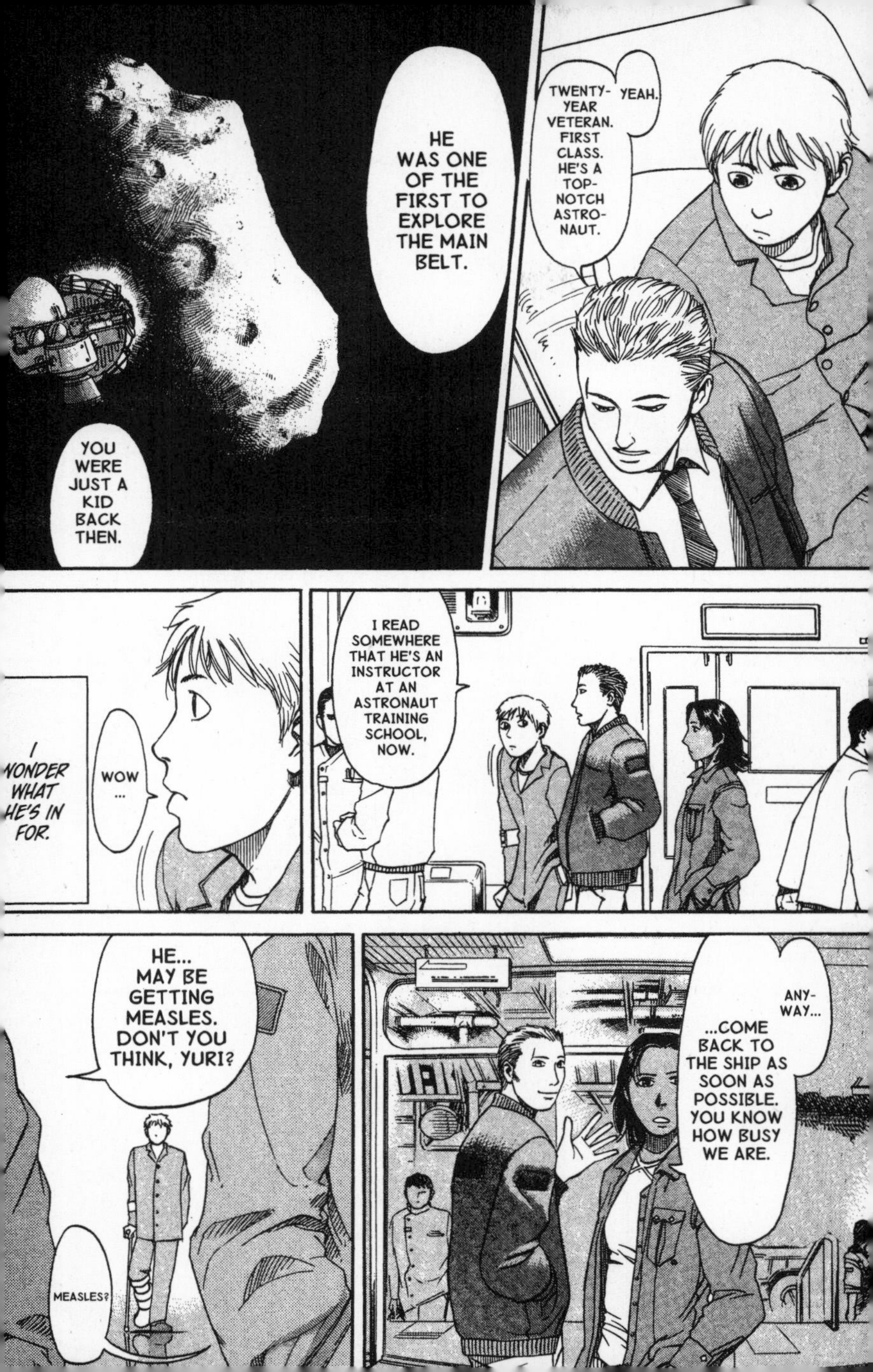
YEAH.
TWENTY-YEAR VETERAN. FIRST CLASS. HE'S A TOP-NOTCH ASTRONAUT.
HE WAS ONE OF THE FIRST TO EXPLORE THE MAIN BELT.
YOU WERE JUST A KID BACK THEN.
I READ SOMEWHERE THAT HE'S AN INSTRUCTOR AT AN ASTRONAUT TRAINING SCHOOL, NOW.
WOW ...
I WONDER WHAT HE'S IN FOR.
ANY-WAY...
...COME BACK TO THE SHIP AS SOON AS POSSIBLE. YOU KNOW HOW BUSY WE ARE.
HE... MAY BE GETTING MEASLES. DON'T YOU THINK, YURI?
MEASLES?

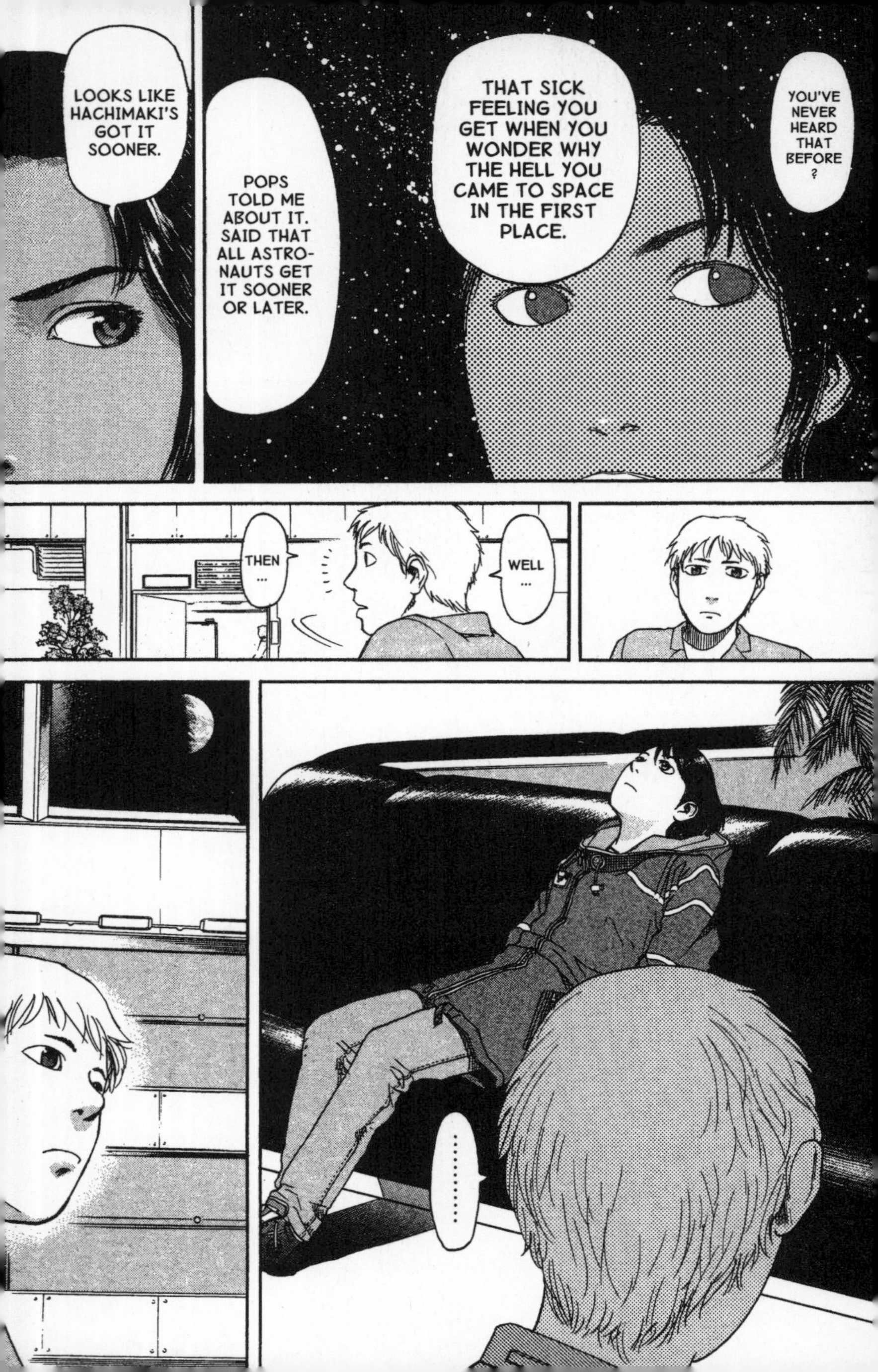
YOU'VE NEVER HEARD THAT BEFORE?
THAT SICK FEELING YOU GET WHEN YOU WONDER WHY THE HELL YOU CAME TO SPACE IN THE FIRST PLACE.
POPS TOLD ME ABOUT IT. SAID THAT ALL ASTRO-NAUTS GET IT SOONER OR LATER.
LOOKS LIKE HACHIMAKI'S GOT IT SOONER.
WELL ...
THEN ...
......

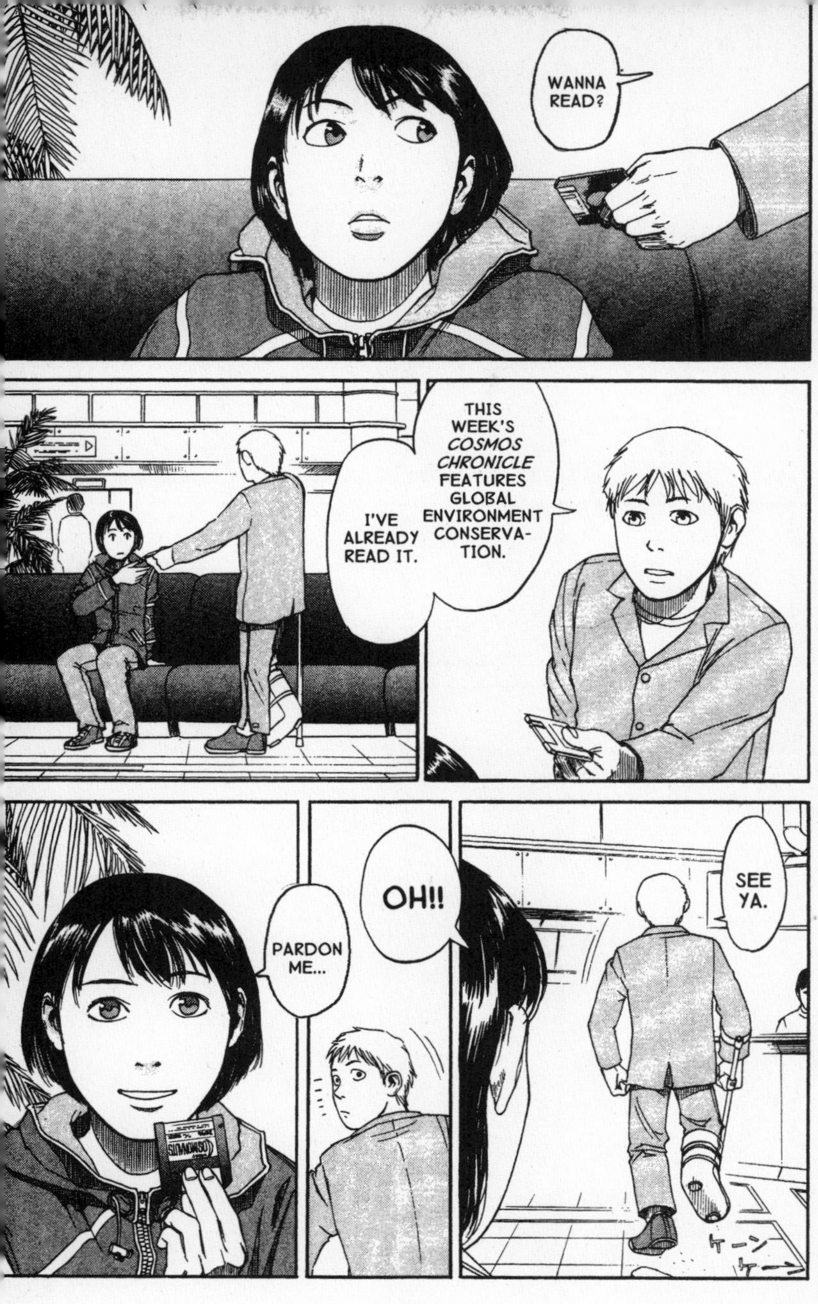
WANNA READ?
THIS WEEK'S *COSMOS CHRONICLE* FEATURES GLOBAL ENVIRONMENT CONSERVA-TION.
I'VE ALREADY READ IT.
SEE YA.
ケーン
ケー
OH!!
PARDON ME...

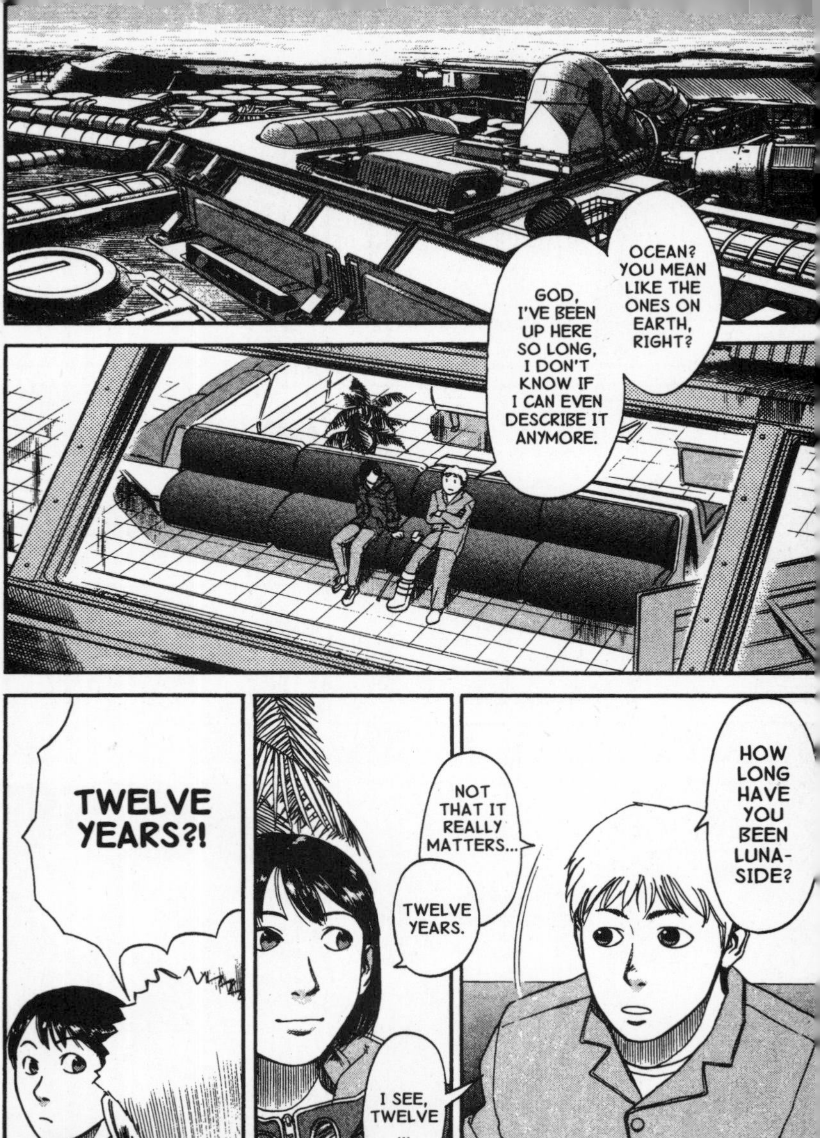
OCEAN? YOU MEAN LIKE THE ONES ON EARTH, RIGHT?
GOD, I'VE BEEN UP HERE SO LONG, I DON'T KNOW IF I CAN EVEN DESCRIBE IT ANYMORE.
HOW LONG HAVE YOU BEEN LUNA-SIDE?
NOT THAT IT REALLY MATTERS...
TWELVE YEARS.
I SEE, TWELVE ...
TWELVE YEARS?!

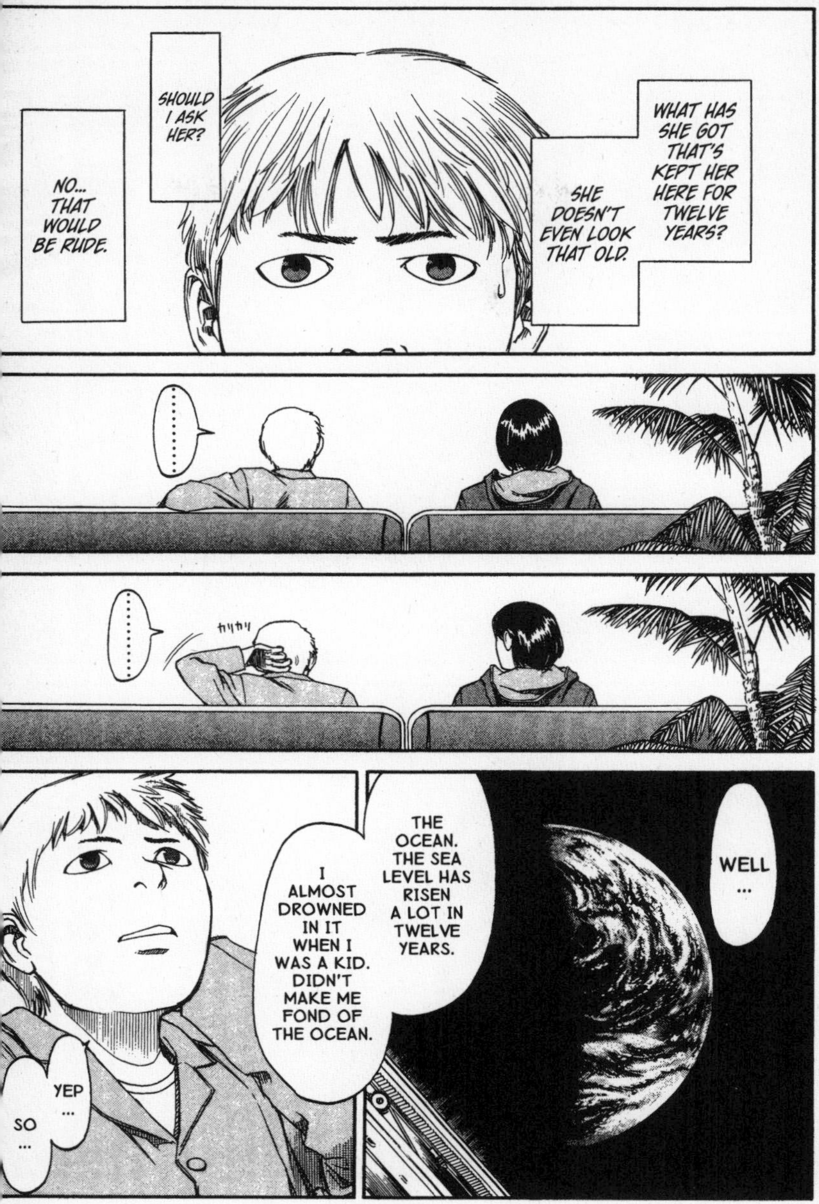
WHAT HAS SHE GOT THAT'S KEPT HER HERE FOR TWELVE YEARS?
SHE DOESN'T EVEN LOOK THAT OLD.
SHOULD I ASK HER?
NO... THAT WOULD BE RUDE.
......
カリカリ
......
WELL ...
THE OCEAN. THE SEA LEVEL HAS RISEN A LOT IN TWELVE YEARS.
I ALMOST DROWNED IN IT WHEN I WAS A KID. DIDN'T MAKE ME FOND OF THE OCEAN.
YEP ...
SO ...

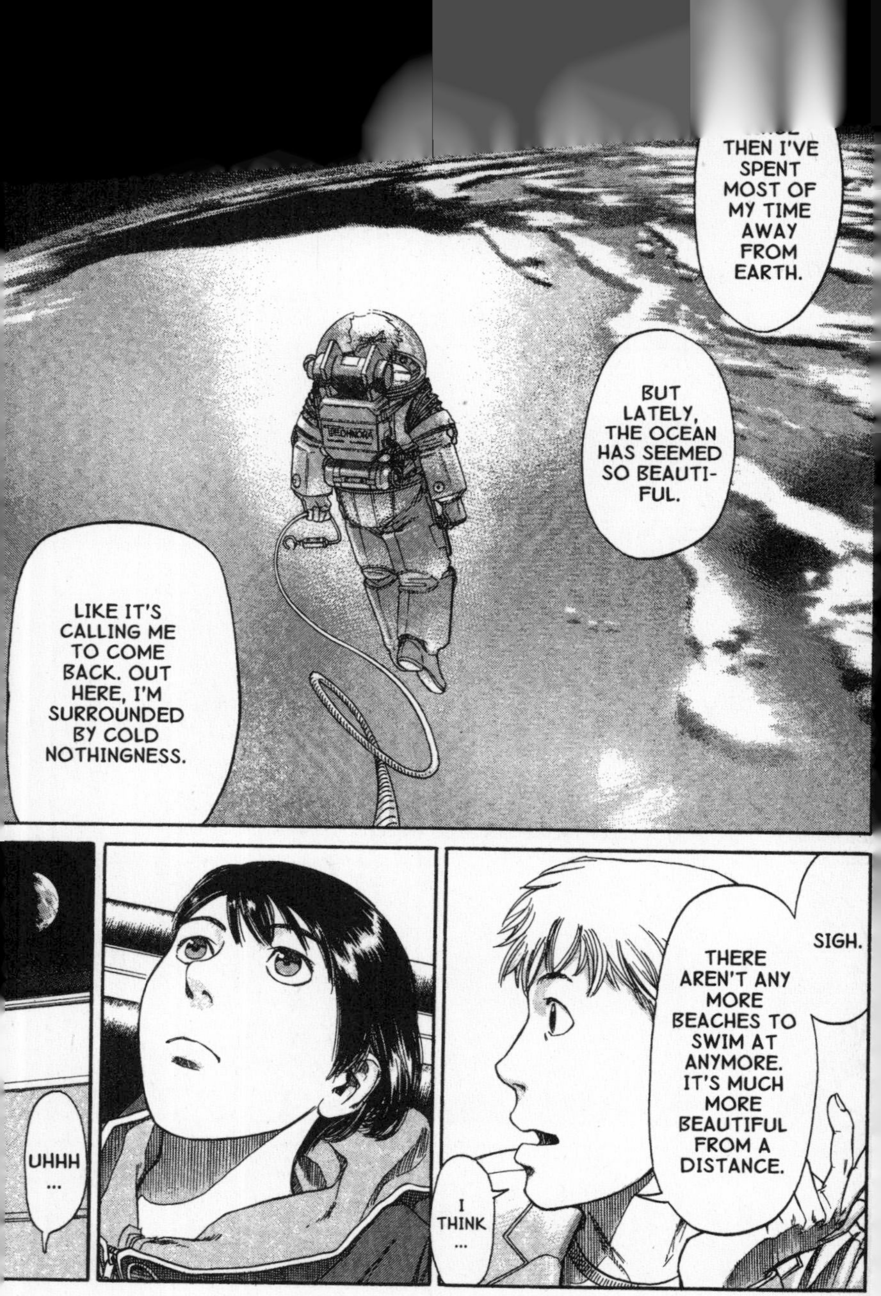
THEN I'VE SPENT MOST OF MY TIME AWAY FROM EARTH.
BUT LATELY, THE OCEAN HAS SEEMED SO BEAUTI-FUL.
LIKE IT'S CALLING ME TO COME BACK. OUT HERE, I'M SURROUNDED BY COLD NOTHINGNESS.
SIGH.
THERE AREN'T ANY MORE BEACHES TO SWIM AT ANYMORE. IT'S MUCH MORE BEAUTIFUL FROM A DISTANCE.
I THINK ...
UHHH ...

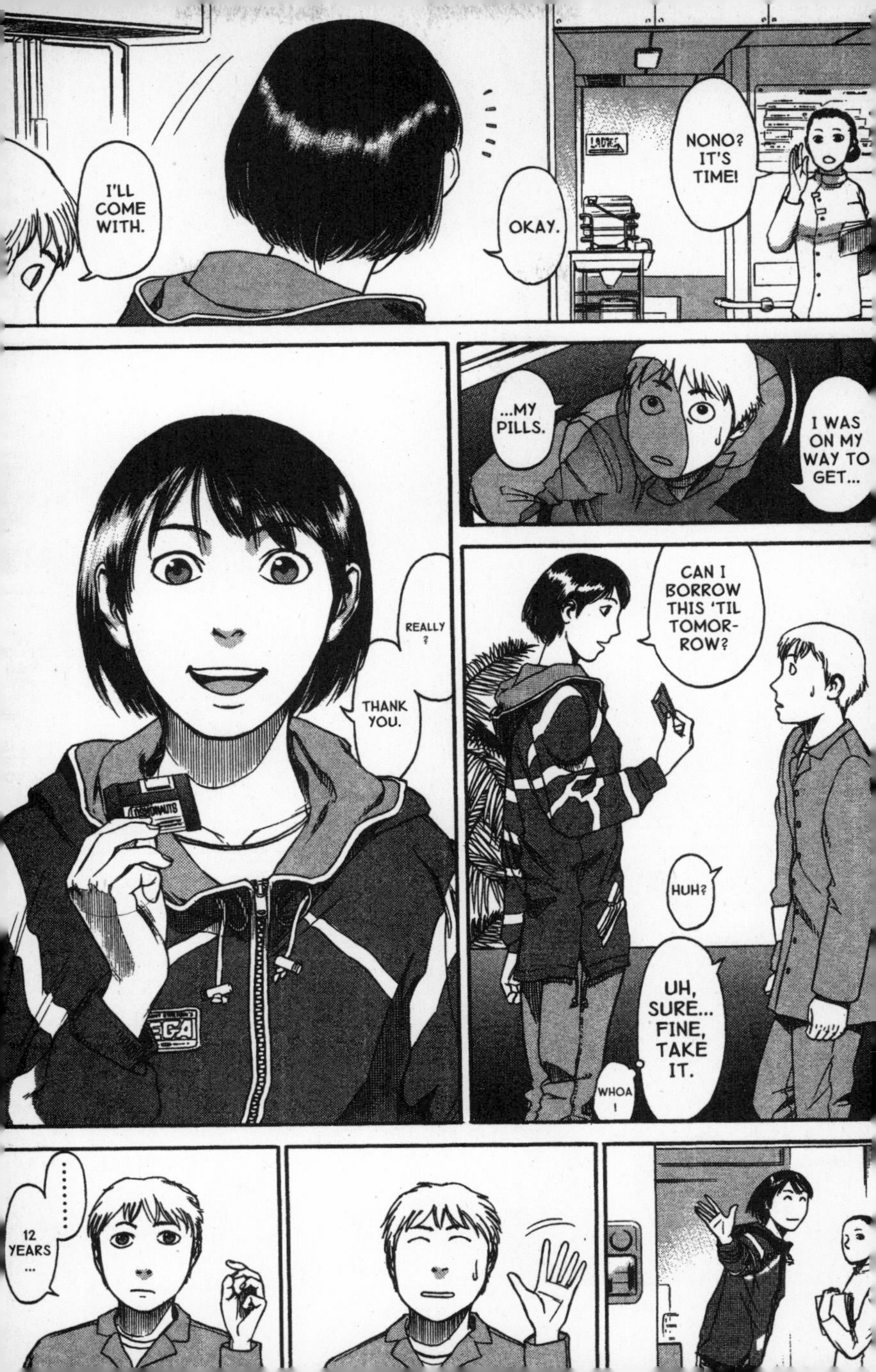
NONO? IT'S TIME!
OKAY.
I'LL COME WITH.
I WAS ON MY WAY TO GET...
...MY PILLS.
CAN I BORROW THIS 'TIL TOMOR-ROW?
HUH?
UH, SURE... FINE, TAKE IT.
WHOA!
REALLY?
THANK YOU.
......
12 YEARS...

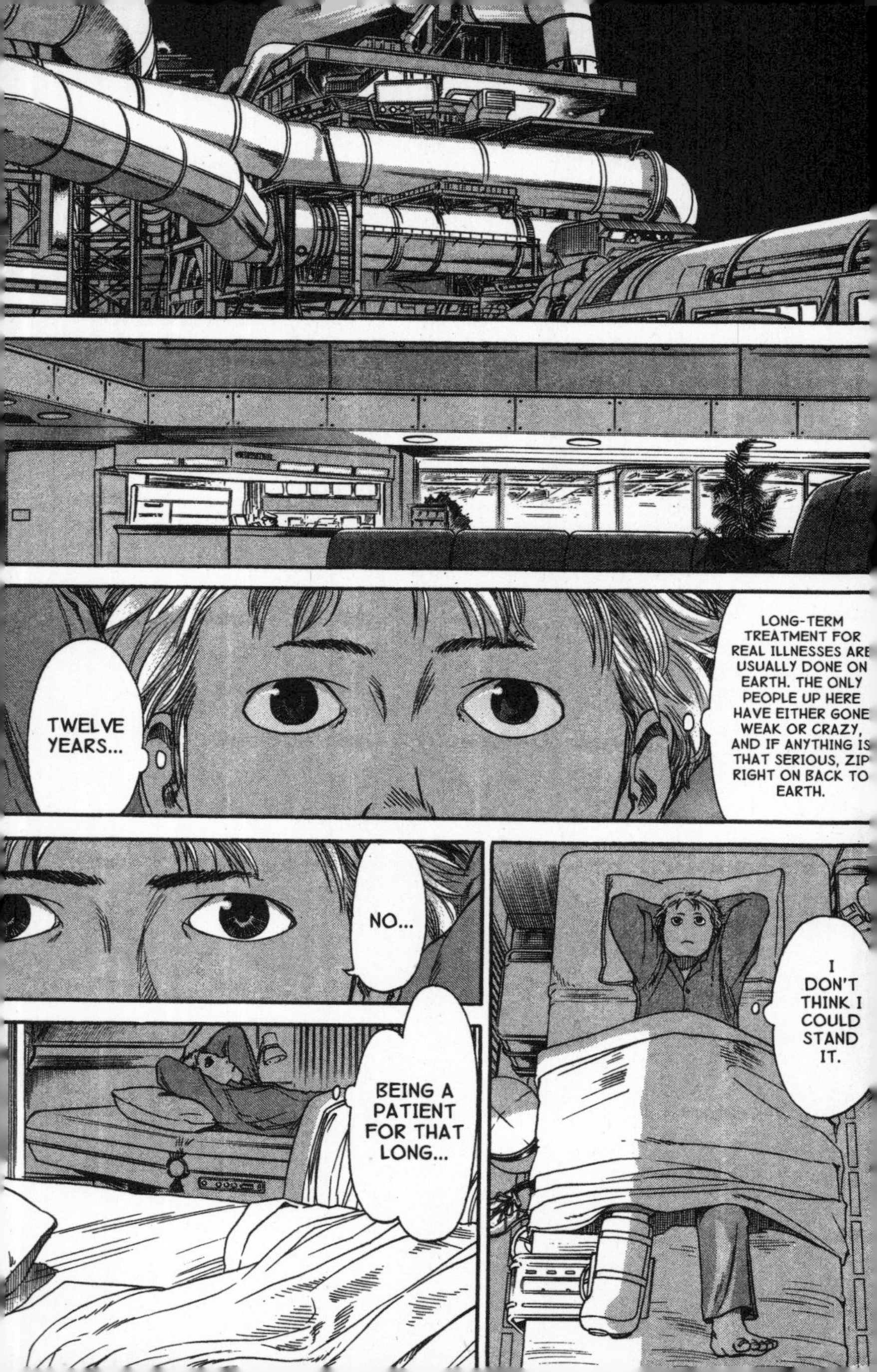
LONG-TERM TREATMENT FOR REAL ILLNESSES ARE USUALLY DONE ON EARTH. THE ONLY PEOPLE UP HERE HAVE EITHER GONE WEAK OR CRAZY, AND IF ANYTHING IS THAT SERIOUS, ZIP RIGHT ON BACK TO EARTH.
TWELVE YEARS...
I DON'T THINK I COULD STAND IT.
NO...
BEING A PATIENT FOR THAT LONG...

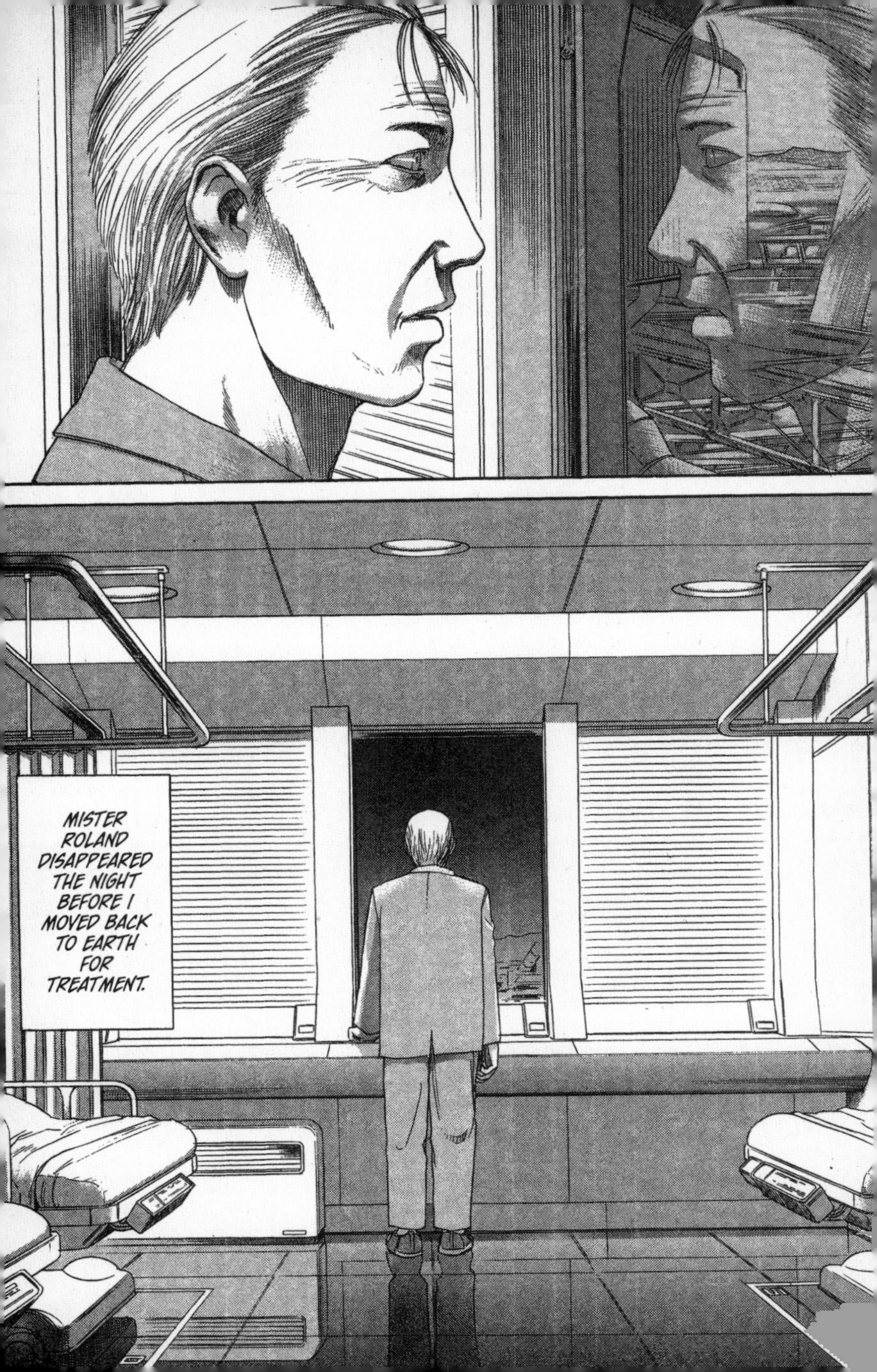
MISTER ROLAND DISAPPEARED THE NIGHT BEFORE I MOVED BACK TO EARTH FOR TREATMENT.

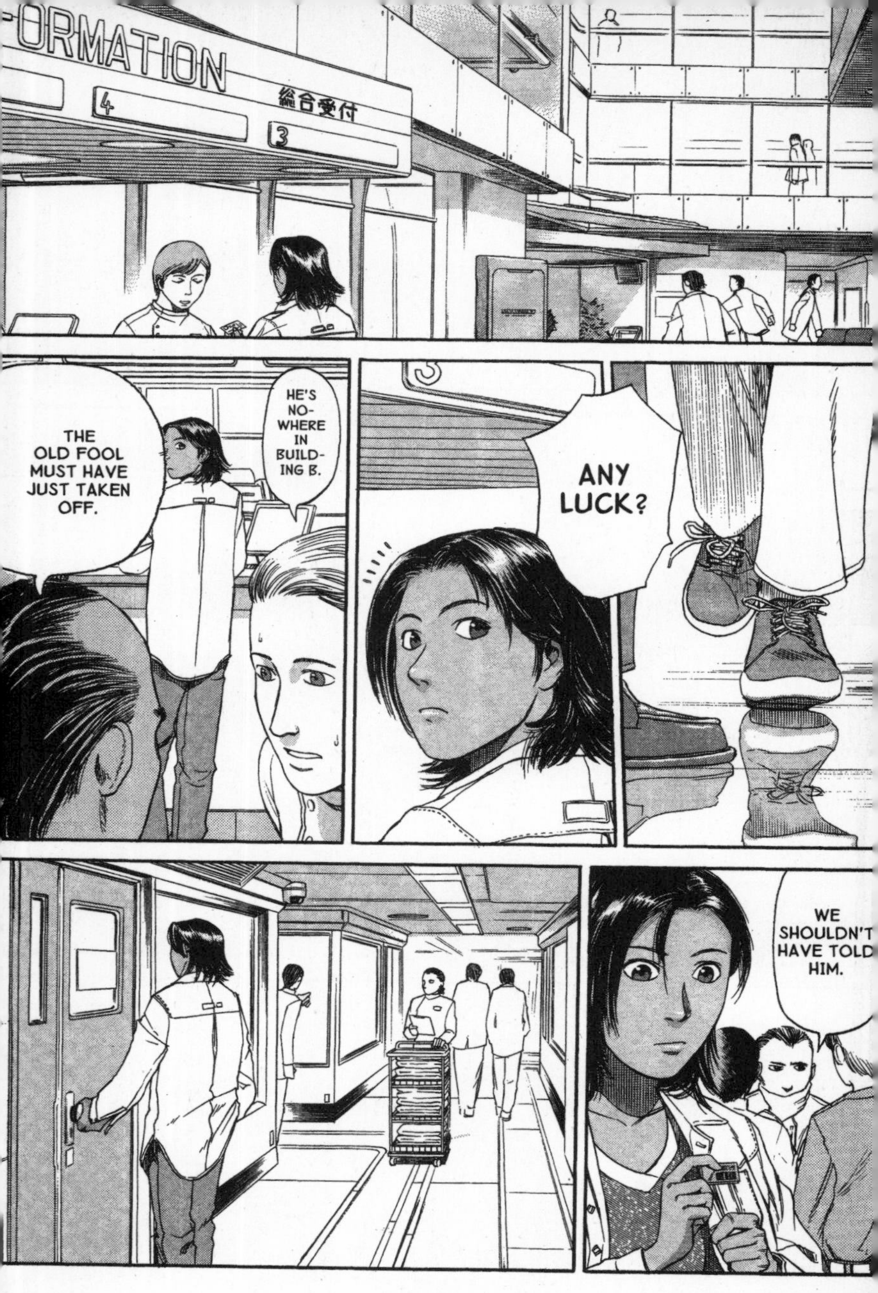
ORMATION
総合受付
4
3
ANY LUCK?
HE'S NO-WHERE IN BUILD-ING B.
THE OLD FOOL MUST HAVE JUST TAKEN OFF.
WE SHOULDN'T HAVE TOLD HIM.

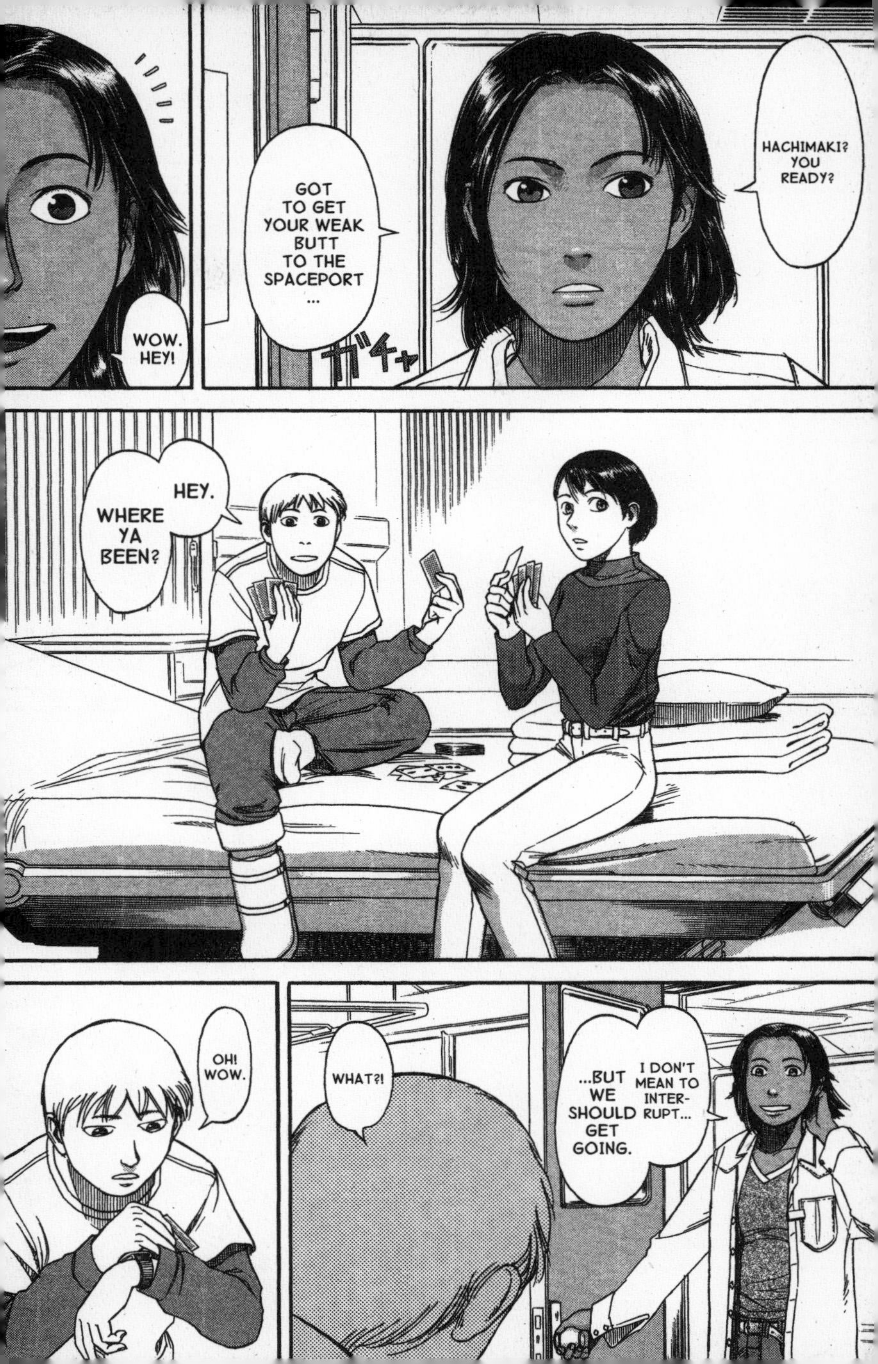
HACHIMAKI? YOU READY?
GOT TO GET YOUR WEAK BUTT TO THE SPACEPORT ...
ガチャ
WOW. HEY!
HEY. WHERE YA BEEN?
I DON'T MEAN TO INTER-RUPT...
...BUT WE SHOULD GET GOING.
WHAT?!
OH! WOW.

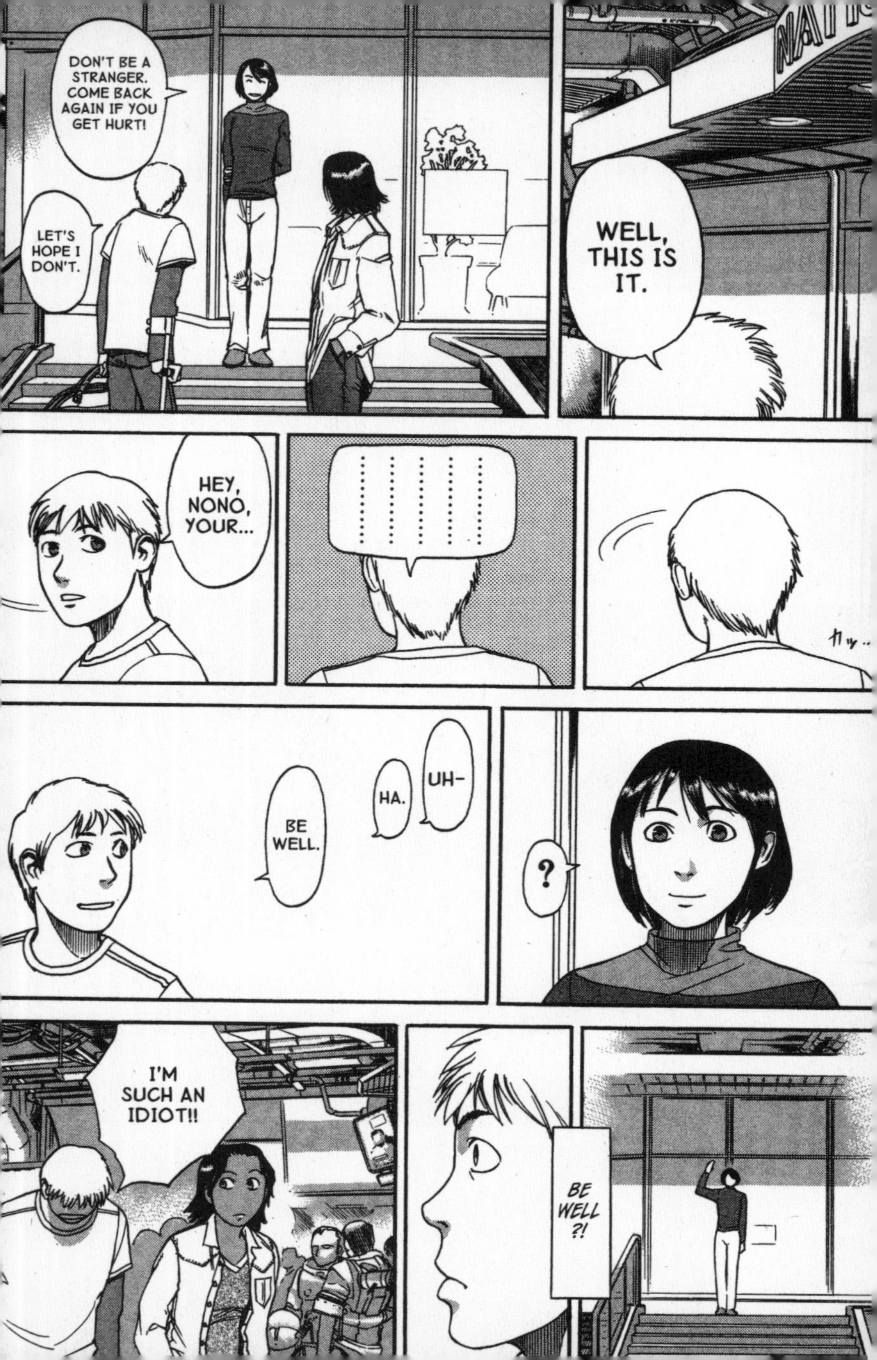
WELL, THIS IS IT.
DON'T BE A STRANGER. COME BACK AGAIN IF YOU GET HURT!
LET'S HOPE I DON'T.
......
HEY, NONO, YOUR...
?
UH-
HA.
BE WELL.
BE WELL ?!
I'M SUCH AN IDIOT!!

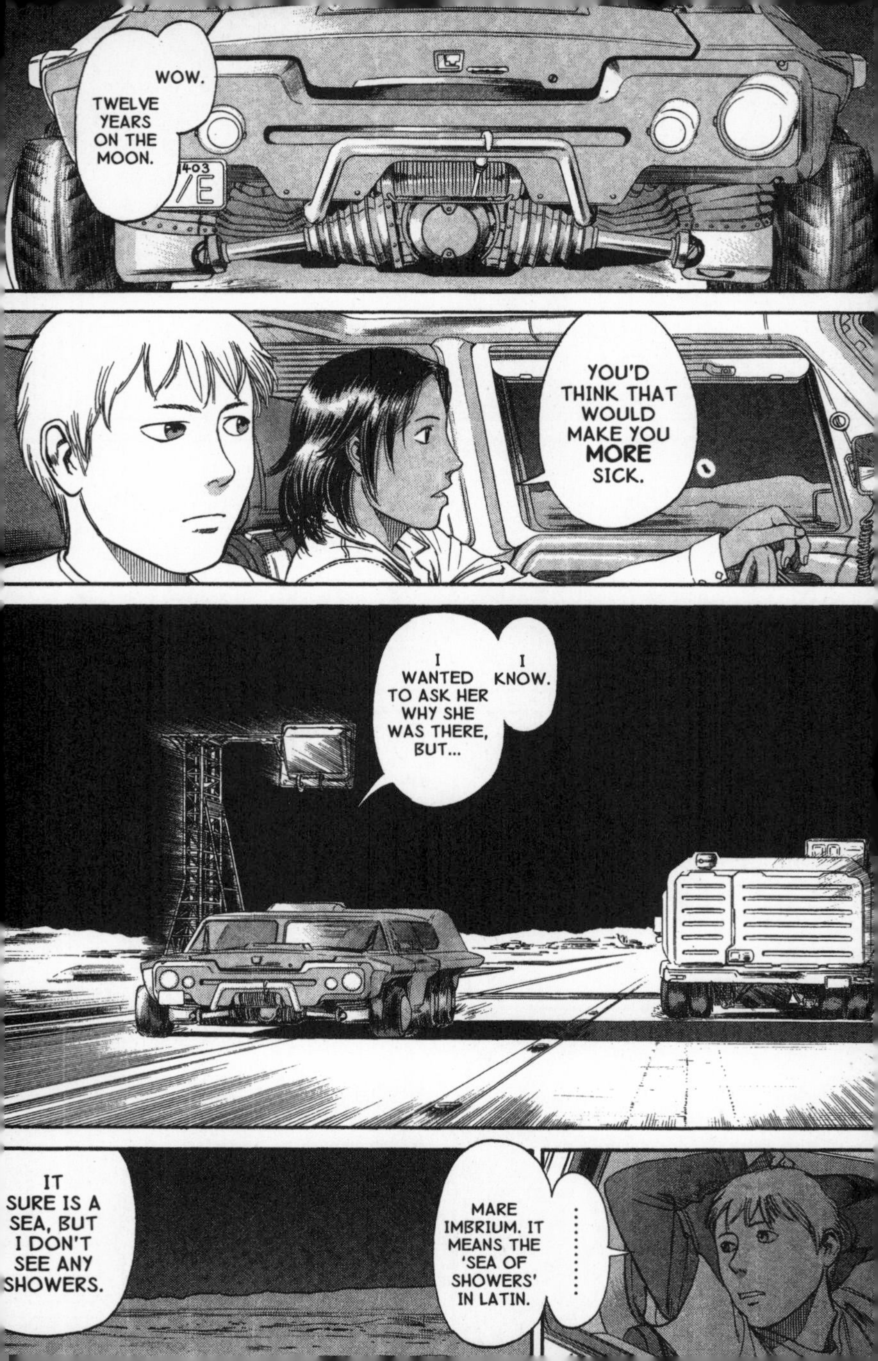
WOW. TWELVE YEARS ON THE MOON.
YOU'D THINK THAT WOULD MAKE YOU **MORE** SICK.
I KNOW.
I WANTED TO ASK HER WHY SHE WAS THERE, BUT...
......
MARE IMBRIUM. IT MEANS THE 'SEA OF SHOWERS' IN LATIN.
IT SURE IS A SEA, BUT I DON'T SEE ANY SHOWERS.

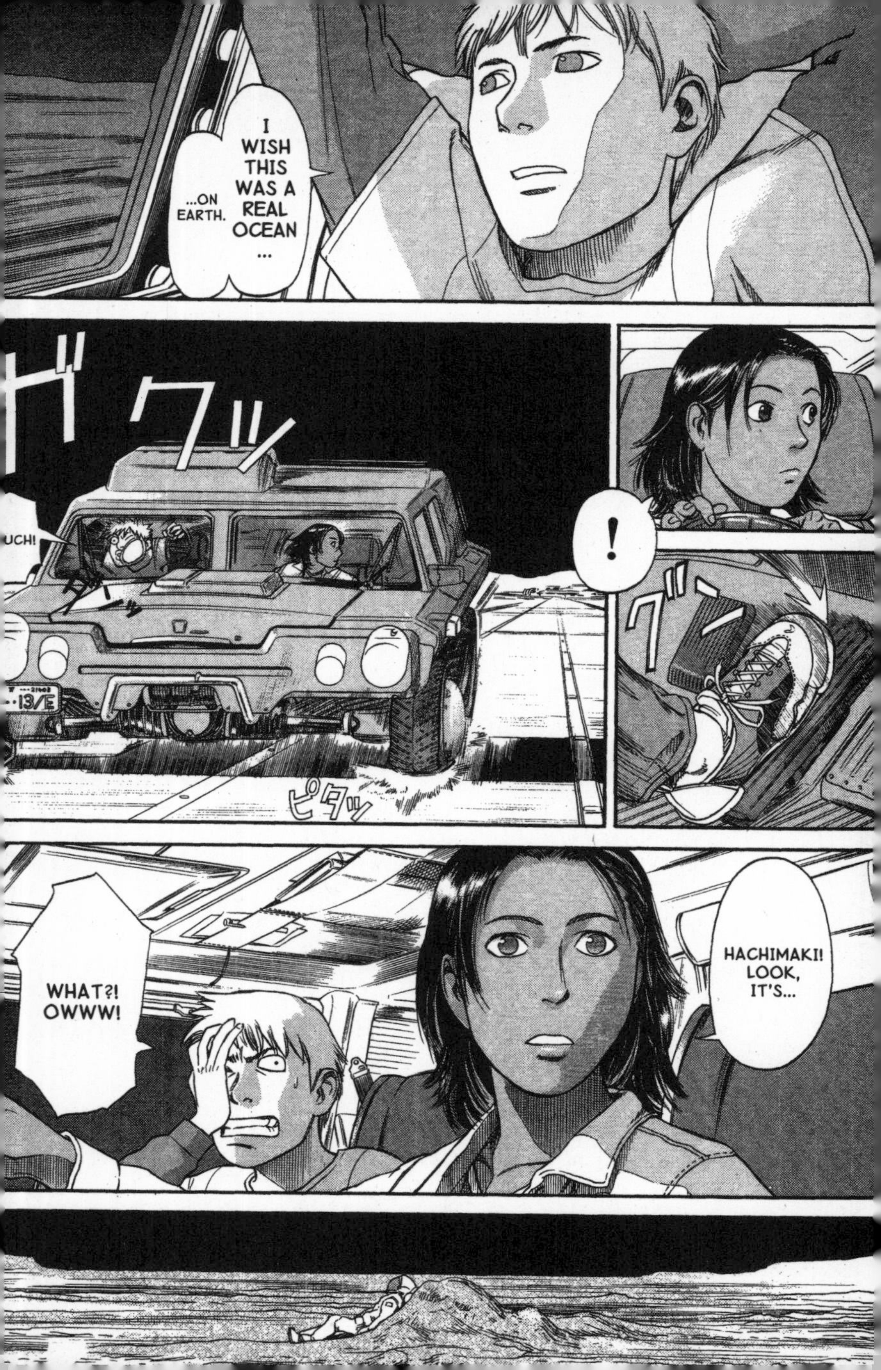

I WISH THIS WAS A REAL OCEAN ...
...ON EARTH.
!
ガクッ
UCH!
ピタッ
HACHIMAKI! LOOK, IT'S...
WHAT?! OWWW!

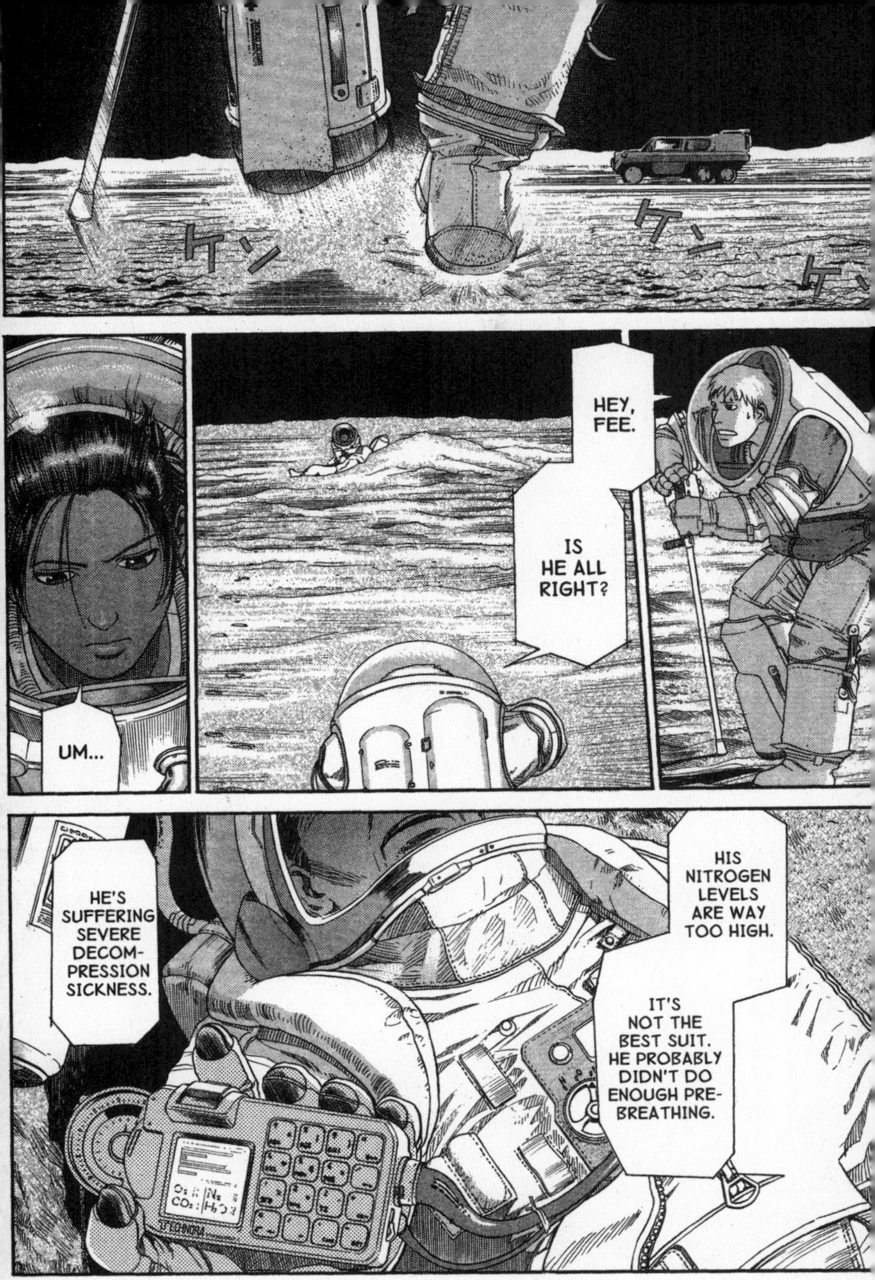
ケン
ケン
ケン
HEY, FEE.
IS HE ALL RIGHT?
UM...
HIS NITROGEN LEVELS ARE WAY TOO HIGH.
IT'S NOT THE BEST SUIT. HE PROBABLY DIDN'T DO ENOUGH PRE-BREATHING.
HE'S SUFFERING SEVERE DECOM-PRESSION SICKNESS.

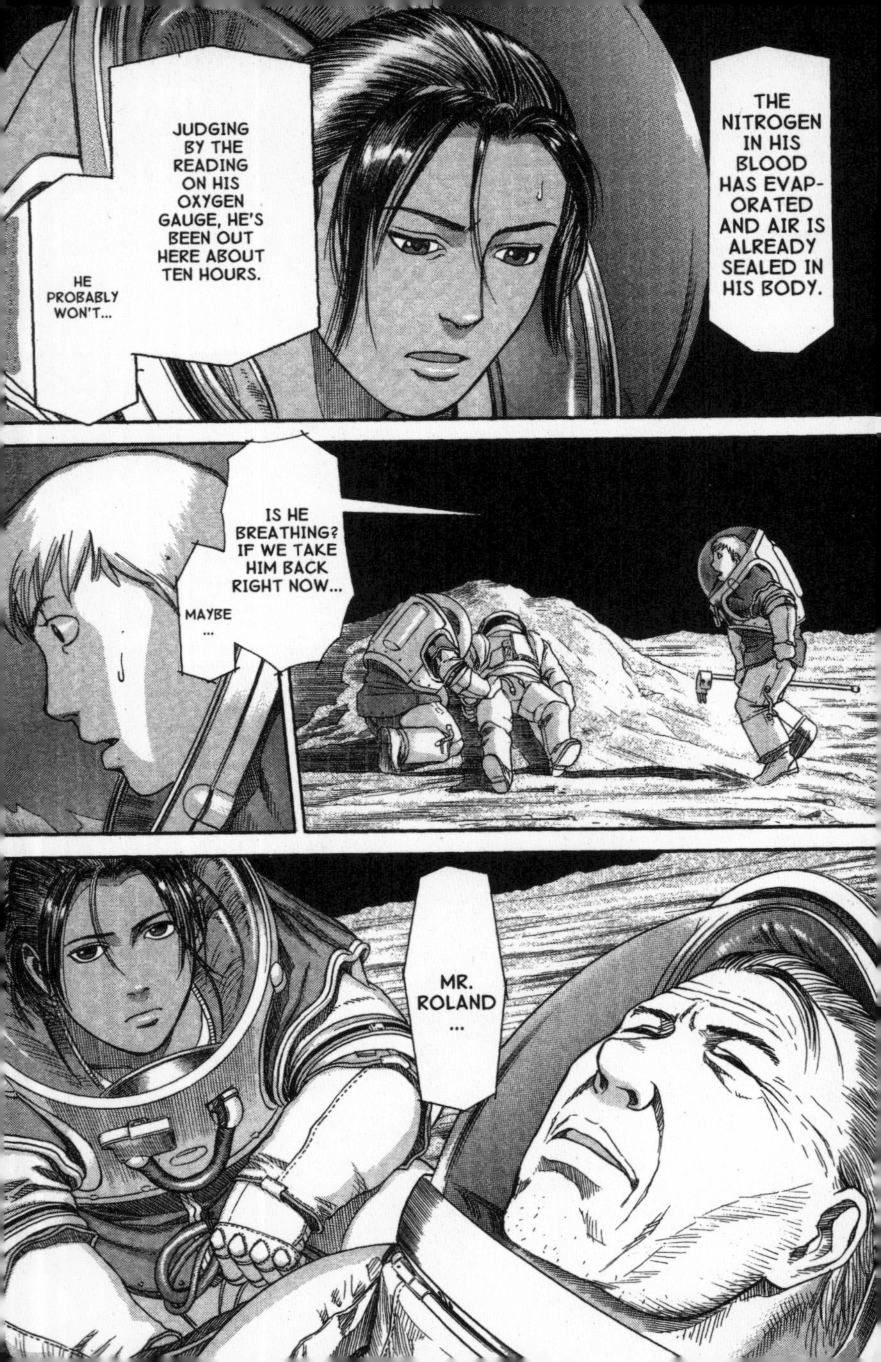
THE NITROGEN IN HIS BLOOD HAS EVAPORATED AND AIR IS ALREADY SEALED IN HIS BODY.
JUDGING BY THE READING ON HIS OXYGEN GAUGE, HE'S BEEN OUT HERE ABOUT TEN HOURS.
HE PROBABLY WON'T...
IS HE BREATHING? IF WE TAKE HIM BACK RIGHT NOW...
MAYBE ...
MR. ROLAND ...

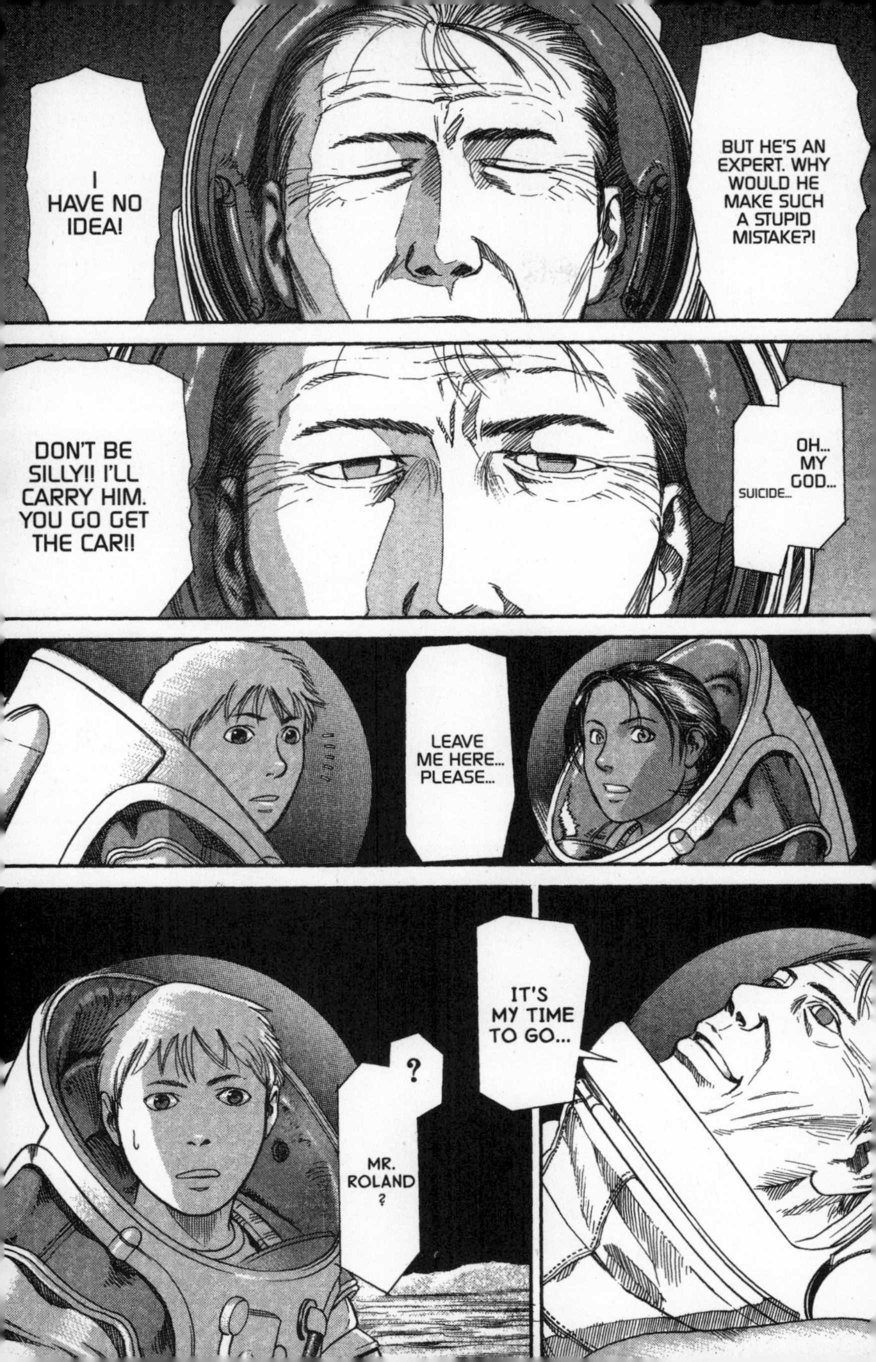
BUT HE'S AN EXPERT. WHY WOULD HE MAKE SUCH A STUPID MISTAKE?!
I HAVE NO IDEA!
OH... MY GOD...
SUICIDE...
DON'T BE SILLY!! I'LL CARRY HIM. YOU GO GET THE CAR!!
LEAVE ME HERE... PLEASE...
IT'S MY TIME TO GO...
?
MR. ROLAND ?

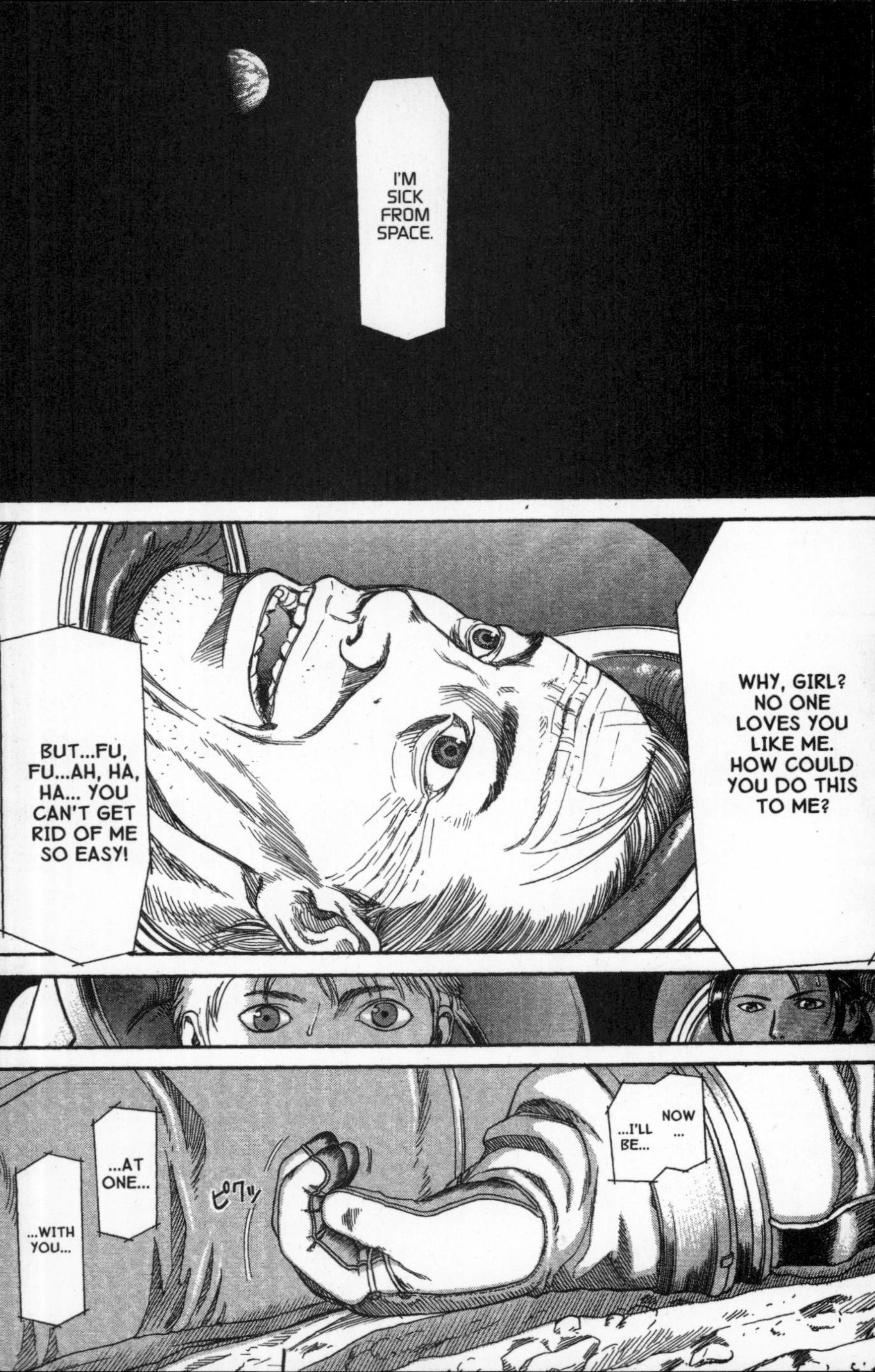
I'M SICK FROM SPACE.
WHY, GIRL? NO ONE LOVES YOU LIKE ME. HOW COULD YOU DO THIS TO ME?
BUT...FU, FU...AH, HA, HA... YOU CAN'T GET RID OF ME SO EASY!
NOW ...
...I'LL BE...
ピクッ
...AT ONE...
...WITH YOU...

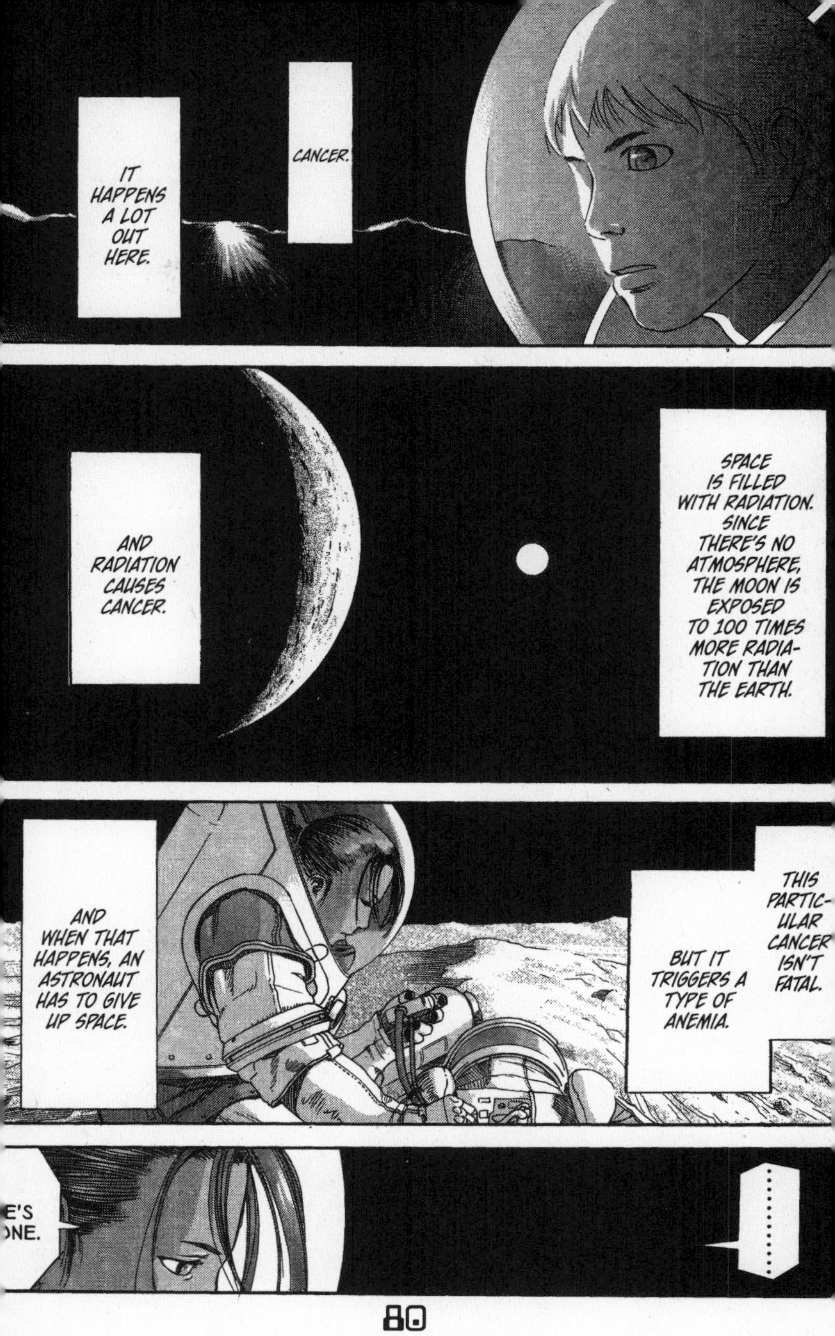
CANCER.
IT HAPPENS A LOT OUT HERE.
SPACE IS FILLED WITH RADIATION. SINCE THERE'S NO ATMOSPHERE, THE MOON IS EXPOSED TO 100 TIMES MORE RADIATION THAN THE EARTH.
AND RADIATION CAUSES CANCER.
THIS PARTICULAR CANCER ISN'T FATAL.
BUT IT TRIGGERS A TYPE OF ANEMIA.
AND WHEN THAT HAPPENS, AN ASTRONAUT HAS TO GIVE UP SPACE.
......
E'S ONE.

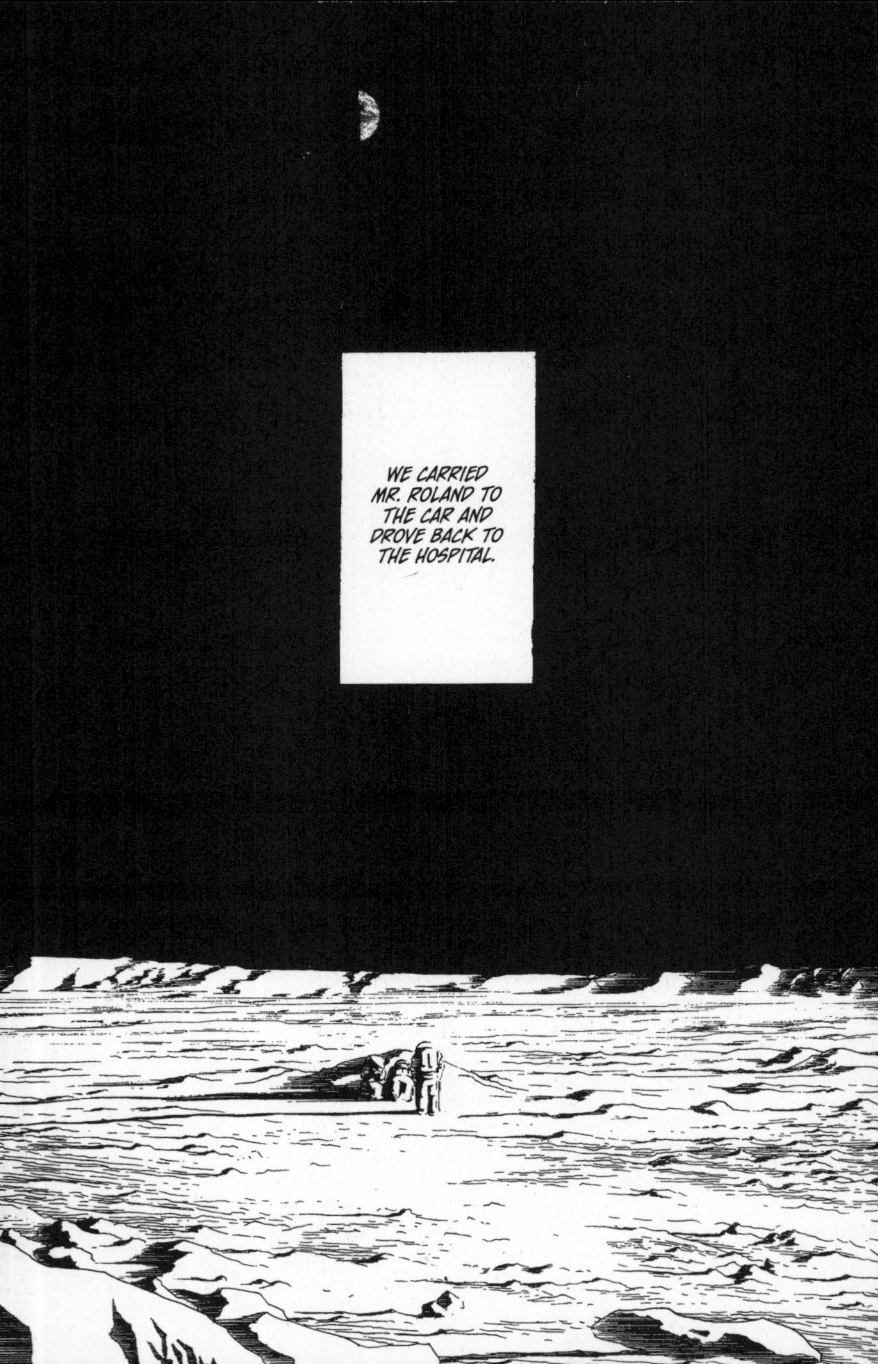
WE CARRIED MR. ROLAND TO THE CAR AND DROVE BACK TO THE HOSPITAL.

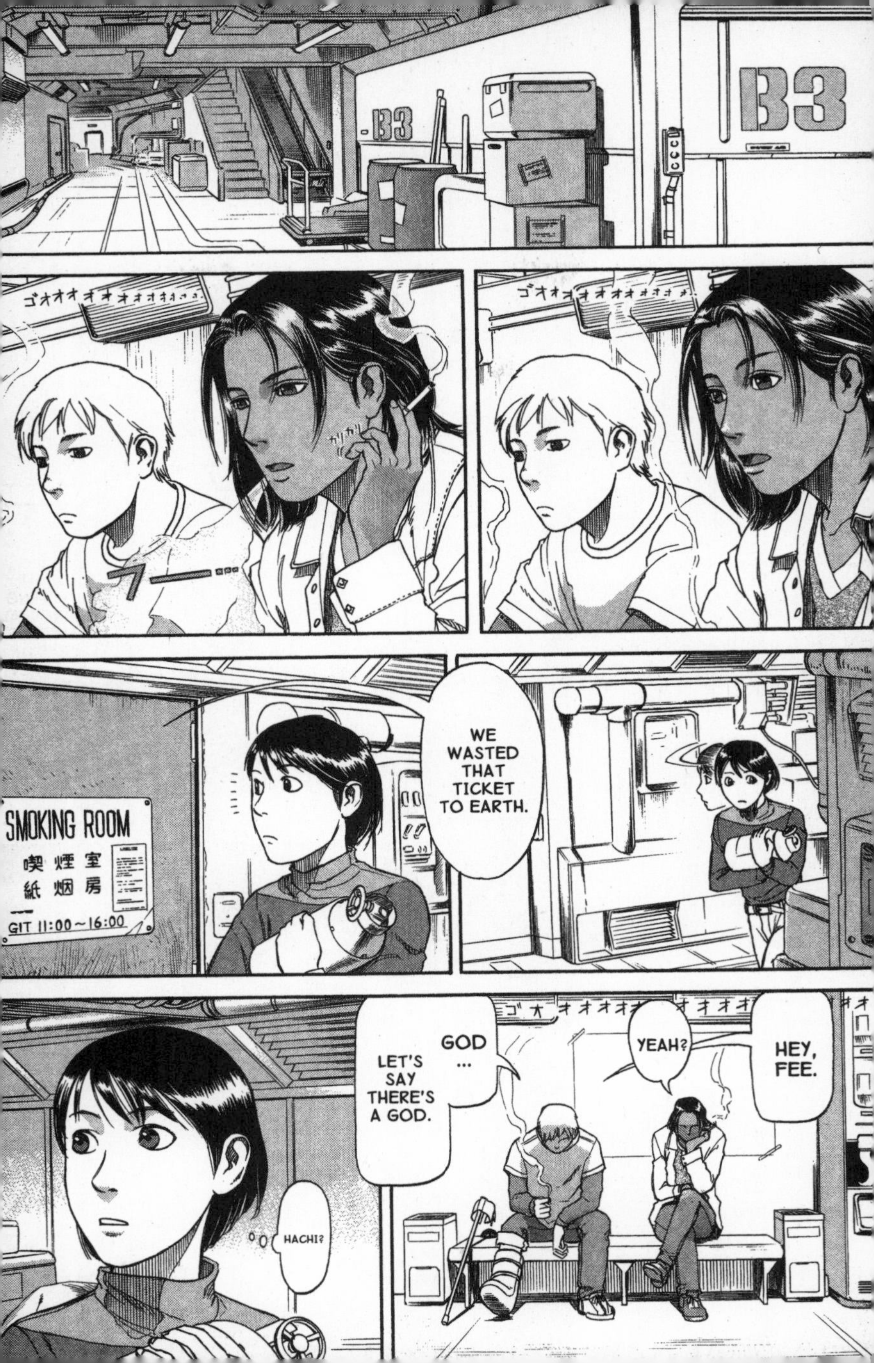
B3
B3
ゴオオオオオオオオ
ゴオオオオオオオオ
カリカリ
フー
WE WASTED THAT TICKET TO EARTH.
SMOKING ROOM
喫煙室
紙烟房
GIT 11:00~16:00
HEY, FEE.
YEAH?
GOD ...
LET'S SAY THERE'S A GOD.
ゴオオオオオオオオ
HACHI?

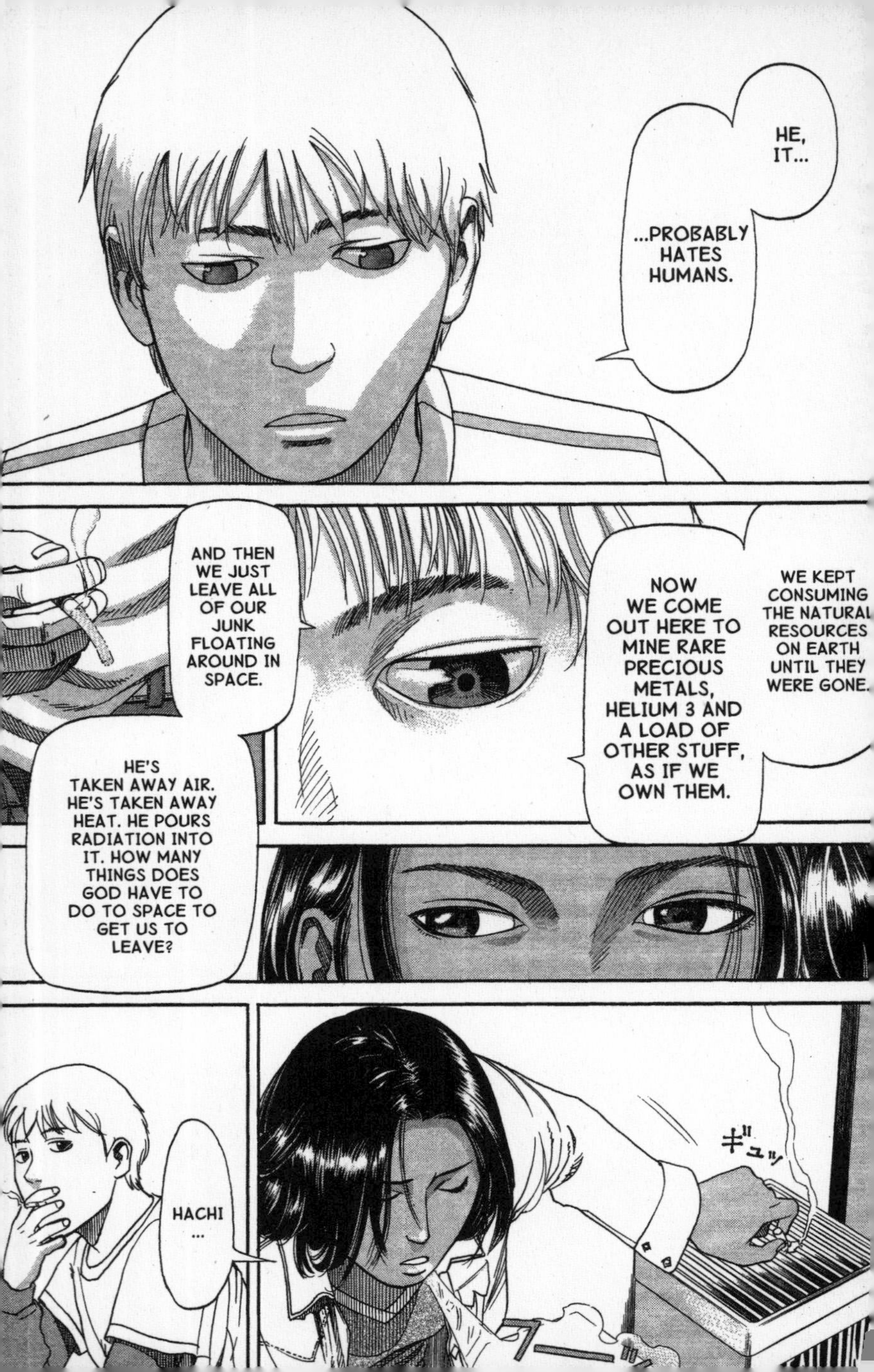
HE, IT...
...PROBABLY HATES HUMANS.
WE KEPT CONSUMING THE NATURAL RESOURCES ON EARTH UNTIL THEY WERE GONE.
NOW WE COME OUT HERE TO MINE RARE PRECIOUS METALS, HELIUM 3 AND A LOAD OF OTHER STUFF, AS IF WE OWN THEM.
AND THEN WE JUST LEAVE ALL OF OUR JUNK FLOATING AROUND IN SPACE.
HE'S TAKEN AWAY AIR. HE'S TAKEN AWAY HEAT. HE POURS RADIATION INTO IT. HOW MANY THINGS DOES GOD HAVE TO DO TO SPACE TO GET US TO LEAVE?
ギュッ
HACHI ...

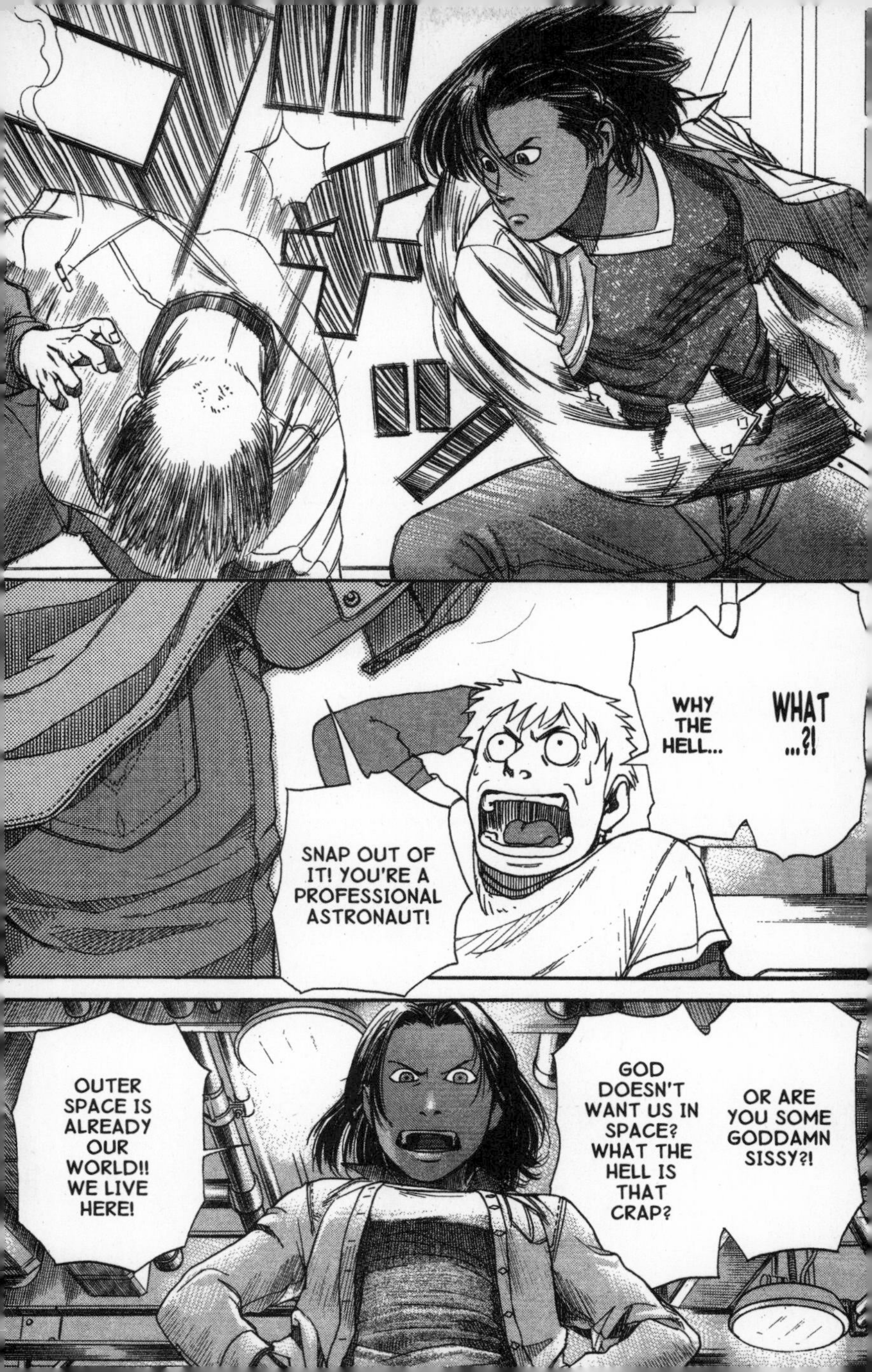
WHAT ...?!
WHY THE HELL...
SNAP OUT OF IT! YOU'RE A PROFESSIONAL ASTRONAUT!
OR ARE YOU SOME GODDAMN SISSY?!
GOD DOESN'T WANT US IN SPACE? WHAT THE HELL IS THAT CRAP?
OUTER SPACE IS ALREADY OUR WORLD!! WE LIVE HERE!

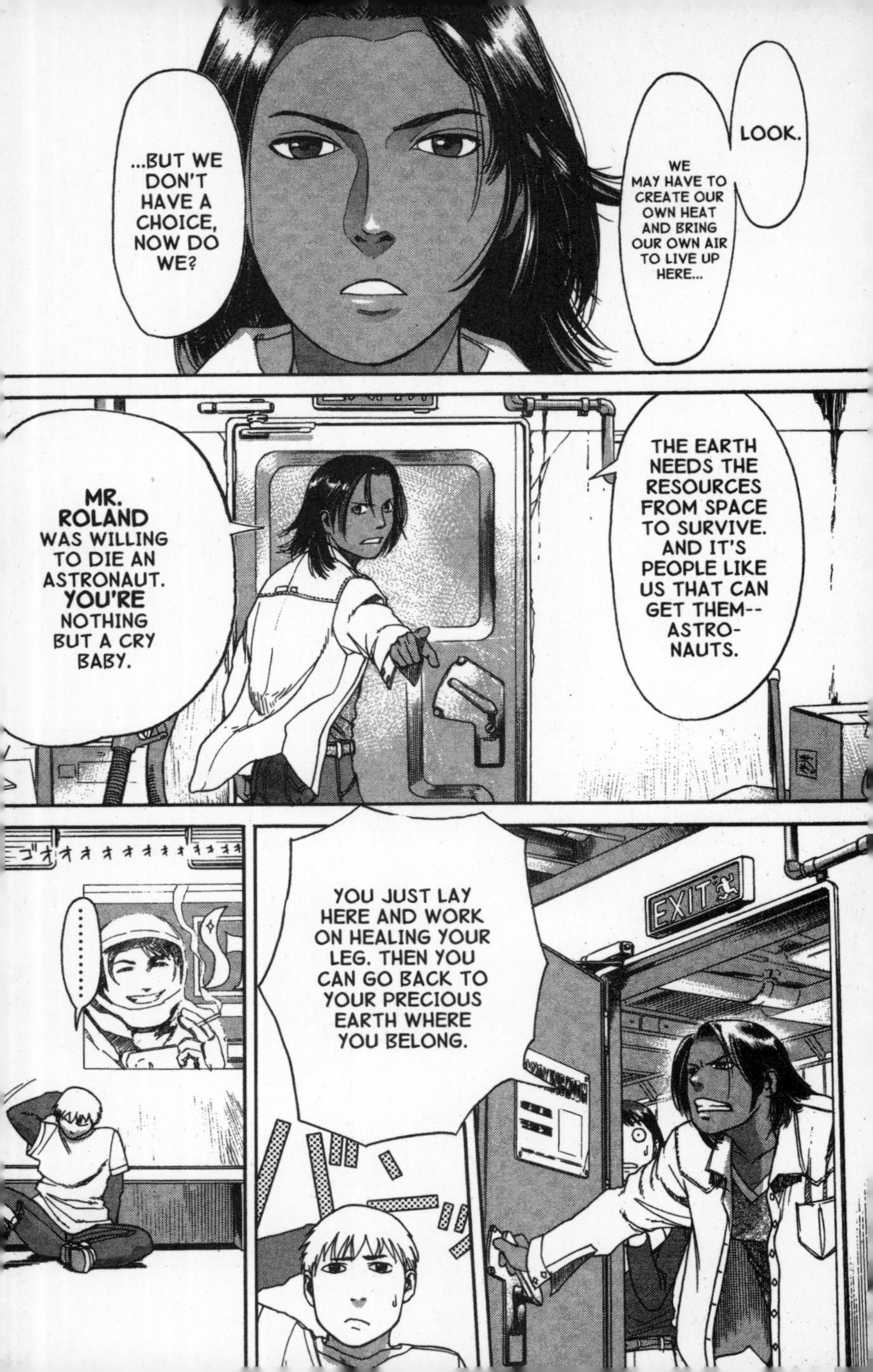
LOOK.
WE MAY HAVE TO CREATE OUR OWN HEAT AND BRING OUR OWN AIR TO LIVE UP HERE...
...BUT WE DON'T HAVE A CHOICE, NOW DO WE?
THE EARTH NEEDS THE RESOURCES FROM SPACE TO SURVIVE. AND IT'S PEOPLE LIKE US THAT CAN GET THEM-- ASTRONAUTS.
MR. ROLAND WAS WILLING TO DIE AN ASTRONAUT. YOU'RE NOTHING BUT A CRY BABY.
EXIT
YOU JUST LAY HERE AND WORK ON HEALING YOUR LEG. THEN YOU CAN GO BACK TO YOUR PRECIOUS EARTH WHERE YOU BELONG.
ゴオオオオオオオオオオオ
....

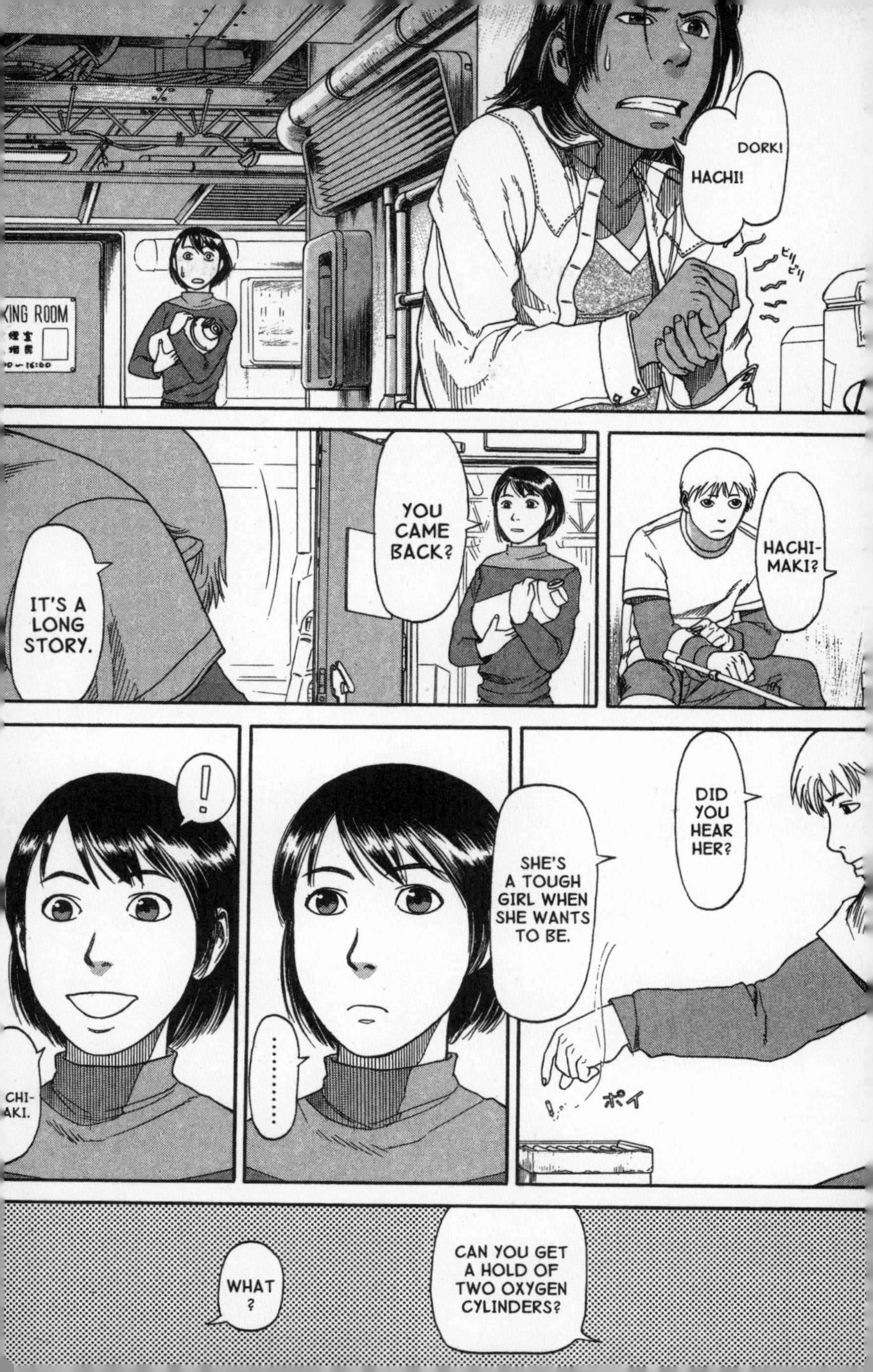
DORK!
HACHI!
ビリビリ
KING ROOM
HACHI-MAKI?
YOU CAME BACK?
IT'S A LONG STORY.
DID YOU HEAR HER?
SHE'S A TOUGH GIRL WHEN SHE WANTS TO BE.
ポイ
......
!
CHI-AKI.
CAN YOU GET A HOLD OF TWO OXYGEN CYLINDERS?
WHAT?

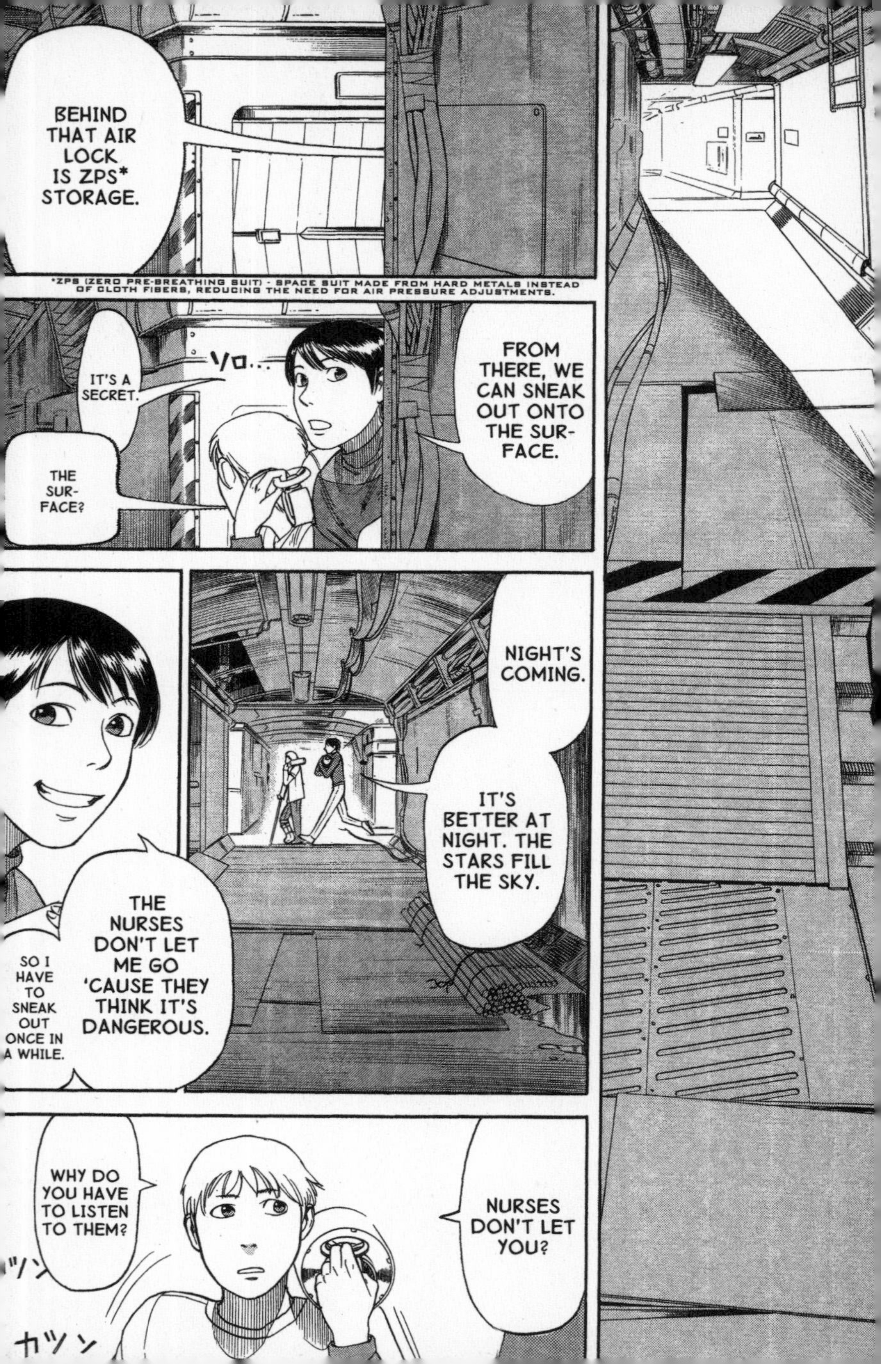
BEHIND THAT AIR LOCK IS ZPS* STORAGE.
*ZPS (ZERO PRE-BREATHING SUIT) - SPACE SUIT MADE FROM HARD METALS INSTEAD OF CLOTH FIBERS, REDUCING THE NEED FOR AIR PRESSURE ADJUSTMENTS.
FROM THERE, WE CAN SNEAK OUT ONTO THE SUR-FACE.
ソロ...
IT'S A SECRET.
THE SUR-FACE?
NIGHT'S COMING.
IT'S BETTER AT NIGHT. THE STARS FILL THE SKY.
THE NURSES DON'T LET ME GO 'CAUSE THEY THINK IT'S DANGEROUS.
SO I HAVE TO SNEAK OUT ONCE IN A WHILE.
NURSES DON'T LET YOU?
WHY DO YOU HAVE TO LISTEN TO THEM?
ツン
カツン

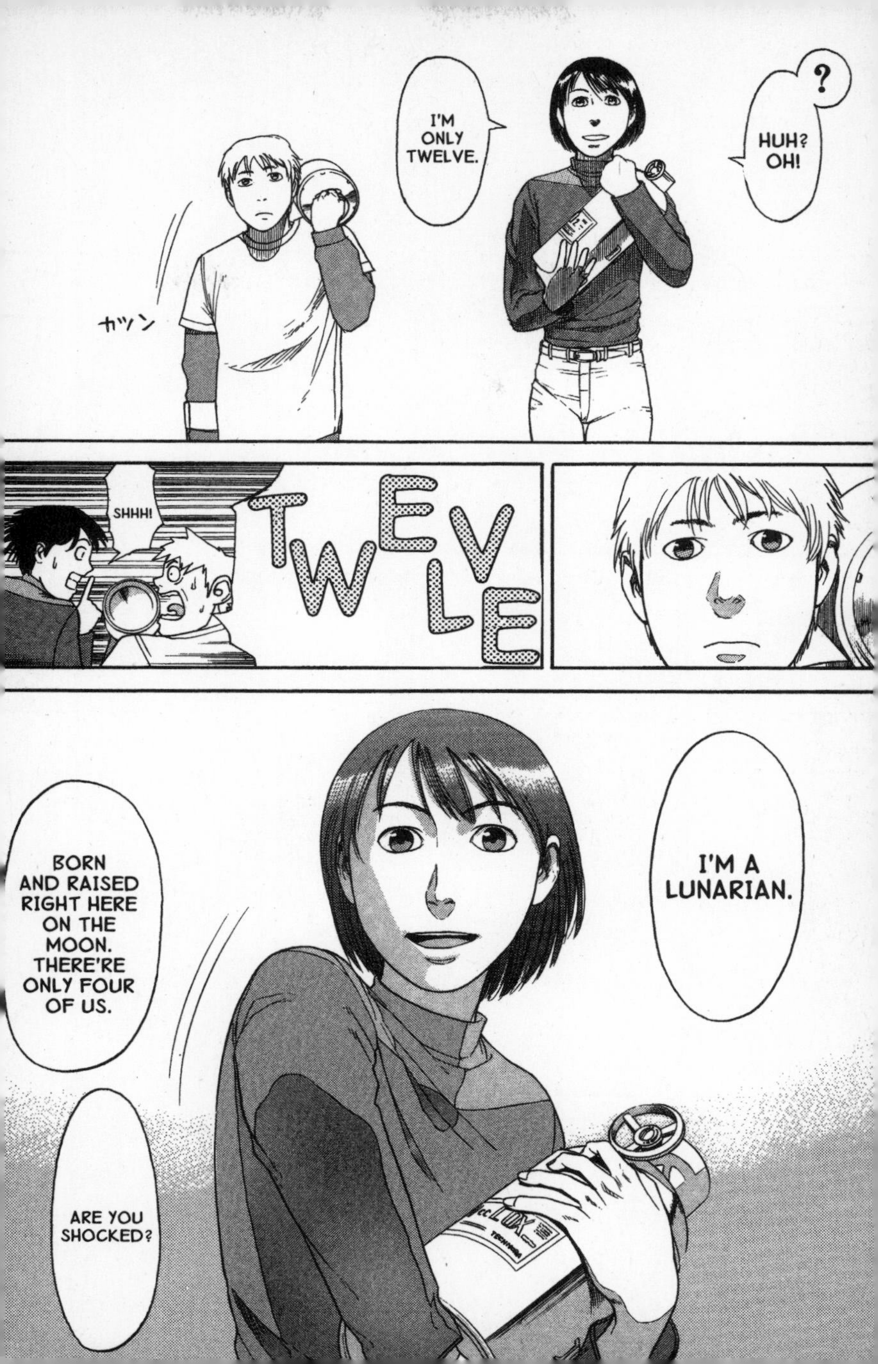
?
HUH? OH!
I'M ONLY TWELVE.
カツン
TWELVE
SHHH!
I'M A LUNARIAN.
BORN AND RAISED RIGHT HERE ON THE MOON. THERE'RE ONLY FOUR OF US.
ARE YOU SHOCKED?

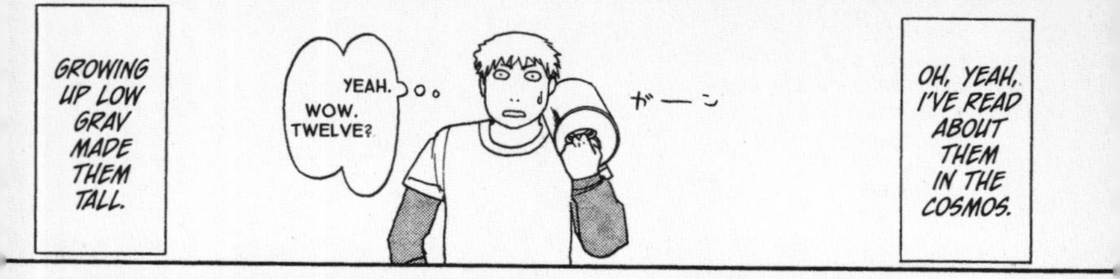
OH, YEAH, I'VE READ ABOUT THEM IN THE COSMOS.
ガーン
YEAH. WOW. TWELVE?
GROWING UP LOW GRAV MADE THEM TALL.

*ILMENITE – IRON TITANIUM OXIDE. ON EARTH, IT IS ONE OF THE BEST ORE SOURCES FOR TITANIUM, A LIGHT-WEIGHT, NON-CORROSIVE METAL THAT HAS SUPPLANTED MANY OTHER COMMERCIAL METALS. ITS DISCOVERY ON THE MOON SPURRED MASSIVE MINING OPERATIONS THERE.

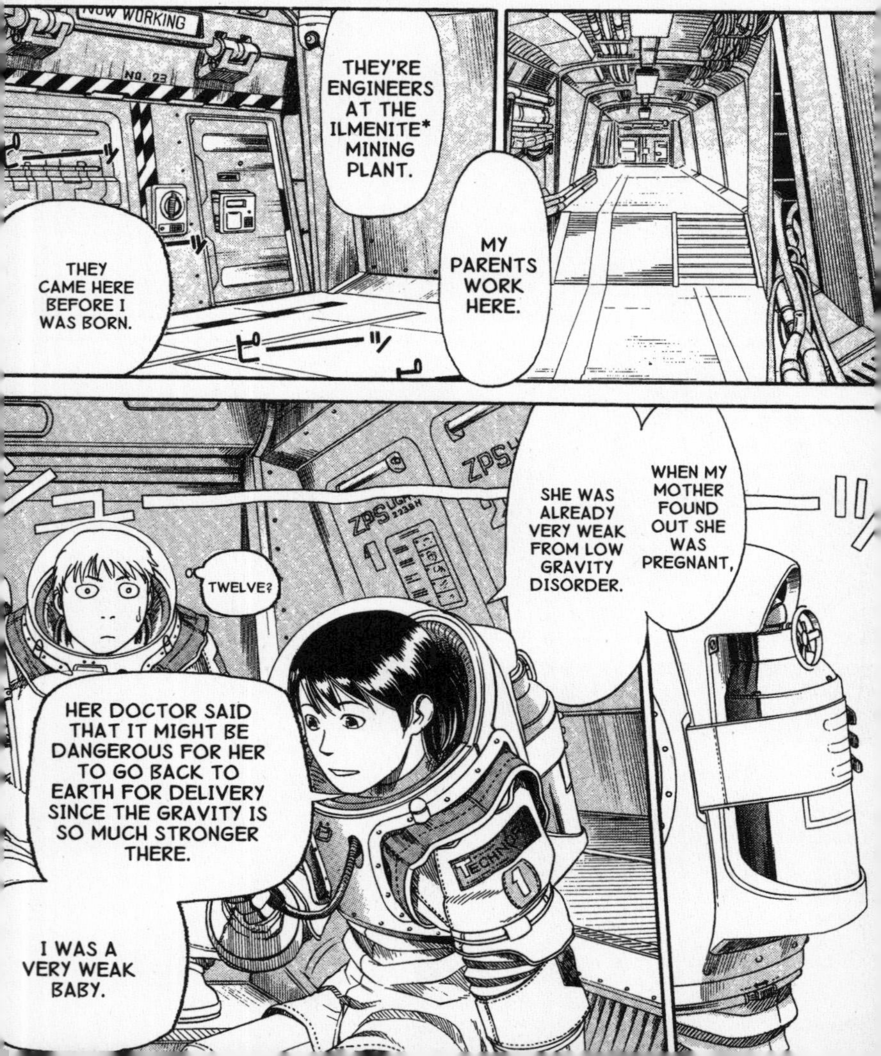
MY PARENTS WORK HERE.
NOW WORKING
NO. 23
THEY'RE ENGINEERS AT THE ILMENITE* MINING PLANT.
THEY CAME HERE BEFORE I WAS BORN.
WHEN MY MOTHER FOUND OUT SHE WAS PREGNANT,
SHE WAS ALREADY VERY WEAK FROM LOW GRAVITY DISORDER.
TWELVE?
HER DOCTOR SAID THAT IT MIGHT BE DANGEROUS FOR HER TO GO BACK TO EARTH FOR DELIVERY SINCE THE GRAVITY IS SO MUCH STRONGER THERE.
I WAS A VERY WEAK BABY.

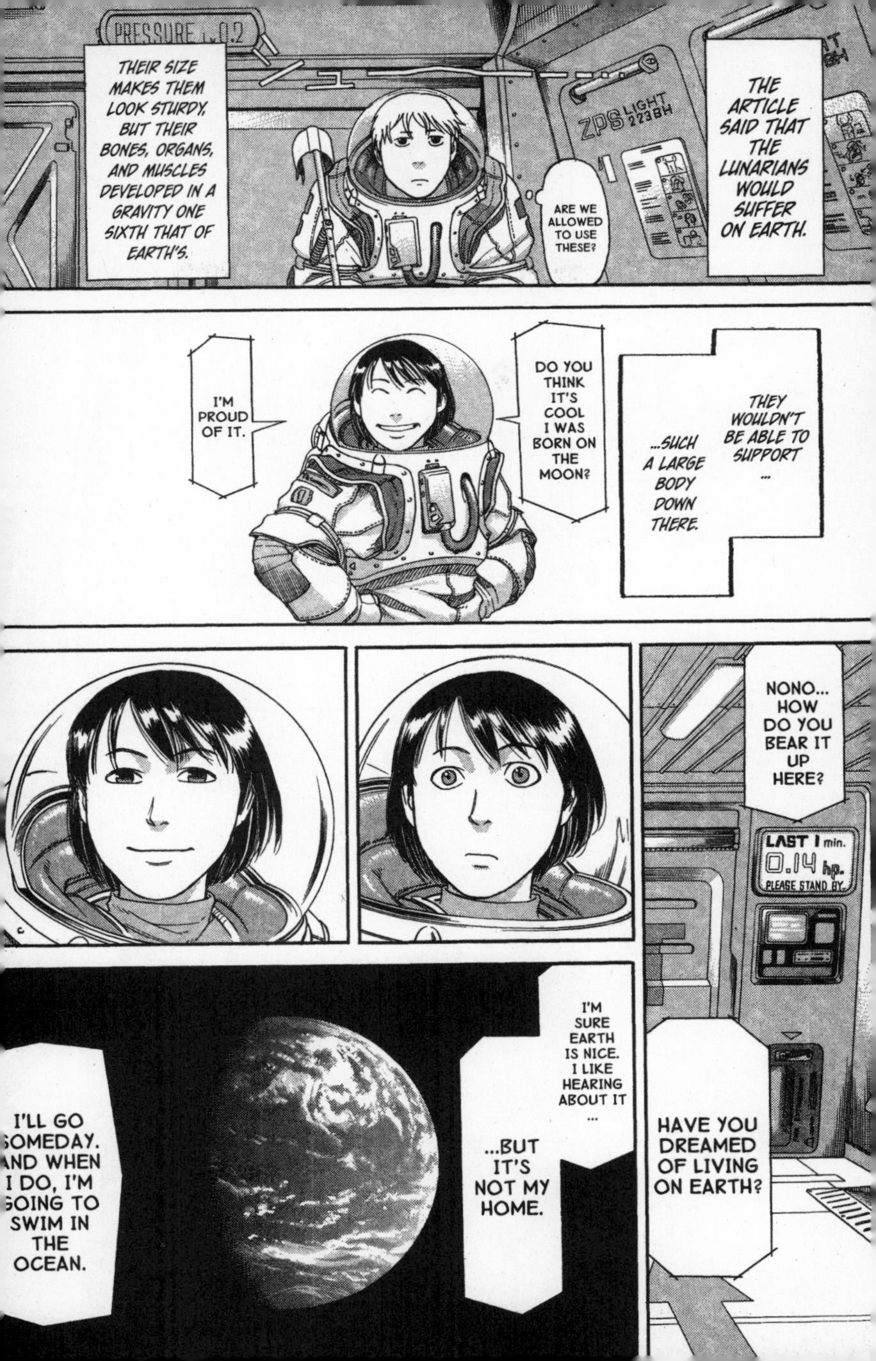
PRESSURE 0.2
THE ARTICLE SAID THAT THE LUNARIANS WOULD SUFFER ON EARTH.
ZPS LIGHT 223BH
ARE WE ALLOWED TO USE THESE?
THEIR SIZE MAKES THEM LOOK STURDY, BUT THEIR BONES, ORGANS, AND MUSCLES DEVELOPED IN A GRAVITY ONE SIXTH THAT OF EARTH'S.
THEY WOULDN'T BE ABLE TO SUPPORT ...
...SUCH A LARGE BODY DOWN THERE.
DO YOU THINK IT'S COOL I WAS BORN ON THE MOON?
I'M PROUD OF IT.
NONO... HOW DO YOU BEAR IT UP HERE?
LAST 1 min.
0.14 hp.
PLEASE STAND BY.
HAVE YOU DREAMED OF LIVING ON EARTH?
I'M SURE EARTH IS NICE. I LIKE HEARING ABOUT IT ...
...BUT IT'S NOT MY HOME.
I'LL GO SOMEDAY. AND WHEN I DO, I'M GOING TO SWIM IN THE OCEAN.

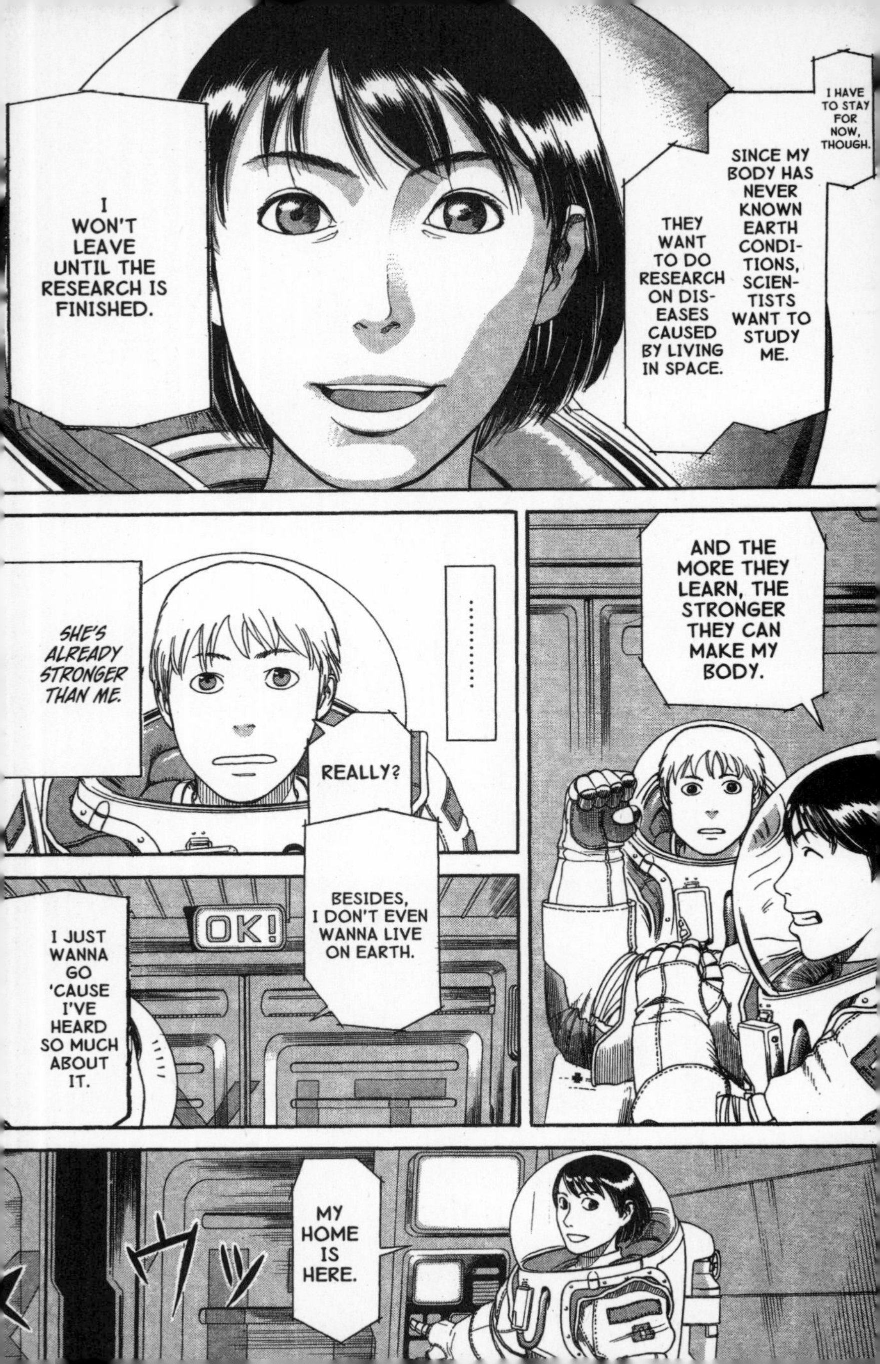
I HAVE TO STAY FOR NOW, THOUGH.
SINCE MY BODY HAS NEVER KNOWN EARTH CONDITIONS, SCIENTISTS WANT TO STUDY ME.
THEY WANT TO DO RESEARCH ON DISEASES CAUSED BY LIVING IN SPACE.
I WON'T LEAVE UNTIL THE RESEARCH IS FINISHED.
AND THE MORE THEY LEARN, THE STRONGER THEY CAN MAKE MY BODY.
....
REALLY?
SHE'S ALREADY STRONGER THAN ME.
BESIDES, I DON'T EVEN WANNA LIVE ON EARTH.
OK!
I JUST WANNA GO 'CAUSE I'VE HEARD SO MUCH ABOUT IT.
MY HOME IS HERE.

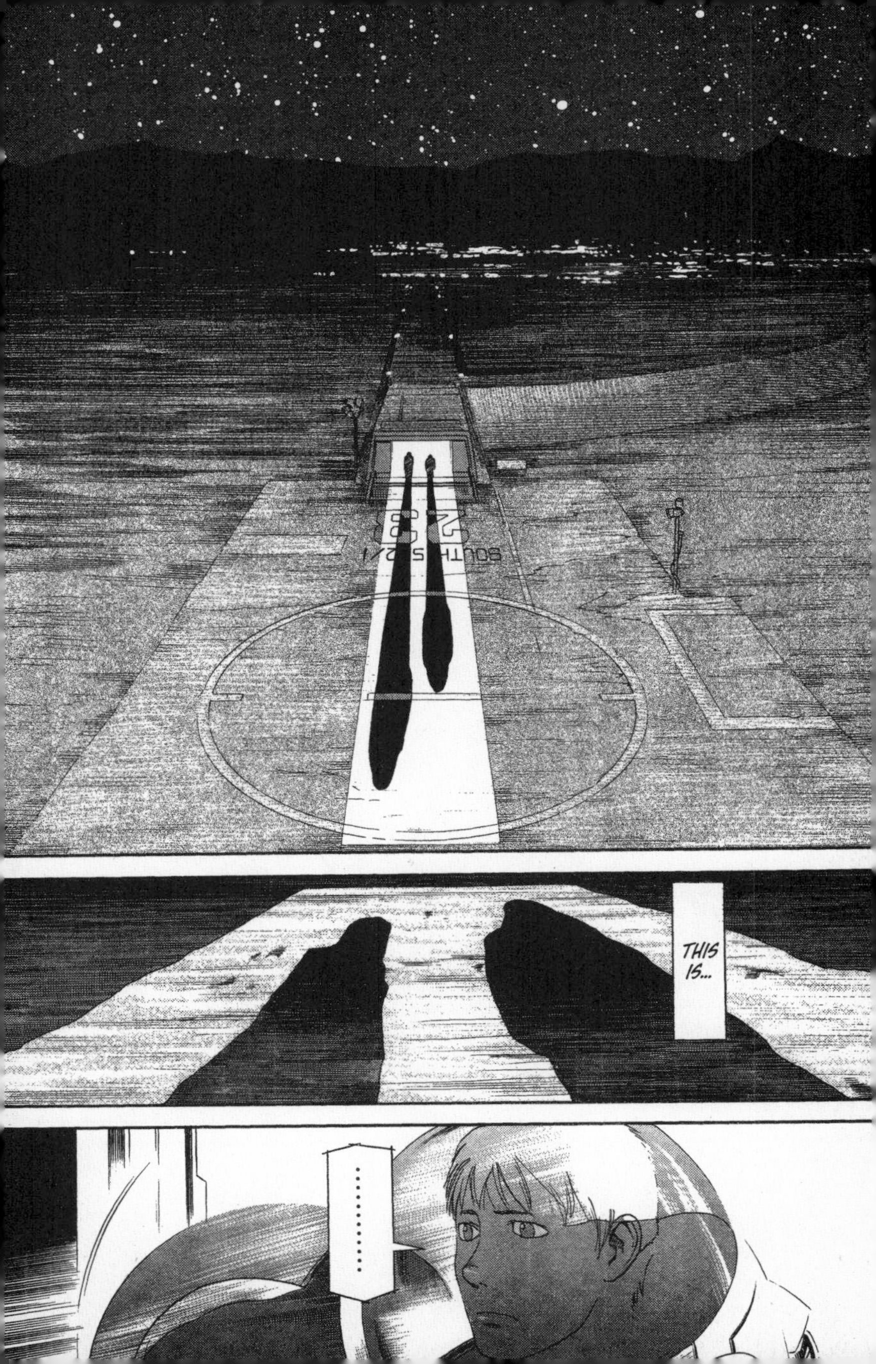
THIS IS...
....

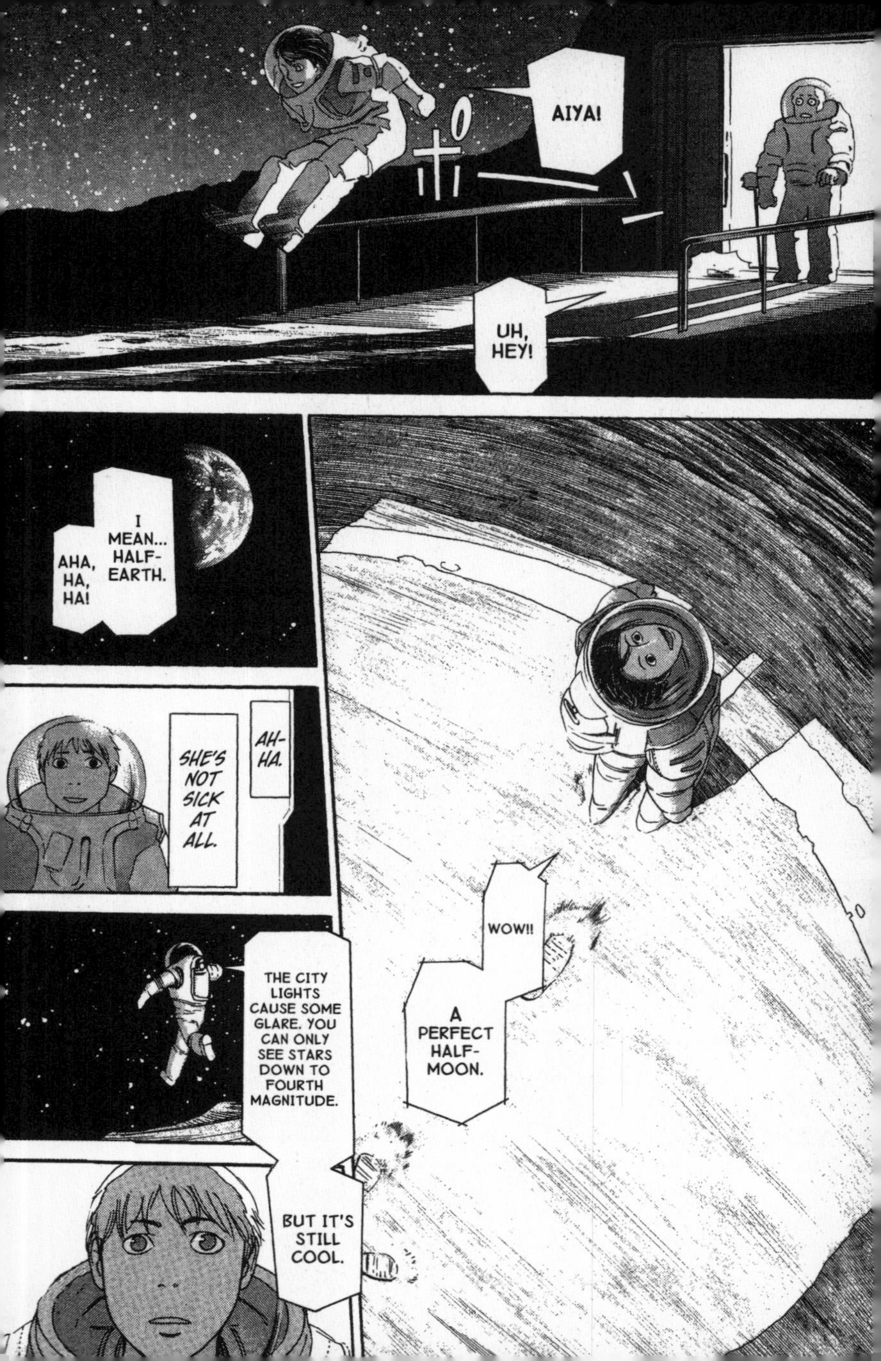
AIYA!
UH, HEY!
WOW!!
A PERFECT HALF-MOON.
I MEAN... HALF-EARTH.
AHA, HA, HA!
AH-HA.
SHE'S NOT SICK AT ALL.
THE CITY LIGHTS CAUSE SOME GLARE. YOU CAN ONLY SEE STARS DOWN TO FOURTH MAGNITUDE.
BUT IT'S STILL COOL.

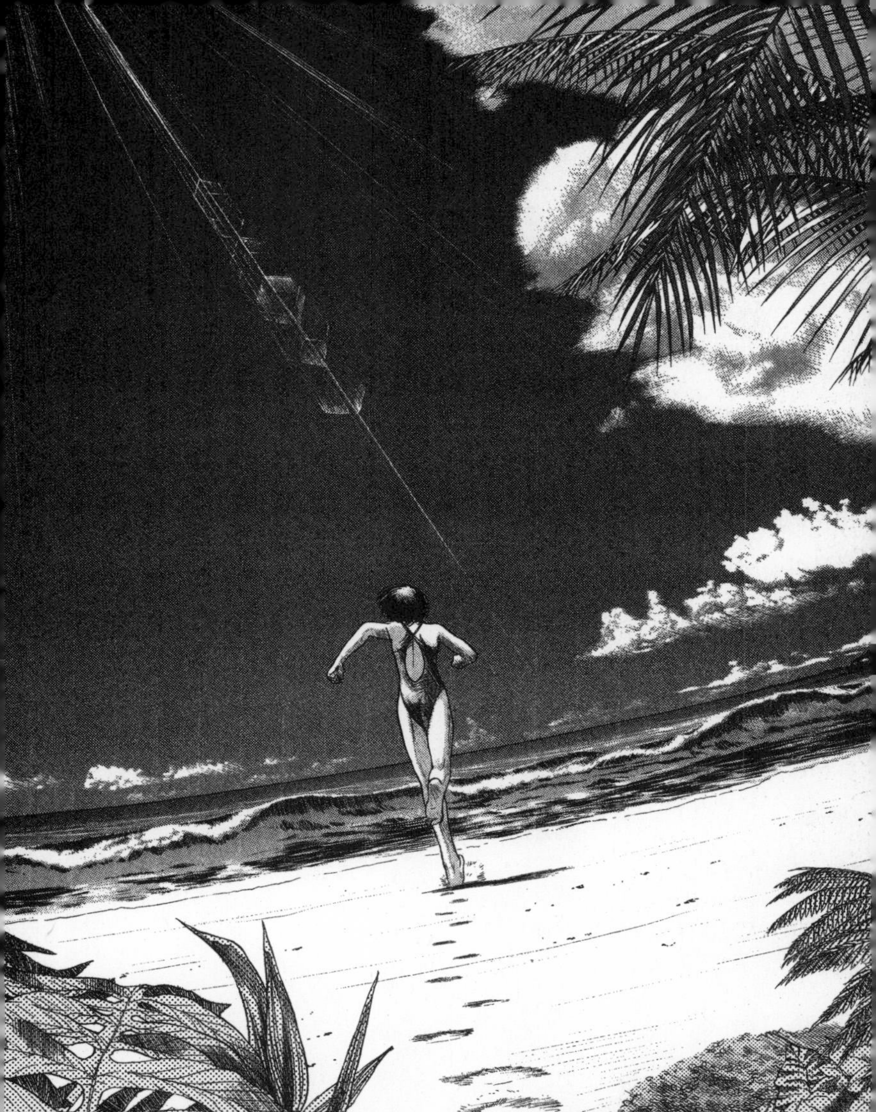
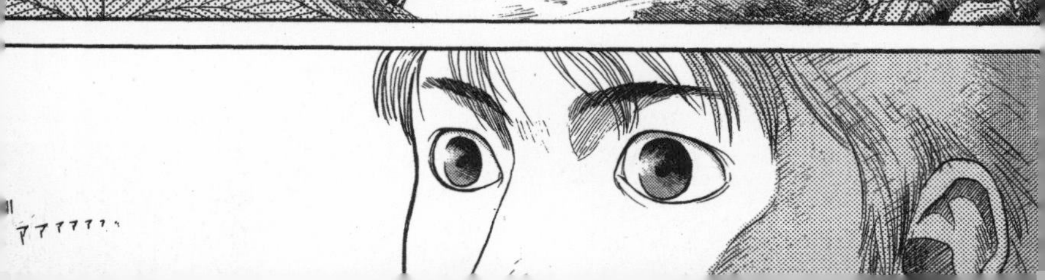
アアァァァァ…

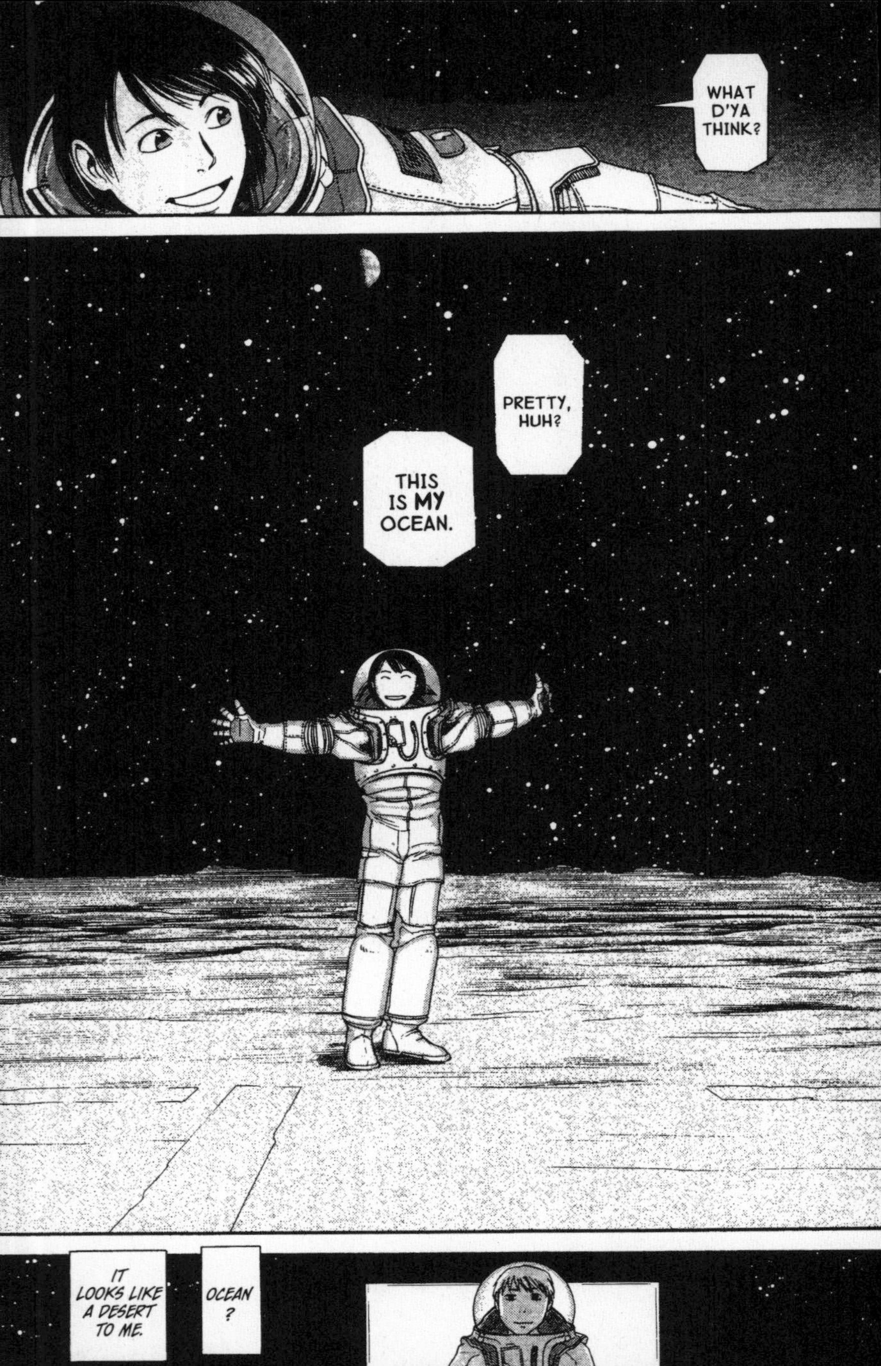

WHAT D'YA THINK?
PRETTY, HUH?
THIS IS MY OCEAN.
OCEAN?
IT LOOKS LIKE A DESERT TO ME.

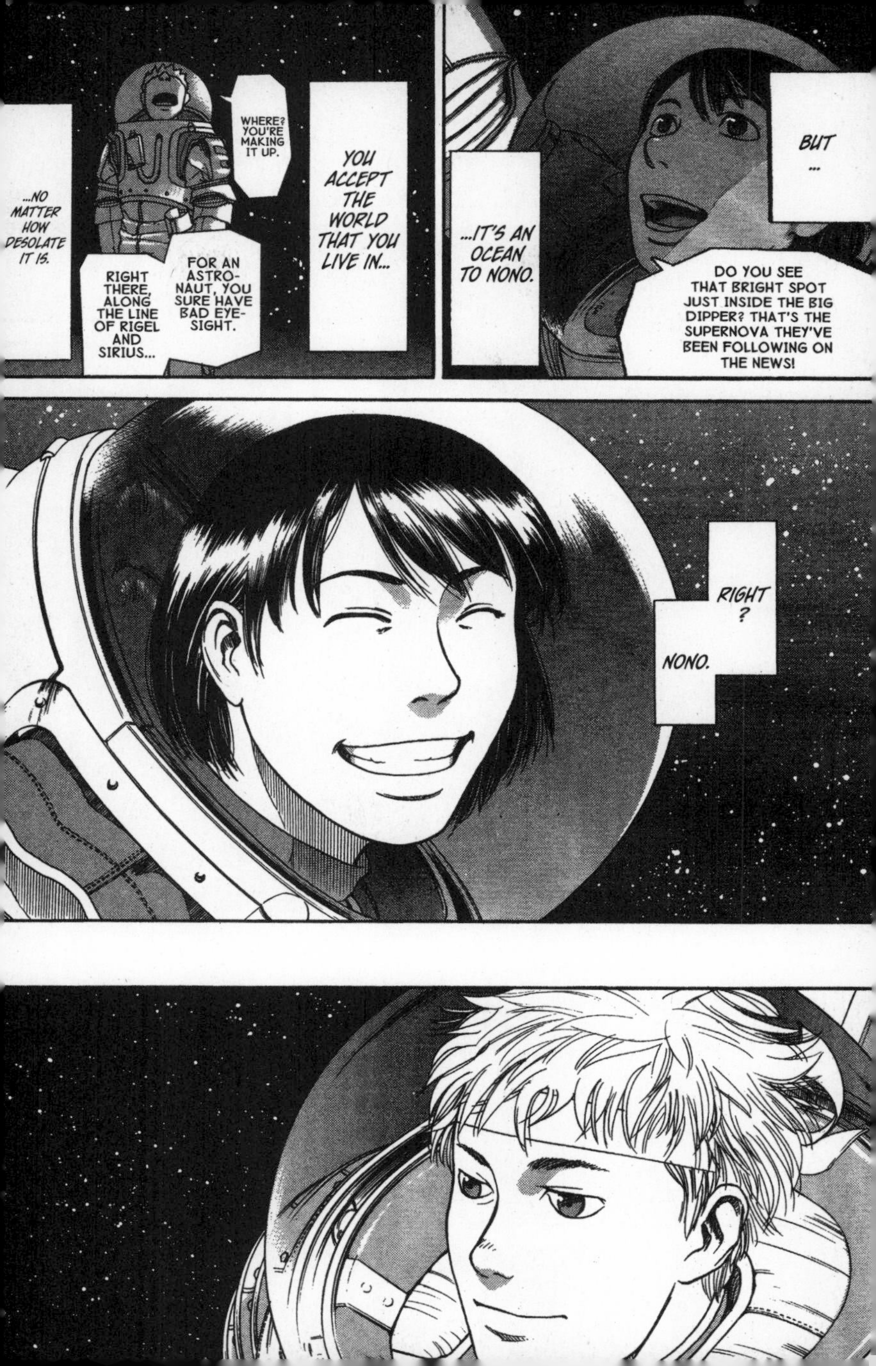
BUT ...
DO YOU SEE THAT BRIGHT SPOT JUST INSIDE THE BIG DIPPER? THAT'S THE SUPERNOVA THEY'VE BEEN FOLLOWING ON THE NEWS!
...IT'S AN OCEAN TO NONO.
YOU ACCEPT THE WORLD THAT YOU LIVE IN...
WHERE? YOU'RE MAKING IT UP.
FOR AN ASTRONAUT, YOU SURE HAVE BAD EYESIGHT.
...NO MATTER HOW DESOLATE IT IS.
RIGHT THERE, ALONG THE LINE OF RIGEL AND SIRIUS...
RIGHT ?
NONO.

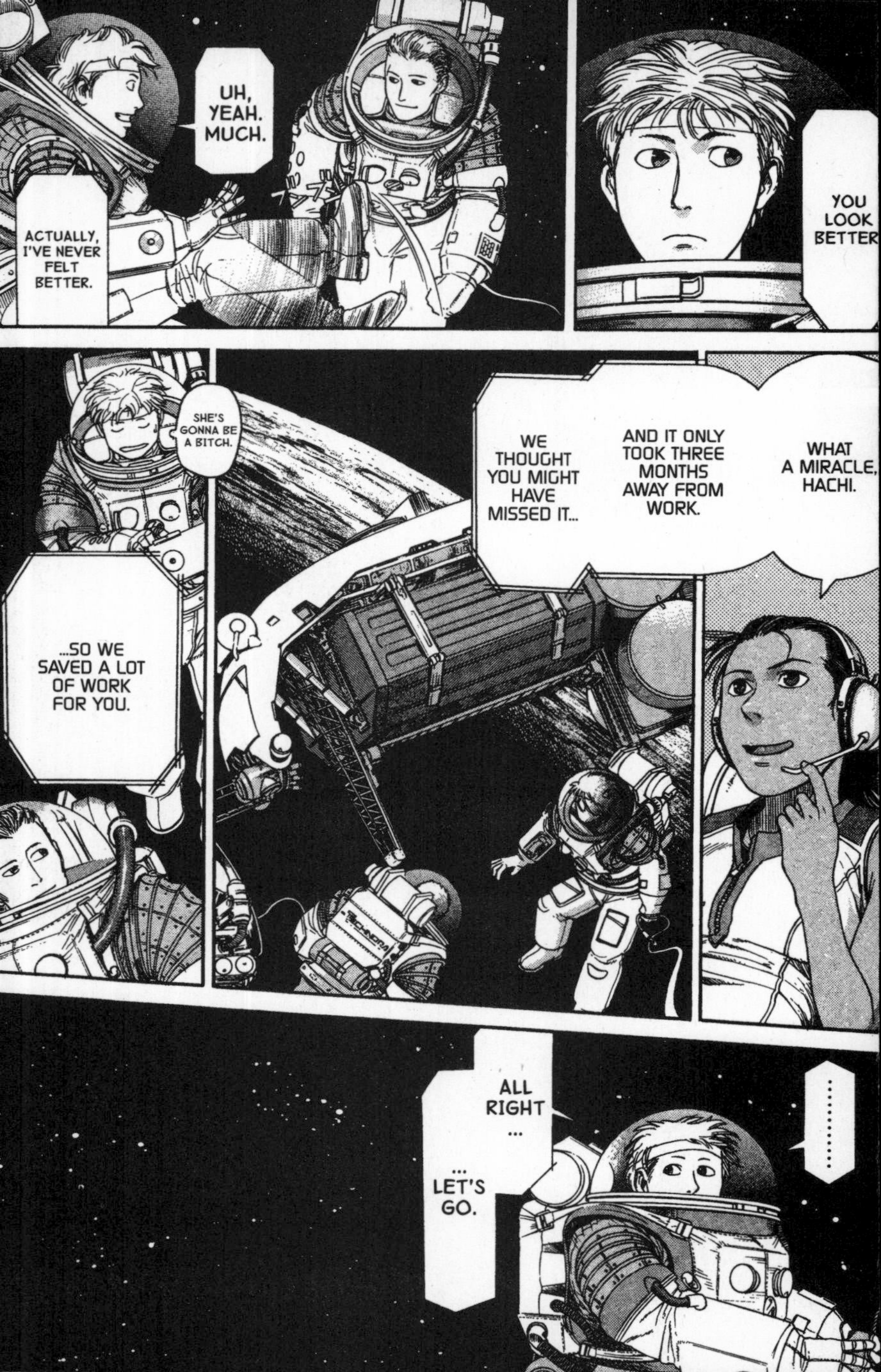
YOU LOOK BETTER
UH, YEAH. MUCH.
ACTUALLY, I'VE NEVER FELT BETTER.
WHAT A MIRACLE, HACHI.
AND IT ONLY TOOK THREE MONTHS AWAY FROM WORK.
WE THOUGHT YOU MIGHT HAVE MISSED IT...
SHE'S GONNA BE A BITCH.
...SO WE SAVED A LOT OF WORK FOR YOU.
....
ALL RIGHT ...
... LET'S GO.

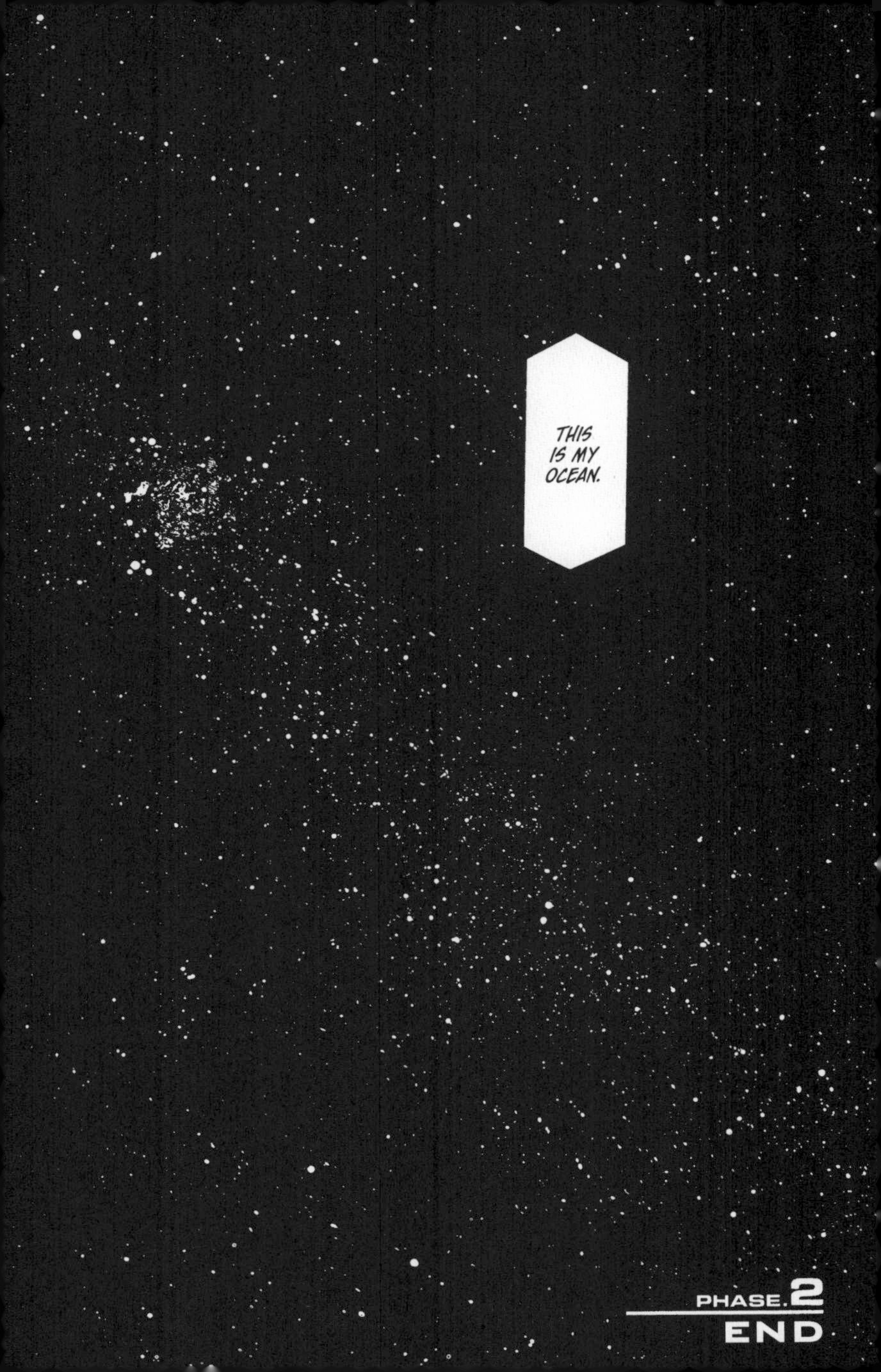
THIS IS MY OCEAN.
PHASE.2 END

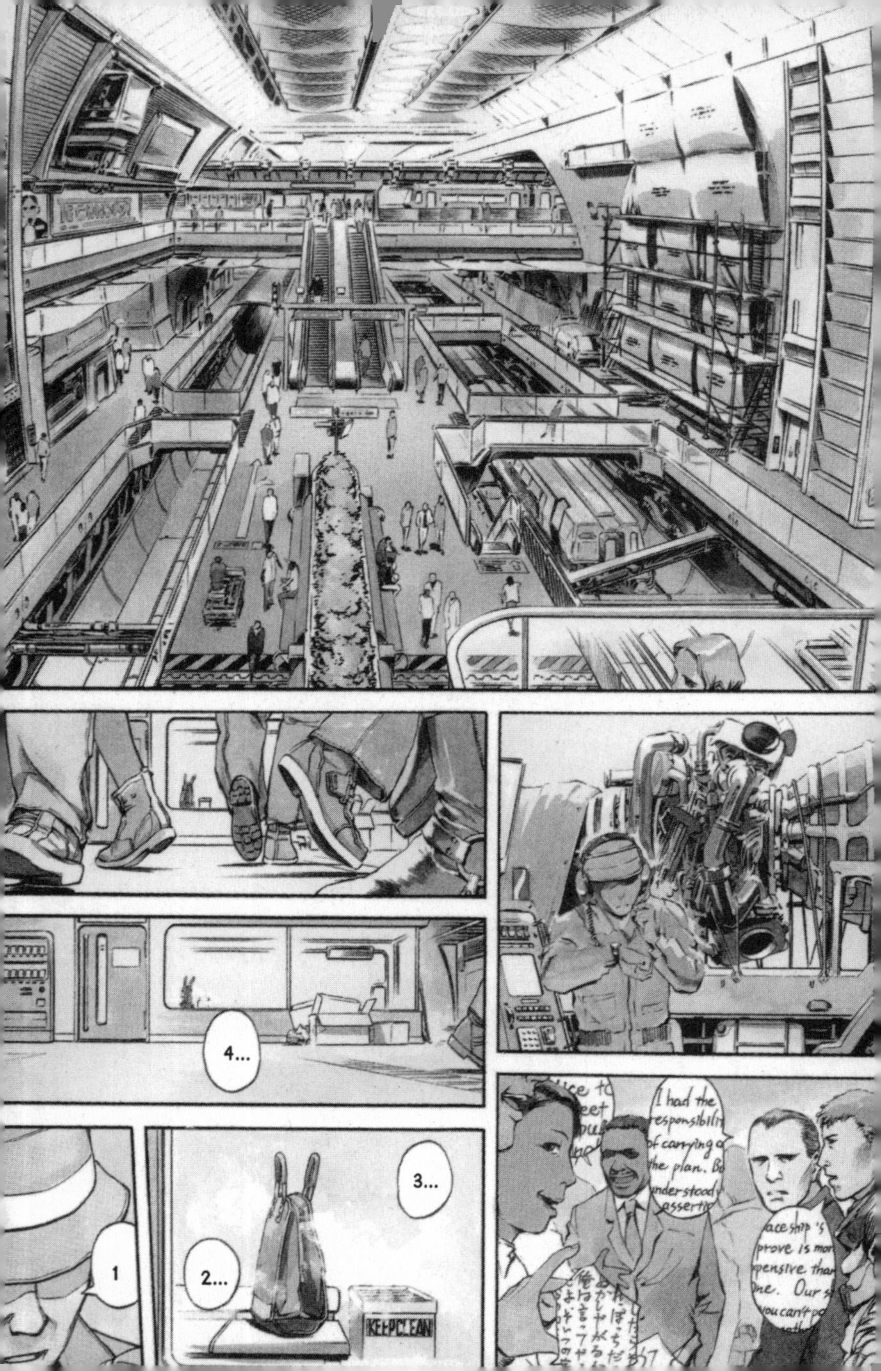
4...
ace ship's prove is mor pensive tha one. Our s you can't p
I had the responsibili of carrying o the plan. B understood assertio
3...
2...
KEEPCLEAN
1

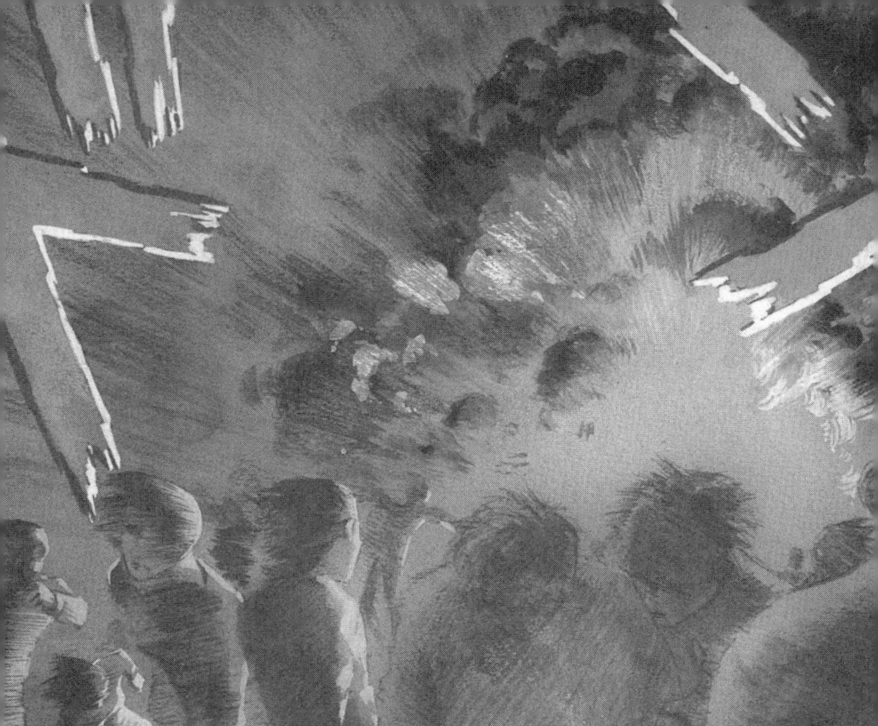

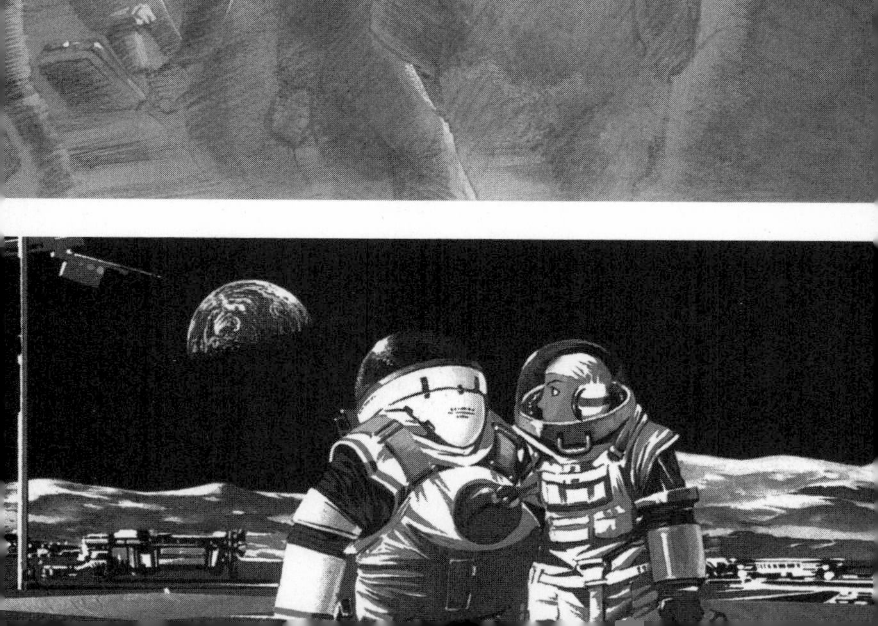

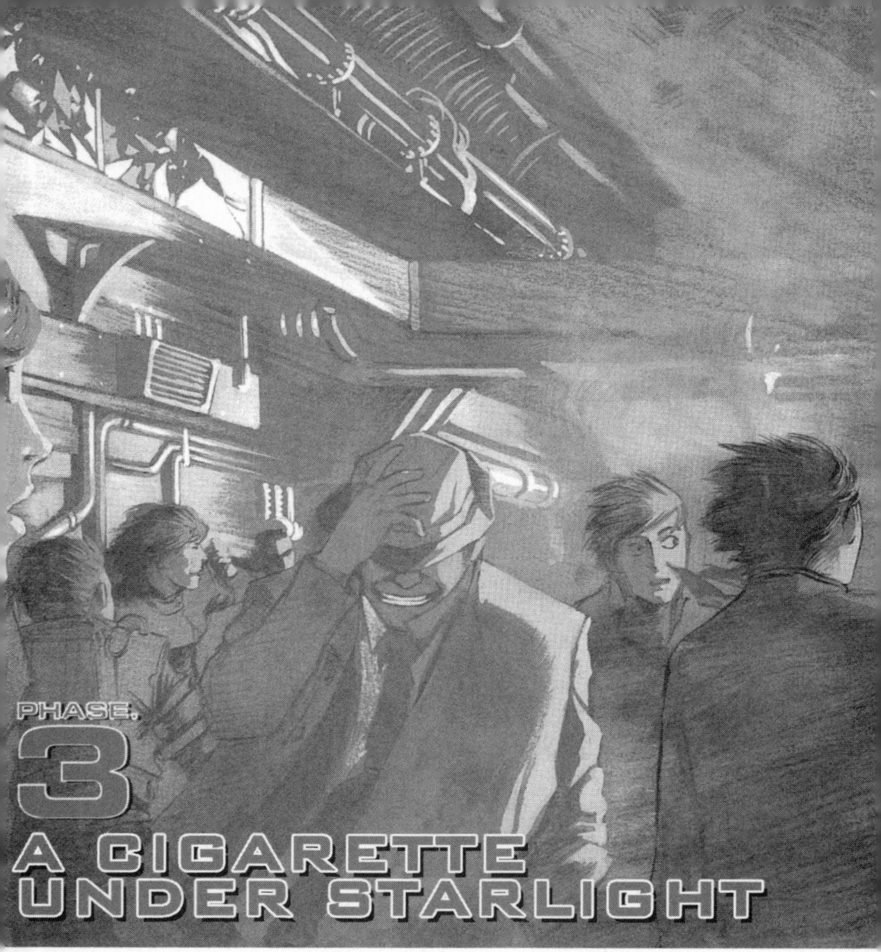
PHASE.
3
A CIGARETTE
UNDER STARLIGHT

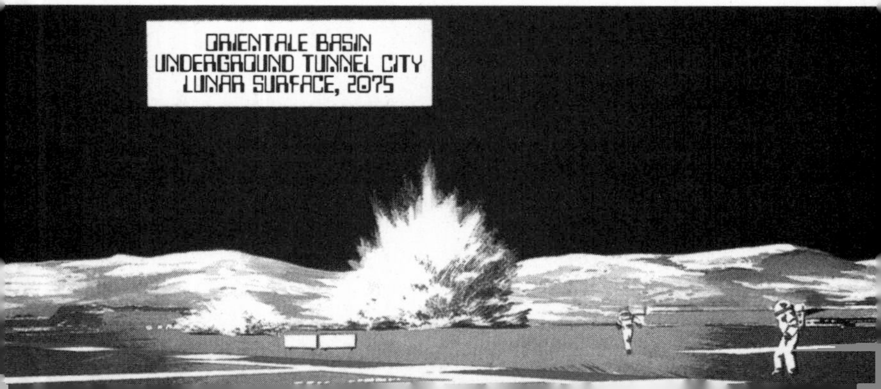
ORIENTALE BASIN
UNDERGROUND TUNNEL CITY
LUNAR SURFACE, 2075

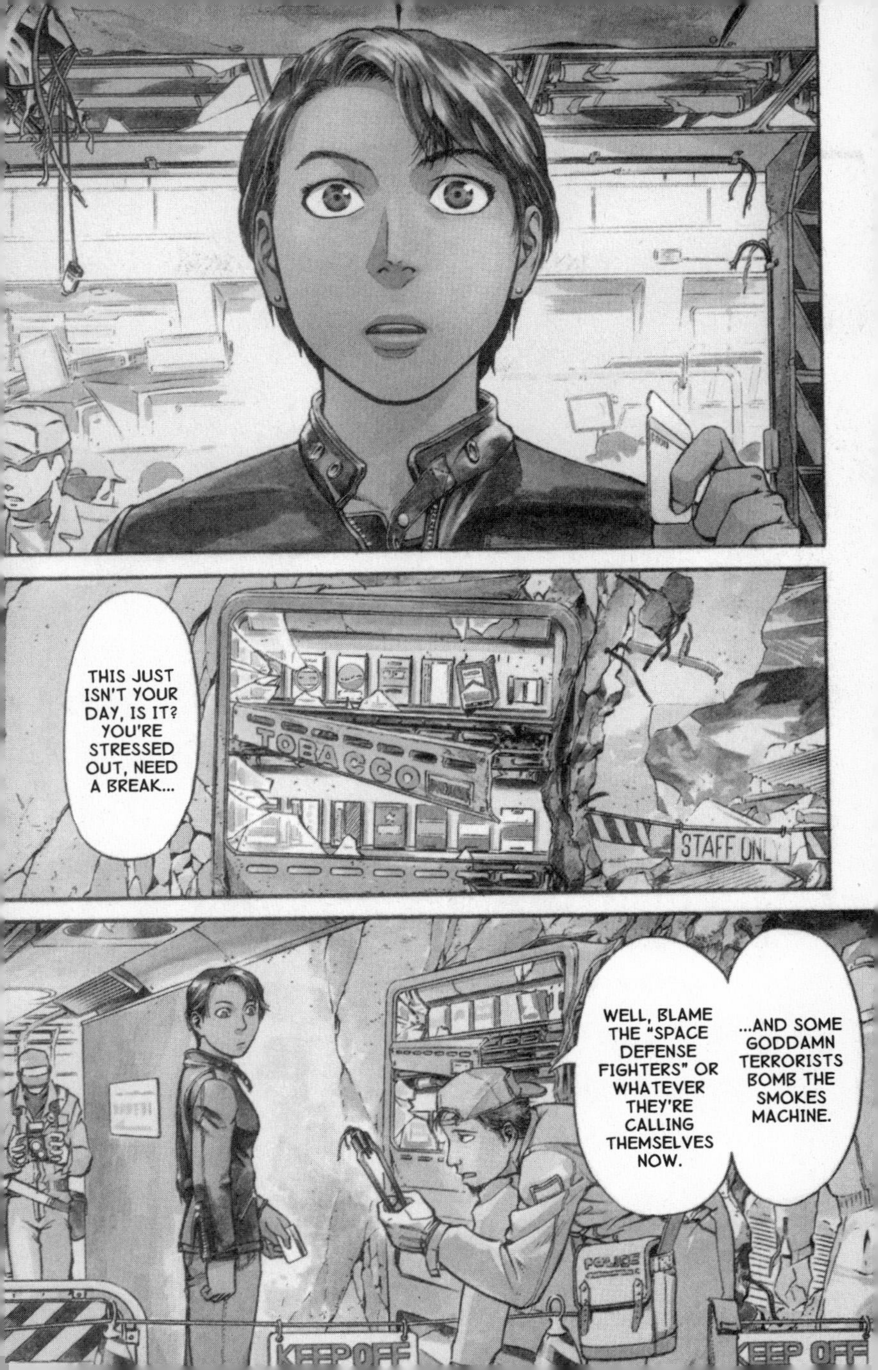
THIS JUST ISN'T YOUR DAY, IS IT? YOU'RE STRESSED OUT, NEED A BREAK...
TOBACCO
STAFF ONL
...AND SOME GODDAMN TERRORISTS BOMB THE SMOKES MACHINE.
WELL, BLAME THE "SPACE DEFENSE FIGHTERS" OR WHATEVER THEY'RE CALLING THEMSELVES NOW.
KEEP OFF
KEEPOFF

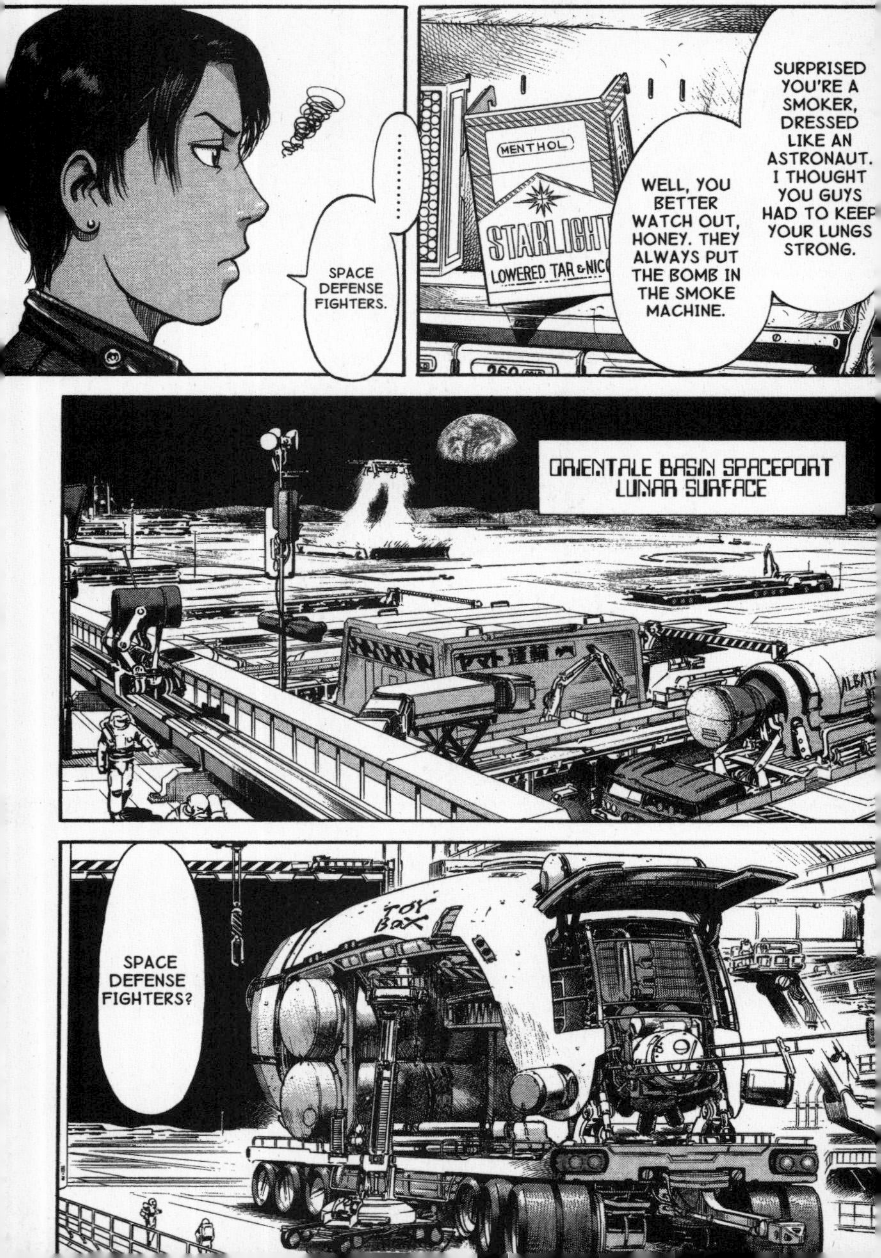
MENTHOL
STARLIGHT
SURPRISED YOU'RE A SMOKER, DRESSED LIKE AN ASTRONAUT. I THOUGHT YOU GUYS HAD TO KEEP YOUR LUNGS STRONG.
WELL, YOU BETTER WATCH OUT, HONEY. THEY ALWAYS PUT THE BOMB IN THE SMOKE MACHINE.
......
SPACE DEFENSE FIGHTERS.
ORIENTALE BASIN SPACEPORT
LUNAR SURFACE
SPACE DEFENSE FIGHTERS?
TOY BOX

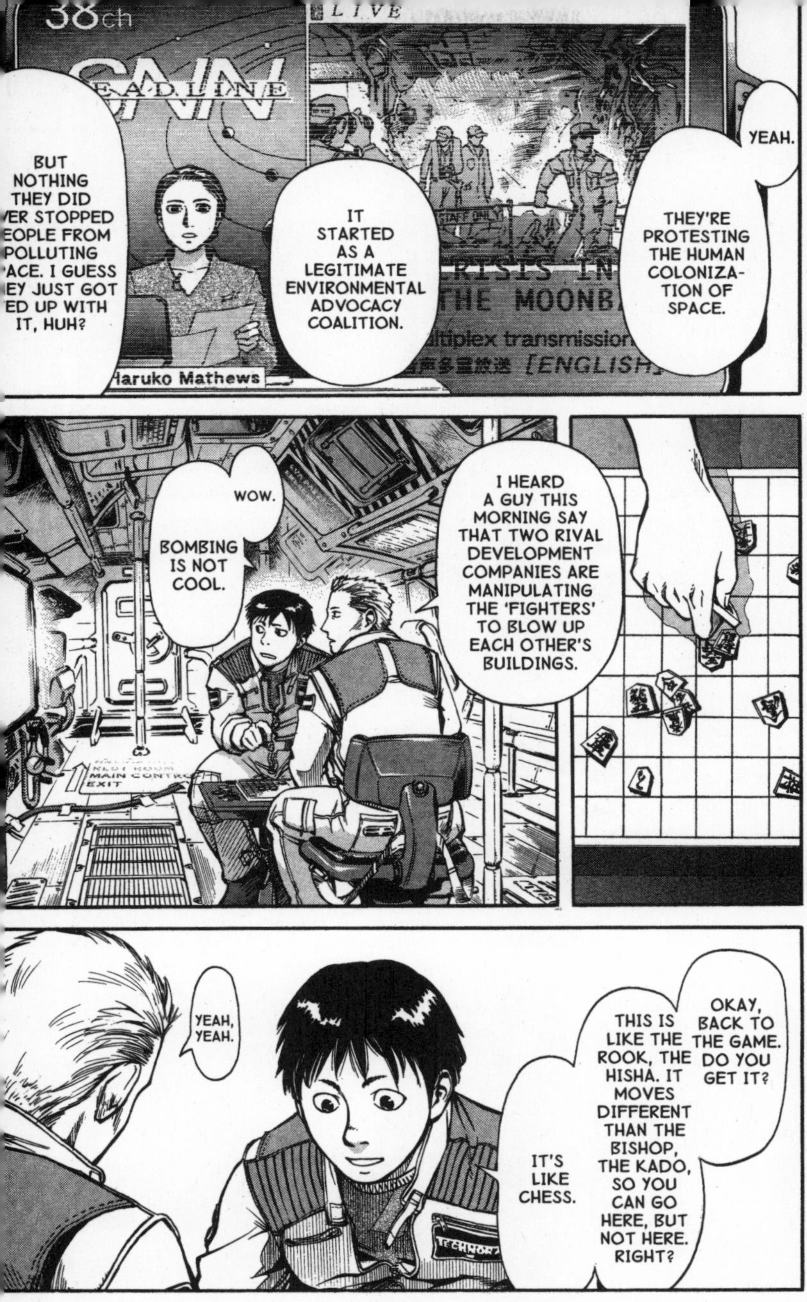
38ch
LIVE
YEAH.
THEY'RE PROTESTING THE HUMAN COLONIZA-TION OF SPACE.
IT STARTED AS A LEGITIMATE ENVIRONMENTAL ADVOCACY COALITION.
BUT NOTHING THEY DID /ER STOPPED EOPLE FROM POLLUTING PACE. I GUESS EY JUST GOT ED UP WITH IT, HUH?
Haruko Mathews
[ENGLISH]
I HEARD A GUY THIS MORNING SAY THAT TWO RIVAL DEVELOPMENT COMPANIES ARE MANIPULATING THE 'FIGHTERS' TO BLOW UP EACH OTHER'S BUILDINGS.
WOW.
BOMBING IS NOT COOL.
OKAY, BACK TO THE GAME. DO YOU GET IT?
THIS IS LIKE THE ROOK, THE HISHA. IT MOVES DIFFERENT THAN THE BISHOP, THE KADO, SO YOU CAN GO HERE, BUT NOT HERE. RIGHT?
IT'S LIKE CHESS.
YEAH, YEAH.

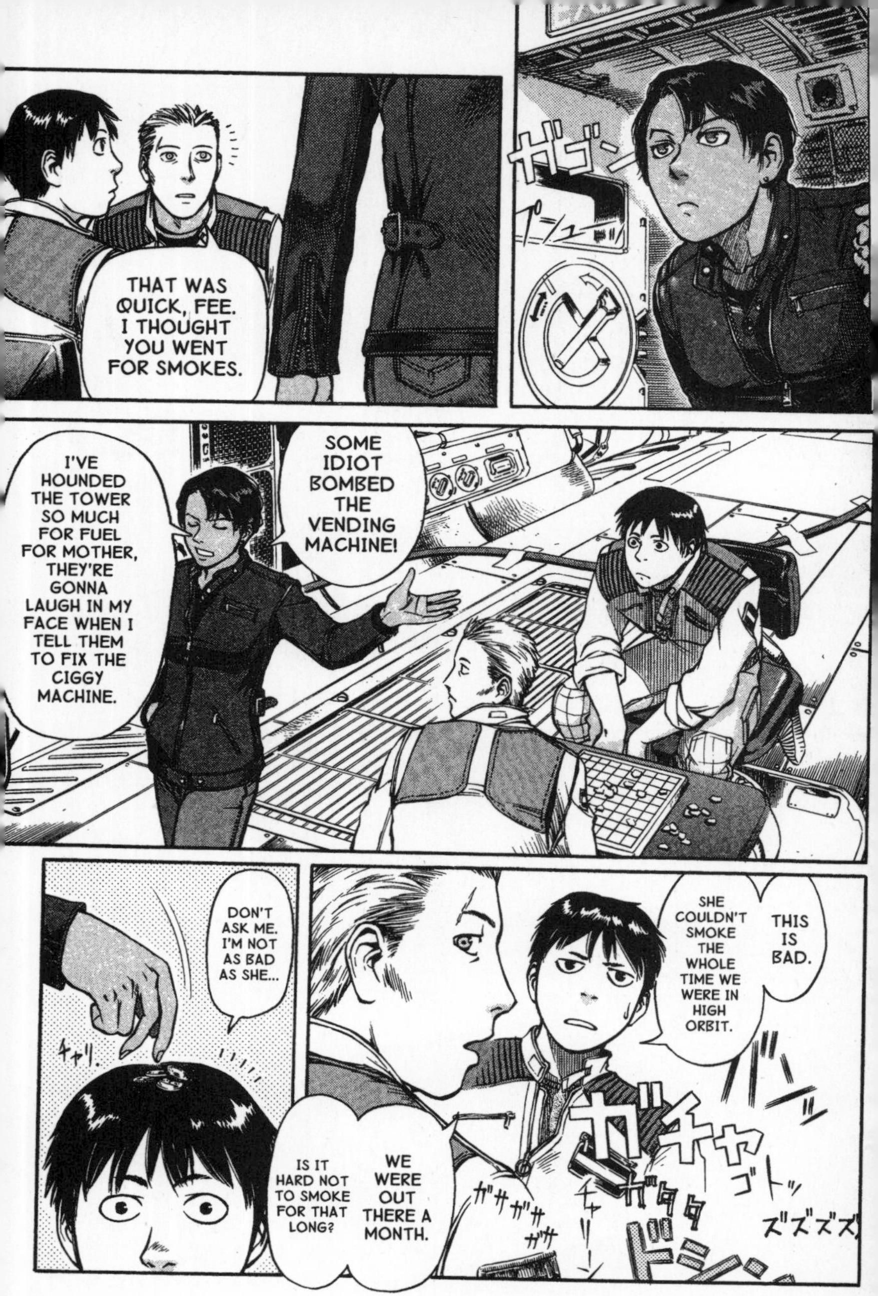
THAT WAS QUICK, FEE. I THOUGHT YOU WENT FOR SMOKES.
SOME IDIOT BOMBED THE VENDING MACHINE!
I'VE HOUNDED THE TOWER SO MUCH FOR FUEL FOR MOTHER, THEY'RE GONNA LAUGH IN MY FACE WHEN I TELL THEM TO FIX THE CIGGY MACHINE.
THIS IS BAD.
SHE COULDN'T SMOKE THE WHOLE TIME WE WERE IN HIGH ORBIT.
WE WERE OUT THERE A MONTH.
IS IT HARD NOT TO SMOKE FOR THAT LONG?
DON'T ASK ME. I'M NOT AS BAD AS SHE...

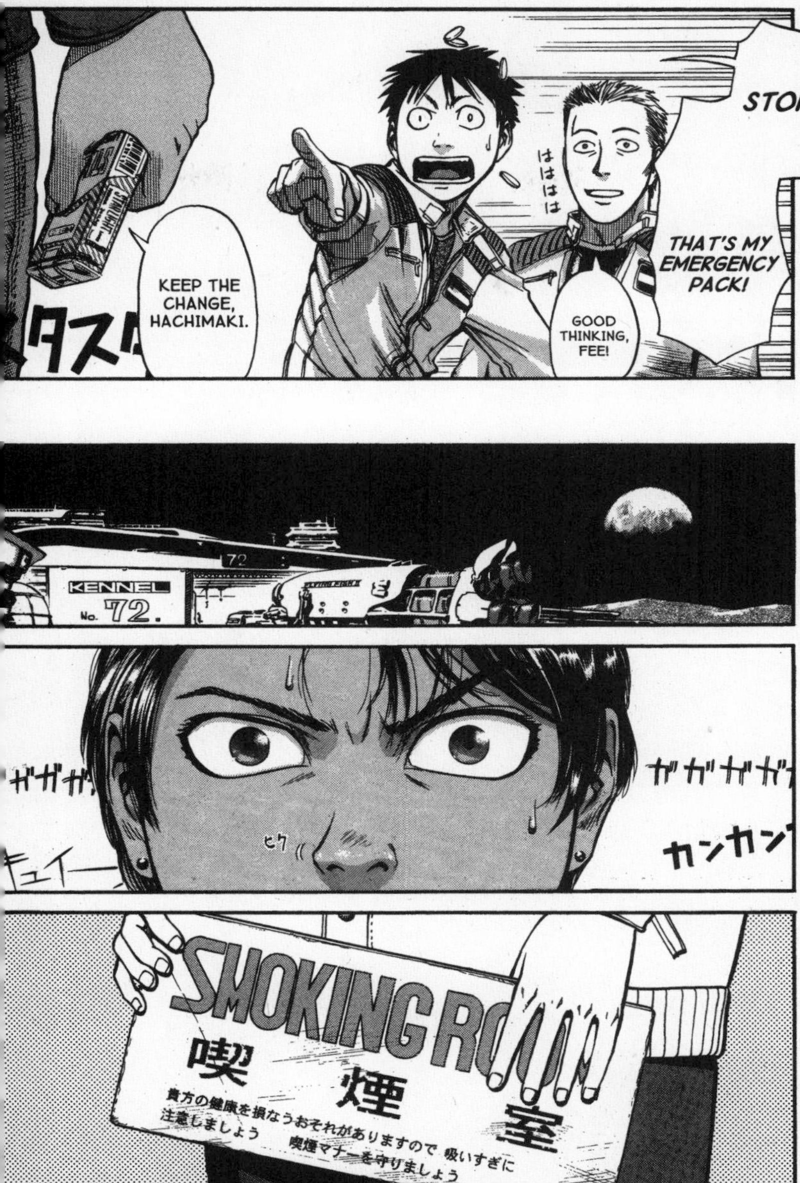
STOP!
THAT'S MY EMERGENCY PACK!
ははははは
GOOD THINKING, FEE!
KEEP THE CHANGE, HACHIMAKI.
KENNEL
No. 72.
ガガガガ
カンカン
ヒク
キュイー
SMOKING RO
喫煙室
貴方の健康を損なうおそれがありますので 吸いすぎに注意しましょう
喫煙マナーを守りましょう

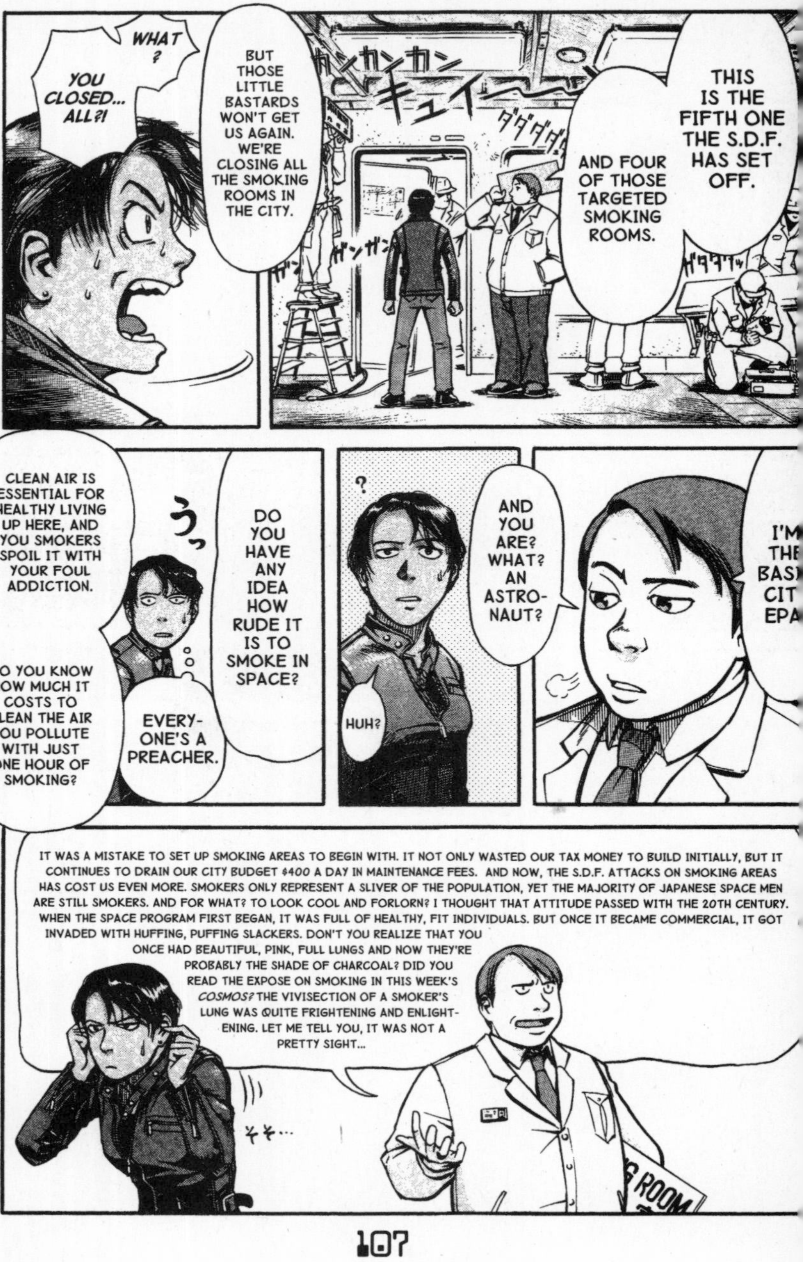
THIS IS THE FIFTH ONE THE S.D.F. HAS SET OFF.
AND FOUR OF THOSE TARGETED SMOKING ROOMS.
BUT THOSE LITTLE BASTARDS WON'T GET US AGAIN. WE'RE CLOSING ALL THE SMOKING ROOMS IN THE CITY.
WHAT?
YOU CLOSED... ALL?!
I'M THE BAS CIT EPA
AND YOU ARE? WHAT? AN ASTRO-NAUT?
?
HUH?
DO YOU HAVE ANY IDEA HOW RUDE IT IS TO SMOKE IN SPACE?
CLEAN AIR IS ESSENTIAL FOR HEALTHY LIVING UP HERE, AND YOU SMOKERS SPOIL IT WITH YOUR FOUL ADDICTION.
DO YOU KNOW HOW MUCH IT COSTS TO CLEAN THE AIR YOU POLLUTE WITH JUST ONE HOUR OF SMOKING?
EVERY-ONE'S A PREACHER.
IT WAS A MISTAKE TO SET UP SMOKING AREAS TO BEGIN WITH. IT NOT ONLY WASTED OUR TAX MONEY TO BUILD INITIALLY, BUT IT CONTINUES TO DRAIN OUR CITY BUDGET $400 A DAY IN MAINTENANCE FEES. AND NOW, THE S.D.F. ATTACKS ON SMOKING AREAS HAS COST US EVEN MORE. SMOKERS ONLY REPRESENT A SLIVER OF THE POPULATION, YET THE MAJORITY OF JAPANESE SPACE MEN ARE STILL SMOKERS. AND FOR WHAT? TO LOOK COOL AND FORLORN? I THOUGHT THAT ATTITUDE PASSED WITH THE 20TH CENTURY. WHEN THE SPACE PROGRAM FIRST BEGAN, IT WAS FULL OF HEALTHY, FIT INDIVIDUALS. BUT ONCE IT BECAME COMMERCIAL, IT GOT INVADED WITH HUFFING, PUFFING SLACKERS. DON'T YOU REALIZE THAT YOU ONCE HAD BEAUTIFUL, PINK, FULL LUNGS AND NOW THEY'RE PROBABLY THE SHADE OF CHARCOAL? DID YOU READ THE EXPOSE ON SMOKING IN THIS WEEK'S *COSMOS?* THE VIVISECTION OF A SMOKER'S LUNG WAS QUITE FRIGHTENING AND ENLIGHT-ENING. LET ME TELL YOU, IT WAS NOT A PRETTY SIGHT...
G ROOM

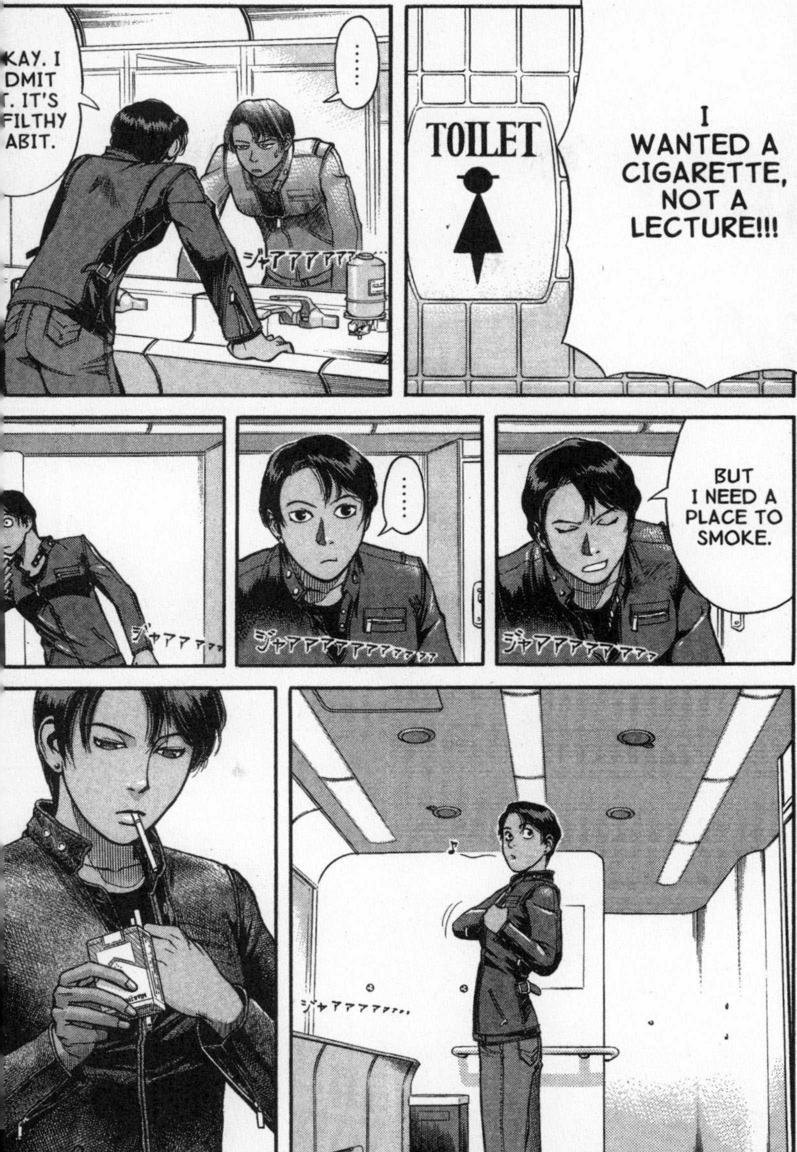
I WANTED A CIGARETTE, NOT A LECTURE!!!
......
KAY. I DMIT T. IT'S FILTHY ABIT.
ジャアアアアア
BUT I NEED A PLACE TO SMOKE.
ジャアアアアアアア
......
ジャアアアアアアアア
ジャアアアア
ジャアアアアア

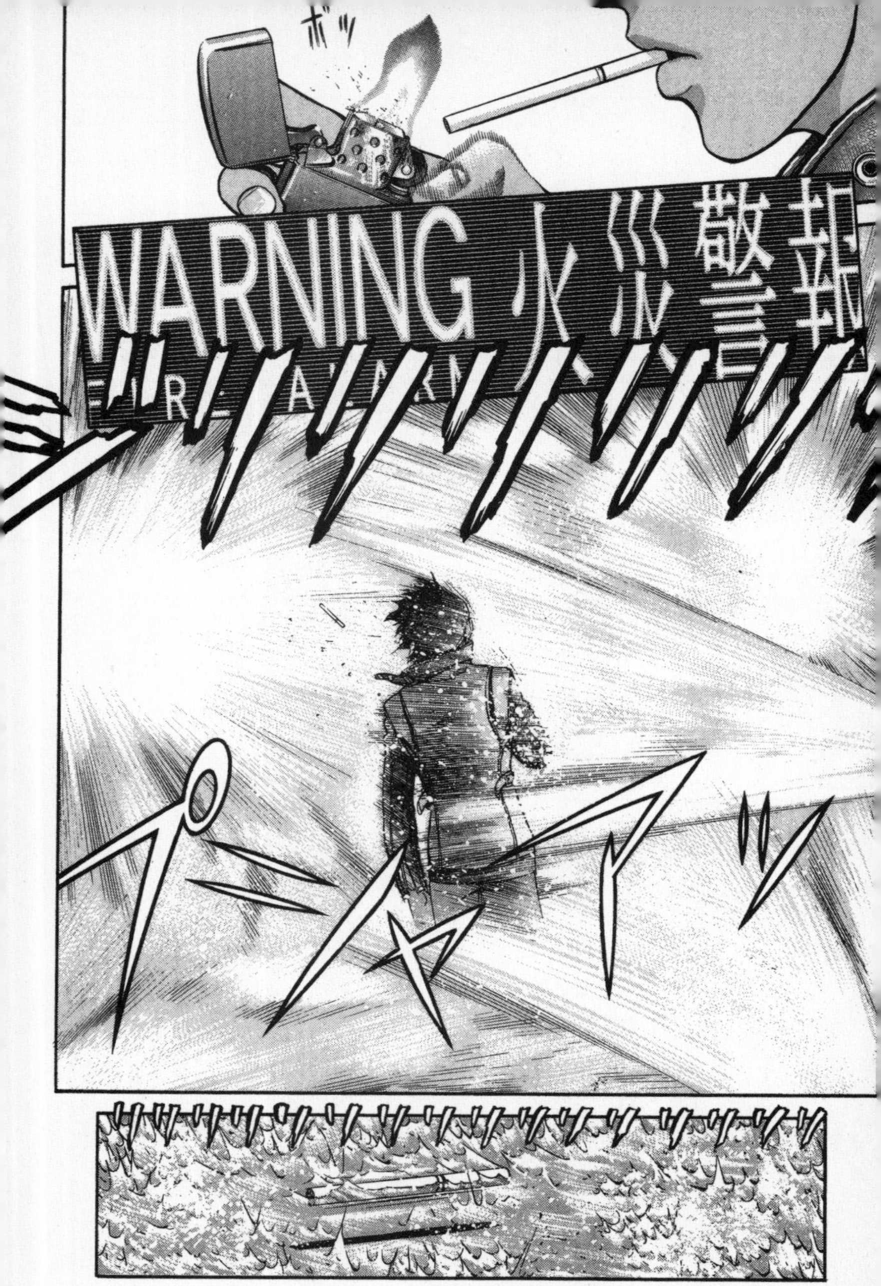
ボッ
WARNING 火災警報

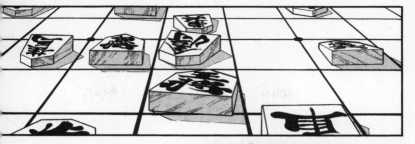

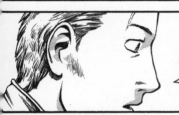

IS THIS CHECK-MATE? I MEAN... 'OUT'?

AM I DOING IT RIGHT, HACHI?

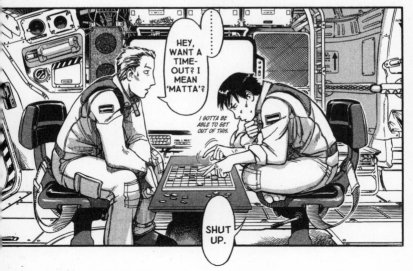

HEY, WANT A TIME-OUT? I MEAN 'MATTA'?

I GOTTA BE ABLE TO GET OUT OF THIS.

SHUT UP.

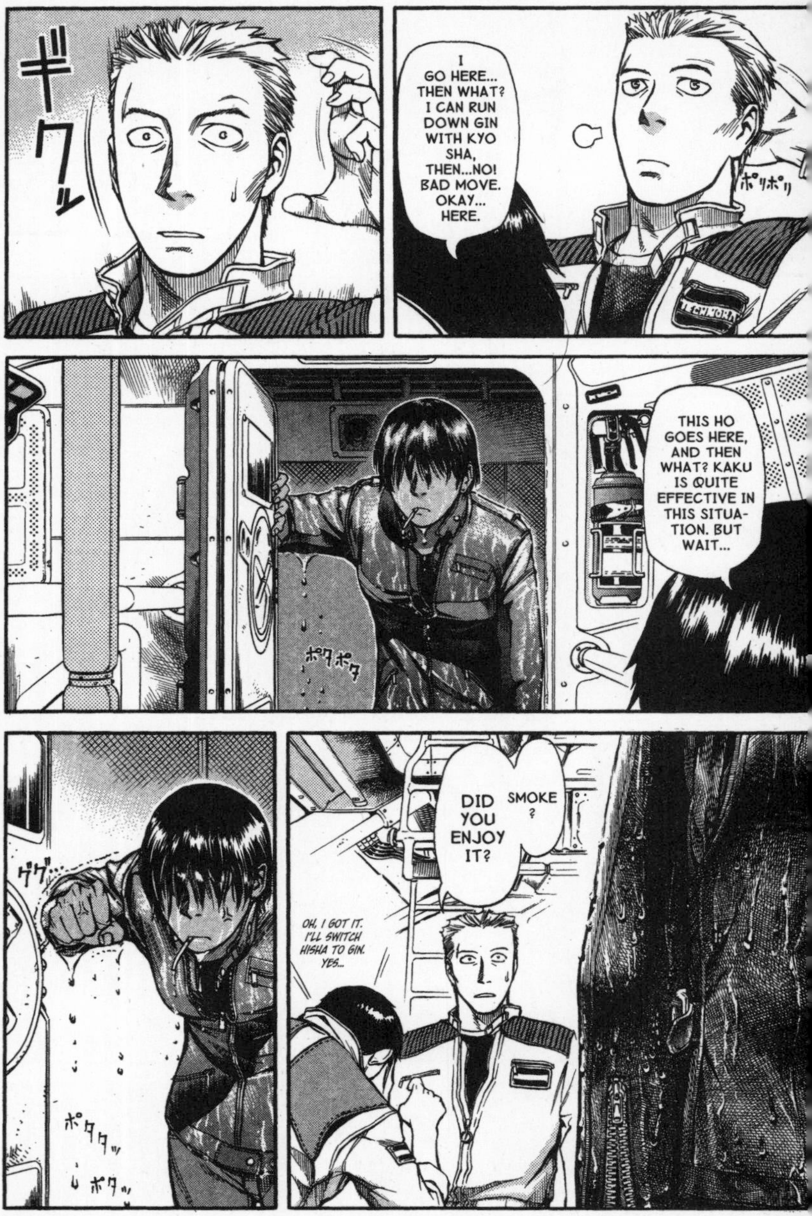
I GO HERE... THEN WHAT? I CAN RUN DOWN GIN WITH KYO SHA, THEN...NO! BAD MOVE. OKAY... HERE.
ポリポリ
ギクッ
THIS HO GOES HERE, AND THEN WHAT? KAKU IS QUITE EFFECTIVE IN THIS SITUATION. BUT WAIT...
ポタポタ
SMOKE?
DID YOU ENJOY IT?
OH, I GOT IT. I'LL SWITCH HISHA TO GIN. YES...
ググ
ポタタッ
ポタッ

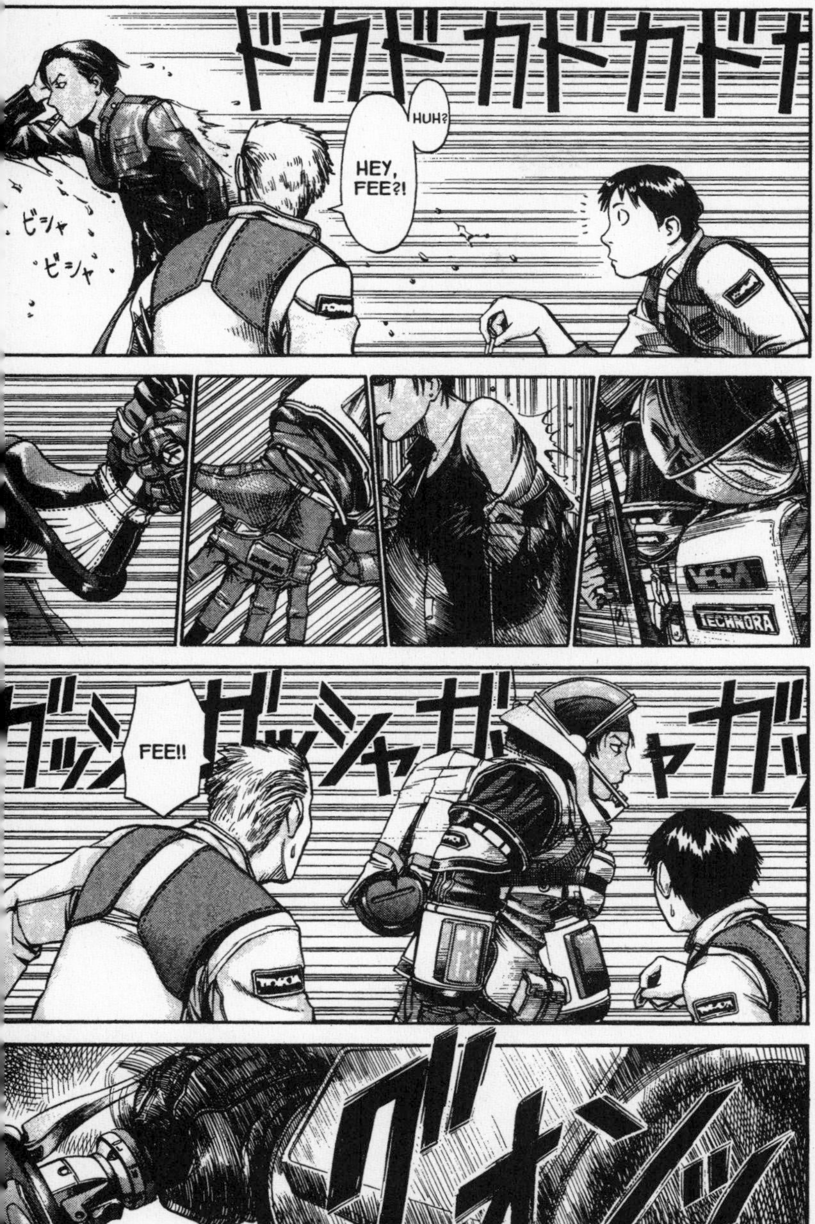
ドカドカドカドカ
HUH?
HEY, FEE?!
ビシャ
ビシャ
TECHNORA
ガッシャガッシャガッ
FEE!!

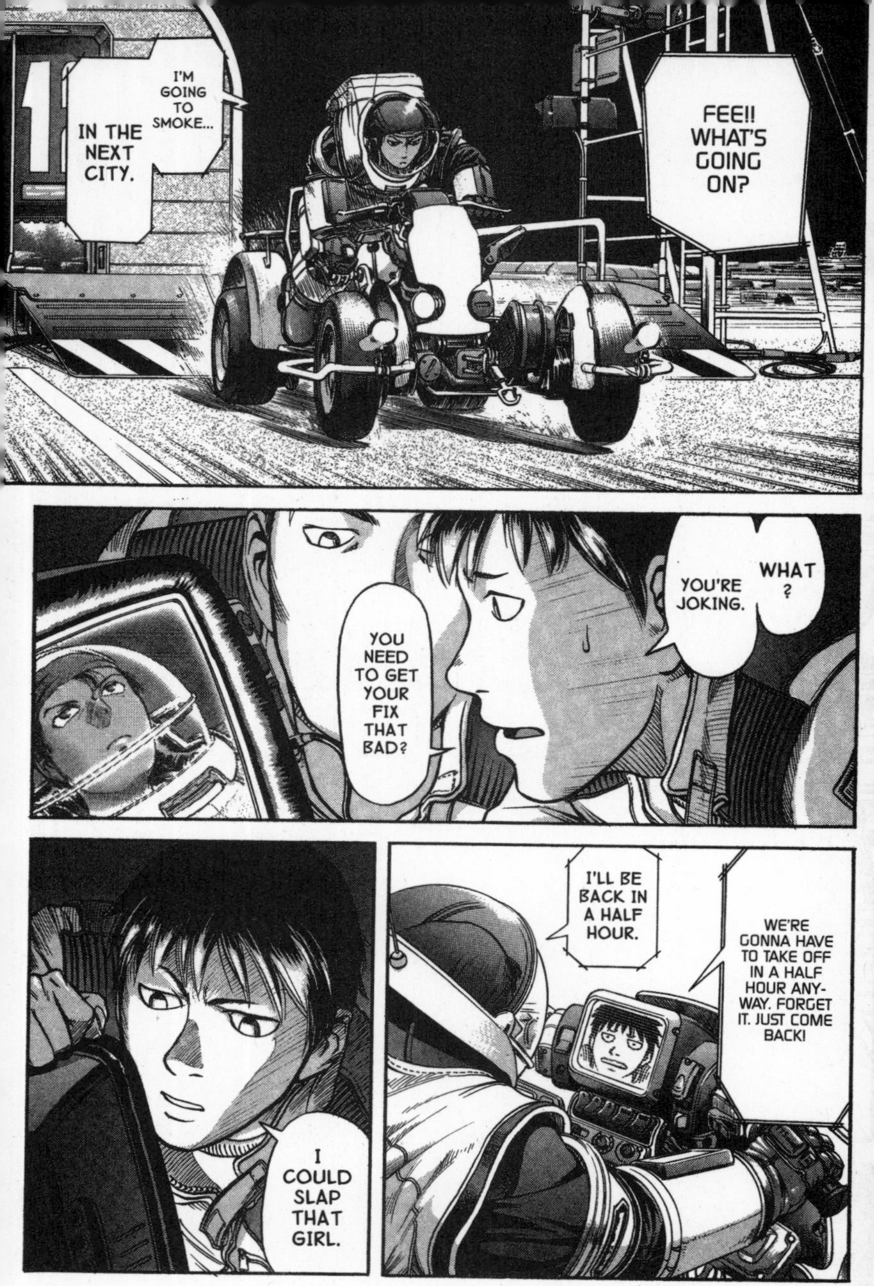
FEE!! WHAT'S GOING ON?
I'M GOING TO SMOKE...
IN THE NEXT CITY.
WHAT ?
YOU'RE JOKING.
YOU NEED TO GET YOUR FIX THAT BAD?
WE'RE GONNA HAVE TO TAKE OFF IN A HALF HOUR ANY-WAY. FORGET IT. JUST COME BACK!
I'LL BE BACK IN A HALF HOUR.
I COULD SLAP THAT GIRL.

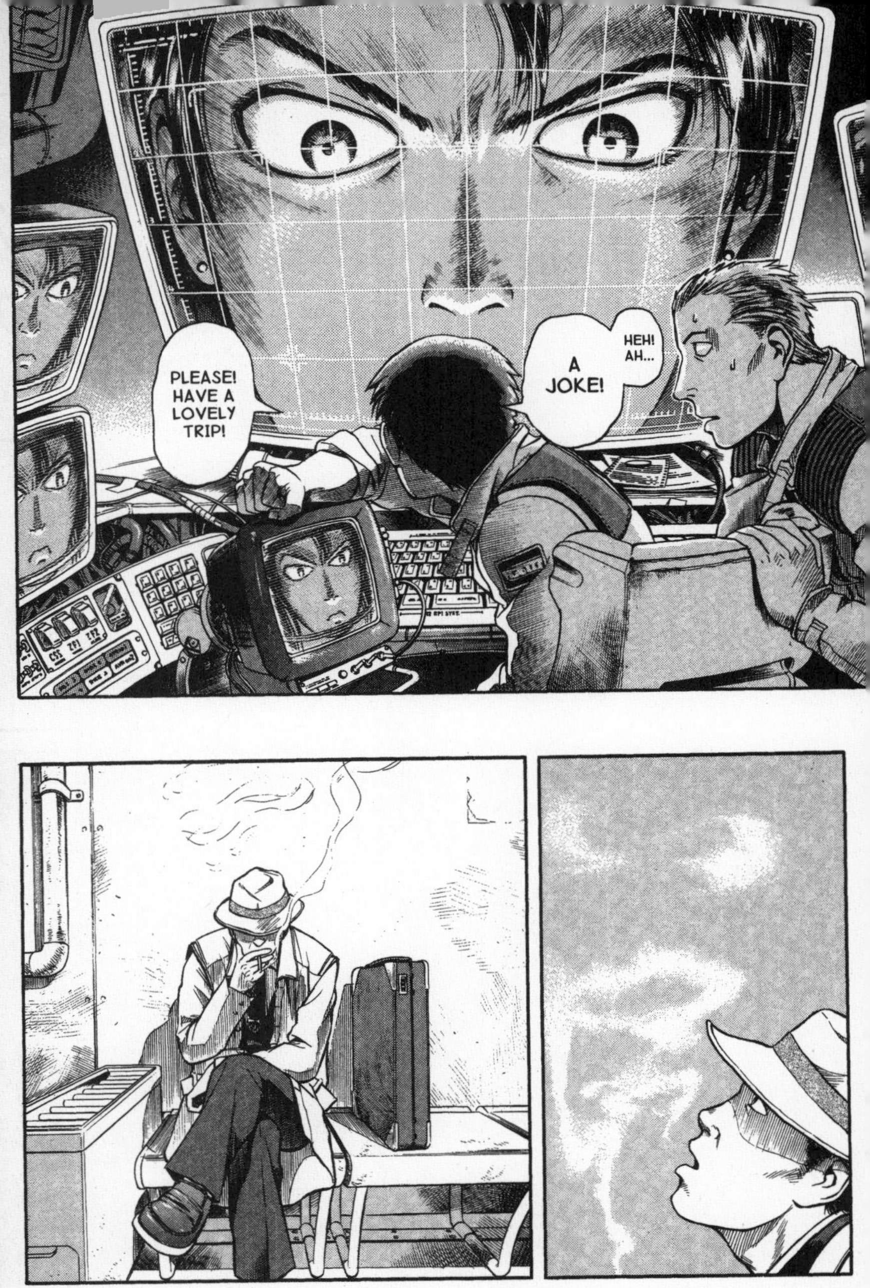
HEH! AH...
A JOKE!
PLEASE! HAVE A LOVELY TRIP!

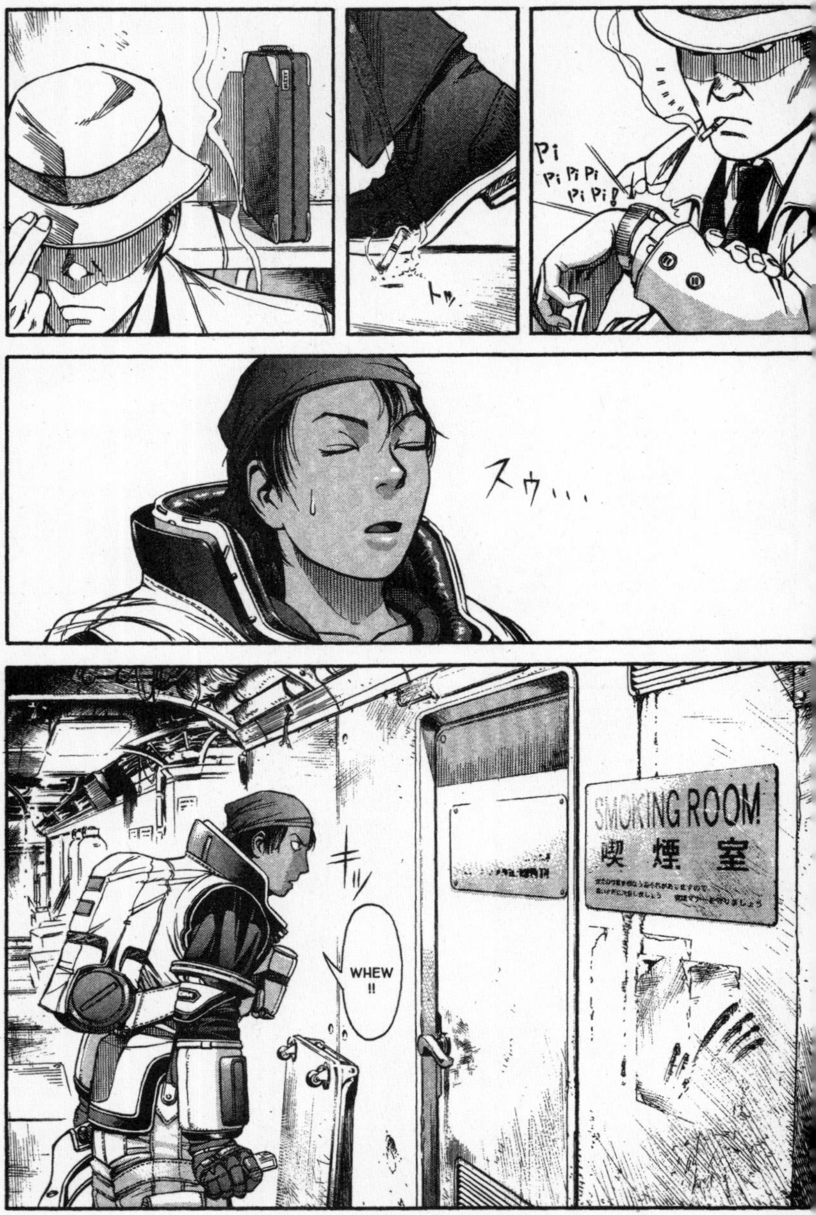
Pi Pi Pi Pi Pi Pi!
トッ
スゥ...
SMOKING ROOM
喫煙室
ギッ
WHEW !!

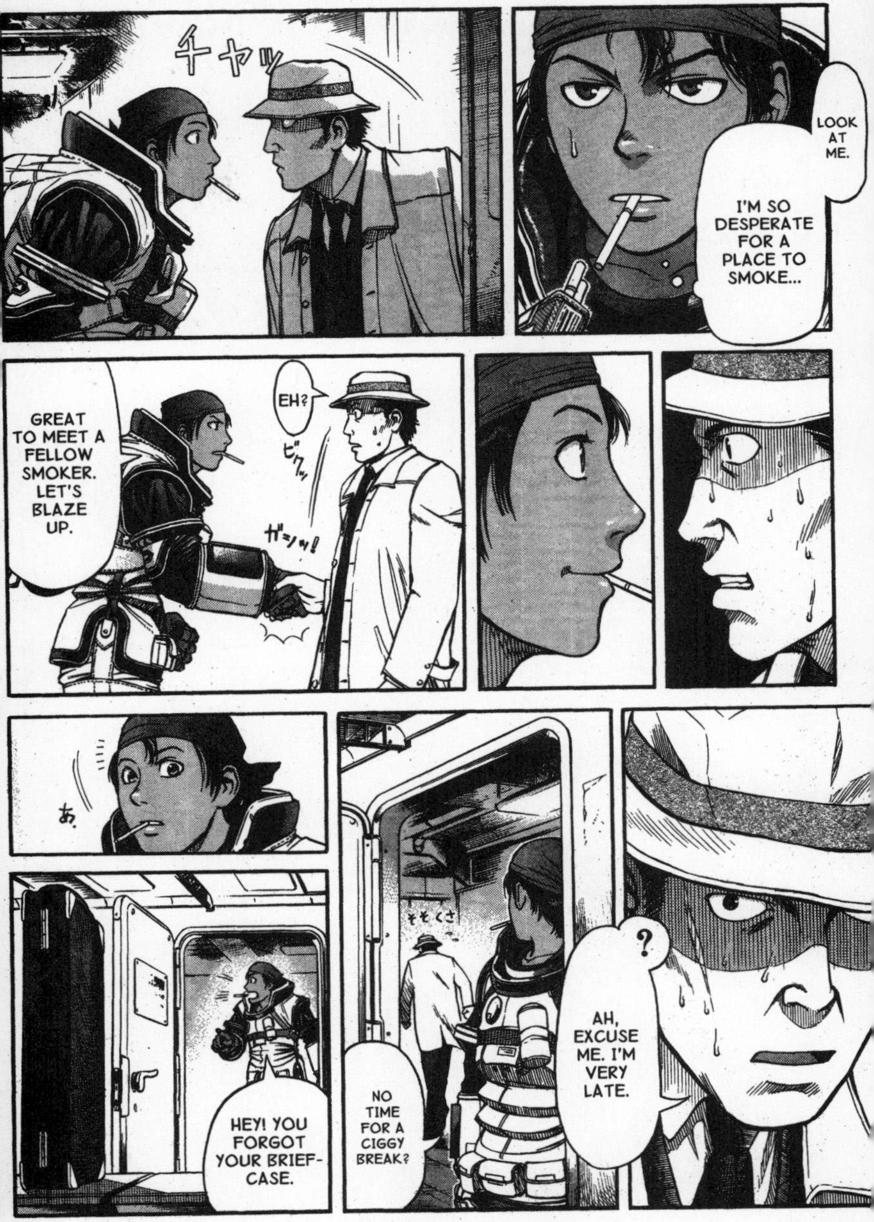
LOOK AT ME.
I'M SO DESPERATE FOR A PLACE TO SMOKE...
チャッ
EH?
GREAT TO MEET A FELLOW SMOKER. LET'S BLAZE UP.
ビクッ
ガシッ!
?
AH, EXCUSE ME. I'M VERY LATE.
そそくさ
NO TIME FOR A CIGGY BREAK?
あ.
HEY! YOU FORGOT YOUR BRIEF-CASE.

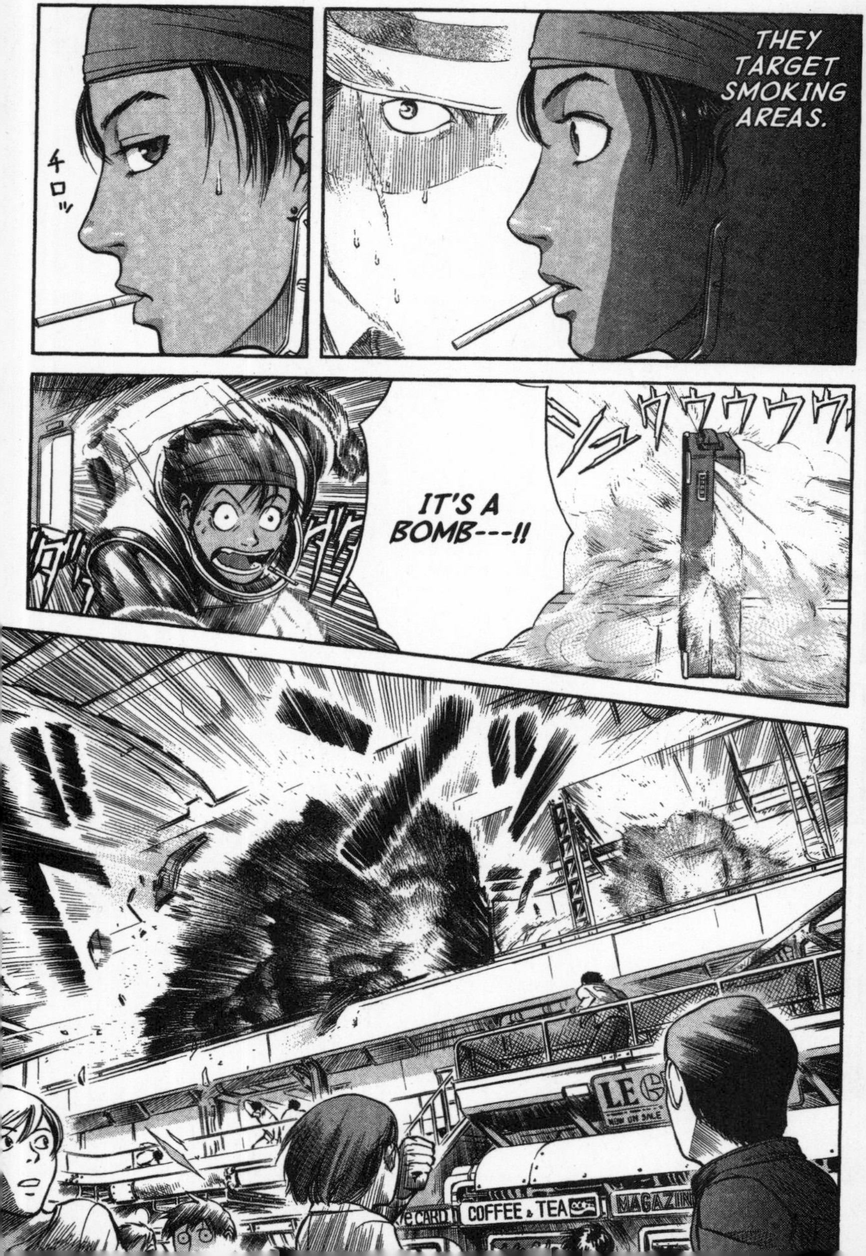
THEY TARGET SMOKING AREAS.
チロッ
シュウウウウウ
IT'S A BOMB---!!
COFFEE & TEA

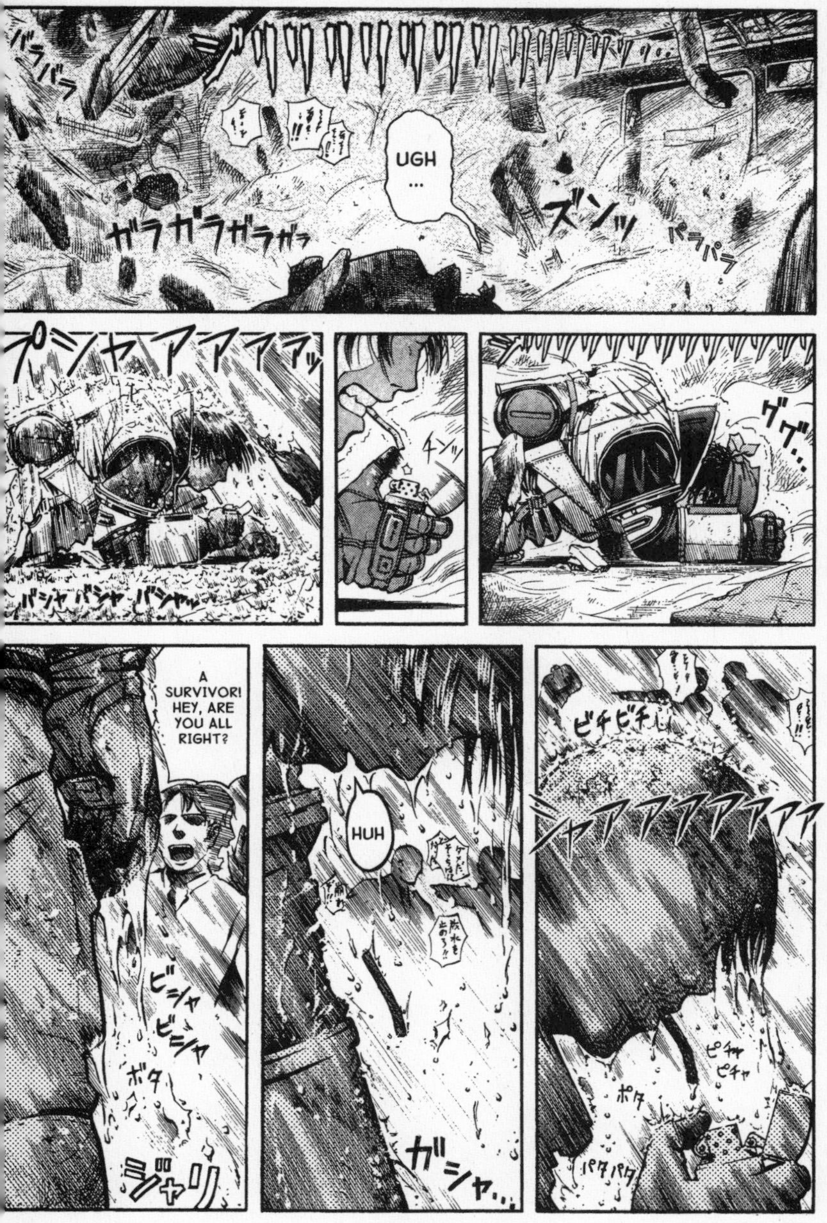
ズンッ
パラパラ
UGH ...
ガラガラガラガラ
バラバラ
ググ...
プシャアアアアッ
バシャバシャバシャ
ビチビチ
シャアアアアアア
ピチャピチャ
ポタ
パタパタ
HUH
ガシャ...
A SURVIVOR! HEY, ARE YOU ALL RIGHT?
ビシャビシャ
ポタ
ジャリ

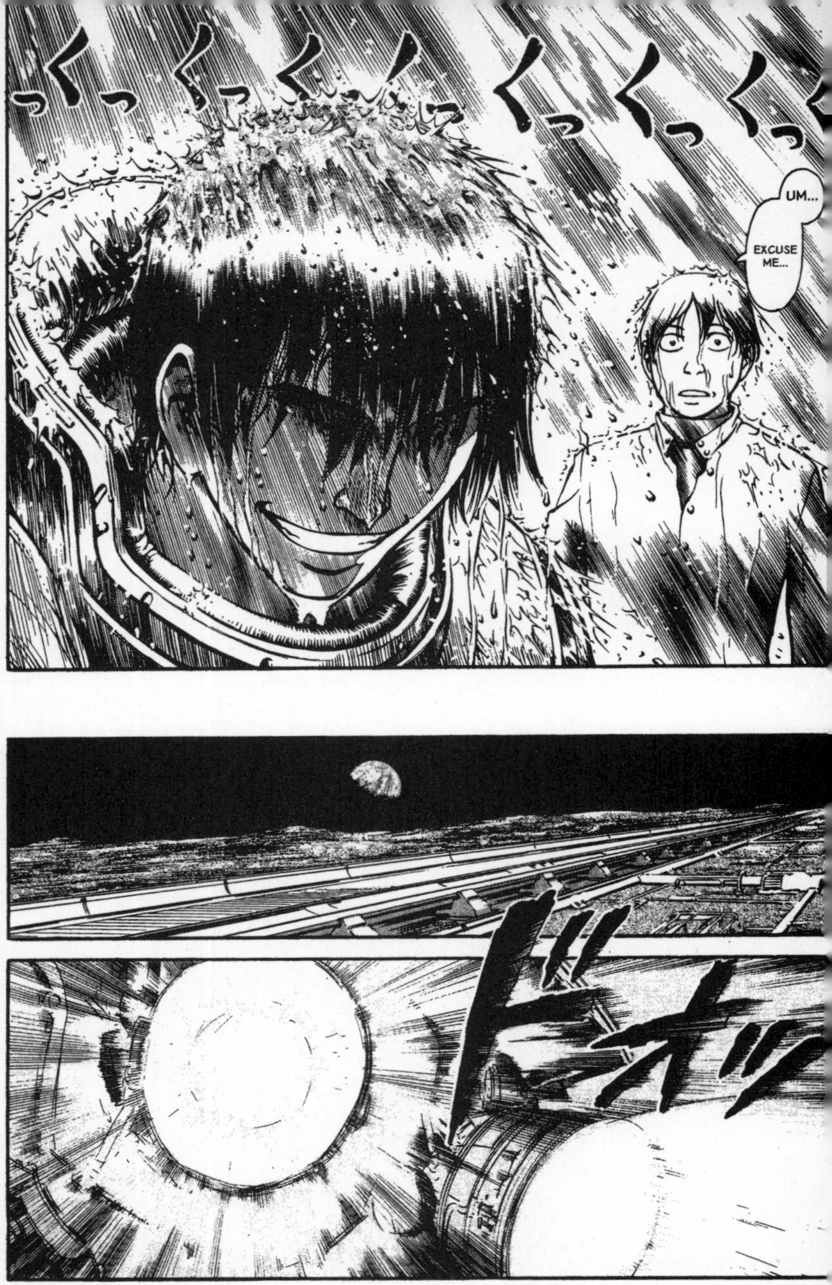
UM...
EXCUSE ME...

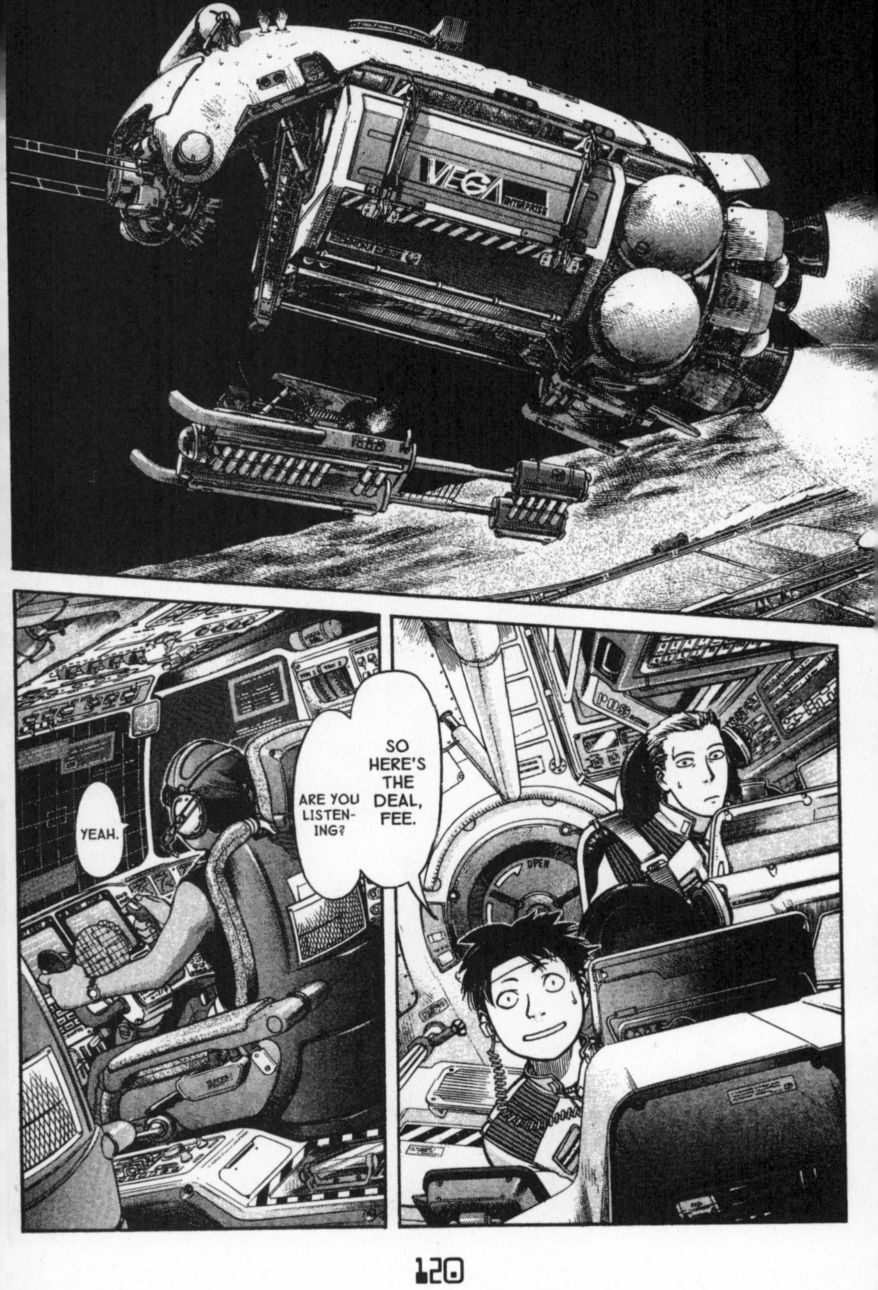
VEGA
SO HERE'S THE DEAL, FEE.
ARE YOU LISTEN-ING?
YEAH.

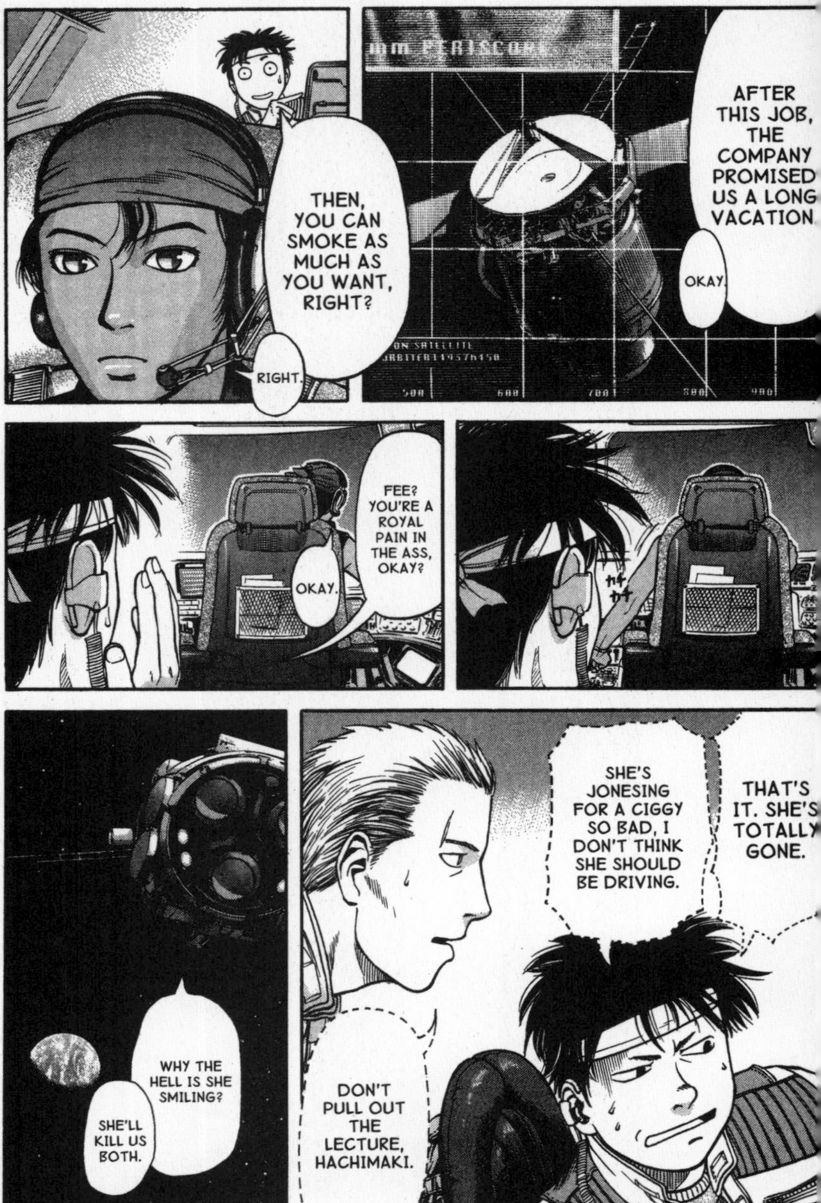
AFTER THIS JOB, THE COMPANY PROMISED US A LONG VACATION.
OKAY.
THEN, YOU CAN SMOKE AS MUCH AS YOU WANT, RIGHT?
RIGHT.
FEE? YOU'RE A ROYAL PAIN IN THE ASS, OKAY?
OKAY.
THAT'S IT. SHE'S TOTALLY GONE.
SHE'S JONESING FOR A CIGGY SO BAD, I DON'T THINK SHE SHOULD BE DRIVING.
DON'T PULL OUT THE LECTURE, HACHIMAKI.
WHY THE HELL IS SHE SMILING?
SHE'LL KILL US BOTH.

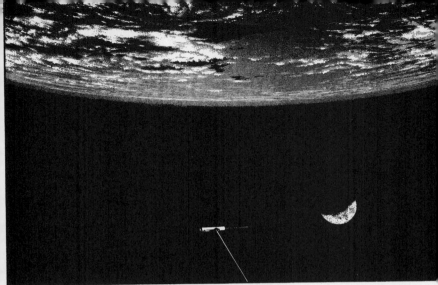

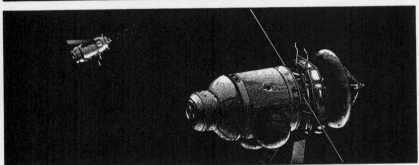

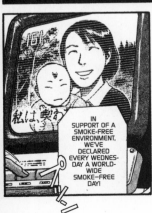

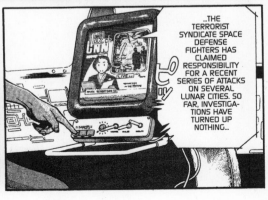

...THE TERRORIST SYNDICATE SPACE DEFENSE FIGHTERS HAS CLAIMED RESPONSIBILITY FOR A RECENT SERIES OF ATTACKS ON SEVERAL LUNAR CITIES. SO FAR, INVESTIGATIONS HAVE TURNED UP NOTHING...
IN SUPPORT OF A SMOKE-FREE ENVIRONMENT, WE'VE DECLARED EVERY WEDNESDAY A WORLD-WIDE SMOKE-FREE DAY!

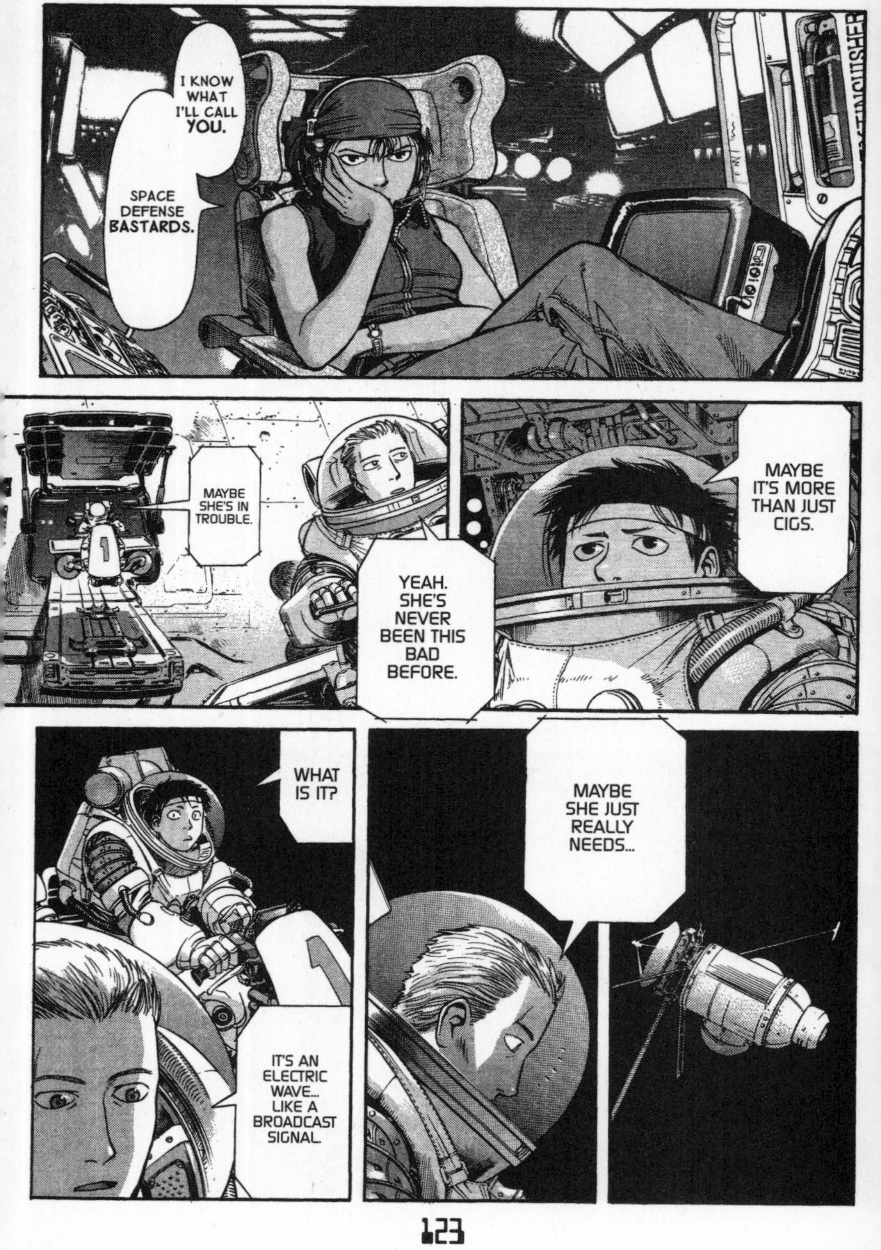
I KNOW WHAT I'LL CALL YOU.
SPACE DEFENSE BASTARDS.
MAYBE IT'S MORE THAN JUST CIGS.
MAYBE SHE'S IN TROUBLE.
YEAH. SHE'S NEVER BEEN THIS BAD BEFORE.
MAYBE SHE JUST REALLY NEEDS...
WHAT IS IT?
IT'S AN ELECTRIC WAVE... LIKE A BROADCAST SIGNAL.

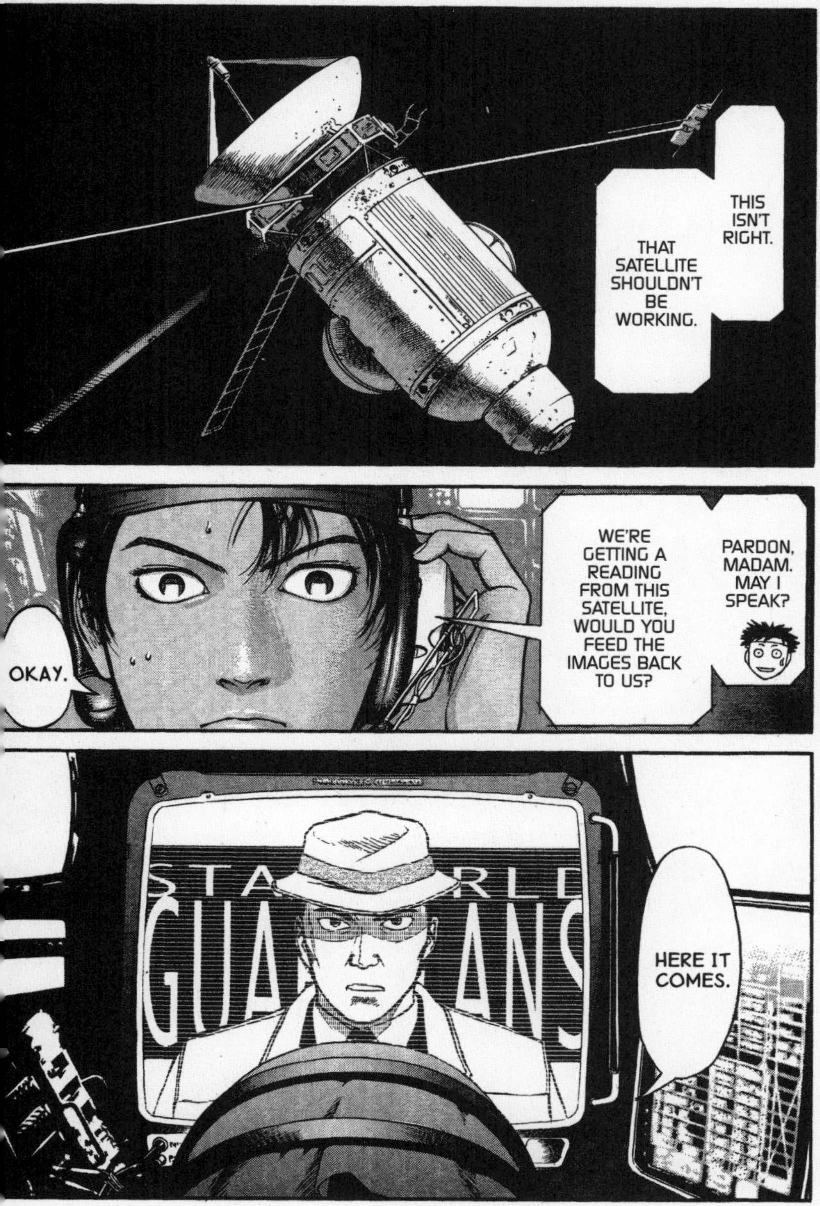
THIS ISN'T RIGHT.
THAT SATELLITE SHOULDN'T BE WORKING.
PARDON, MADAM. MAY I SPEAK?
WE'RE GETTING A READING FROM THIS SATELLITE, WOULD YOU FEED THE IMAGES BACK TO US?
OKAY.
HERE IT COMES.

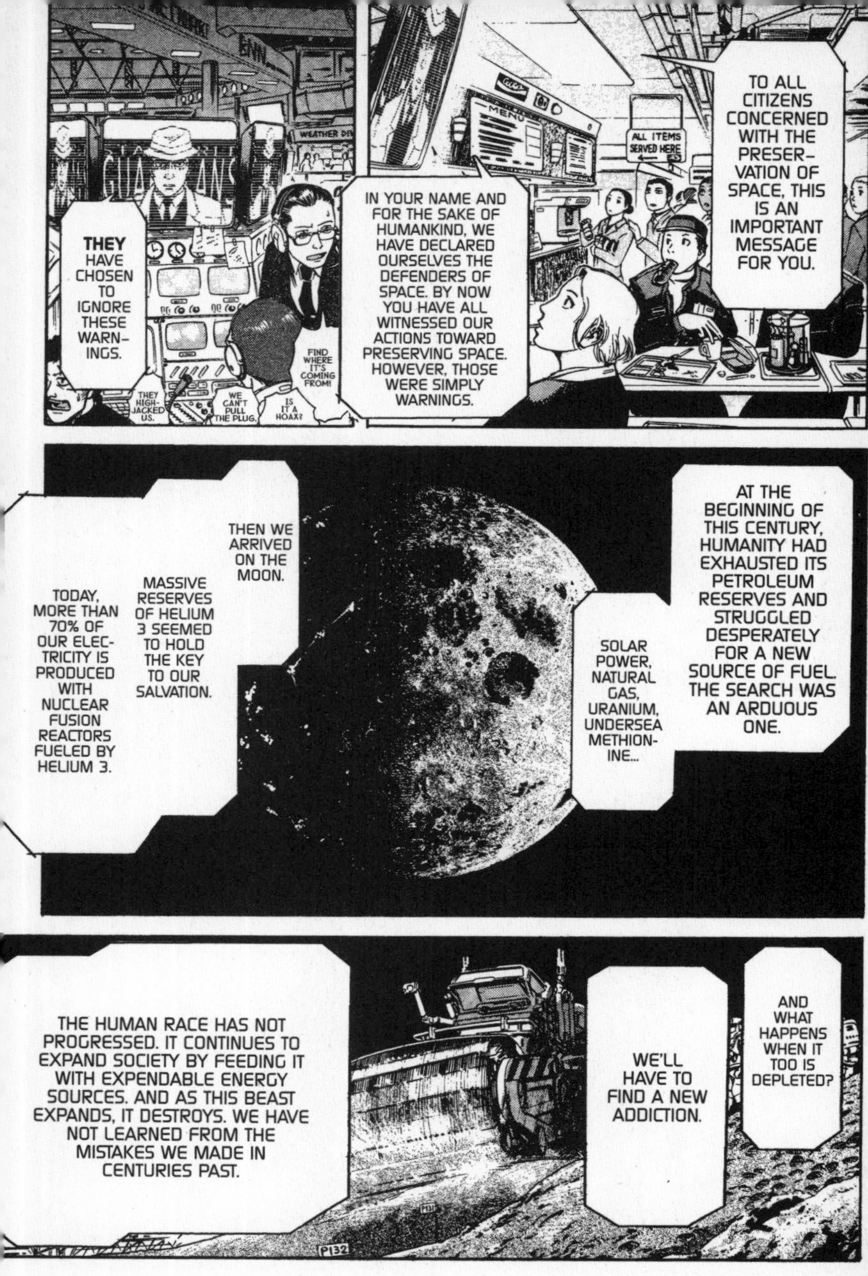
TO ALL CITIZENS CONCERNED WITH THE PRESER-VATION OF SPACE, THIS IS AN IMPORTANT MESSAGE FOR YOU.
ALL ITEMS SERVED HERE
MENU
IN YOUR NAME AND FOR THE SAKE OF HUMANKIND, WE HAVE DECLARED OURSELVES THE DEFENDERS OF SPACE. BY NOW YOU HAVE ALL WITNESSED OUR ACTIONS TOWARD PRESERVING SPACE. HOWEVER, THOSE WERE SIMPLY WARNINGS.
THEY HAVE CHOSEN TO IGNORE THESE WARN-INGS.
FIND WHERE IT'S COMING FROM!
IS IT A HOAX?
WE CAN'T PULL THE PLUG.
THEY HIGH-JACKED US.
AT THE BEGINNING OF THIS CENTURY, HUMANITY HAD EXHAUSTED ITS PETROLEUM RESERVES AND STRUGGLED DESPERATELY FOR A NEW SOURCE OF FUEL. THE SEARCH WAS AN ARDUOUS ONE.
SOLAR POWER, NATURAL GAS, URANIUM, UNDERSEA METHION-INE...
THEN WE ARRIVED ON THE MOON.
MASSIVE RESERVES OF HELIUM 3 SEEMED TO HOLD THE KEY TO OUR SALVATION.
TODAY, MORE THAN 70% OF OUR ELEC-TRICITY IS PRODUCED WITH NUCLEAR FUSION REACTORS FUELED BY HELIUM 3.
AND WHAT HAPPENS WHEN IT TOO IS DEPLETED?
WE'LL HAVE TO FIND A NEW ADDICTION.
THE HUMAN RACE HAS NOT PROGRESSED. IT CONTINUES TO EXPAND SOCIETY BY FEEDING IT WITH EXPENDABLE ENERGY SOURCES. AND AS THIS BEAST EXPANDS, IT DESTROYS. WE HAVE NOT LEARNED FROM THE MISTAKES WE MADE IN CENTURIES PAST.

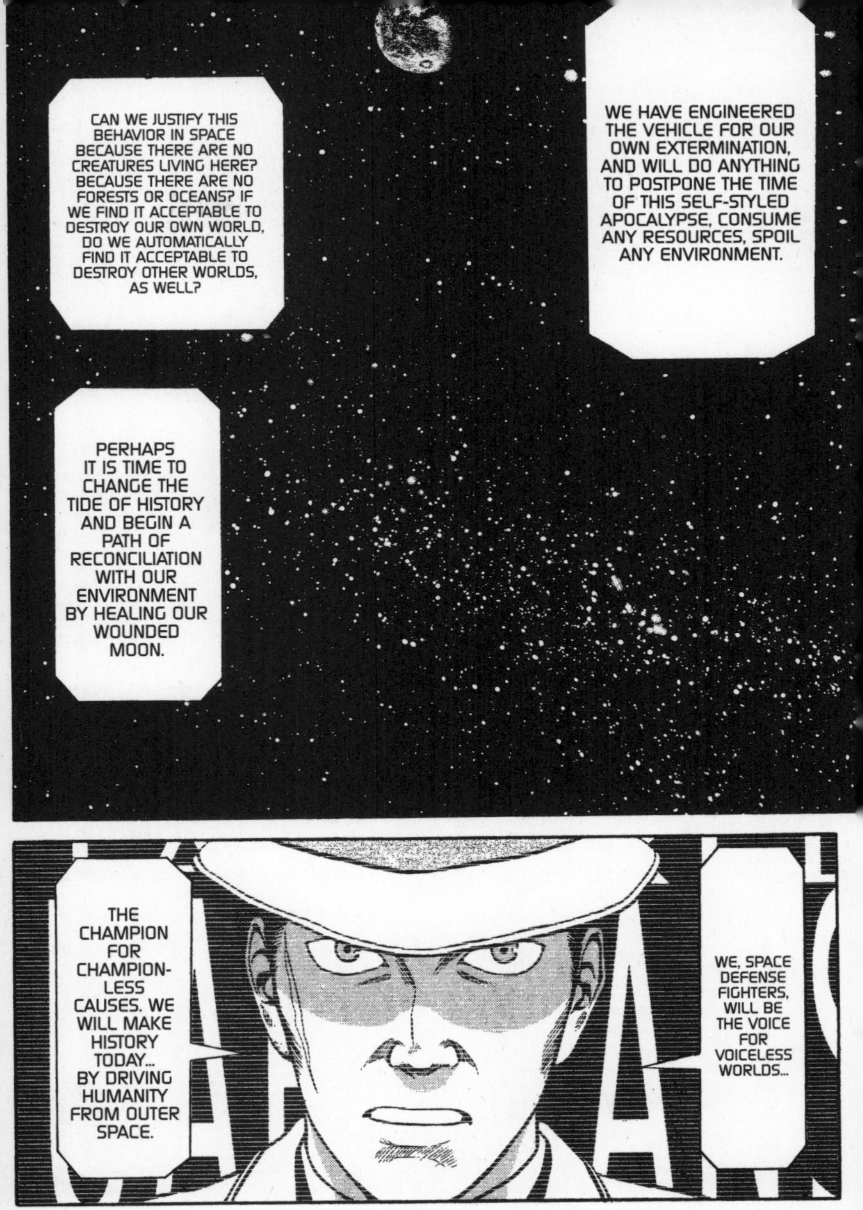
WE HAVE ENGINEERED THE VEHICLE FOR OUR OWN EXTERMINATION, AND WILL DO ANYTHING TO POSTPONE THE TIME OF THIS SELF-STYLED APOCALYPSE, CONSUME ANY RESOURCES, SPOIL ANY ENVIRONMENT.
CAN WE JUSTIFY THIS BEHAVIOR IN SPACE BECAUSE THERE ARE NO CREATURES LIVING HERE? BECAUSE THERE ARE NO FORESTS OR OCEANS? IF WE FIND IT ACCEPTABLE TO DESTROY OUR OWN WORLD, DO WE AUTOMATICALLY FIND IT ACCEPTABLE TO DESTROY OTHER WORLDS, AS WELL?
PERHAPS IT IS TIME TO CHANGE THE TIDE OF HISTORY AND BEGIN A PATH OF RECONCILIATION WITH OUR ENVIRONMENT BY HEALING OUR WOUNDED MOON.
WE, SPACE DEFENSE FIGHTERS, WILL BE THE VOICE FOR VOICELESS WORLDS...
THE CHAMPION FOR CHAMPION-LESS CAUSES. WE WILL MAKE HISTORY TODAY... BY DRIVING HUMANITY FROM OUTER SPACE.

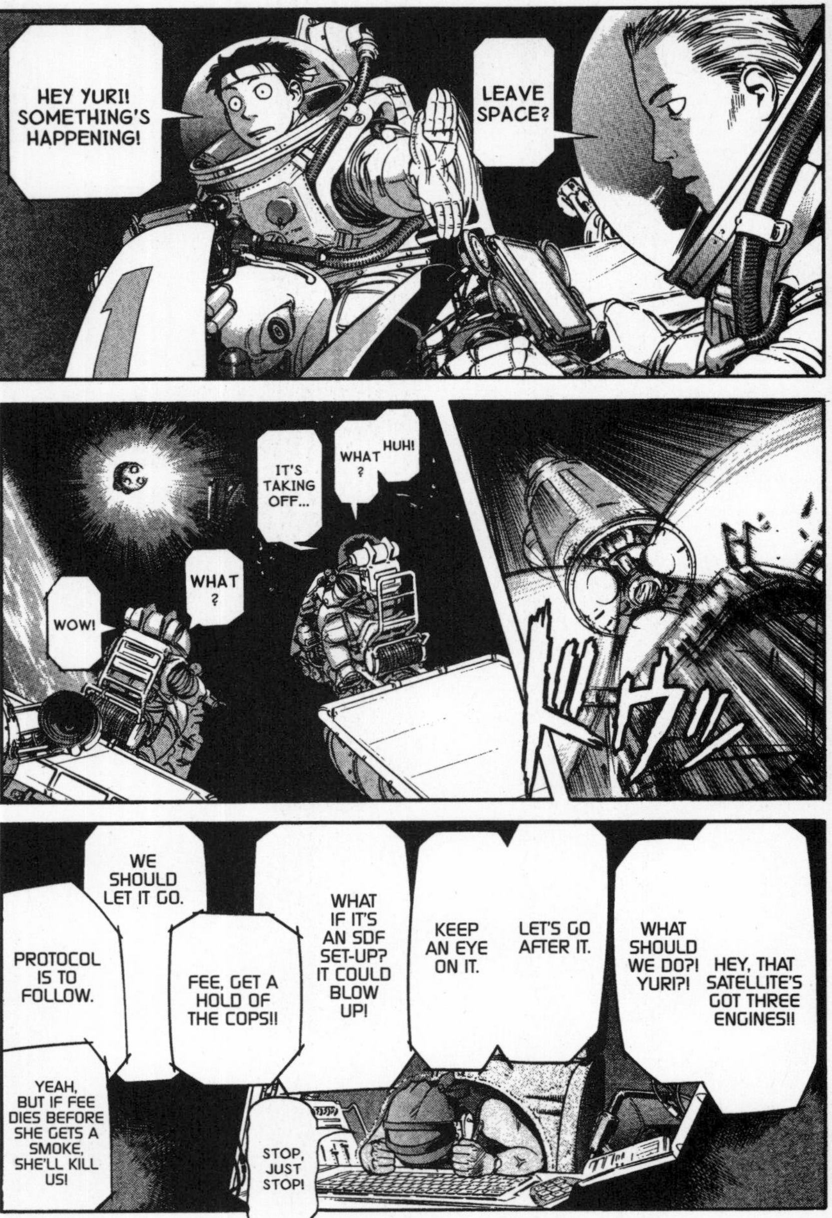
LEAVE SPACE?
HEY YURI! SOMETHING'S HAPPENING!
HUH!
WHAT ?
IT'S TAKING OFF...
WHAT ?
WOW!
HEY, THAT SATELLITE'S GOT THREE ENGINES!!
WHAT SHOULD WE DO?! YURI?!
LET'S GO AFTER IT.
KEEP AN EYE ON IT.
WHAT IF IT'S AN SDF SET-UP? IT COULD BLOW UP!
WE SHOULD LET IT GO.
FEE, GET A HOLD OF THE COPS!!
PROTOCOL IS TO FOLLOW.
STOP, JUST STOP!
YEAH, BUT IF FEE DIES BEFORE SHE GETS A SMOKE, SHE'LL KILL US!

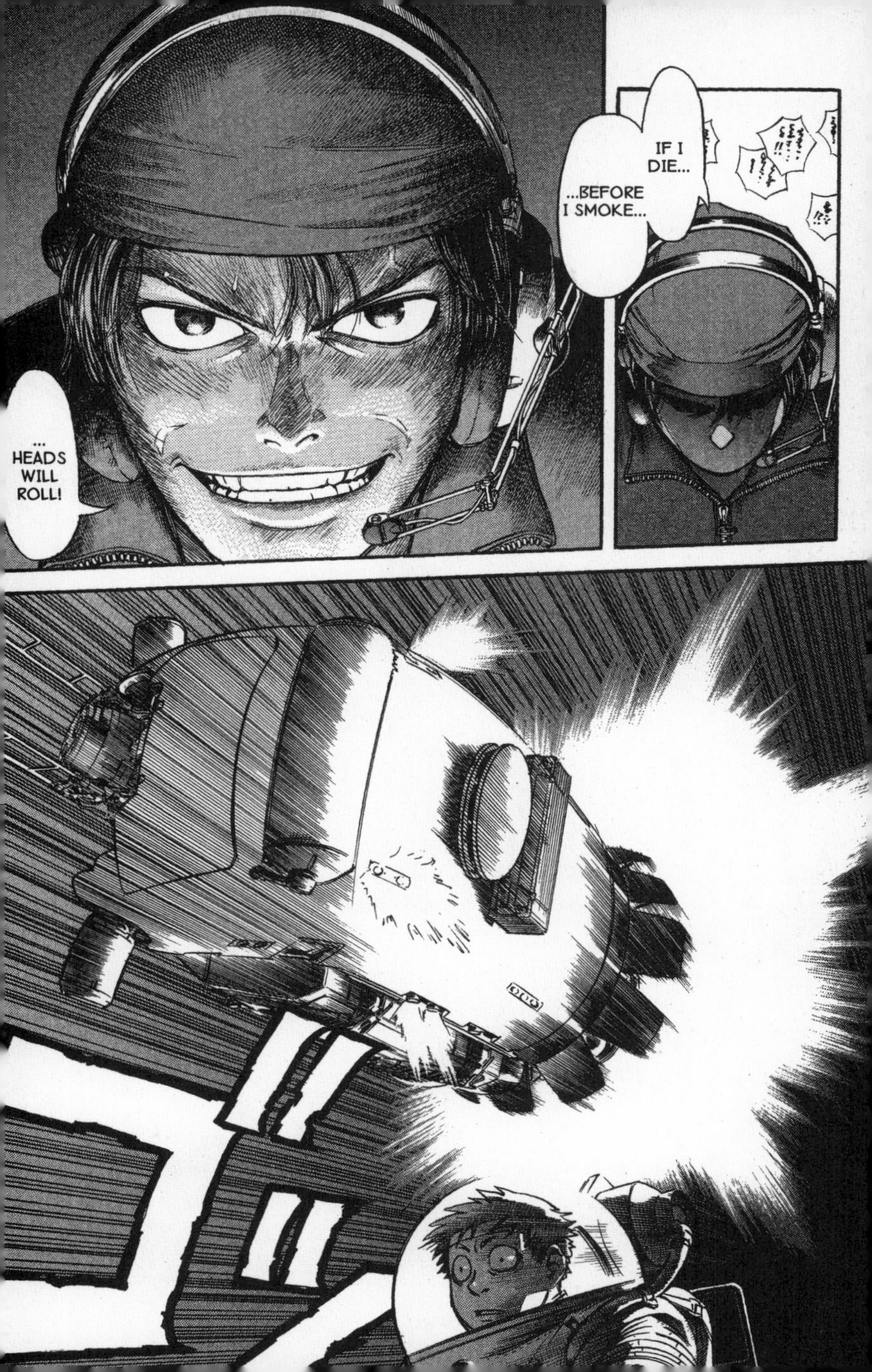
IF I DIE...
...BEFORE I SMOKE...
...HEADS WILL ROLL!

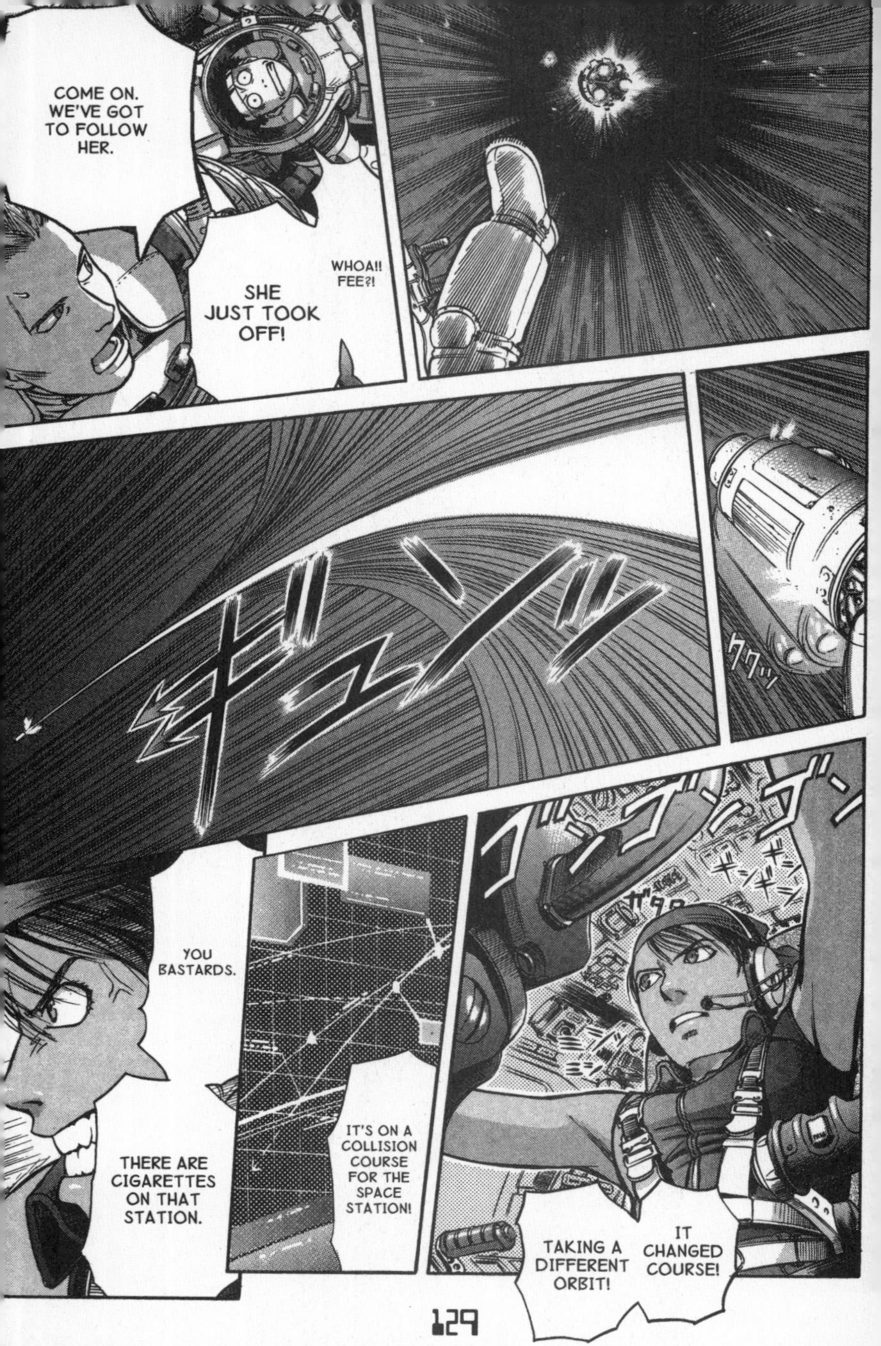
WHOA!! FEE?!
SHE JUST TOOK OFF!
COME ON. WE'VE GOT TO FOLLOW HER.
ギュンッ
IT CHANGED COURSE!
TAKING A DIFFERENT ORBIT!
IT'S ON A COLLISION COURSE FOR THE SPACE STATION!
YOU BASTARDS.
THERE ARE CIGARETTES ON THAT STATION.

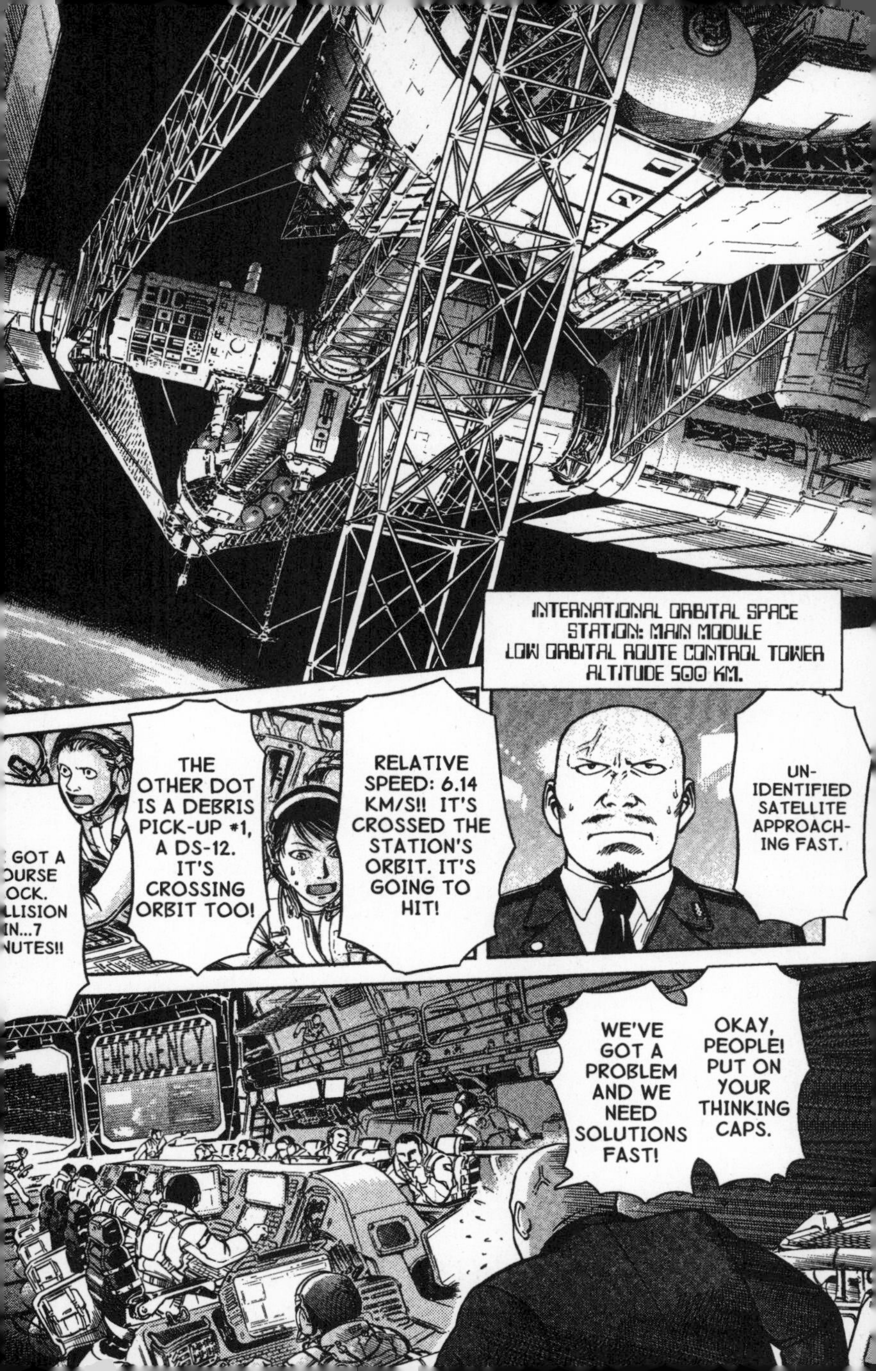
INTERNATIONAL ORBITAL SPACE STATION: MAIN MODULE
LOW ORBITAL ROUTE CONTROL TOWER
ALTITUDE 500 KM.
UN-IDENTIFIED SATELLITE APPROACHING FAST.
RELATIVE SPEED: 6.14 KM/S!! IT'S CROSSED THE STATION'S ORBIT. IT'S GOING TO HIT!
THE OTHER DOT IS A DEBRIS PICK-UP #1, A DS-12. IT'S CROSSING ORBIT TOO!
GOT A OURSE OCK. LLISION IN...7 NUTES!!
EMERGENCY
OKAY, PEOPLE! PUT ON YOUR THINKING CAPS.
WE'VE GOT A PROBLEM AND WE NEED SOLUTIONS FAST!

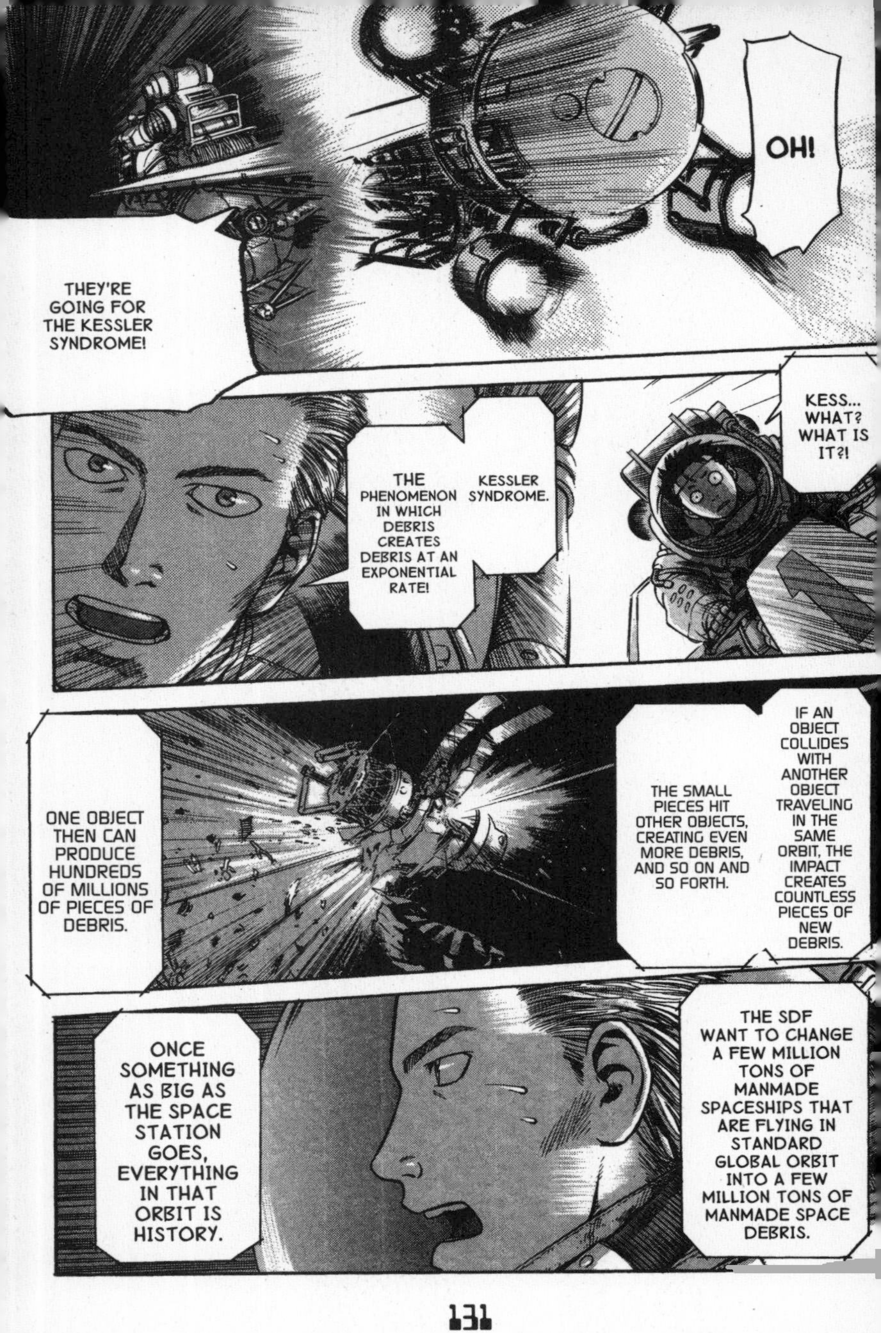
OH!
THEY'RE GOING FOR THE KESSLER SYNDROME!
KESS... WHAT? WHAT IS IT?!
KESSLER SYNDROME.
THE PHENOMENON IN WHICH DEBRIS CREATES DEBRIS AT AN EXPONENTIAL RATE!
IF AN OBJECT COLLIDES WITH ANOTHER OBJECT TRAVELING IN THE SAME ORBIT, THE IMPACT CREATES COUNTLESS PIECES OF NEW DEBRIS.
THE SMALL PIECES HIT OTHER OBJECTS, CREATING EVEN MORE DEBRIS, AND SO ON AND SO FORTH.
ONE OBJECT THEN CAN PRODUCE HUNDREDS OF MILLIONS OF PIECES OF DEBRIS.
THE SDF WANT TO CHANGE A FEW MILLION TONS OF MANMADE SPACESHIPS THAT ARE FLYING IN STANDARD GLOBAL ORBIT INTO A FEW MILLION TONS OF MANMADE SPACE DEBRIS.
ONCE SOMETHING AS BIG AS THE SPACE STATION GOES, EVERYTHING IN THAT ORBIT IS HISTORY.

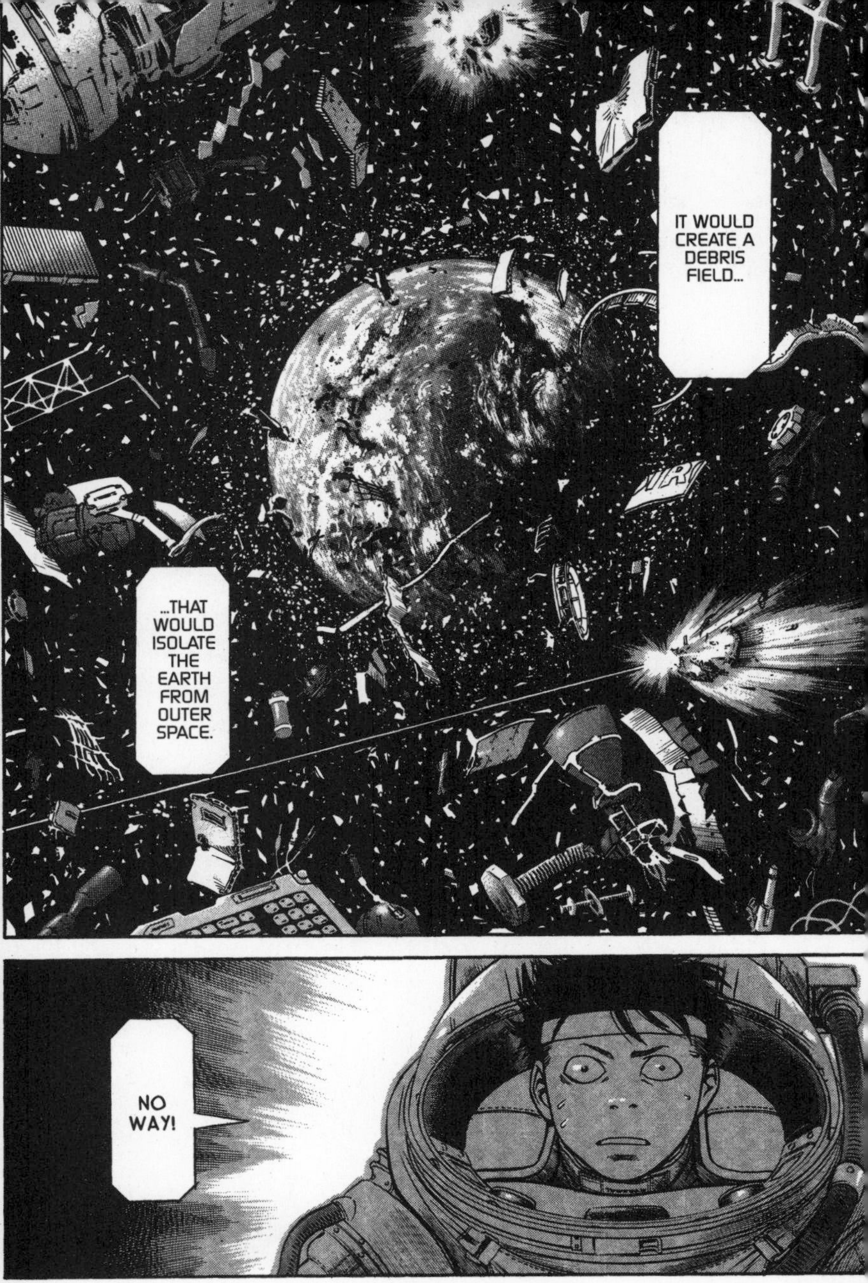
IT WOULD CREATE A DEBRIS FIELD...
...THAT WOULD ISOLATE THE EARTH FROM OUTER SPACE.
NO WAY!

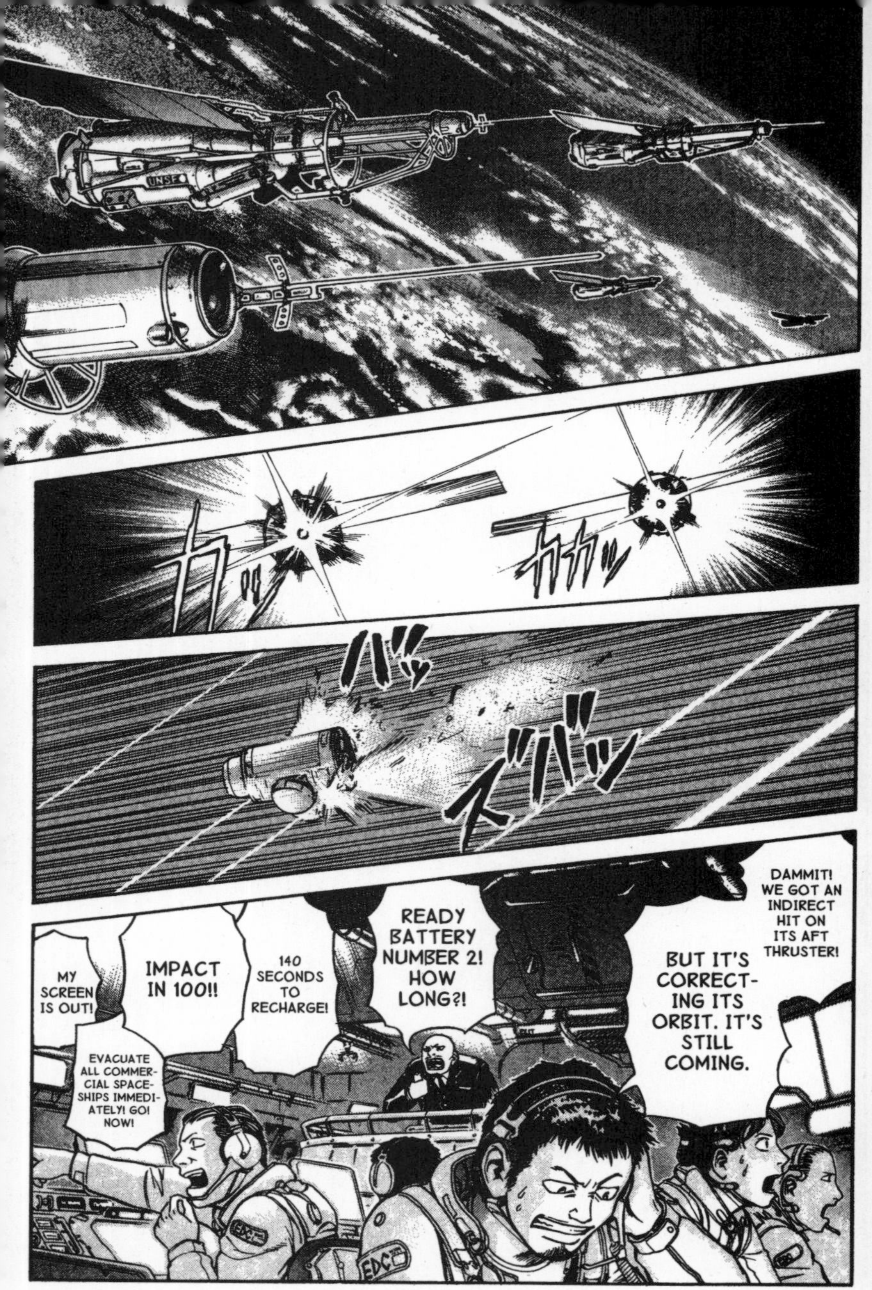

UNSF
カカッ
カッ
バッ
ズバッ
DAMMIT! WE GOT AN INDIRECT HIT ON ITS AFT THRUSTER!
BUT IT'S CORRECT-ING ITS ORBIT. IT'S STILL COMING.
READY BATTERY NUMBER 2! HOW LONG?!
140 SECONDS TO RECHARGE!
IMPACT IN 100!!
MY SCREEN IS OUT!
EVACUATE ALL COMMER-CIAL SPACE-SHIPS IMMEDI-ATELY! GO! NOW!
EDC

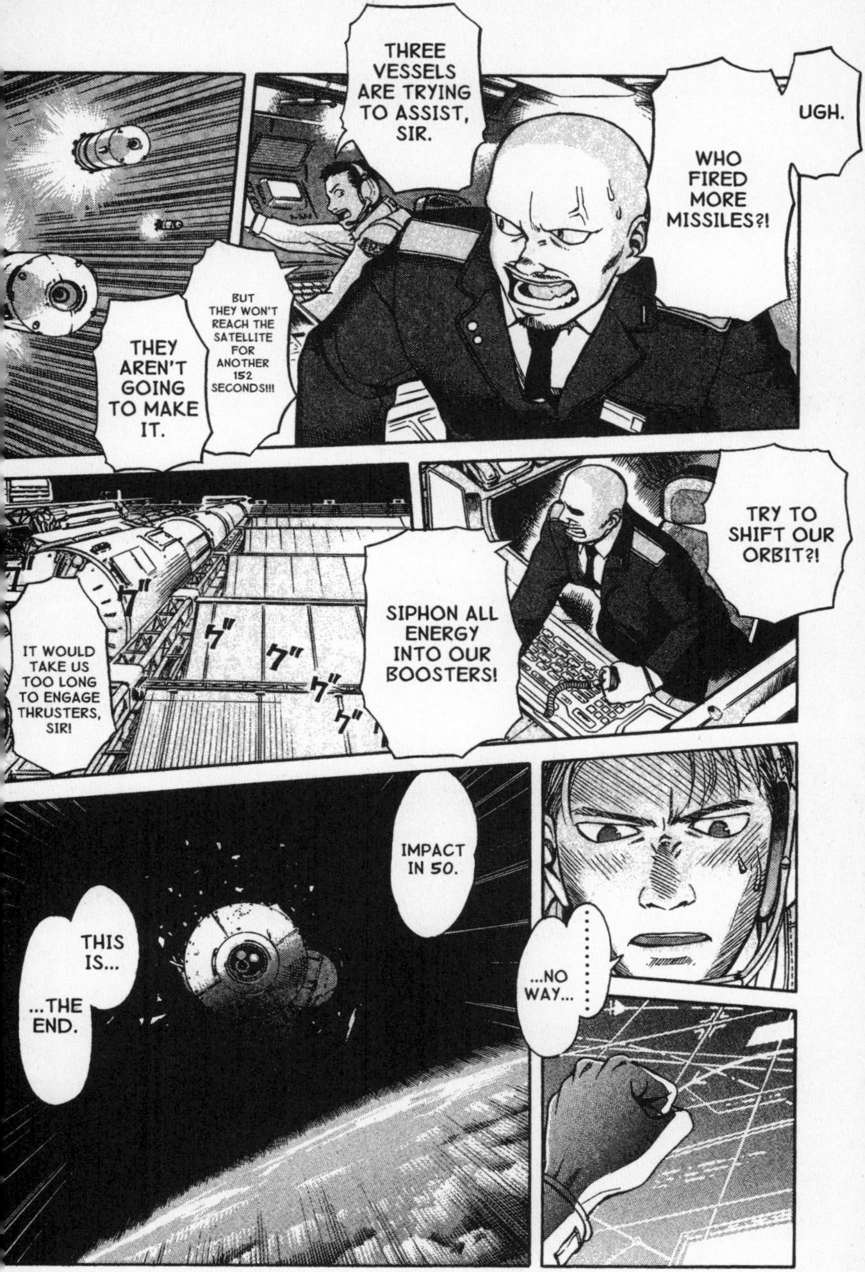
UGH.
WHO FIRED MORE MISSILES?!
THREE VESSELS ARE TRYING TO ASSIST, SIR.
BUT THEY WON'T REACH THE SATELLITE FOR ANOTHER 152 SECONDS!!!
THEY AREN'T GOING TO MAKE IT.
TRY TO SHIFT OUR ORBIT?!
SIPHON ALL ENERGY INTO OUR BOOSTERS!
IT WOULD TAKE US TOO LONG TO ENGAGE THRUSTERS, SIR!
......NO WAY...
IMPACT IN 50.
THIS IS...
...THE END.

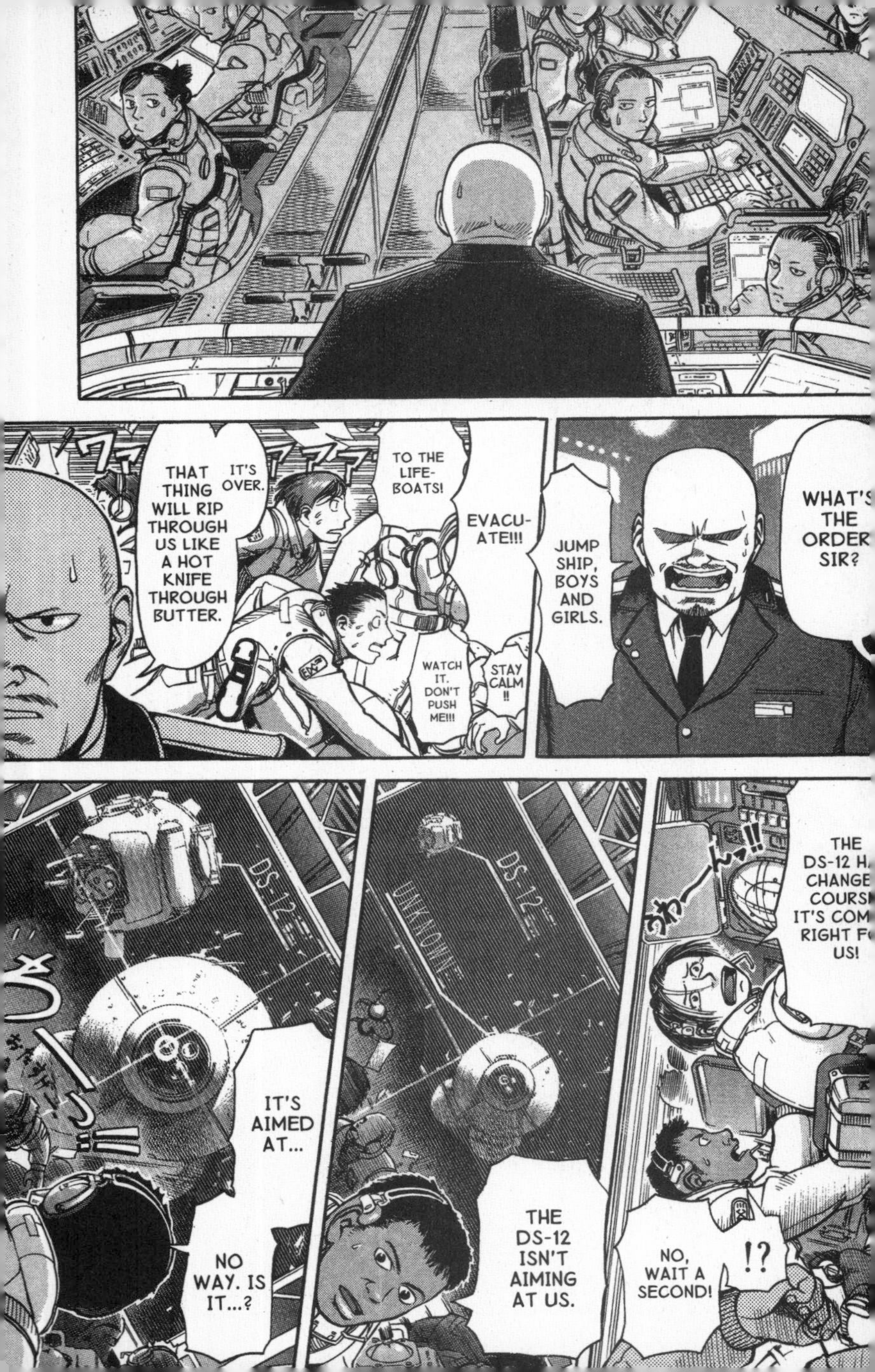

WHAT'S THE ORDER SIR?
JUMP SHIP, BOYS AND GIRLS.
TO THE LIFE-BOATS!
EVACUATE!!!
IT'S OVER.
THAT THING WILL RIP THROUGH US LIKE A HOT KNIFE THROUGH BUTTER.
STAY CALM!!
WATCH IT. DON'T PUSH ME!!!
THE DS-12 HA CHANGE COURS IT'S COM RIGHT FO US!
!?
NO, WAIT A SECOND!
DS-12
UNKNOWN
THE DS-12 ISN'T AIMING AT US.
DS-12
IT'S AIMED AT...
NO WAY. IS IT...?

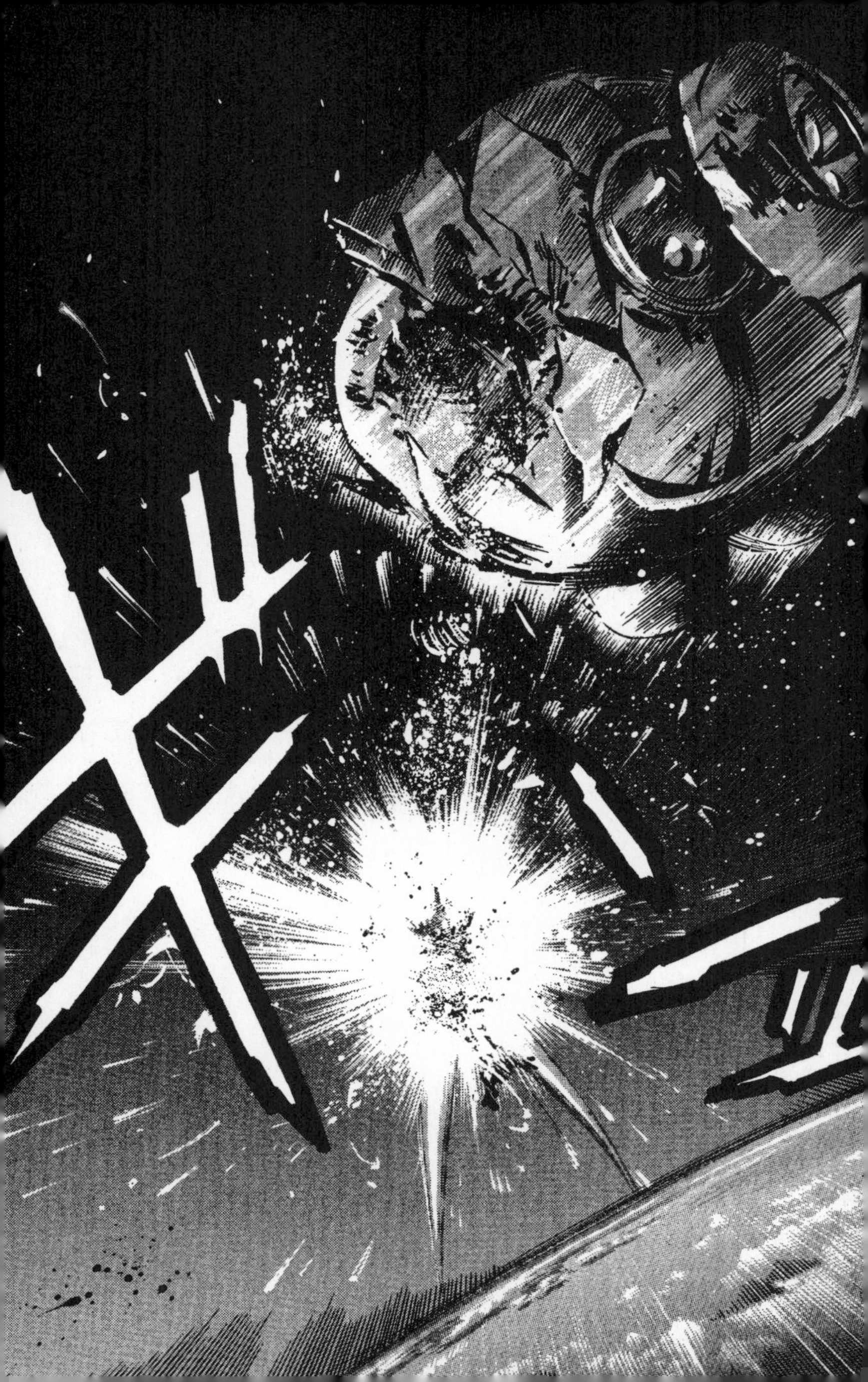

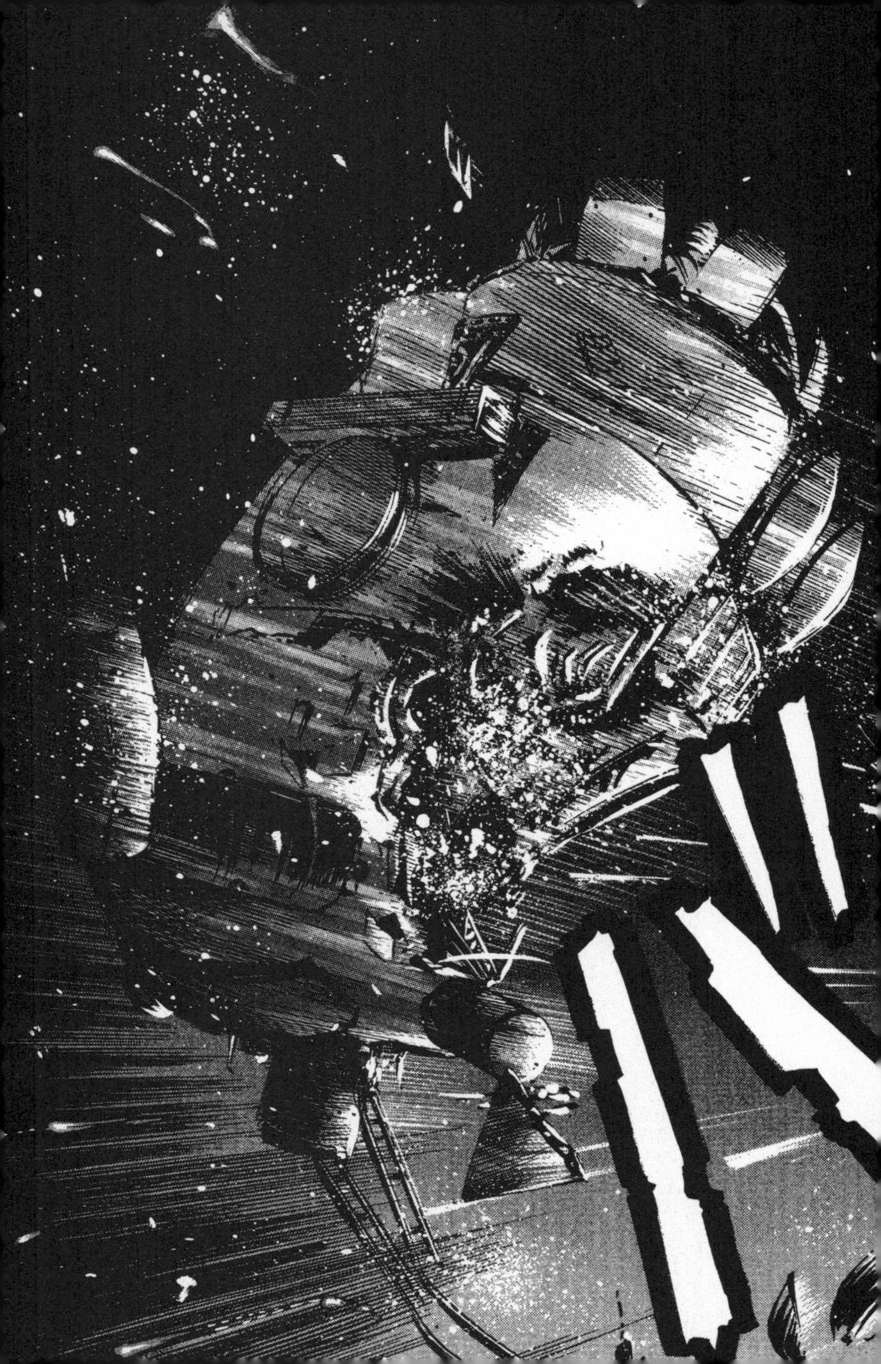

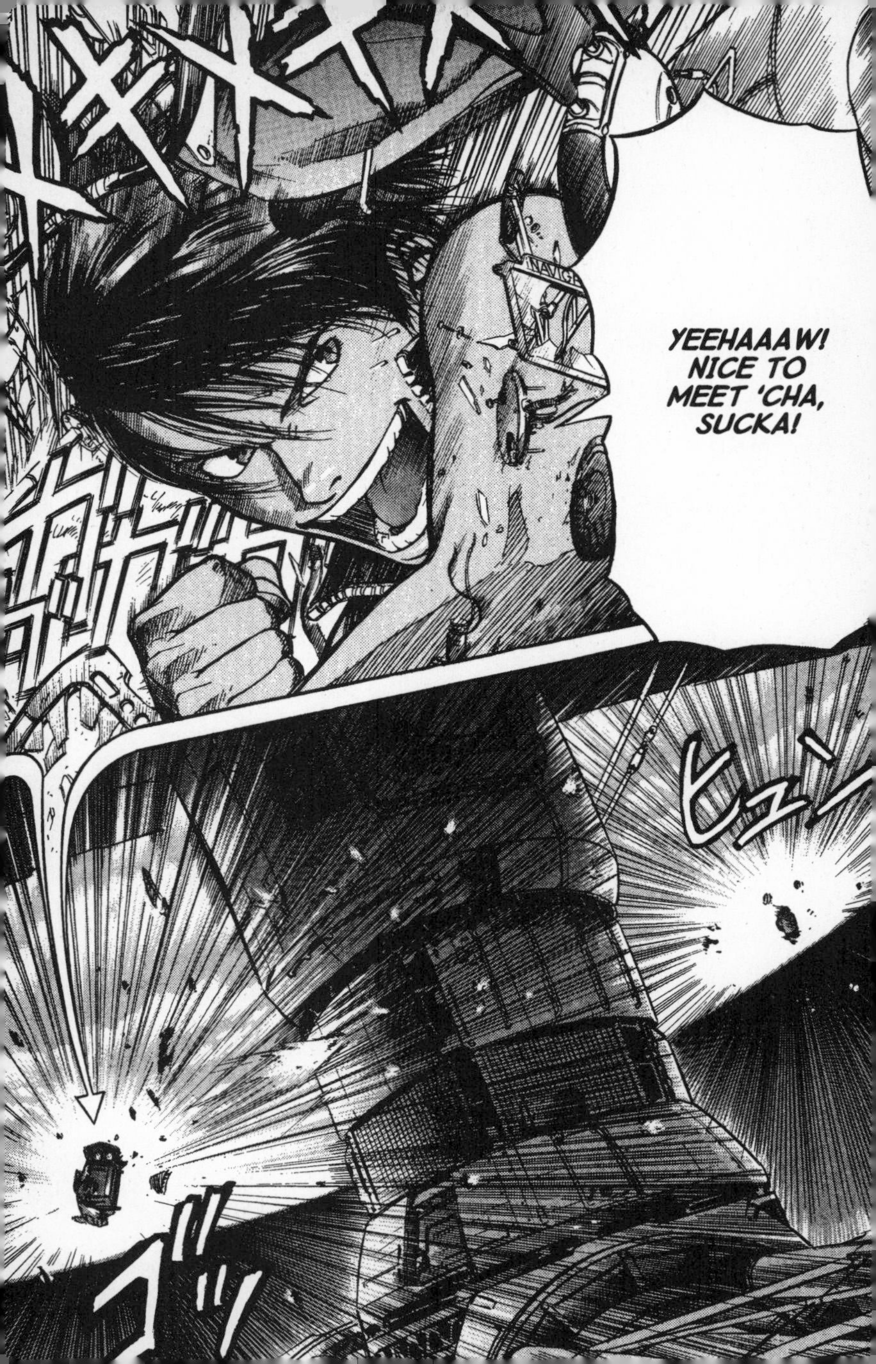
YEEHAAAW! NICE TO MEET 'CHA, SUCKA!

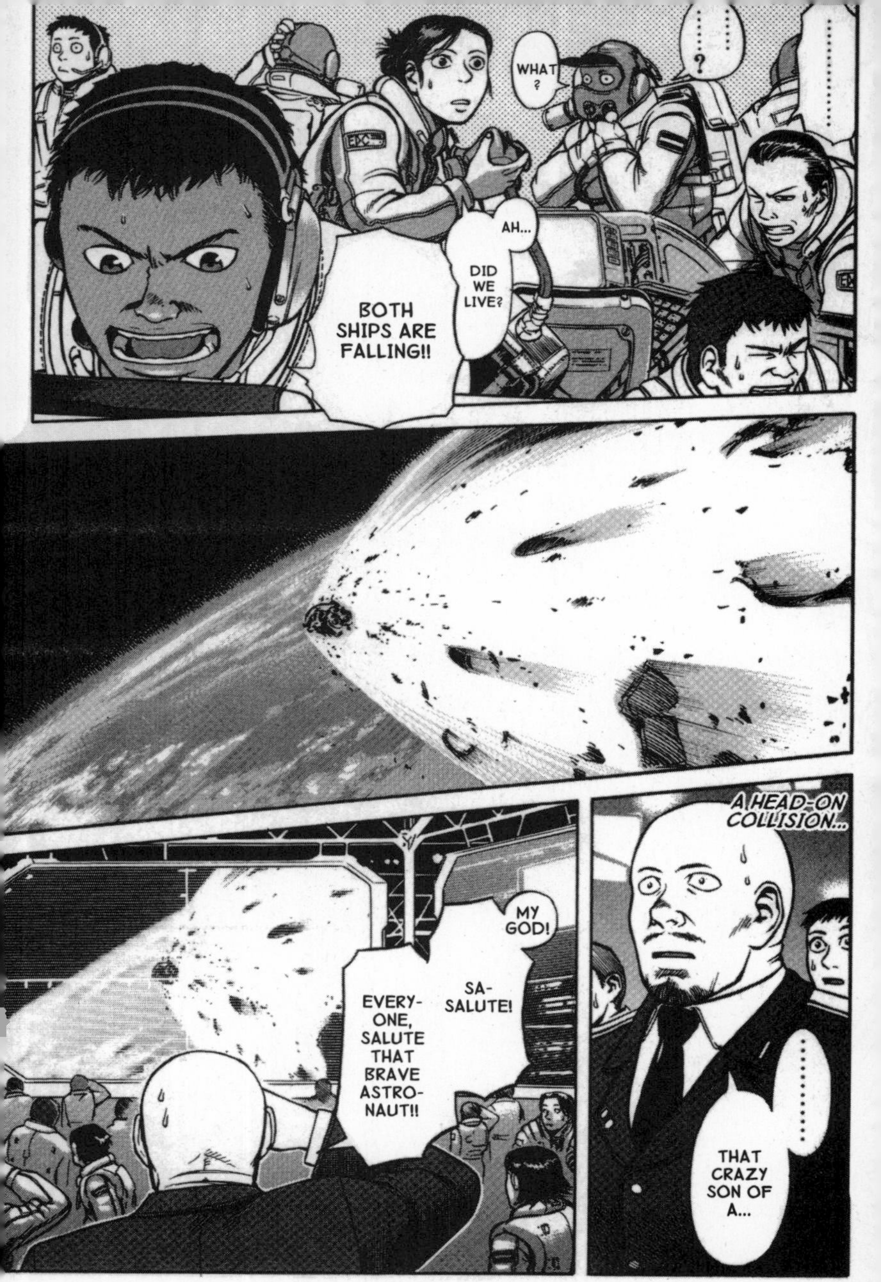
......?
WHAT?
AH...
DID WE LIVE?
BOTH SHIPS ARE FALLING!!
A HEAD-ON COLLISION...
......
THAT CRAZY SON OF A...
MY GOD!
SA-SALUTE!
EVERYONE, SALUTE THAT BRAVE ASTRONAUT!!

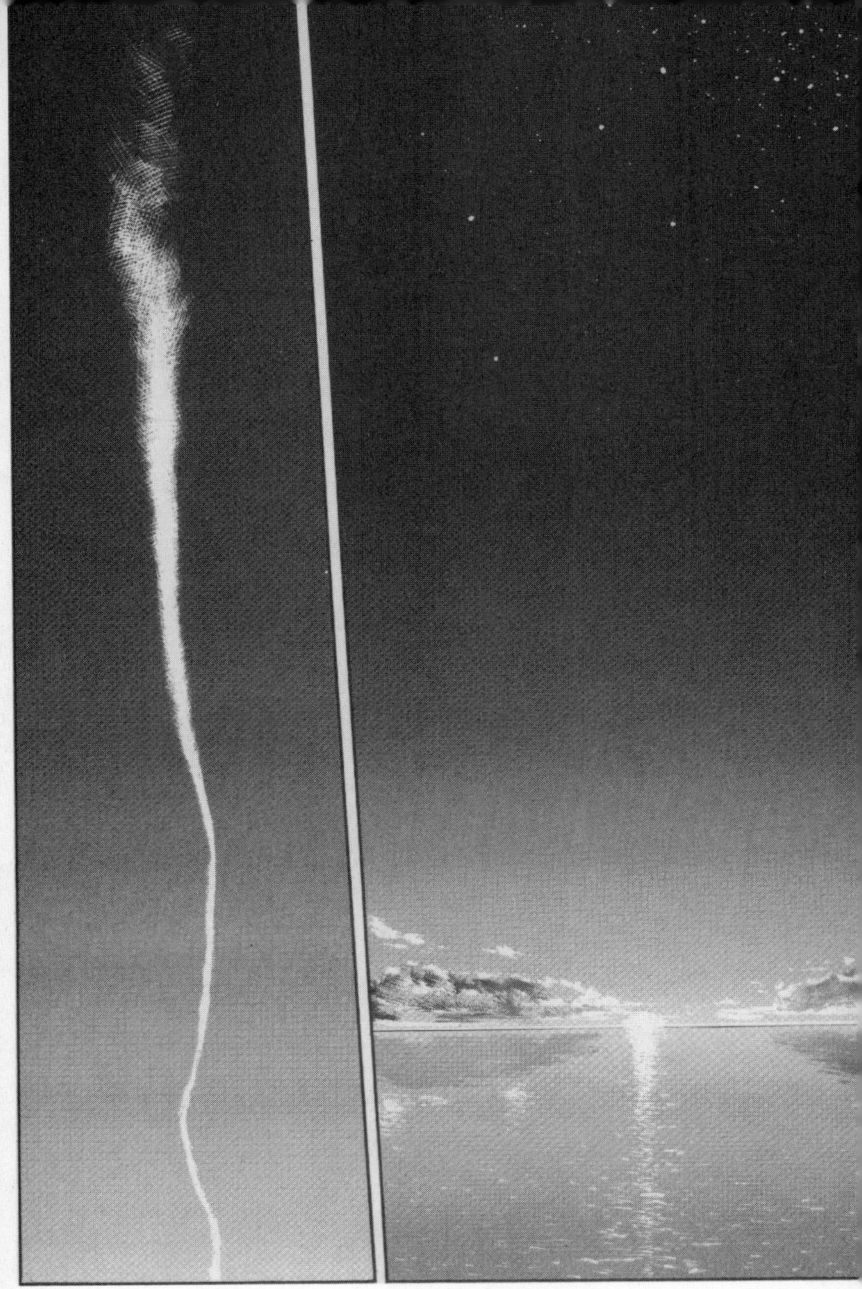

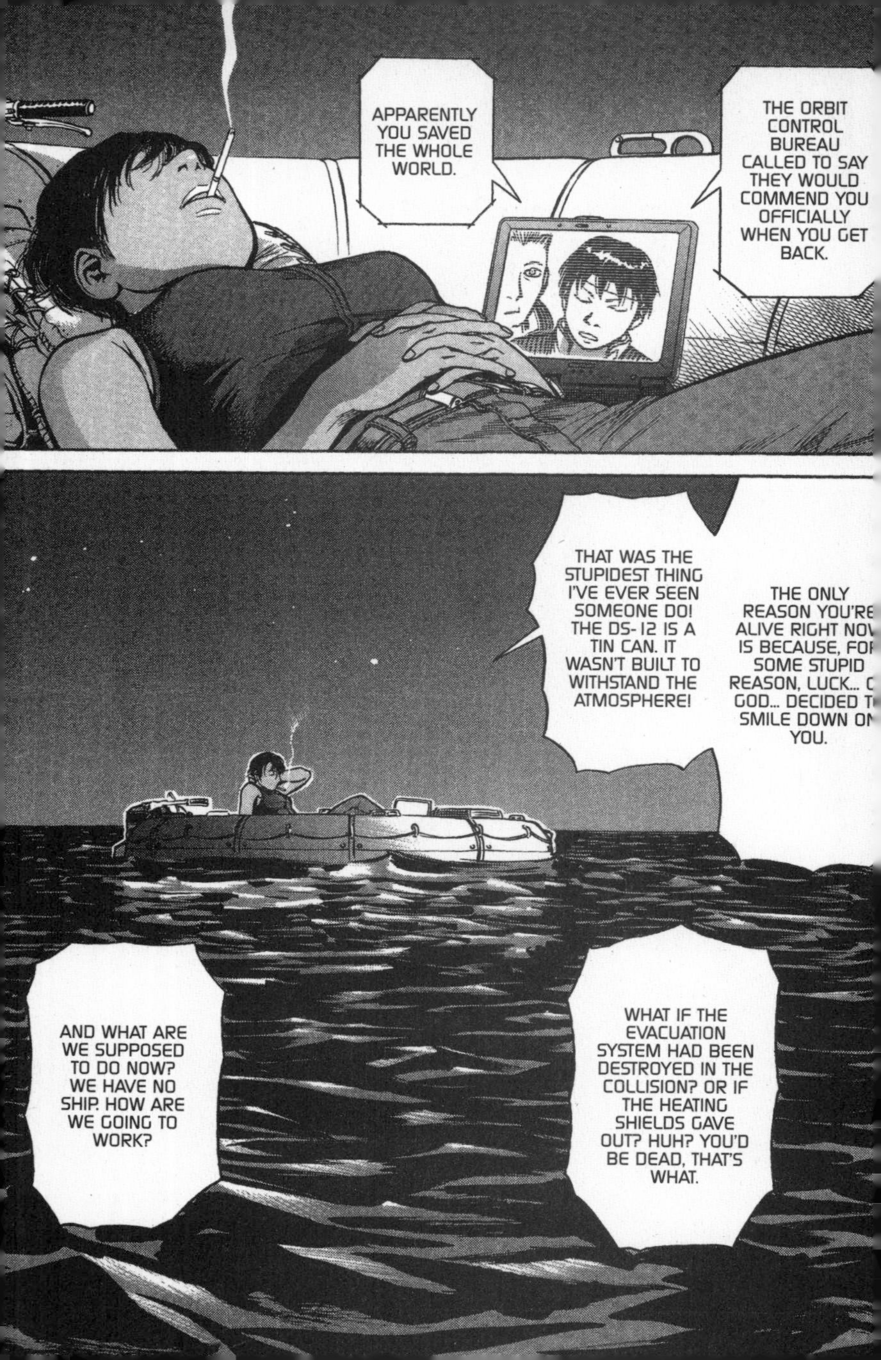
THE ORBIT CONTROL BUREAU CALLED TO SAY THEY WOULD COMMEND YOU OFFICIALLY WHEN YOU GET BACK.
APPARENTLY YOU SAVED THE WHOLE WORLD.
THAT WAS THE STUPIDEST THING I'VE EVER SEEN SOMEONE DO! THE DS-12 IS A TIN CAN. IT WASN'T BUILT TO WITHSTAND THE ATMOSPHERE!
THE ONLY REASON YOU'RE ALIVE RIGHT NOW IS BECAUSE, FOR SOME STUPID REASON, LUCK... OR GOD... DECIDED TO SMILE DOWN ON YOU.
WHAT IF THE EVACUATION SYSTEM HAD BEEN DESTROYED IN THE COLLISION? OR IF THE HEATING SHIELDS GAVE OUT? HUH? YOU'D BE DEAD, THAT'S WHAT.
AND WHAT ARE WE SUPPOSED TO DO NOW? WE HAVE NO SHIP. HOW ARE WE GOING TO WORK?

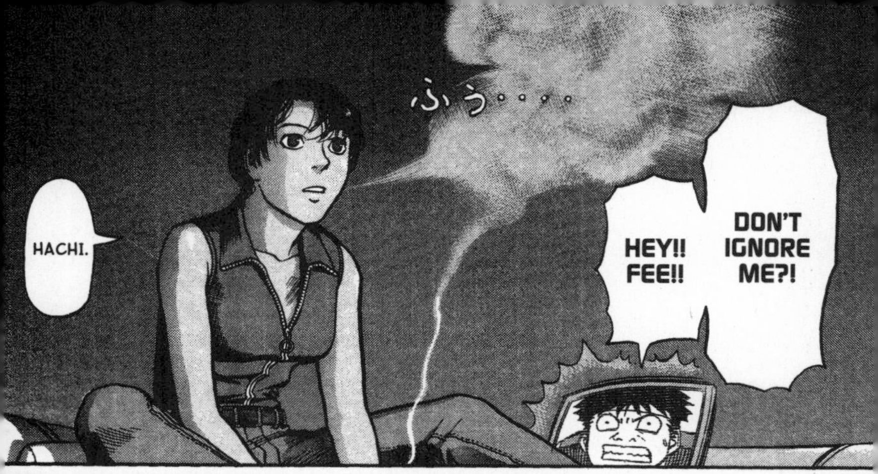
DON'T IGNORE ME?!
HEY!! FEE!!
ふう・・・・
HACHI.

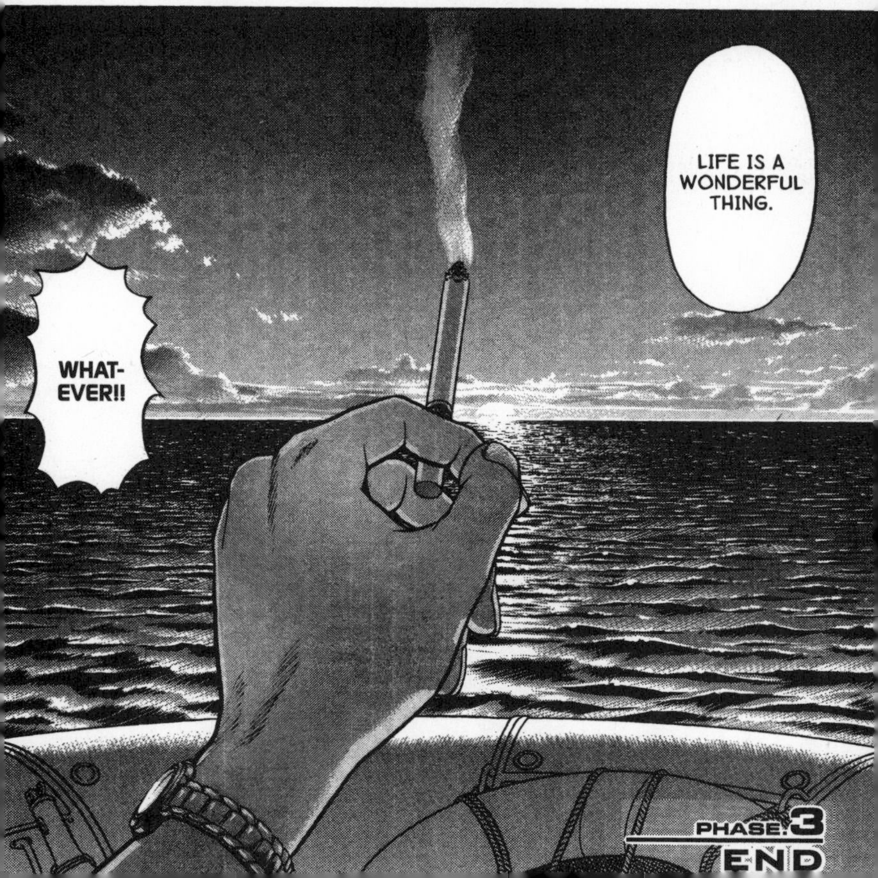
LIFE IS A WONDERFUL THING.
WHAT-EVER!!
PHASE.3 END

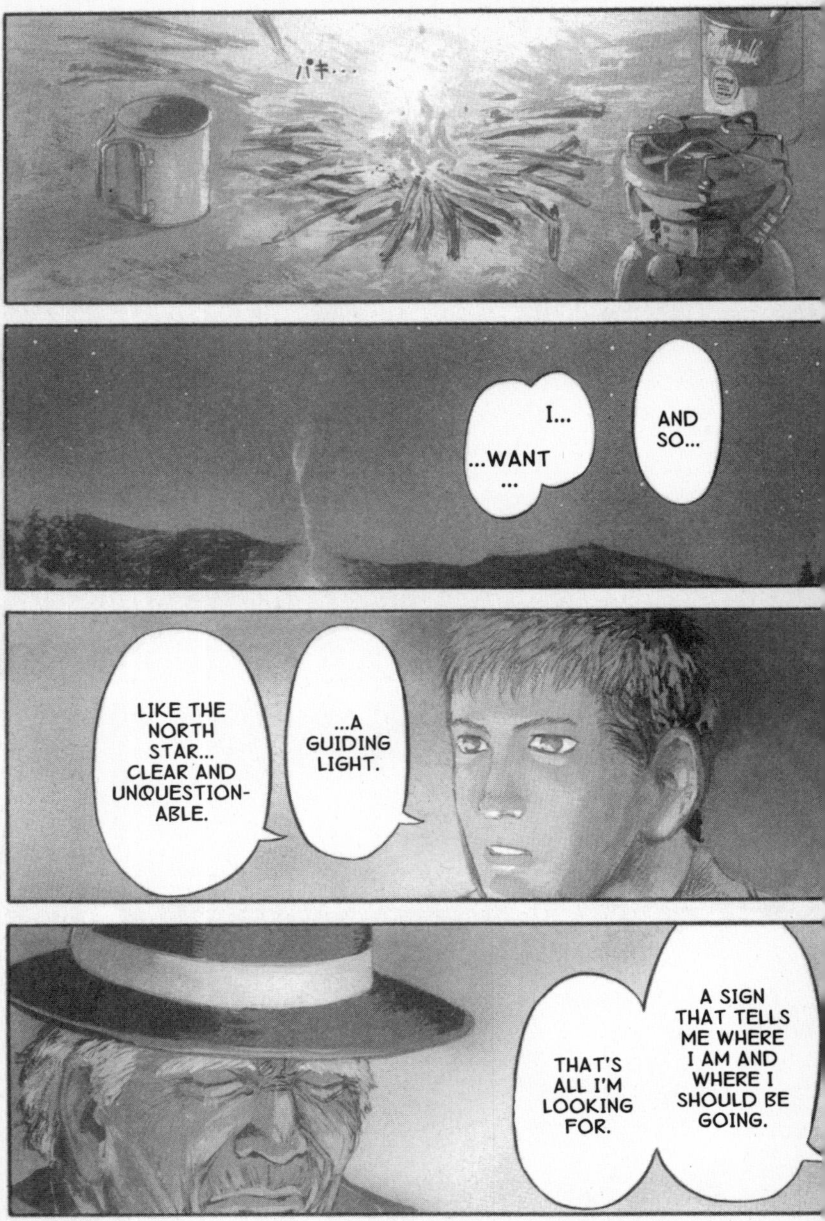
パキ…
AND SO...
I... ...WANT ...
...A GUIDING LIGHT.
LIKE THE NORTH STAR... CLEAR AND UNQUESTION-ABLE.
A SIGN THAT TELLS ME WHERE I AM AND WHERE I SHOULD BE GOING.
THAT'S ALL I'M LOOKING FOR.

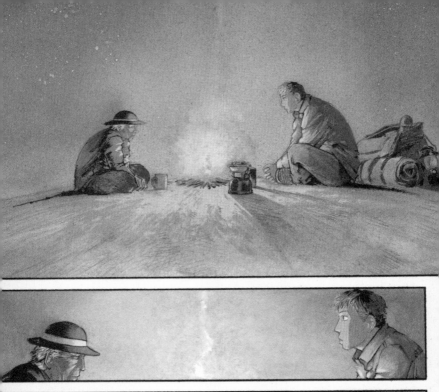

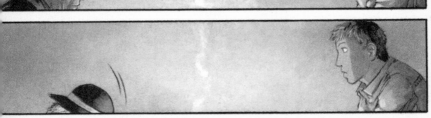

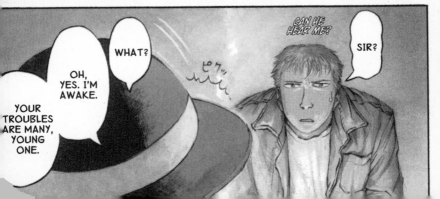

CAN HE HEAR ME?

SIR?

WHAT?

OH, YES. I'M AWAKE.

YOUR TROUBLES ARE MANY, YOUNG ONE.

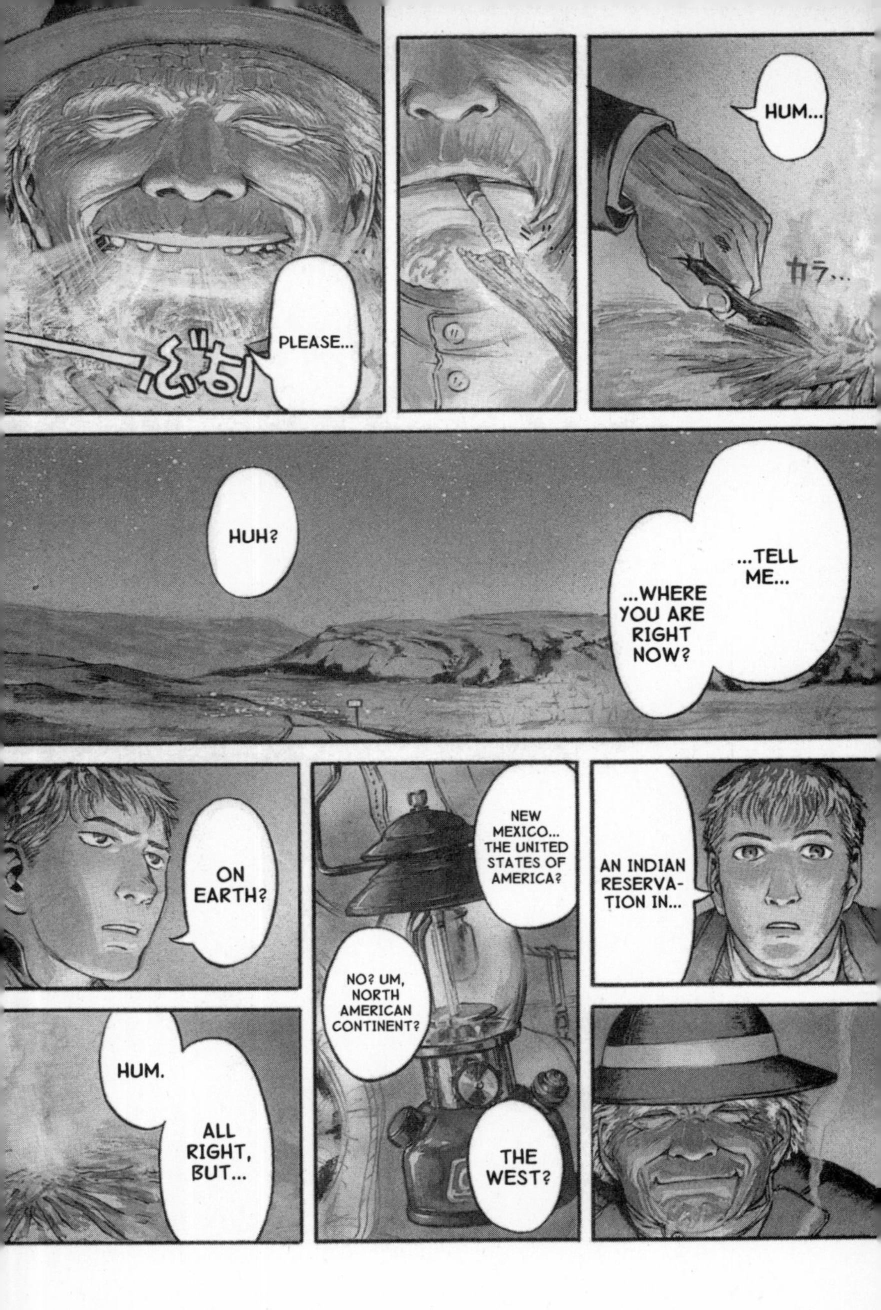
HUM...
カラ...
PLEASE...
...TELL ME...
...WHERE YOU ARE RIGHT NOW?
HUH?
AN INDIAN RESERVATION IN...
NEW MEXICO... THE UNITED STATES OF AMERICA?
NO? UM, NORTH AMERICAN CONTINENT?
THE WEST?
ON EARTH?
HUM.
ALL RIGHT, BUT...

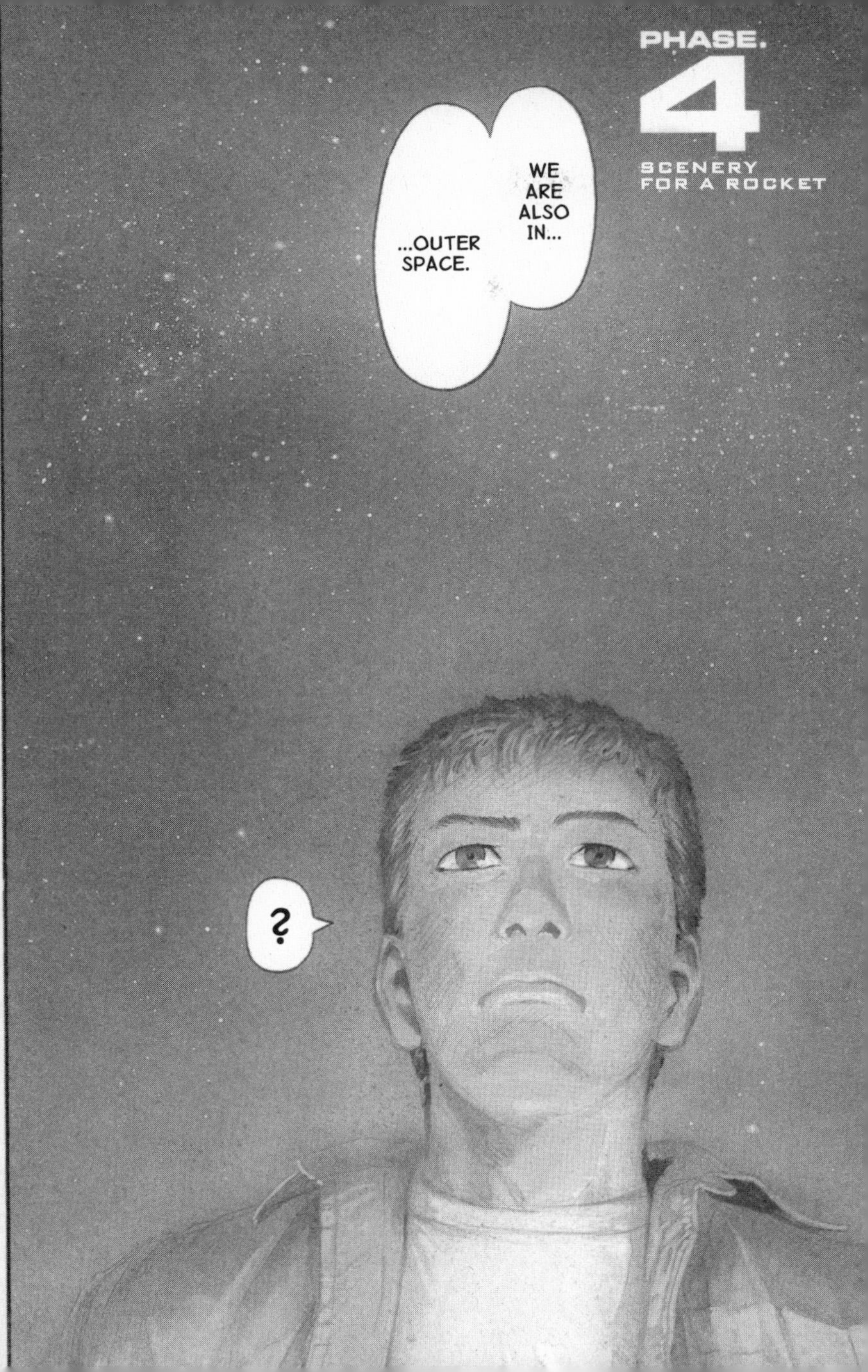
PHASE. 4
SCENERY FOR A ROCKET
WE ARE ALSO IN...
...OUTER SPACE.
?

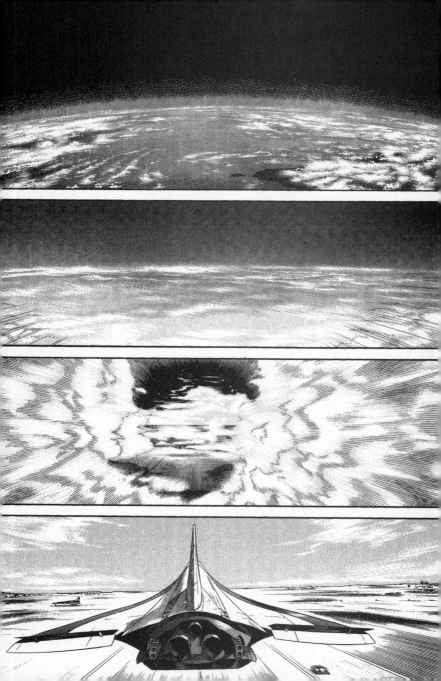

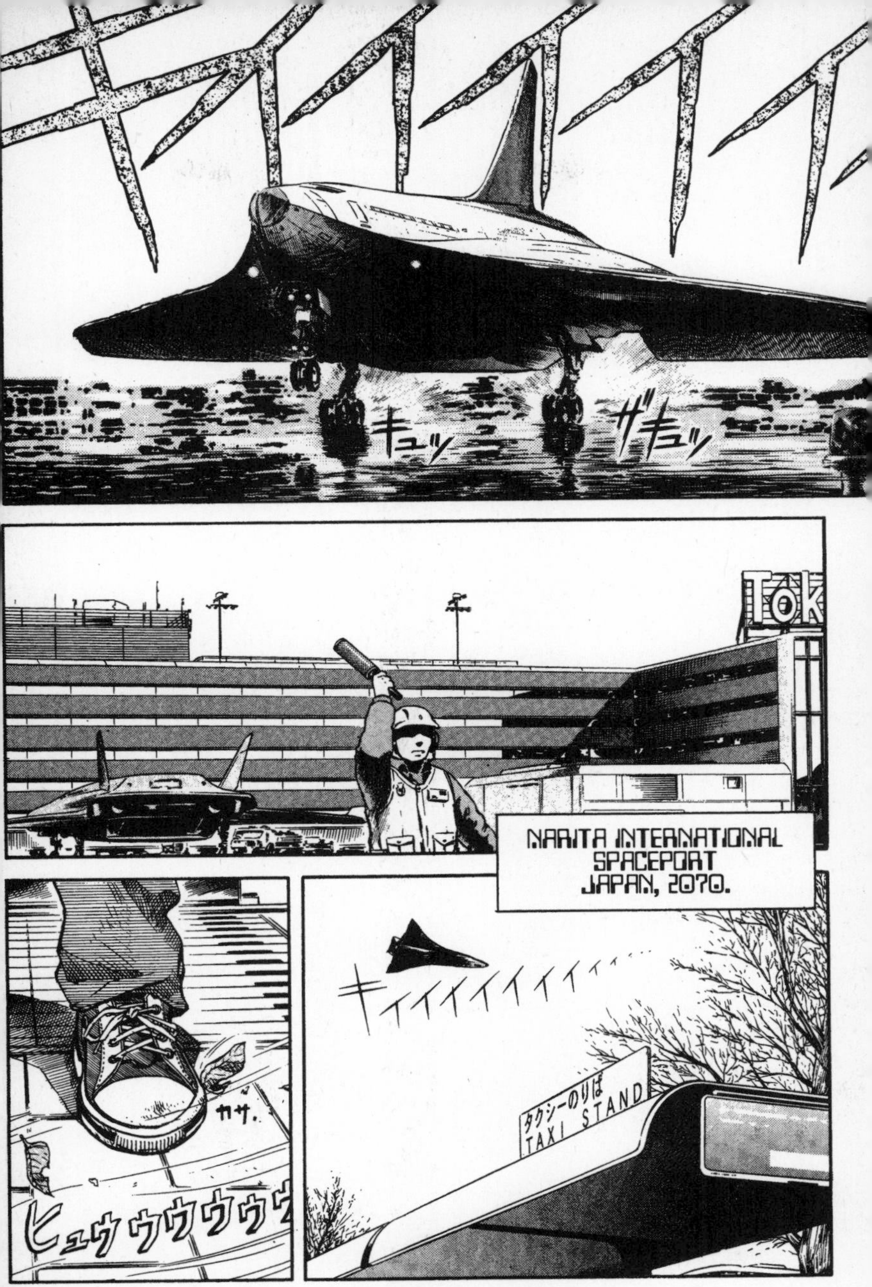
キィイイイイ
ザキュッ
キュッ
Tok
NARITA INTERNATIONAL
SPACEPORT
JAPAN, 2070.
キィイイイイイイィィ…
タクシーのりば
TAXI STAND
カサ.
ヒュウウウウウ

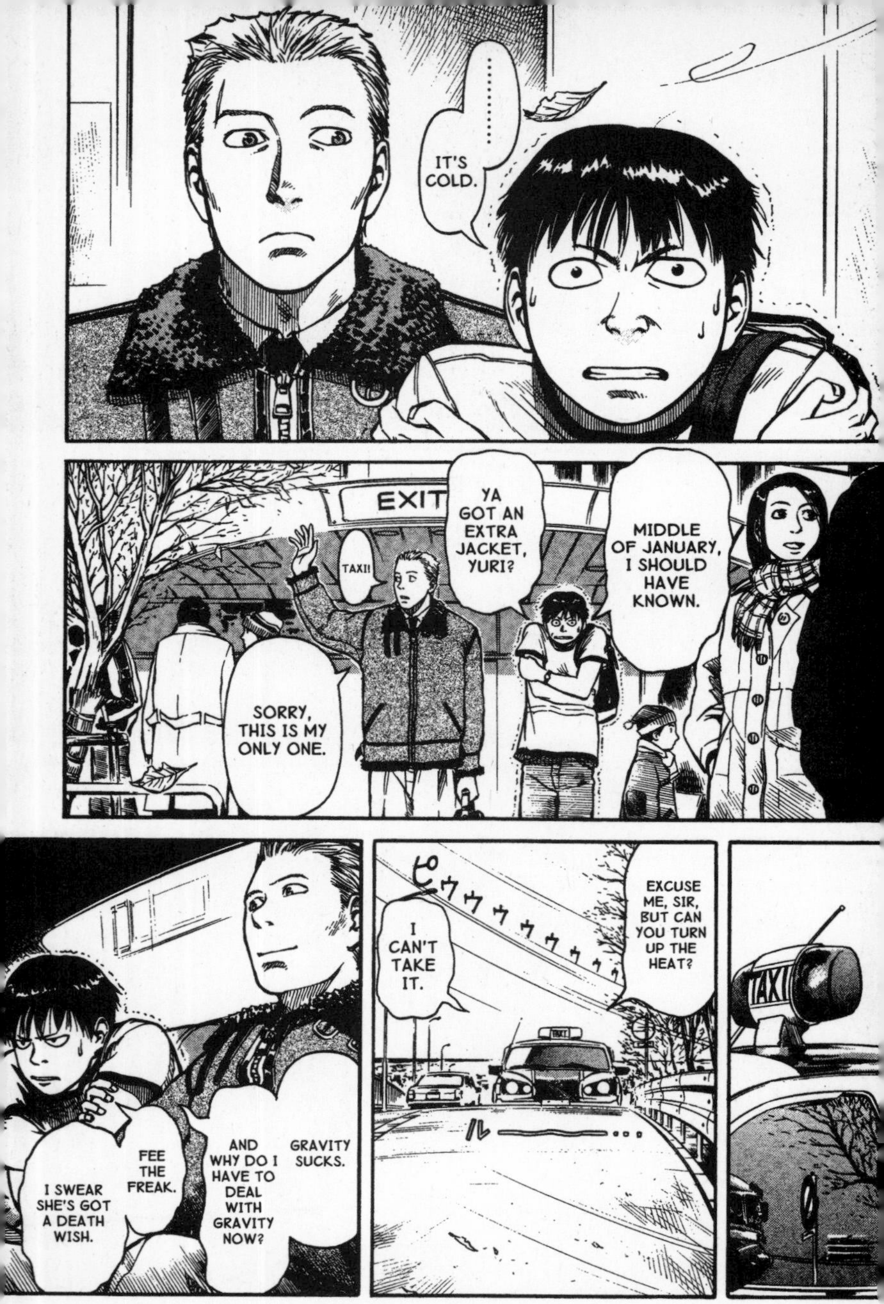
......
IT'S COLD.
MIDDLE OF JANUARY, I SHOULD HAVE KNOWN.
YA GOT AN EXTRA JACKET, YURI?
TAXI!
SORRY, THIS IS MY ONLY ONE.
EXIT
TAXI
EXCUSE ME, SIR, BUT CAN YOU TURN UP THE HEAT?
I CAN'T TAKE IT.
ピウウウウウウウウ
ル——...
GRAVITY SUCKS.
AND WHY DO I HAVE TO DEAL WITH GRAVITY NOW?
FEE THE FREAK.
I SWEAR SHE'S GOT A DEATH WISH.

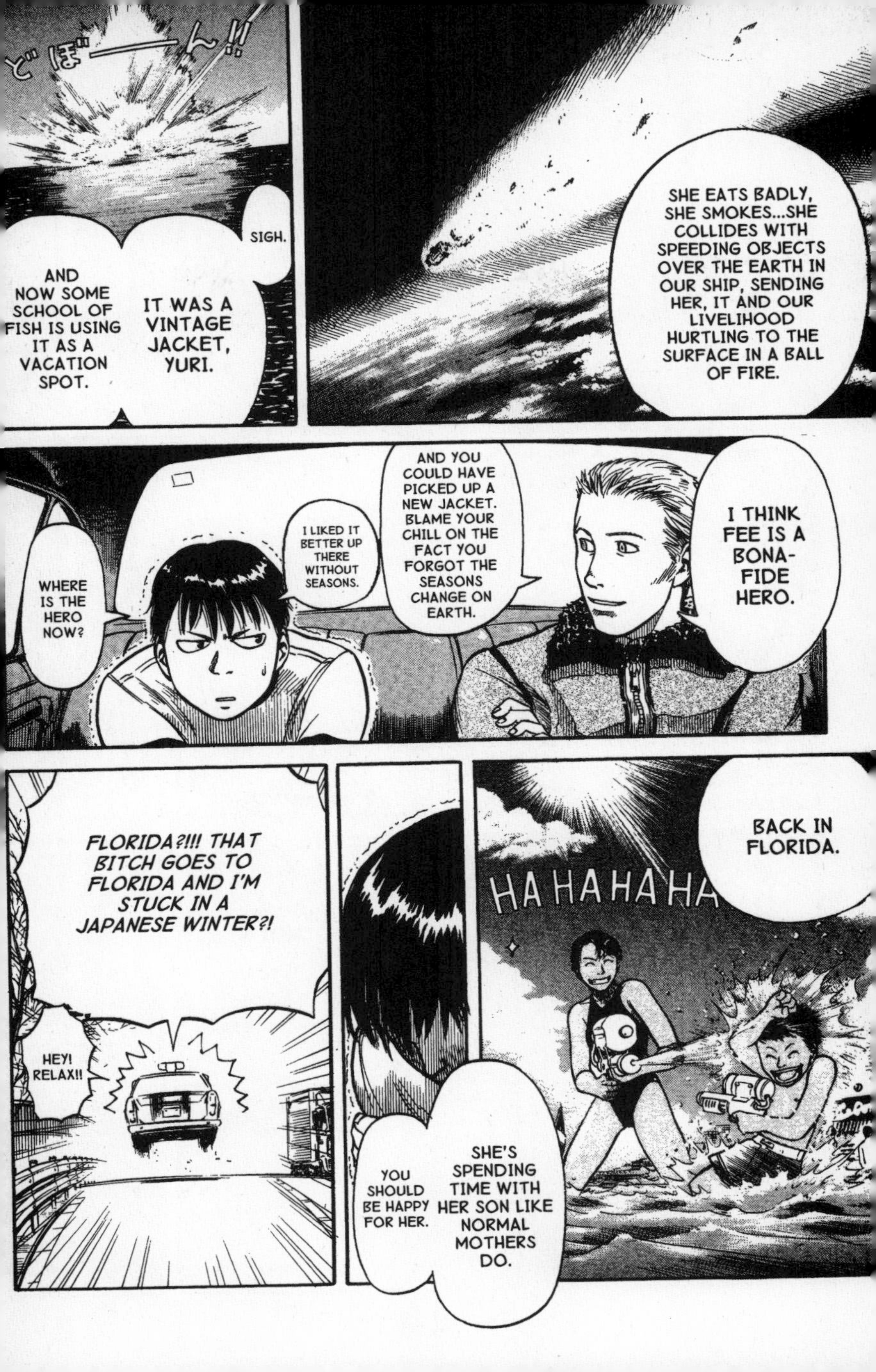
SHE EATS BADLY, SHE SMOKES...SHE COLLIDES WITH SPEEDING OBJECTS OVER THE EARTH IN OUR SHIP, SENDING HER, IT AND OUR LIVELIHOOD HURTLING TO THE SURFACE IN A BALL OF FIRE.
どぼーーん!!
SIGH.
IT WAS A VINTAGE JACKET, YURI.
AND NOW SOME SCHOOL OF FISH IS USING IT AS A VACATION SPOT.
I THINK FEE IS A BONA-FIDE HERO.
AND YOU COULD HAVE PICKED UP A NEW JACKET. BLAME YOUR CHILL ON THE FACT YOU FORGOT THE SEASONS CHANGE ON EARTH.
I LIKED IT BETTER UP THERE WITHOUT SEASONS.
WHERE IS THE HERO NOW?
BACK IN FLORIDA.
HA HA HA HA HA
SHE'S SPENDING TIME WITH HER SON LIKE NORMAL MOTHERS DO.
YOU SHOULD BE HAPPY FOR HER.
FLORIDA?!!! THAT BITCH GOES TO FLORIDA AND I'M STUCK IN A JAPANESE WINTER?!
HEY! RELAX!!

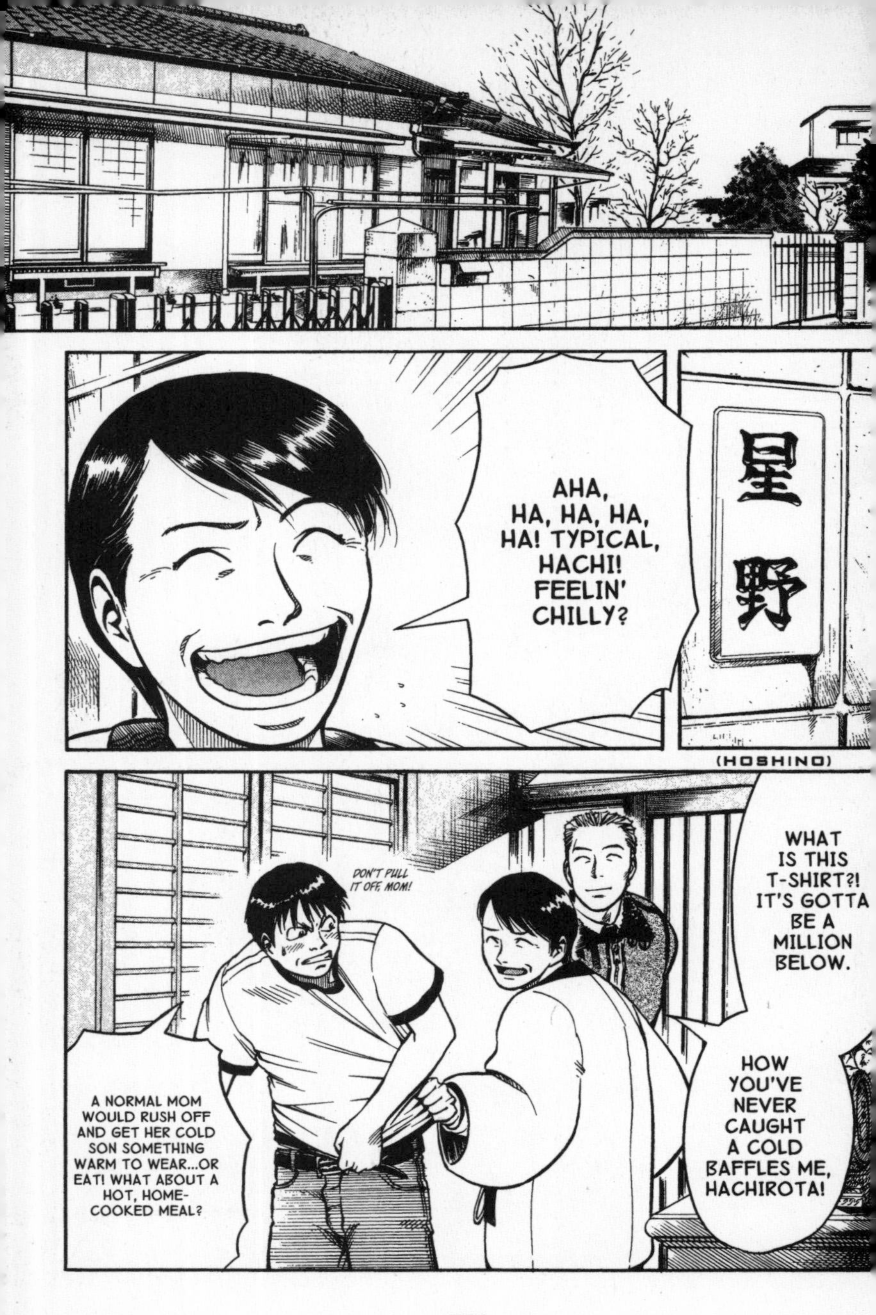
星野
(HOSHINO)
AHA, HA, HA, HA, HA! TYPICAL, HACHI! FEELIN' CHILLY?
WHAT IS THIS T-SHIRT?! IT'S GOTTA BE A MILLION BELOW.
HOW YOU'VE NEVER CAUGHT A COLD BAFFLES ME, HACHIROTA!
DON'T PULL IT OFF, MOM!
A NORMAL MOM WOULD RUSH OFF AND GET HER COLD SON SOMETHING WARM TO WEAR...OR EAT! WHAT ABOUT A HOT, HOME-COOKED MEAL?

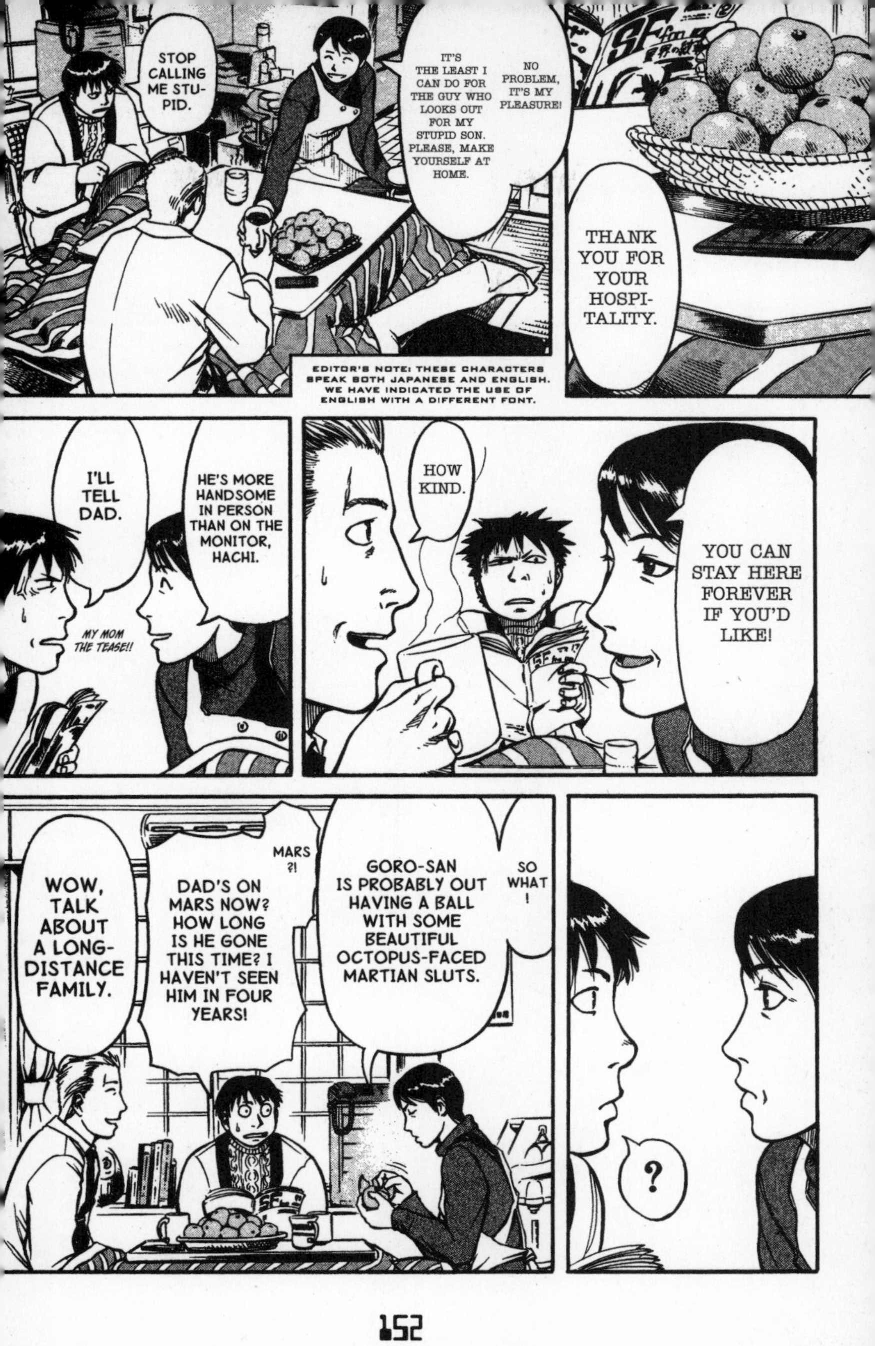
THANK YOU FOR YOUR HOSPI-TALITY.
NO PROBLEM, IT'S MY PLEASURE!
IT'S THE LEAST I CAN DO FOR THE GUY WHO LOOKS OUT FOR MY STUPID SON. PLEASE, MAKE YOURSELF AT HOME.
STOP CALLING ME STU-PID.
EDITOR'S NOTE: THESE CHARACTERS SPEAK BOTH JAPANESE AND ENGLISH. WE HAVE INDICATED THE USE OF ENGLISH WITH A DIFFERENT FONT.
YOU CAN STAY HERE FOREVER IF YOU'D LIKE!
HOW KIND.
HE'S MORE HANDSOME IN PERSON THAN ON THE MONITOR, HACHI.
I'LL TELL DAD.
MY MOM THE TEASE!!
?
SO WHAT!
GORO-SAN IS PROBABLY OUT HAVING A BALL WITH SOME BEAUTIFUL OCTOPUS-FACED MARTIAN SLUTS.
MARS?!
DAD'S ON MARS NOW? HOW LONG IS HE GONE THIS TIME? I HAVEN'T SEEN HIM IN FOUR YEARS!
WOW, TALK ABOUT A LONG-DISTANCE FAMILY.

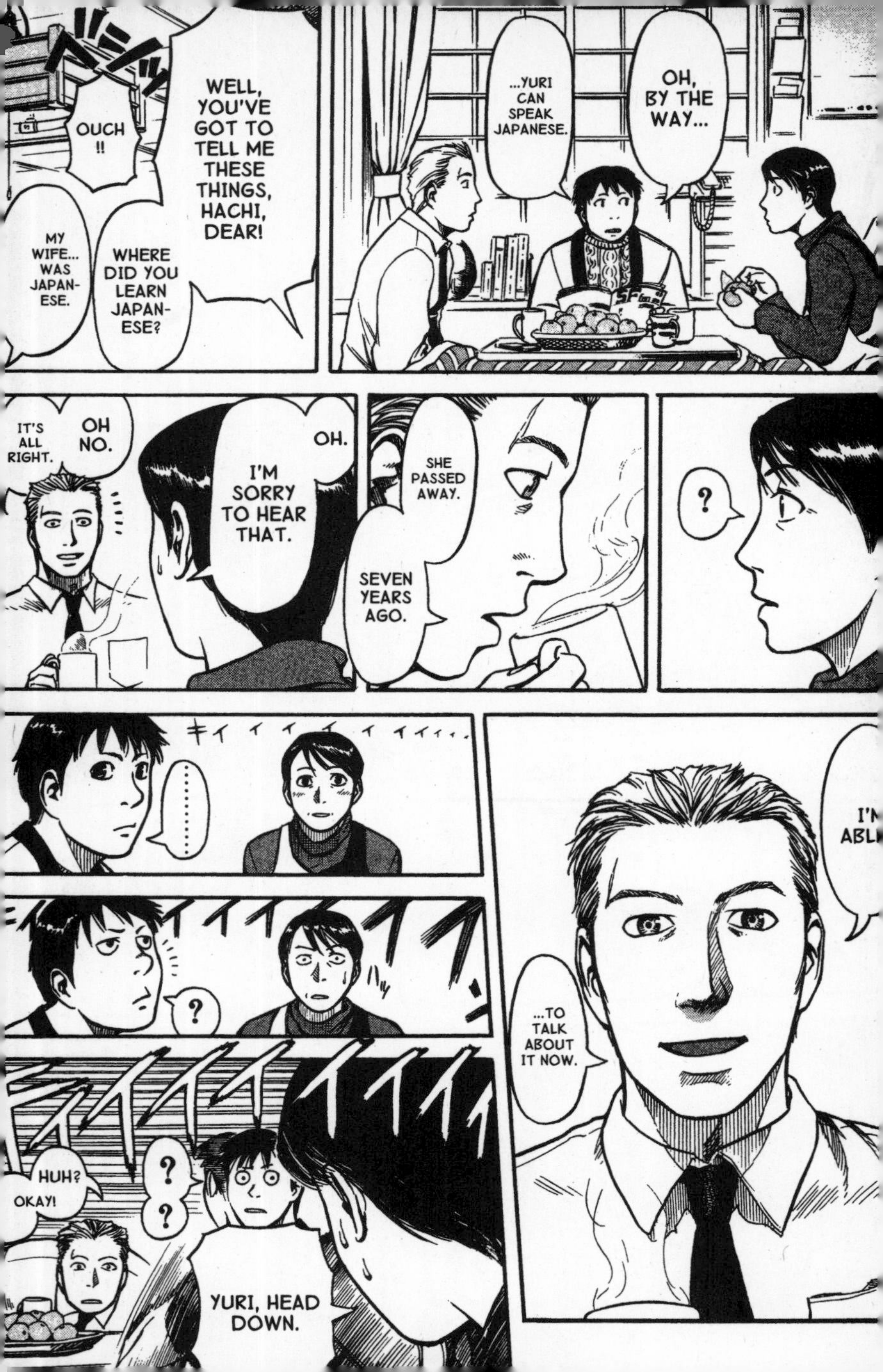
OH, BY THE WAY...
...YURI CAN SPEAK JAPANESE.
WELL, YOU'VE GOT TO TELL ME THESE THINGS, HACHI, DEAR!
OUCH !!
WHERE DID YOU LEARN JAPANESE?
MY WIFE... WAS JAPANESE.
?
SHE PASSED AWAY.
SEVEN YEARS AGO.
OH.
I'M SORRY TO HEAR THAT.
OH NO.
IT'S ALL RIGHT.
I'M ABL
...TO TALK ABOUT IT NOW.
キィィィィィィィィ..
......
?
ハッ
?
?
HUH?
OKAY!
YURI, HEAD DOWN.

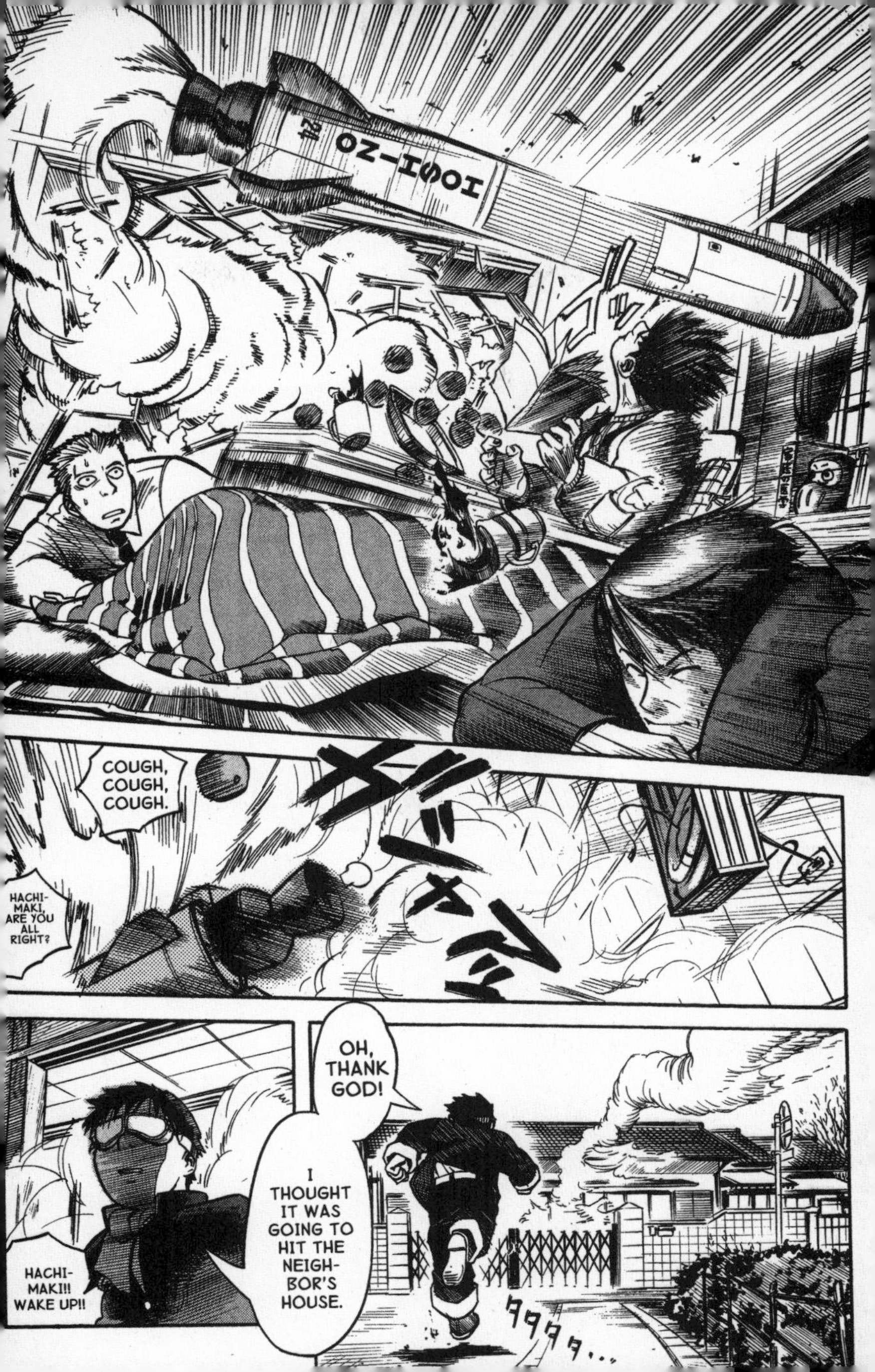
COUGH, COUGH, COUGH.
HACHI-MAKI, ARE YOU ALL RIGHT?
OH, THANK GOD!
I THOUGHT IT WAS GOING TO HIT THE NEIGH-BOR'S HOUSE.
タタタタ...
HACHI-MAKI!! WAKE UP!!

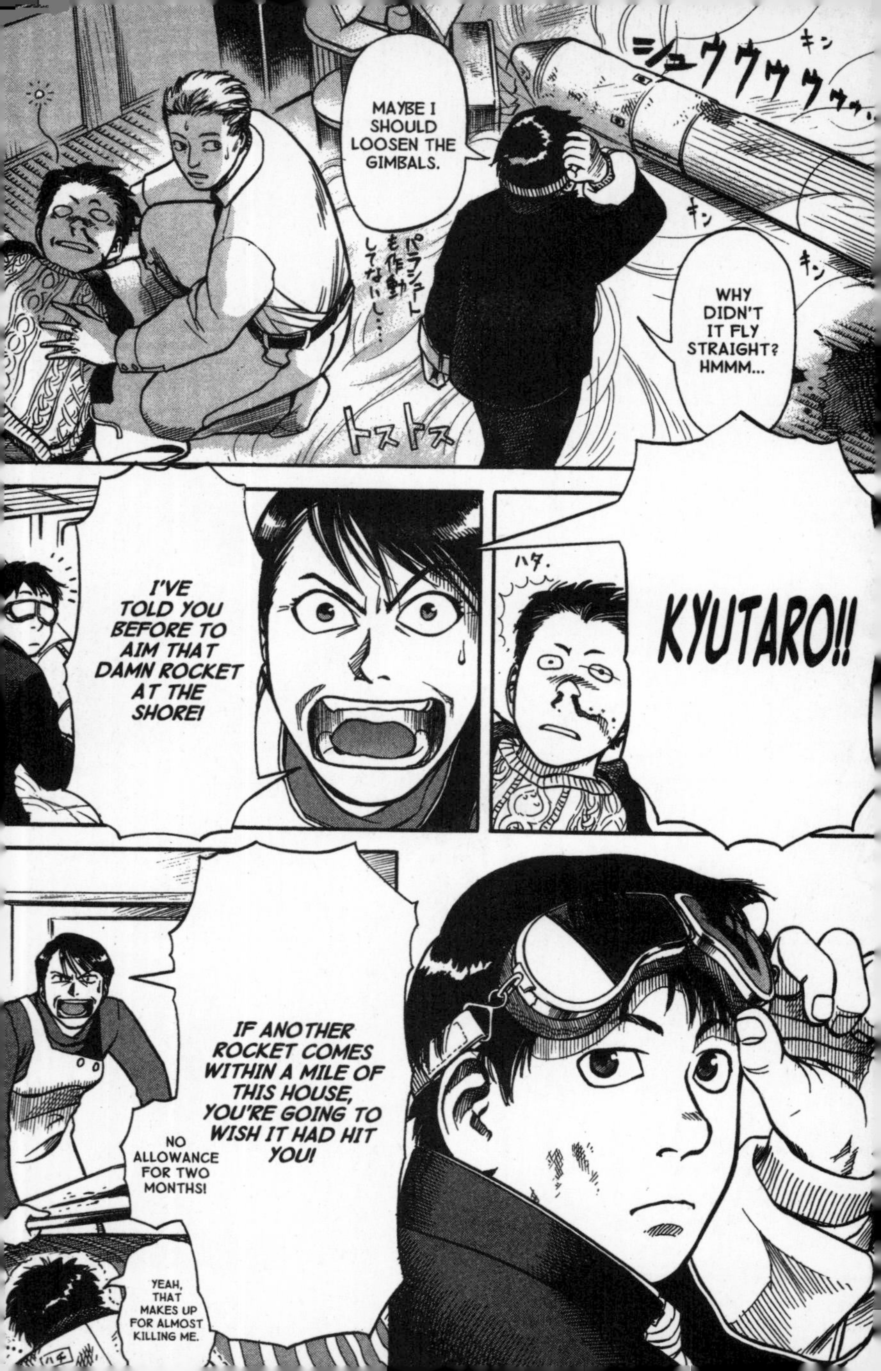
シュウウウウゥ…
キン
WHY DIDN'T IT FLY STRAIGHT? HMMM...
MAYBE I SHOULD LOOSEN THE GIMBALS.
パラシュートも作動してないし…
トストス
KYUTARO!!
ハタ.
I'VE TOLD YOU BEFORE TO AIM THAT DAMN ROCKET AT THE SHORE!
IF ANOTHER ROCKET COMES WITHIN A MILE OF THIS HOUSE, YOU'RE GOING TO WISH IT HAD HIT YOU!
NO ALLOWANCE FOR TWO MONTHS!
YEAH, THAT MAKES UP FOR ALMOST KILLING ME.

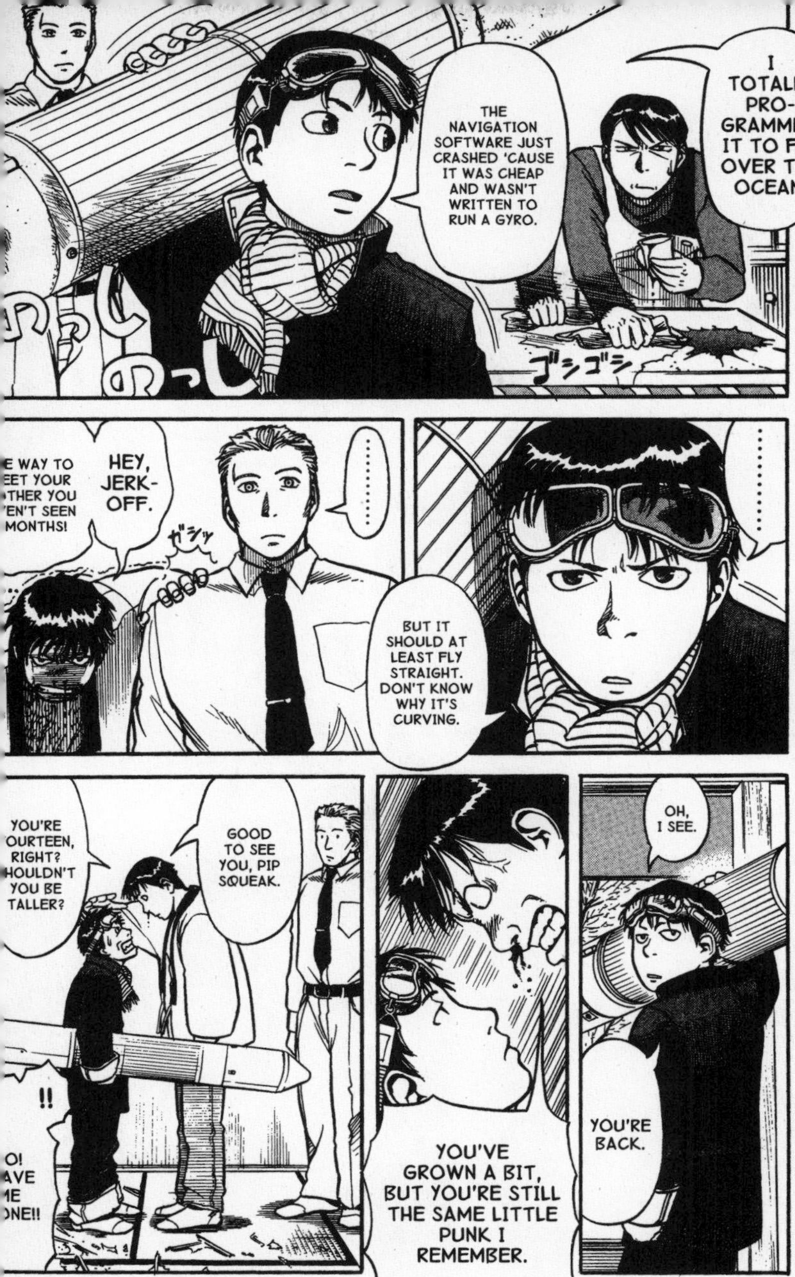
I TOTALLY PRO-GRAMMED IT TO FLY OVER THE OCEAN.
THE NAVIGATION SOFTWARE JUST CRASHED 'CAUSE IT WAS CHEAP AND WASN'T WRITTEN TO RUN A GYRO.
ゴシゴシ
のっし
のっし
......
BUT IT SHOULD AT LEAST FLY STRAIGHT. DON'T KNOW WHY IT'S CURVING.
......
HEY, JERK-OFF.
E WAY TO EET YOUR THER YOU EN'T SEEN MONTHS!
ガシッ
OH, I SEE.
YOU'RE BACK.
YOU'VE GROWN A BIT, BUT YOU'RE STILL THE SAME LITTLE PUNK I REMEMBER.
GOOD TO SEE YOU, PIP SQUEAK.
YOU'RE OURTEEN, RIGHT? HOULDN'T YOU BE TALLER?
!!
O! AVE ME ONE!!

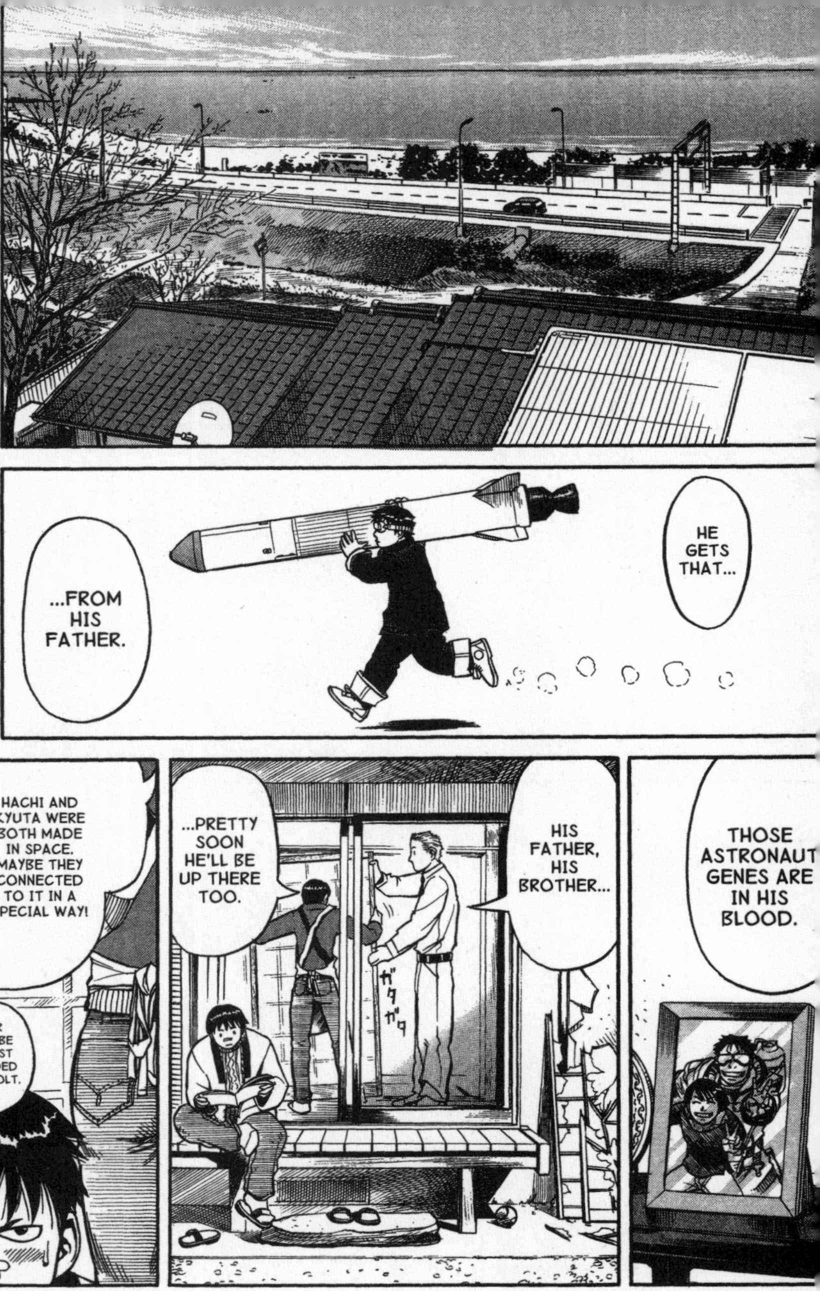
HE GETS THAT...
...FROM HIS FATHER.
THOSE ASTRONAUT GENES ARE IN HIS BLOOD.
HIS FATHER, HIS BROTHER...
...PRETTY SOON HE'LL BE UP THERE TOO.
ガタガタ
HACHI AND KYUTA WERE BOTH MADE IN SPACE. MAYBE THEY CONNECTED TO IT IN A SPECIAL WAY!
OR MAYBE I JUST NEEDED TO BOLT.

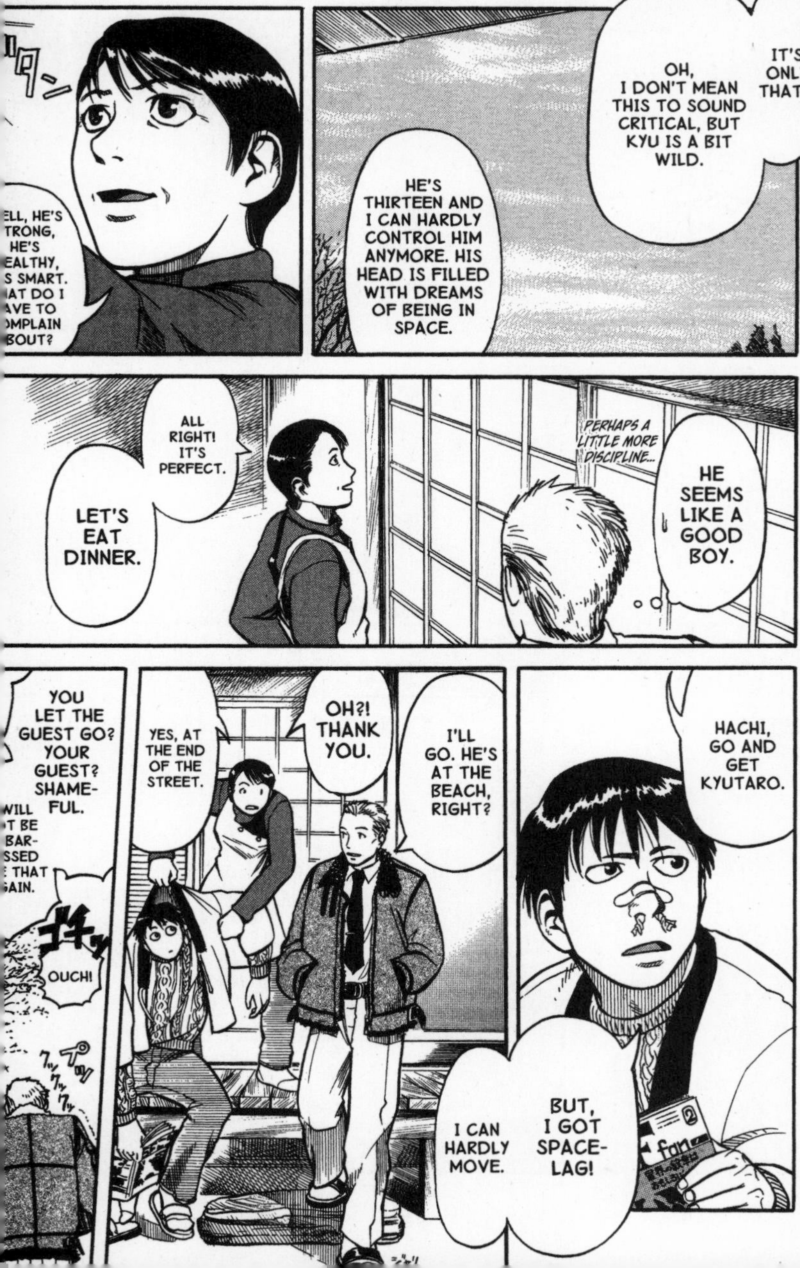
IT'S ONLY THAT...
OH, I DON'T MEAN THIS TO SOUND CRITICAL, BUT KYU IS A BIT WILD.
HE'S THIRTEEN AND I CAN HARDLY CONTROL HIM ANYMORE. HIS HEAD IS FILLED WITH DREAMS OF BEING IN SPACE.
ELL, HE'S TRONG, HE'S EALTHY, S SMART. AT DO I AVE TO OMPLAIN BOUT?
HE SEEMS LIKE A GOOD BOY.
PERHAPS A LITTLE MORE DISCIPLINE...
ALL RIGHT! IT'S PERFECT.
LET'S EAT DINNER.
HACHI, GO AND GET KYUTARO.
BUT, I GOT SPACE-LAG!
I CAN HARDLY MOVE.
I'LL GO. HE'S AT THE BEACH, RIGHT?
OH?! THANK YOU.
YES, AT THE END OF THE STREET.
YOU LET THE GUEST GO? YOUR GUEST? SHAMEFUL.
WILL T BE BAR-SSED E THAT AIN.
OUCH!

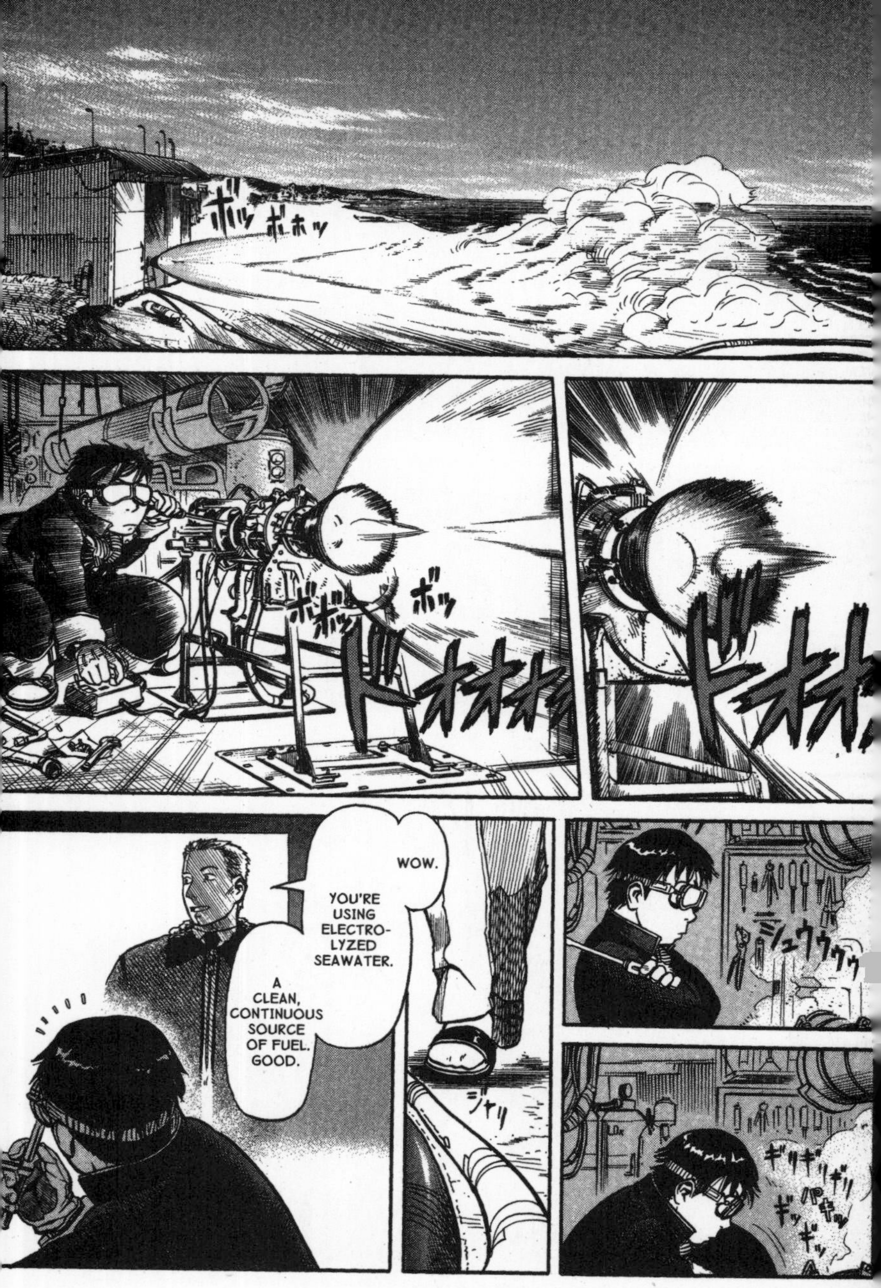
WOW.
YOU'RE USING ELECTRO-LYZED SEAWATER.
A CLEAN, CONTINUOUS SOURCE OF FUEL. GOOD.

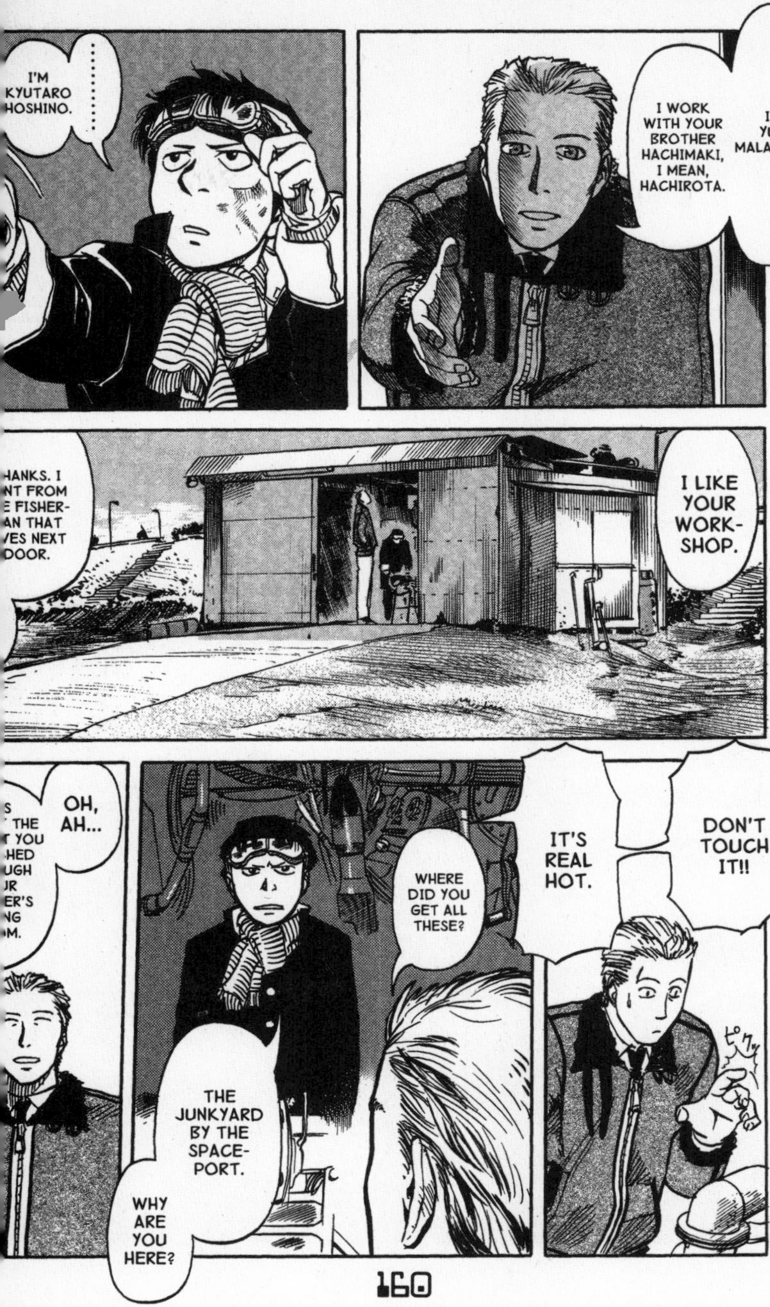
I'M YURI MALAKOFF.
I WORK WITH YOUR BROTHER HACHIMAKI, I MEAN, HACHIROTA.
I'M KYUTARO HOSHINO.
......
I LIKE YOUR WORK-SHOP.
HANKS. I NT FROM E FISHER- AN THAT VES NEXT DOOR.
DON'T TOUCH IT!!
IT'S REAL HOT.
ピクッ
WHERE DID YOU GET ALL THESE?
THE JUNKYARD BY THE SPACE-PORT.
WHY ARE YOU HERE?
OH, AH...

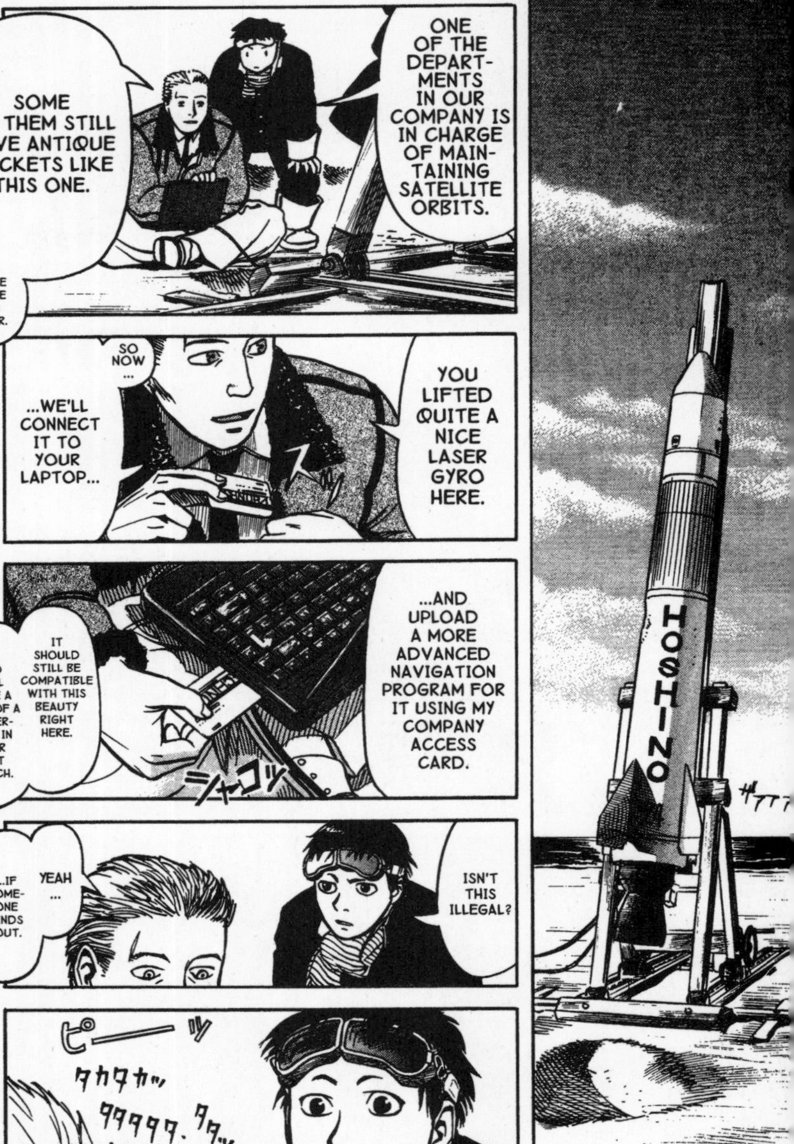
HOSHINO
ONE OF THE DEPARTMENTS IN OUR COMPANY IS IN CHARGE OF MAINTAINING SATELLITE ORBITS.
SOME OF THEM STILL HAVE ANTIQUE ROCKETS LIKE THIS ONE.
OF COURSE THEY'RE MUCH BIGGER.
YOU LIFTED QUITE A NICE LASER GYRO HERE.
SO NOW...
...WE'LL CONNECT IT TO YOUR LAPTOP...
...AND UPLOAD A MORE ADVANCED NAVIGATION PROGRAM FOR IT USING MY COMPANY ACCESS CARD.
IT SHOULD STILL BE COMPATIBLE WITH THIS BEAUTY RIGHT HERE.
AND IT'LL MAKE A HECK OF A DIFFERENCE IN YOUR NEXT LAUNCH.
シャコッ
ISN'T THIS ILLEGAL?
YEAH...
...IF SOMEONE FINDS OUT.
ピーーッ
タカタカッ
タタタタタ
タタッ
カタカタッ

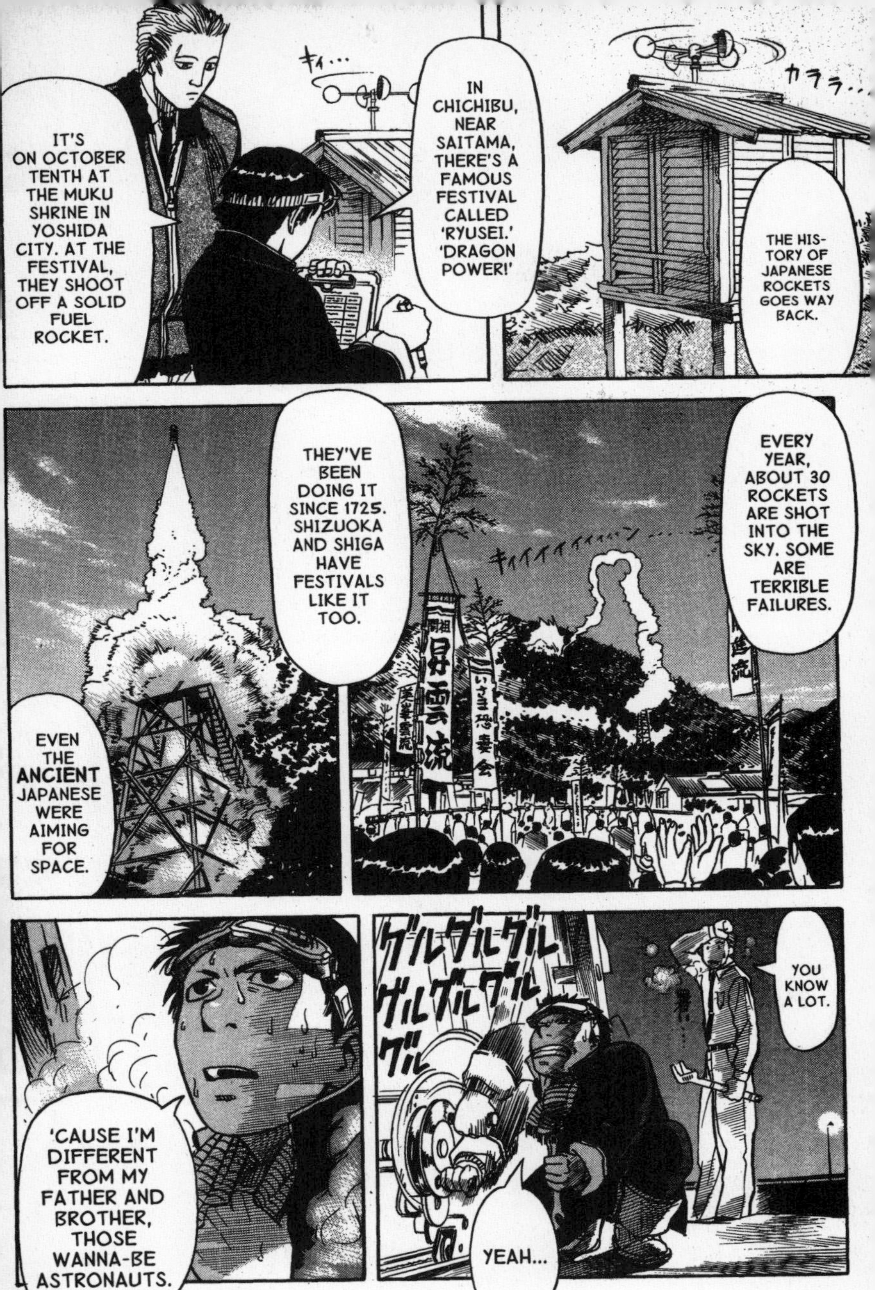
カラララ…
THE HISTORY OF JAPANESE ROCKETS GOES WAY BACK.
キィ…
IN CHICHIBU, NEAR SAITAMA, THERE'S A FAMOUS FESTIVAL CALLED 'RYUSEI.' 'DRAGON POWER!'
IT'S ON OCTOBER TENTH AT THE MUKU SHRINE IN YOSHIDA CITY. AT THE FESTIVAL, THEY SHOOT OFF A SOLID FUEL ROCKET.
EVERY YEAR, ABOUT 30 ROCKETS ARE SHOT INTO THE SKY. SOME ARE TERRIBLE FAILURES.
キィイイイィィバン…
THEY'VE BEEN DOING IT SINCE 1725. SHIZUOKA AND SHIGA HAVE FESTIVALS LIKE IT TOO.
EVEN THE **ANCIENT** JAPANESE WERE AIMING FOR SPACE.
YOU KNOW A LOT.
グルグルグル
グルグルグル
グル
YEAH...
'CAUSE I'M DIFFERENT FROM MY FATHER AND BROTHER, THOSE WANNA-BE ASTRONAUTS.

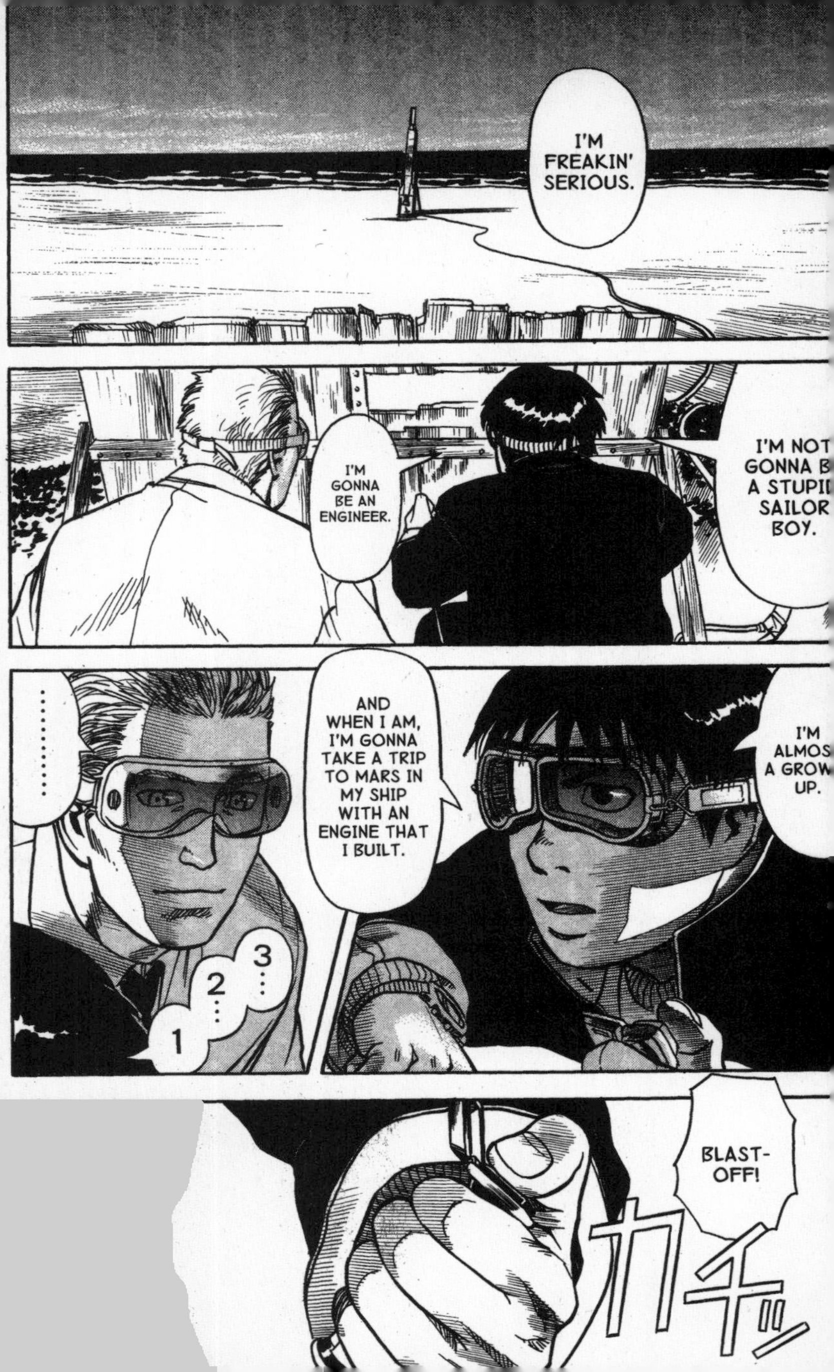
I'M FREAKIN' SERIOUS.
I'M NOT GONNA B A STUPII SAILOR BOY.
I'M GONNA BE AN ENGINEER.
I'M ALMOS A GROW UP.
AND WHEN I AM, I'M GONNA TAKE A TRIP TO MARS IN MY SHIP WITH AN ENGINE THAT I BUILT.
......
3... 2... 1
BLAST-OFF!
カチッ

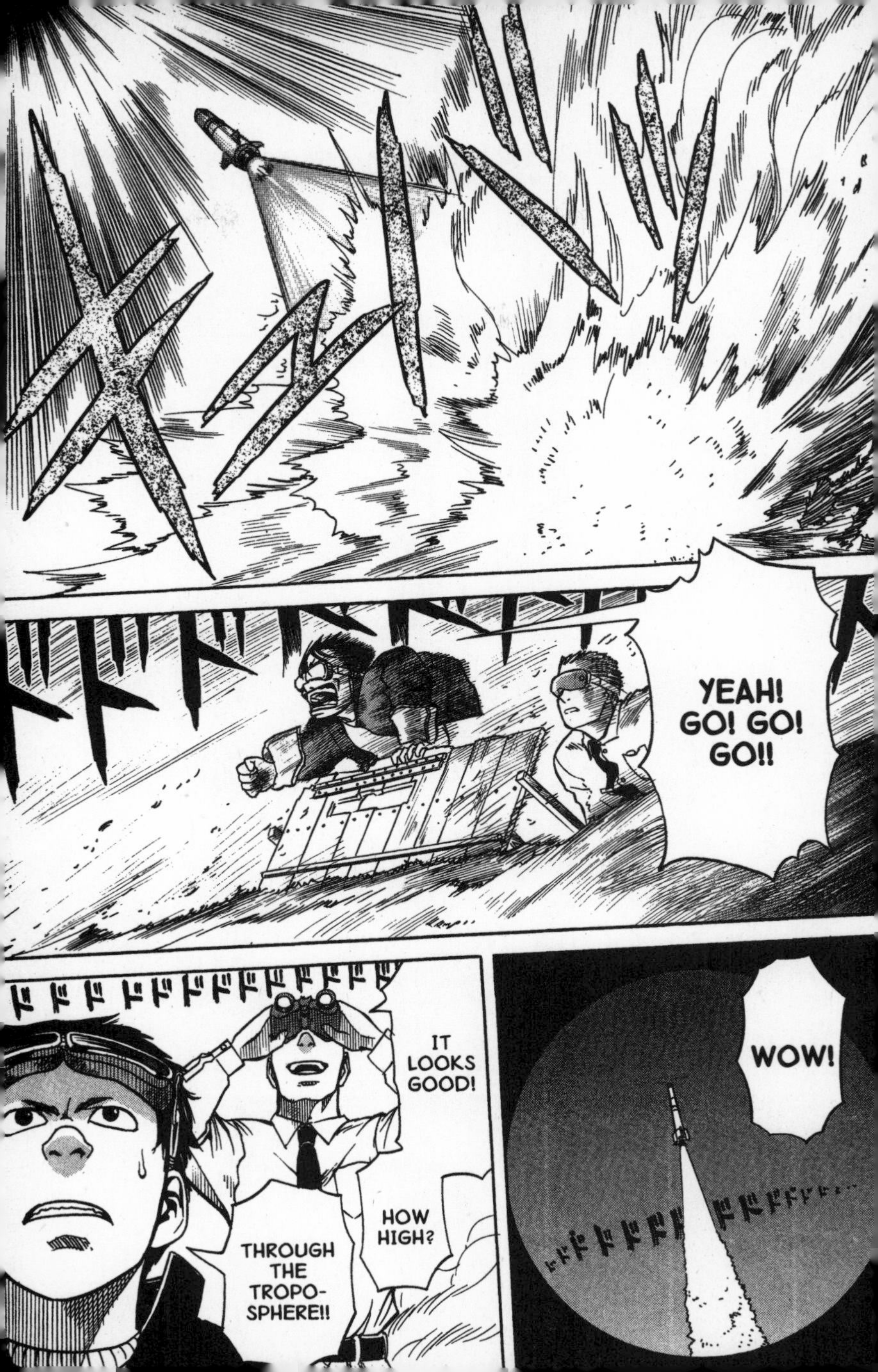
YEAH! GO! GO! GO!!
WOW!
IT LOOKS GOOD!
HOW HIGH?
THROUGH THE TROPO-SPHERE!!

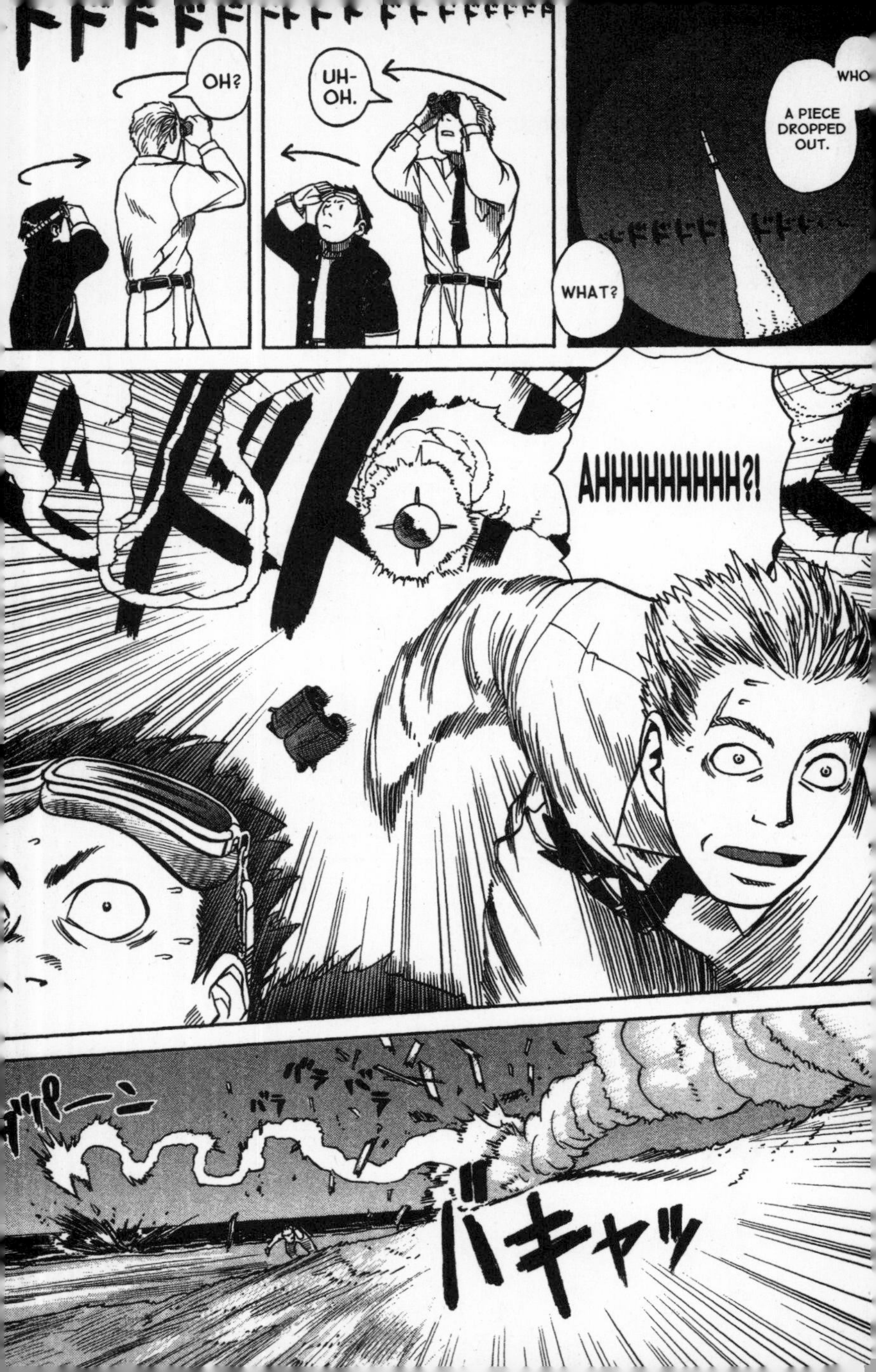
WHO
A PIECE DROPPED OUT.
WHAT?
UH-OH.
OH?
AHHHHHHHHH?!
ザパーン
バラ
バラ
バラ
バキャッ

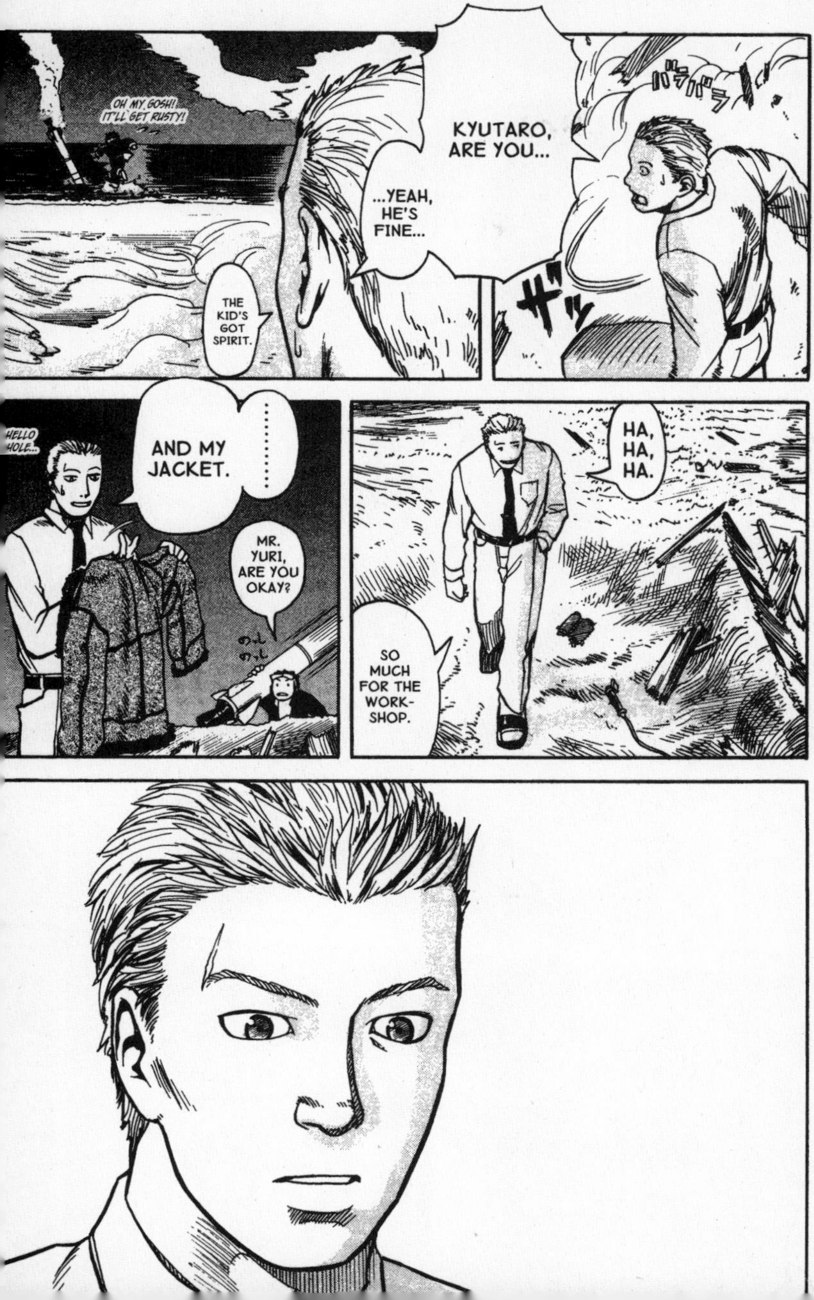
KYUTARO, ARE YOU...
...YEAH, HE'S FINE...
THE KID'S GOT SPIRIT.
OH MY GOSH!! IT'LL GET RUSTY!
HA, HA, HA.
SO MUCH FOR THE WORK-SHOP.
....
AND MY JACKET.
MR. YURI, ARE YOU OKAY?

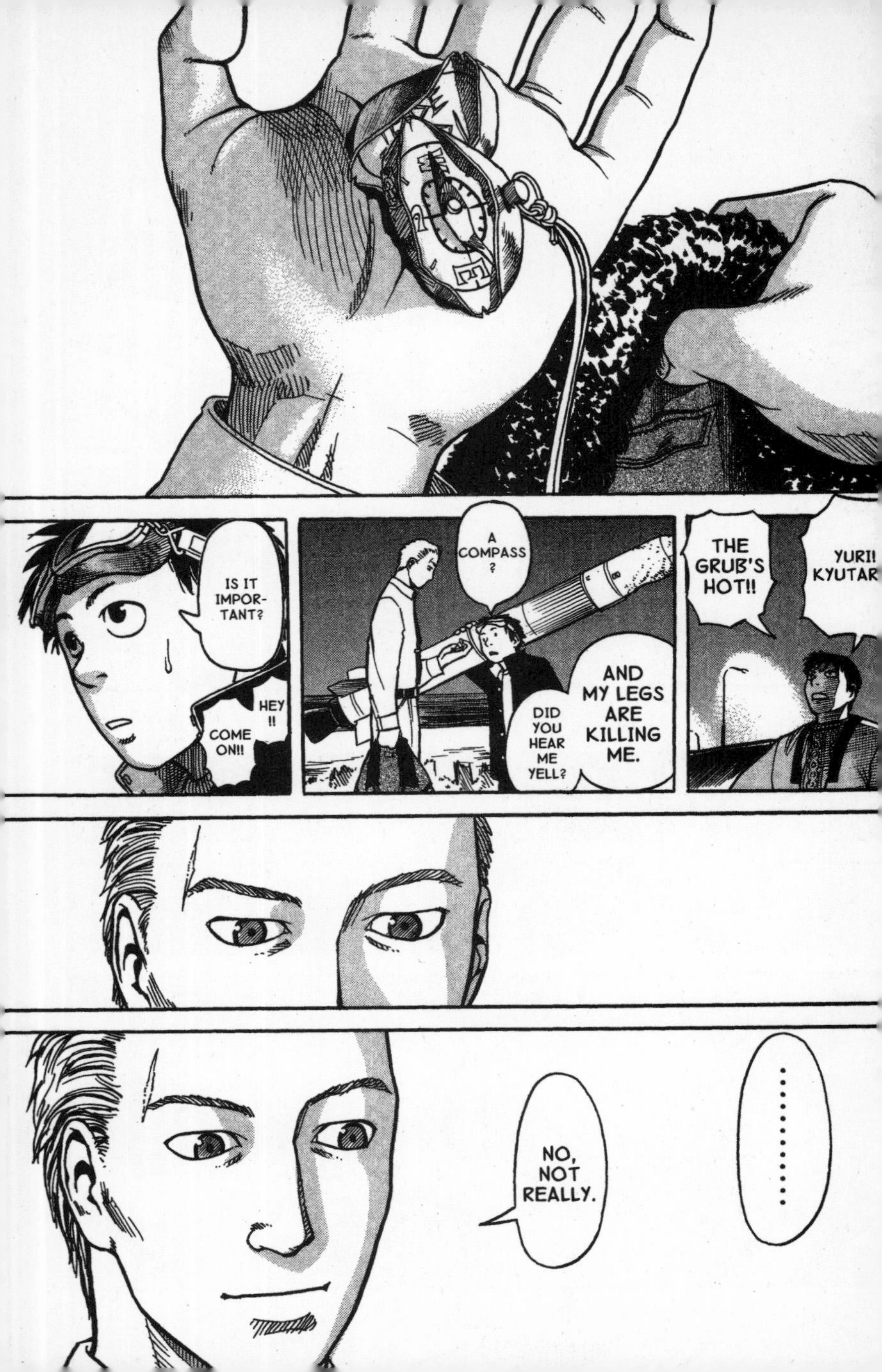
YURI! KYUTAR
THE GRUB'S HOT!!
A COMPASS?
AND MY LEGS ARE KILLING ME.
DID YOU HEAR ME YELL?
IS IT IMPOR-TANT?
HEY!!
COME ON!!
......
NO, NOT REALLY.

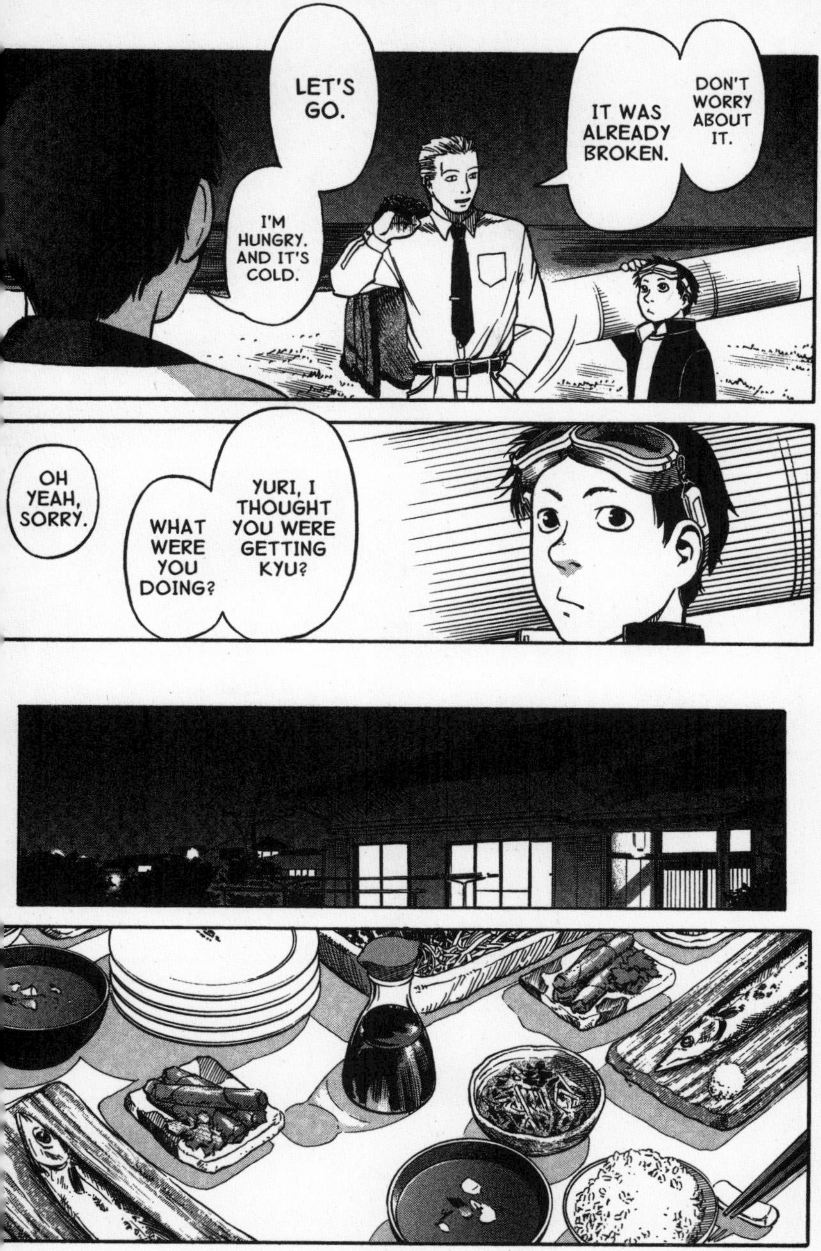
DON'T WORRY ABOUT IT.
IT WAS ALREADY BROKEN.
LET'S GO.
I'M HUNGRY. AND IT'S COLD.
YURI, I THOUGHT YOU WERE GETTING KYU?
WHAT WERE YOU DOING?
OH YEAH, SORRY.

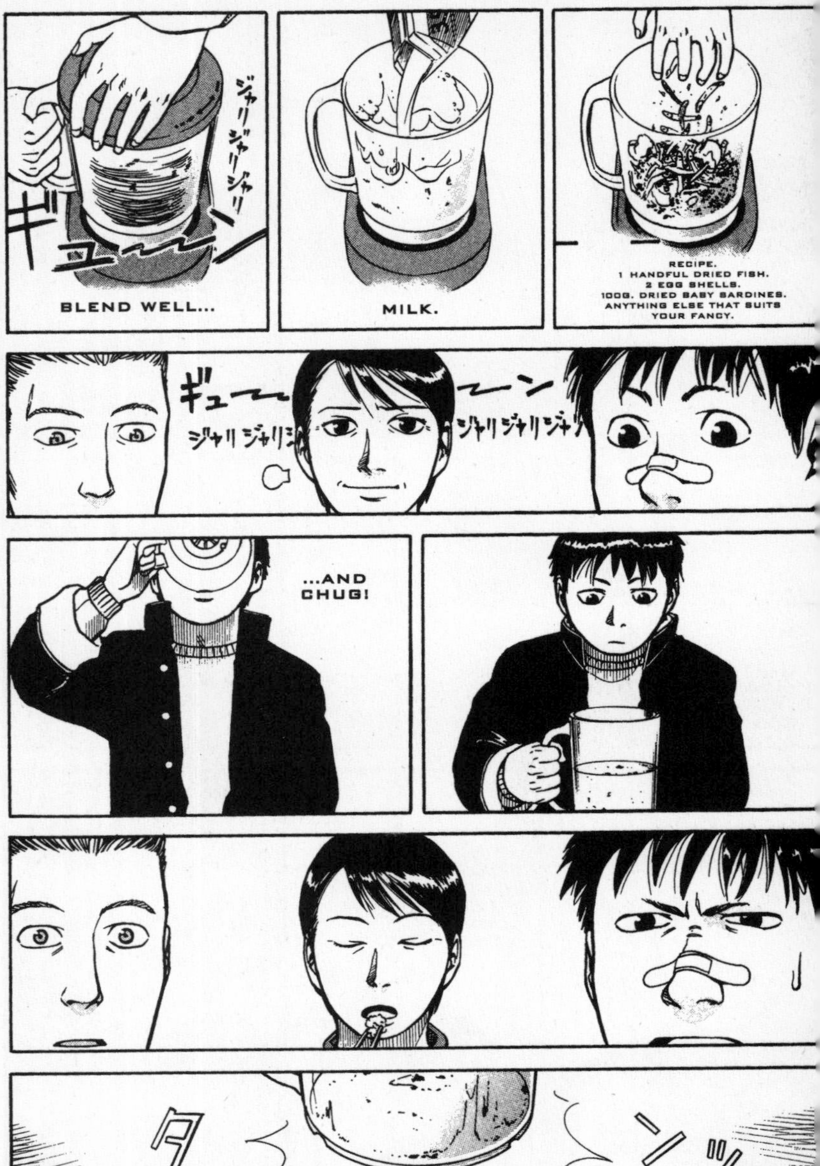
RECIPE.
1 HANDFUL DRIED FISH.
2 EGG SHELLS.
100G. DRIED BABY SARDINES.
ANYTHING ELSE THAT SUITS YOUR FANCY.
MILK.
ジャリジャリジャリ
ギュ～～
BLEND WELL...
...AND CHUG!
タンッ

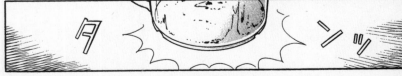

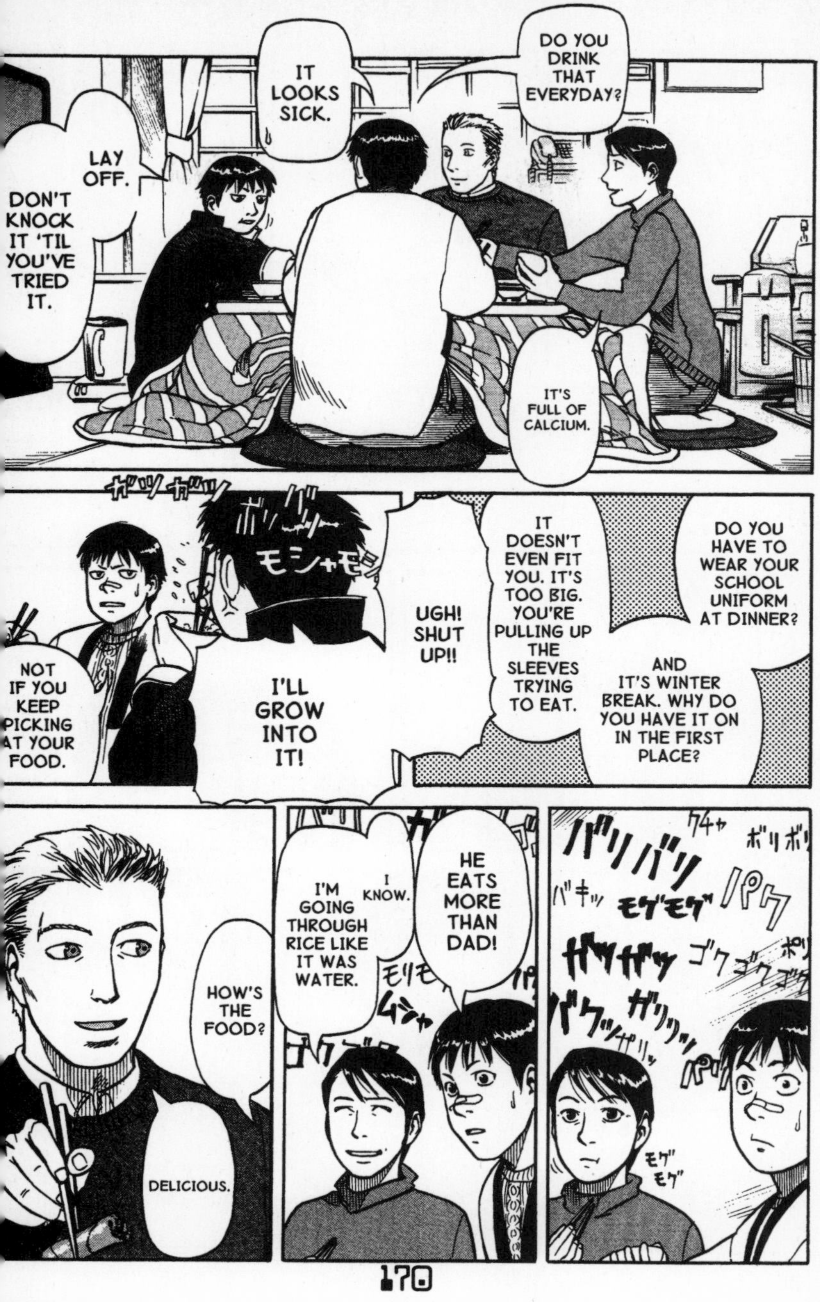
DO YOU DRINK THAT EVERYDAY?
IT LOOKS SICK.
IT'S FULL OF CALCIUM.
LAY OFF.
DON'T KNOCK IT 'TIL YOU'VE TRIED IT.
DO YOU HAVE TO WEAR YOUR SCHOOL UNIFORM AT DINNER?
AND IT'S WINTER BREAK. WHY DO YOU HAVE IT ON IN THE FIRST PLACE?
IT DOESN'T EVEN FIT YOU. IT'S TOO BIG. YOU'RE PULLING UP THE SLEEVES TRYING TO EAT.
UGH! SHUT UP!!
I'LL GROW INTO IT!
NOT IF YOU KEEP PICKING AT YOUR FOOD.
バリバリ
ボリボリ
パク
モグモグ
ガツガツ
ゴクゴク
HE EATS MORE THAN DAD!
I KNOW.
I'M GOING THROUGH RICE LIKE IT WAS WATER.
HOW'S THE FOOD?
DELICIOUS.

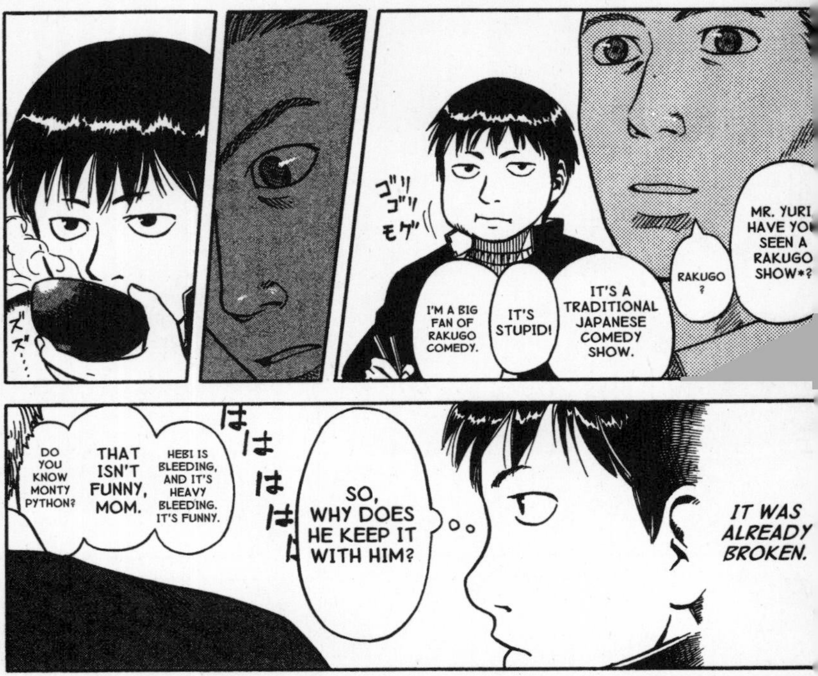
MR. YURI HAVE YO SEEN A RAKUGO SHOW*?
RAKUGO ?
IT'S A TRADITIONAL JAPANESE COMEDY SHOW.
IT'S STUPID!
I'M A BIG FAN OF RAKUGO COMEDY.
ゴリ ゴリ モグ
ズズ…
IT WAS ALREADY BROKEN.
SO, WHY DOES HE KEEP IT WITH HIM?
ははは
HEBI IS BLEEDING, AND IT'S HEAVY BLEEDING. IT'S FUNNY.
THAT ISN'T FUNNY, MOM.
DO YOU KNOW MONTY PYTHON?

* WHEREAS THE WEST HAS ITS STAND-UP COMEDY, THE JAPANESE HAVE THEIR SIT-DOWN COMEDY. A RAKUGO SHOW INVOLVES A PERFORMER SITTING AMONGST HIS AUDIENCE AND TELLING A HUMOROUS STORY FOR WHICH HE ACTS OUT ALL THE PARTS.

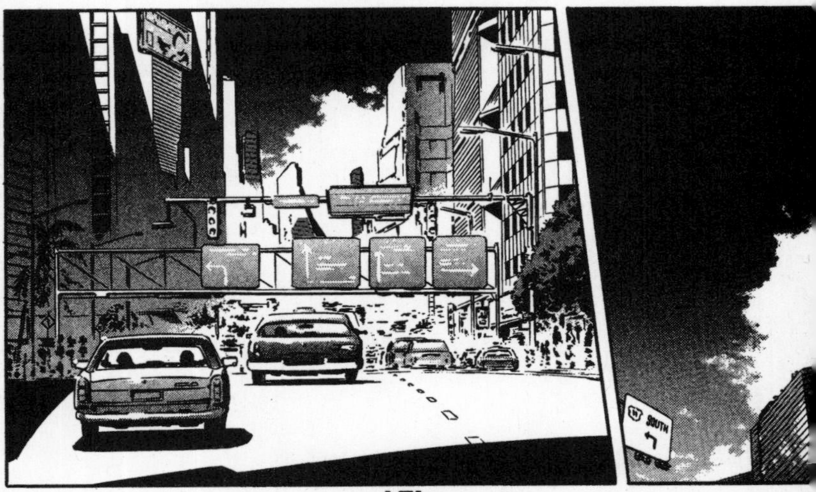
SOUTH

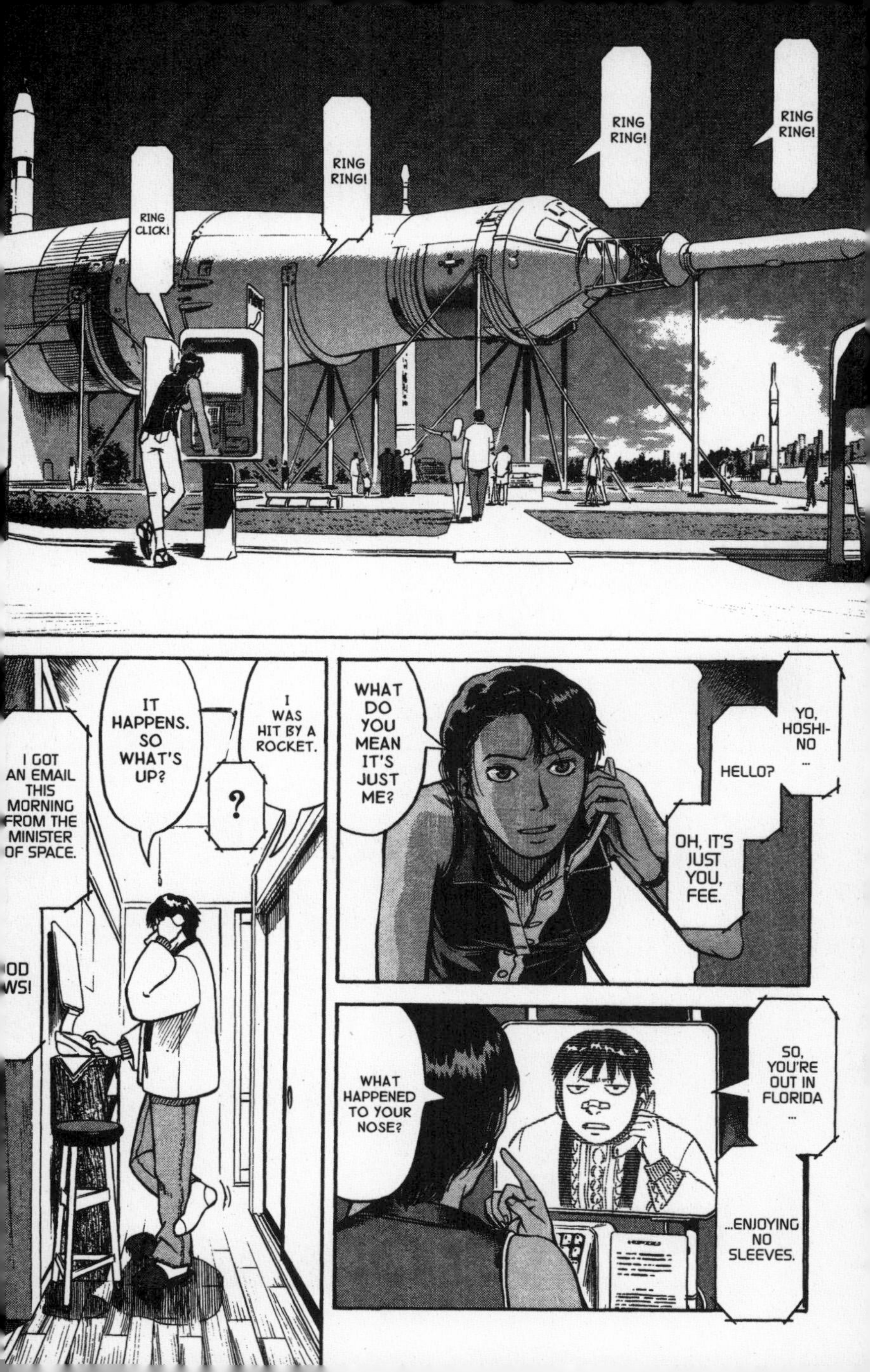
RING RING!
RING RING!
RING RING!
RING CLICK!
YO, HOSHINO ...
HELLO?
OH, IT'S JUST YOU, FEE.
WHAT DO YOU MEAN IT'S JUST ME?
SO, YOU'RE OUT IN FLORIDA ...
...ENJOYING NO SLEEVES.
WHAT HAPPENED TO YOUR NOSE?
I WAS HIT BY A ROCKET.
?
IT HAPPENS. SO WHAT'S UP?
I GOT AN EMAIL THIS MORNING FROM THE MINISTER OF SPACE.

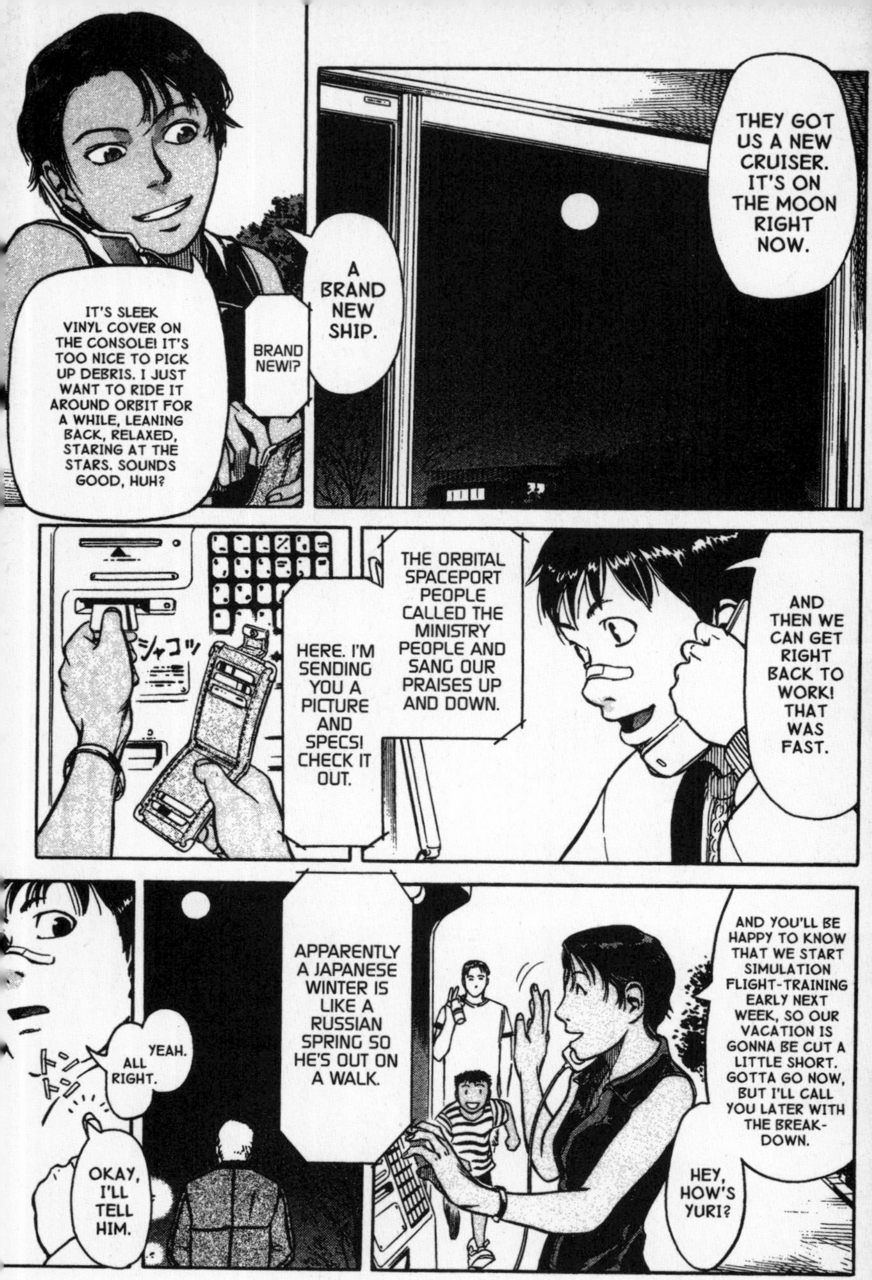
THEY GOT US A NEW CRUISER. IT'S ON THE MOON RIGHT NOW.
A BRAND NEW SHIP.
BRAND NEW!?
IT'S SLEEK VINYL COVER ON THE CONSOLE! IT'S TOO NICE TO PICK UP DEBRIS. I JUST WANT TO RIDE IT AROUND ORBIT FOR A WHILE, LEANING BACK, RELAXED, STARING AT THE STARS. SOUNDS GOOD, HUH?
AND THEN WE CAN GET RIGHT BACK TO WORK! THAT WAS FAST.
THE ORBITAL SPACEPORT PEOPLE CALLED THE MINISTRY PEOPLE AND SANG OUR PRAISES UP AND DOWN.
HERE. I'M SENDING YOU A PICTURE AND SPECS! CHECK IT OUT.
シャコッ
AND YOU'LL BE HAPPY TO KNOW THAT WE START SIMULATION FLIGHT-TRAINING EARLY NEXT WEEK, SO OUR VACATION IS GONNA BE CUT A LITTLE SHORT. GOTTA GO NOW, BUT I'LL CALL YOU LATER WITH THE BREAK-DOWN.
HEY, HOW'S YURI?
APPARENTLY A JAPANESE WINTER IS LIKE A RUSSIAN SPRING SO HE'S OUT ON A WALK.
YEAH. ALL RIGHT.
OKAY, I'LL TELL HIM.

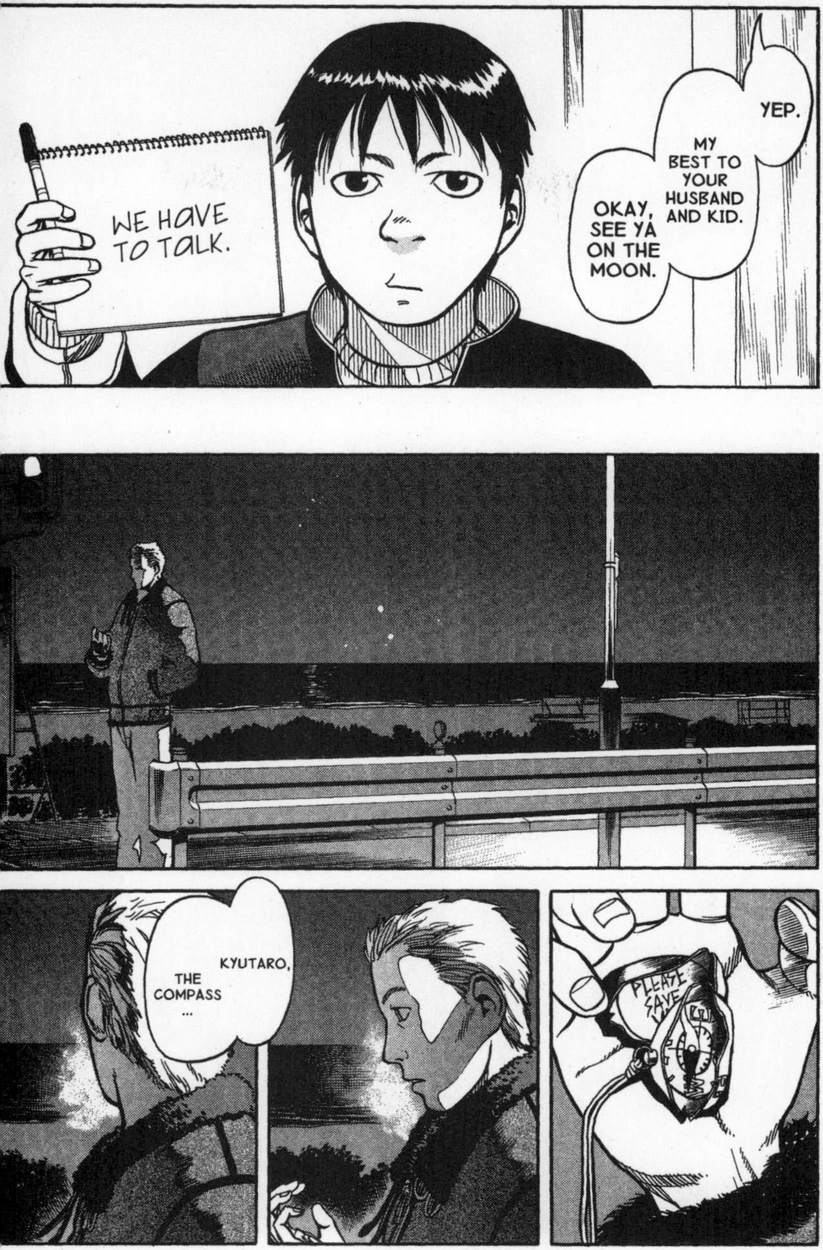
YEP.
MY BEST TO YOUR HUSBAND AND KID.
OKAY, SEE YA ON THE MOON.
WE HAVE TO TALK.
PLEASE SAVE
KYUTARO, THE COMPASS ...

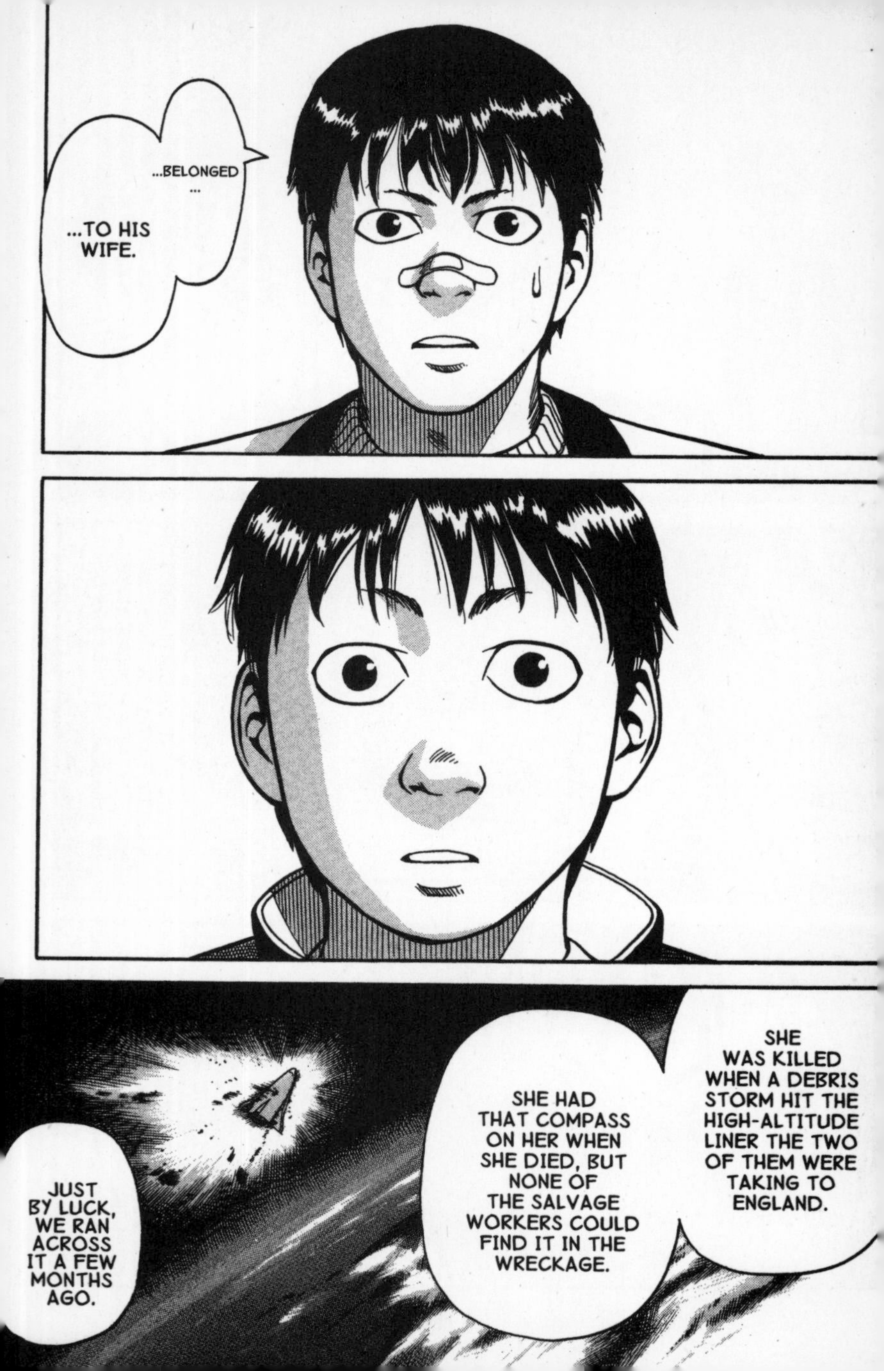
...BELONGED ...
...TO HIS WIFE.
SHE WAS KILLED WHEN A DEBRIS STORM HIT THE HIGH-ALTITUDE LINER THE TWO OF THEM WERE TAKING TO ENGLAND.
SHE HAD THAT COMPASS ON HER WHEN SHE DIED, BUT NONE OF THE SALVAGE WORKERS COULD FIND IT IN THE WRECKAGE.
JUST BY LUCK, WE RAN ACROSS IT A FEW MONTHS AGO.

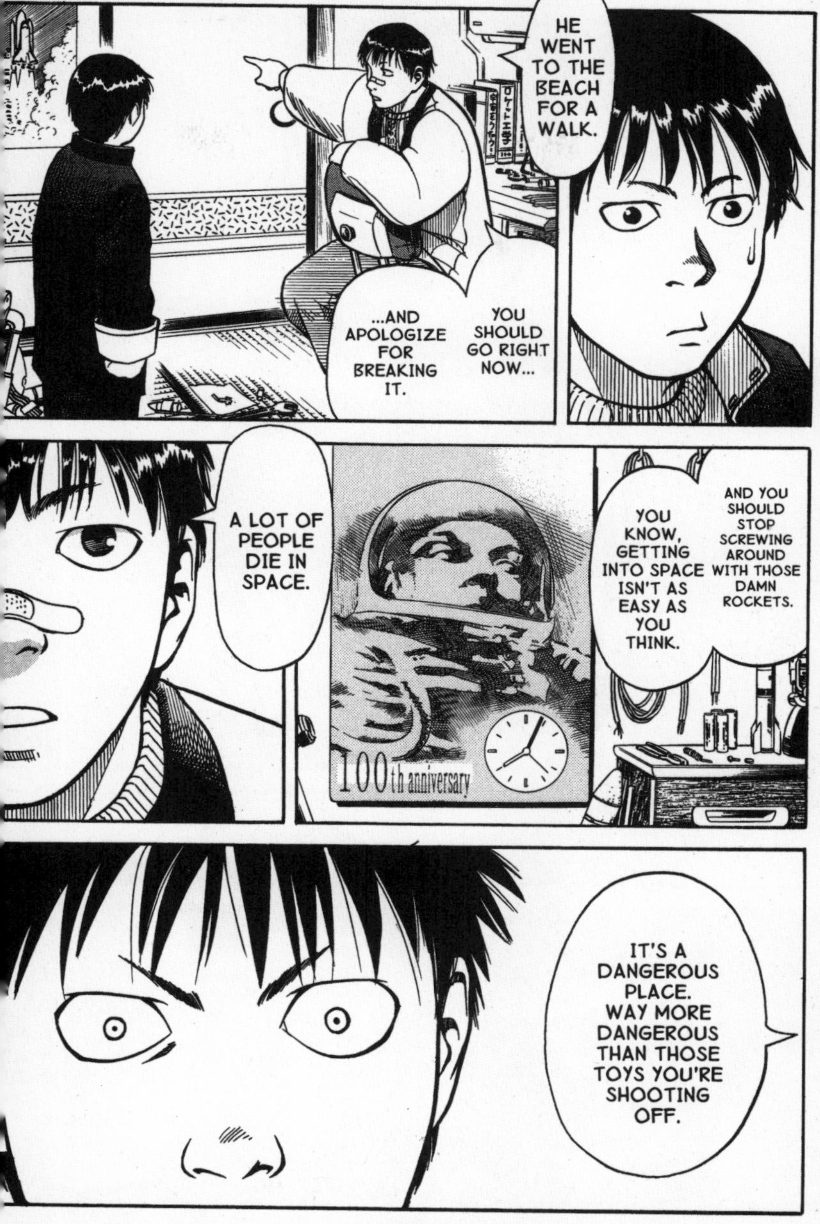
HE WENT TO THE BEACH FOR A WALK.
YOU SHOULD GO RIGHT NOW...
...AND APOLOGIZE FOR BREAKING IT.
AND YOU SHOULD STOP SCREWING AROUND WITH THOSE DAMN ROCKETS.
YOU KNOW, GETTING INTO SPACE ISN'T AS EASY AS YOU THINK.
100th anniversary
A LOT OF PEOPLE DIE IN SPACE.
IT'S A DANGEROUS PLACE. WAY MORE DANGEROUS THAN THOSE TOYS YOU'RE SHOOTING OFF.

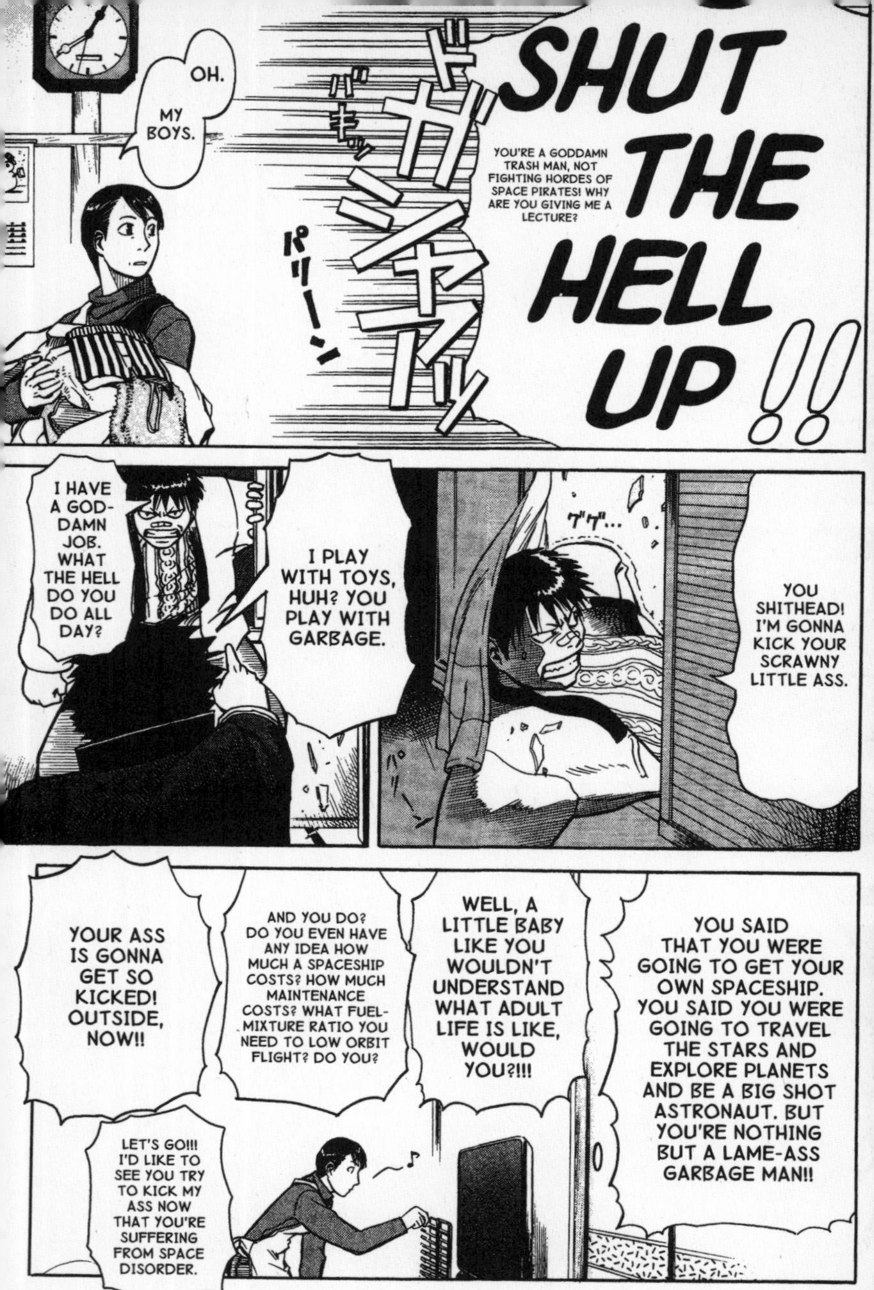
SHUT THE HELL UP!!
YOU'RE A GODDAMN TRASH MAN, NOT FIGHTING HORDES OF SPACE PIRATES! WHY ARE YOU GIVING ME A LECTURE?
ドガシャアッ
バキッ
パリーン
OH. MY BOYS.
YOU SHITHEAD! I'M GONNA KICK YOUR SCRAWNY LITTLE ASS.
ググ…
I PLAY WITH TOYS, HUH? YOU PLAY WITH GARBAGE.
I HAVE A GOD-DAMN JOB. WHAT THE HELL DO YOU DO ALL DAY?
YOU SAID THAT YOU WERE GOING TO GET YOUR OWN SPACESHIP. YOU SAID YOU WERE GOING TO TRAVEL THE STARS AND EXPLORE PLANETS AND BE A BIG SHOT ASTRONAUT. BUT YOU'RE NOTHING BUT A LAME-ASS GARBAGE MAN!!
WELL, A LITTLE BABY LIKE YOU WOULDN'T UNDERSTAND WHAT ADULT LIFE IS LIKE, WOULD YOU?!!!
AND YOU DO? DO YOU EVEN HAVE ANY IDEA HOW MUCH A SPACESHIP COSTS? HOW MUCH MAINTENANCE COSTS? WHAT FUEL-MIXTURE RATIO YOU NEED TO LOW ORBIT FLIGHT? DO YOU?
YOUR ASS IS GONNA GET SO KICKED! OUTSIDE, NOW!!
LET'S GO!!! I'D LIKE TO SEE YOU TRY TO KICK MY ASS NOW THAT YOU'RE SUFFERING FROM SPACE DISORDER.

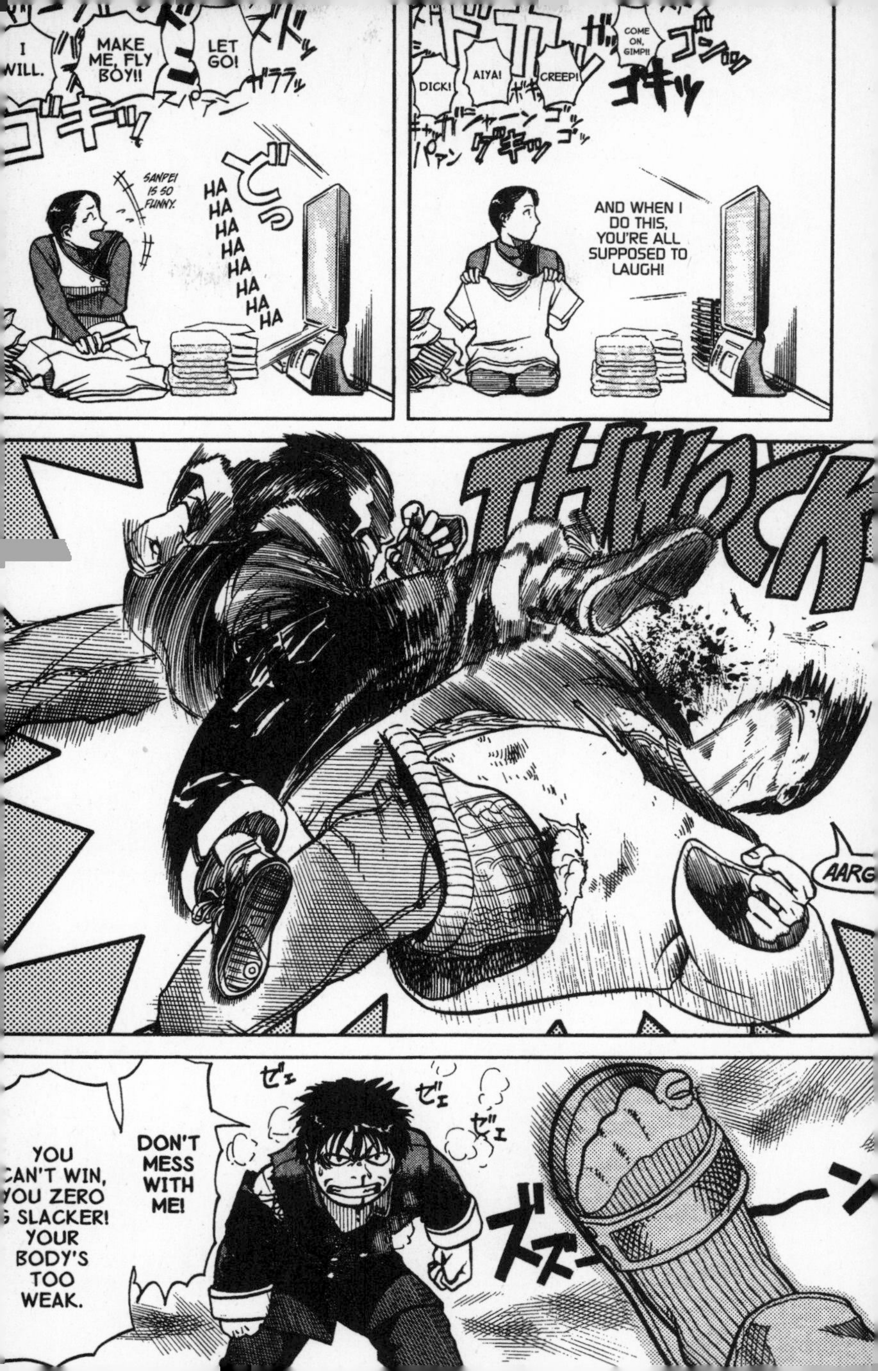
COME ON, GIMP!!
CREEP!
AIYA!
DICK!
AND WHEN I DO THIS, YOU'RE ALL SUPPOSED TO LAUGH!
LET GO!
MAKE ME, FLY BOY!!
I WILL.
HA HA HA HA HA HA HA HA HA
SANPEI IS SO FUNNY.
THWOCK
AARG
DON'T MESS WITH ME!
YOU CAN'T WIN, YOU ZERO G SLACKER! YOUR BODY'S TOO WEAK.

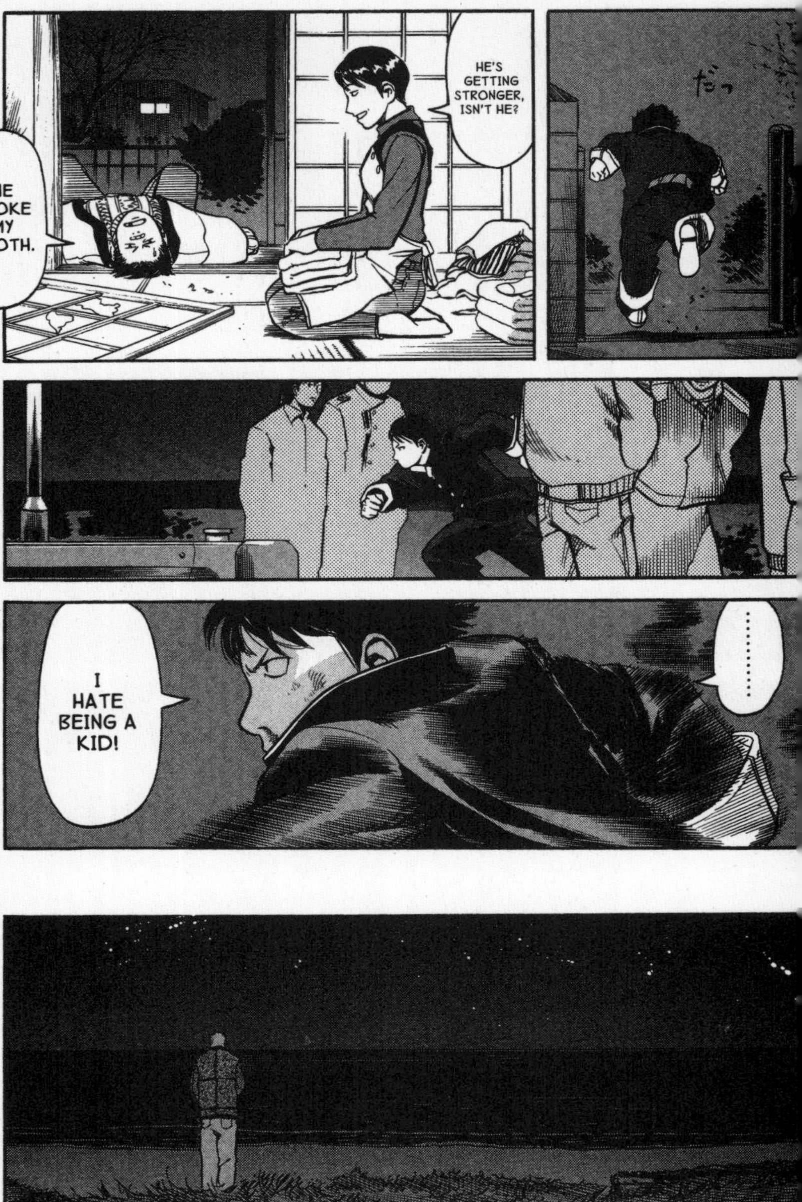
だっ
HE'S GETTING STRONGER, ISN'T HE?
HE BROKE MY TOOTH.
......
I HATE BEING A KID!

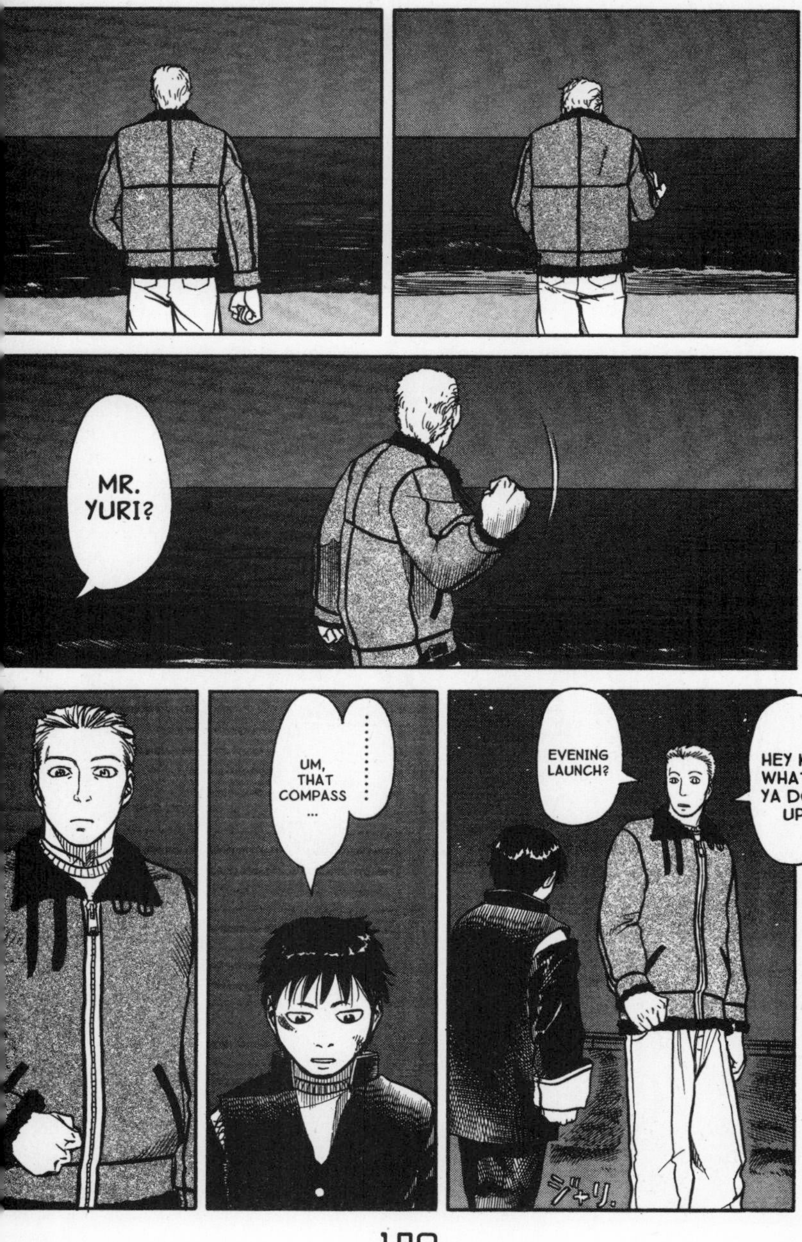
MR. YURI?
HEY KYU. WHAT'RE YA DOIN' UP?
EVENING LAUNCH?
ジャリ。
......
UM, THAT COMPASS ...

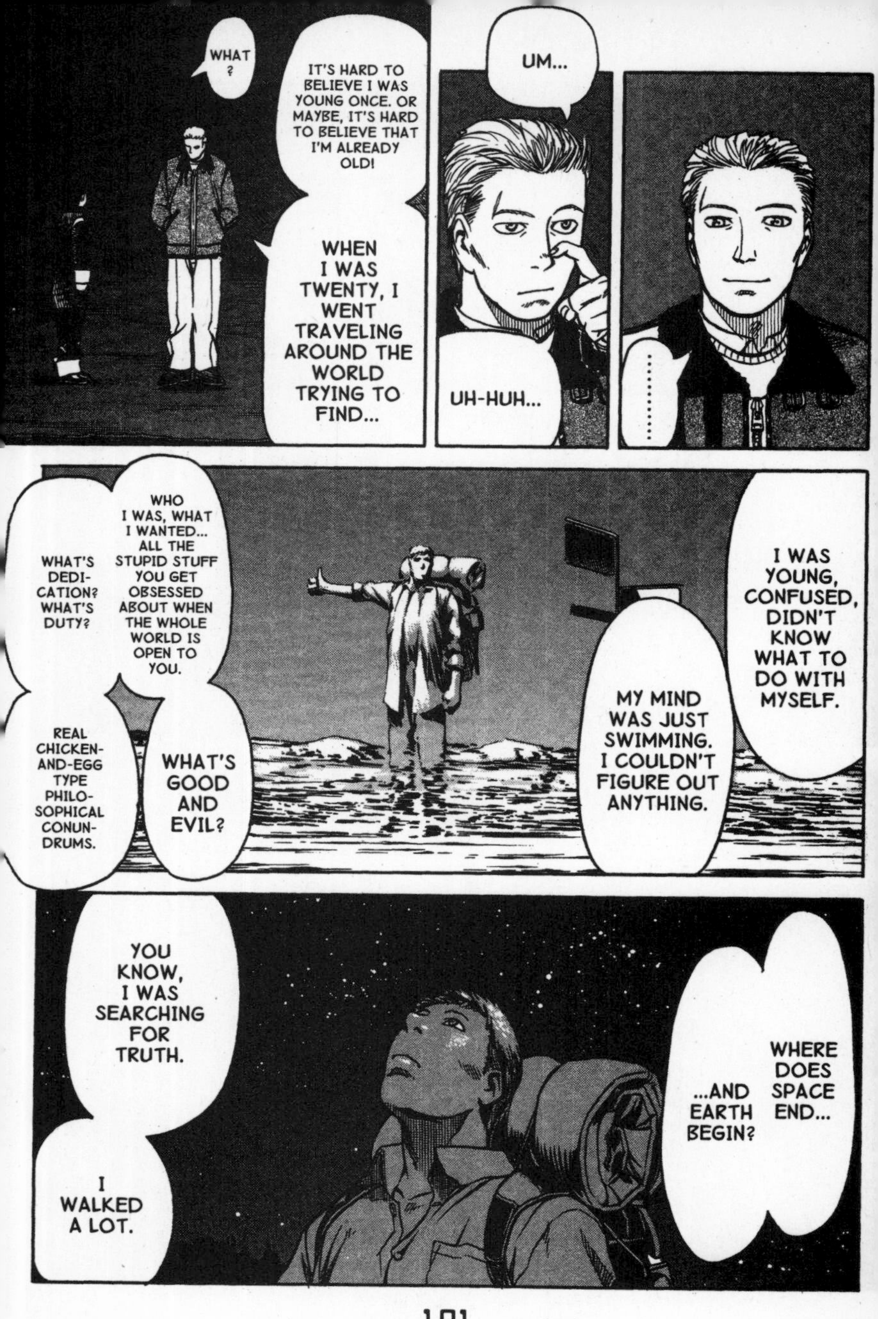
......
UM...
UH-HUH...
WHAT ?
IT'S HARD TO BELIEVE I WAS YOUNG ONCE. OR MAYBE, IT'S HARD TO BELIEVE THAT I'M ALREADY OLD!
WHEN I WAS TWENTY, I WENT TRAVELING AROUND THE WORLD TRYING TO FIND...
I WAS YOUNG, CONFUSED, DIDN'T KNOW WHAT TO DO WITH MYSELF.
MY MIND WAS JUST SWIMMING. I COULDN'T FIGURE OUT ANYTHING.
WHO I WAS, WHAT I WANTED... ALL THE STUPID STUFF YOU GET OBSESSED ABOUT WHEN THE WHOLE WORLD IS OPEN TO YOU.
WHAT'S DEDICATION? WHAT'S DUTY?
WHAT'S GOOD AND EVIL?
REAL CHICKEN-AND-EGG TYPE PHILOSOPHICAL CONUNDRUMS.
WHERE DOES SPACE END...
...AND EARTH BEGIN?
YOU KNOW, I WAS SEARCHING FOR TRUTH.
I WALKED A LOT.

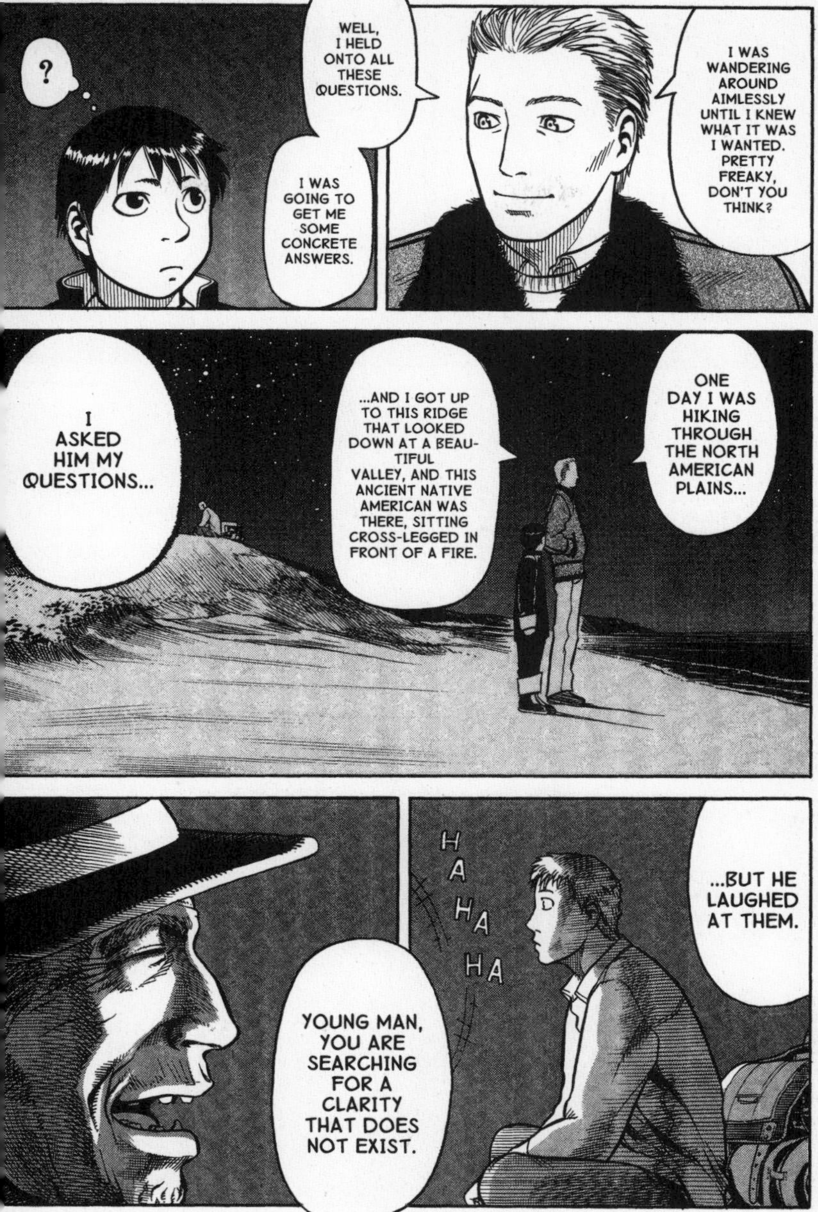
I WAS WANDERING AROUND AIMLESSLY UNTIL I KNEW WHAT IT WAS I WANTED. PRETTY FREAKY, DON'T YOU THINK?
WELL, I HELD ONTO ALL THESE QUESTIONS.
I WAS GOING TO GET ME SOME CONCRETE ANSWERS.
?
ONE DAY I WAS HIKING THROUGH THE NORTH AMERICAN PLAINS...
...AND I GOT UP TO THIS RIDGE THAT LOOKED DOWN AT A BEAUTIFUL VALLEY, AND THIS ANCIENT NATIVE AMERICAN WAS THERE, SITTING CROSS-LEGGED IN FRONT OF A FIRE.
I ASKED HIM MY QUESTIONS...
...BUT HE LAUGHED AT THEM.
HA HA HA HA
YOUNG MAN, YOU ARE SEARCHING FOR A CLARITY THAT DOES NOT EXIST.

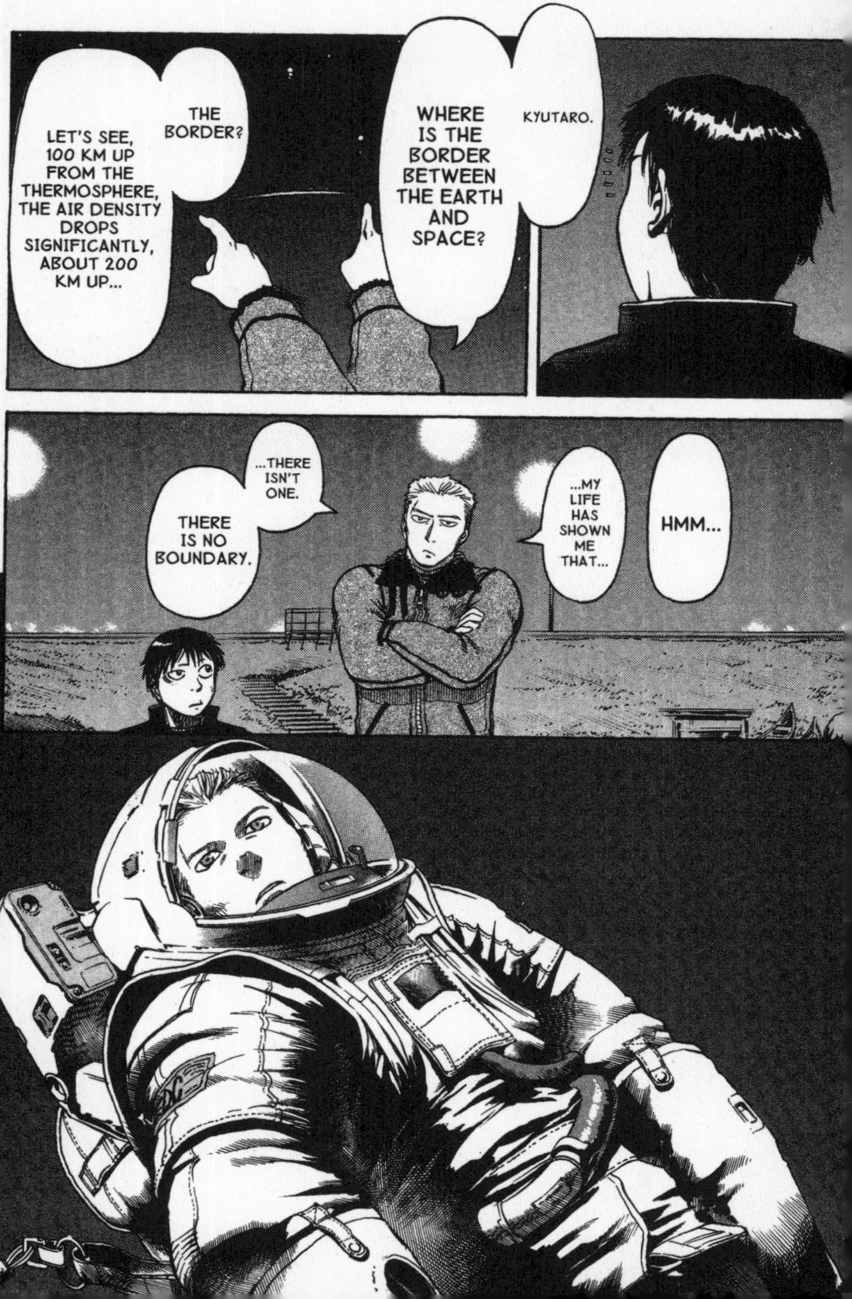
KYUTARO.
WHERE IS THE BORDER BETWEEN THE EARTH AND SPACE?
THE BORDER?
LET'S SEE, 100 KM UP FROM THE THERMOSPHERE, THE AIR DENSITY DROPS SIGNIFICANTLY, ABOUT 200 KM UP...
HMM...
...MY LIFE HAS SHOWN ME THAT...
...THERE ISN'T ONE.
THERE IS NO BOUNDARY.

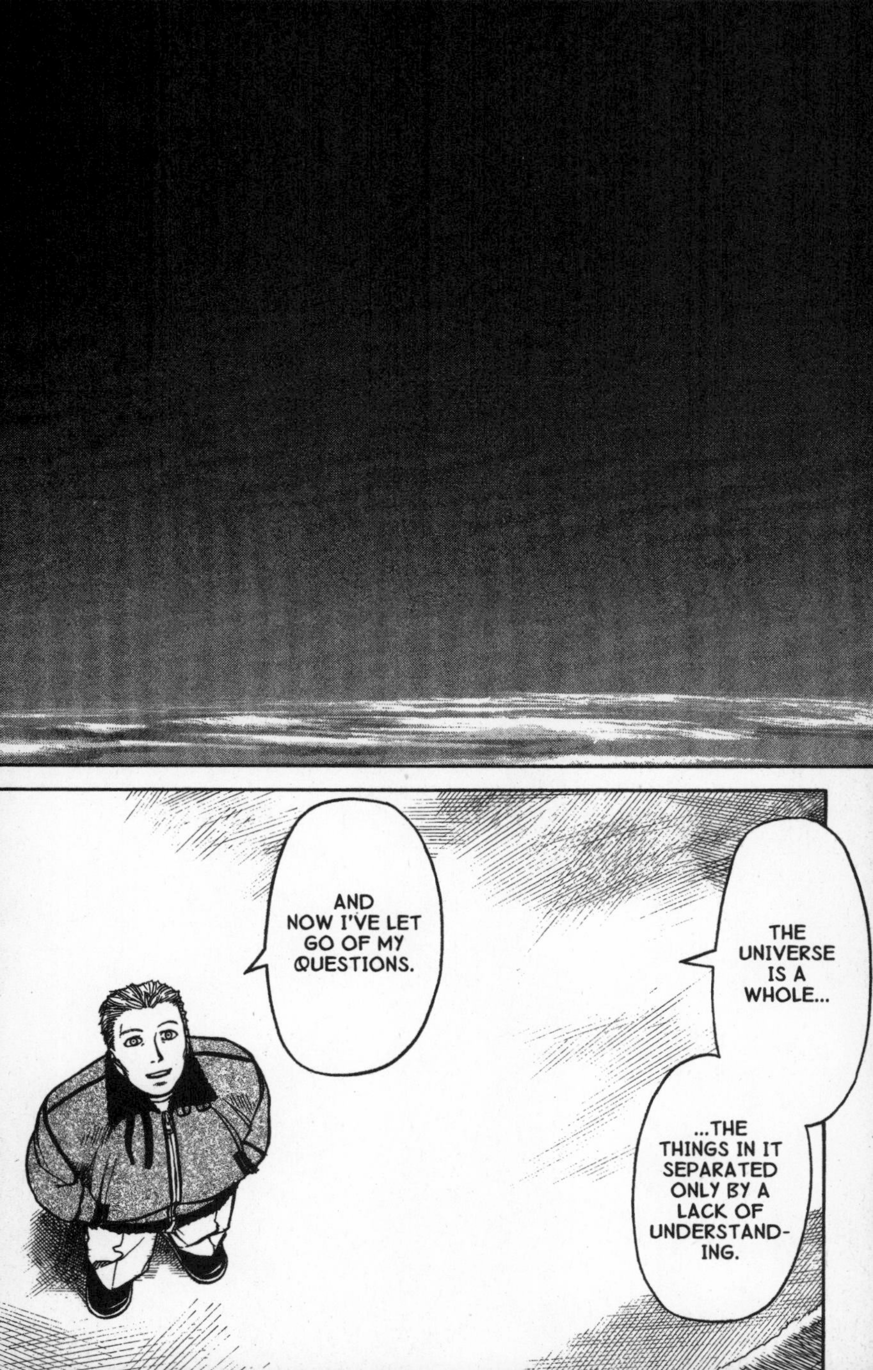
THE UNIVERSE IS A WHOLE...
...THE THINGS IN IT SEPARATED ONLY BY A LACK OF UNDERSTAND-ING.
AND NOW I'VE LET GO OF MY QUESTIONS.

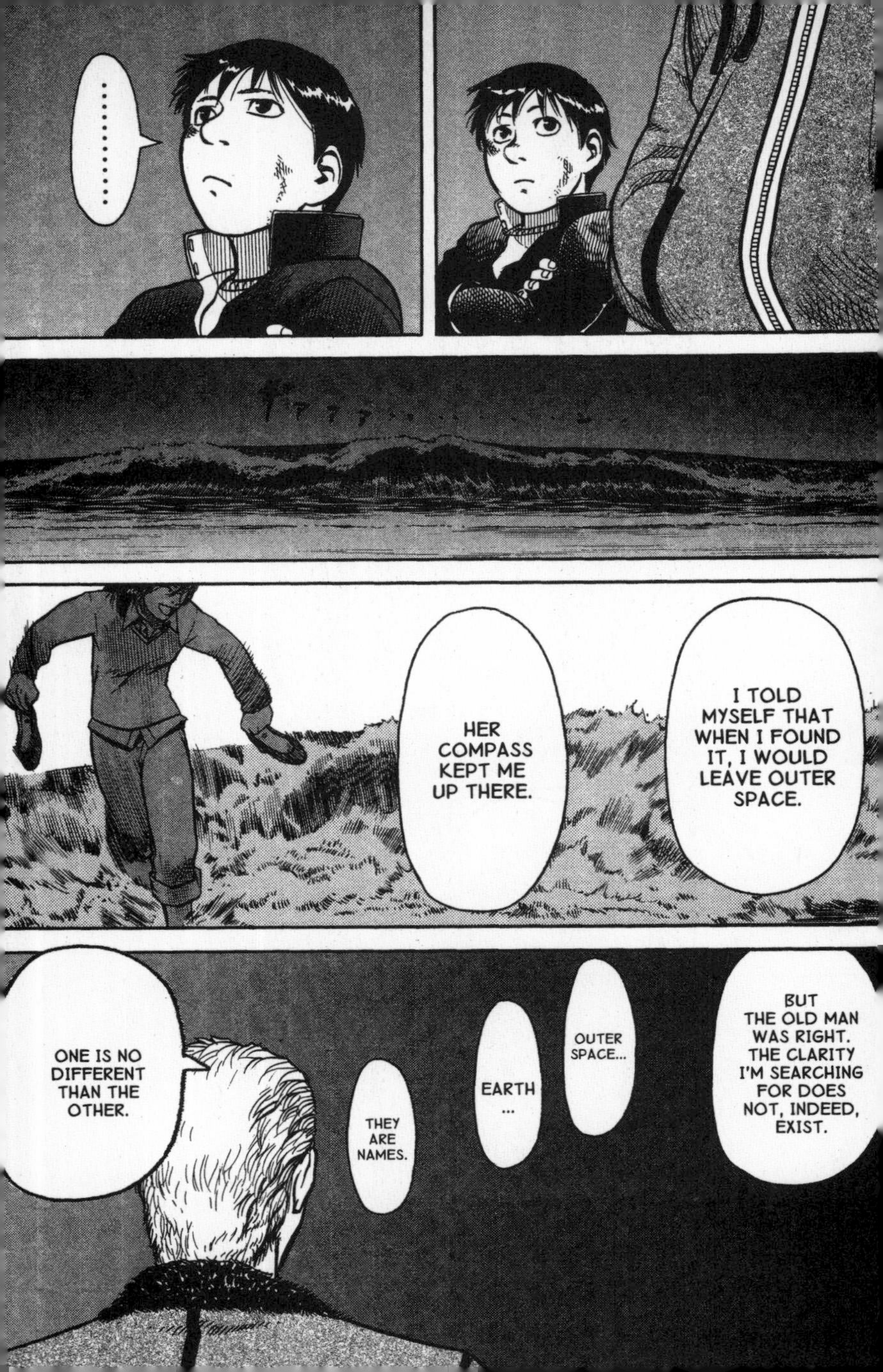
......
I TOLD MYSELF THAT WHEN I FOUND IT, I WOULD LEAVE OUTER SPACE.
HER COMPASS KEPT ME UP THERE.
BUT THE OLD MAN WAS RIGHT. THE CLARITY I'M SEARCHING FOR DOES NOT, INDEED, EXIST.
OUTER SPACE...
EARTH ...
THEY ARE NAMES.
ONE IS NO DIFFERENT THAN THE OTHER.

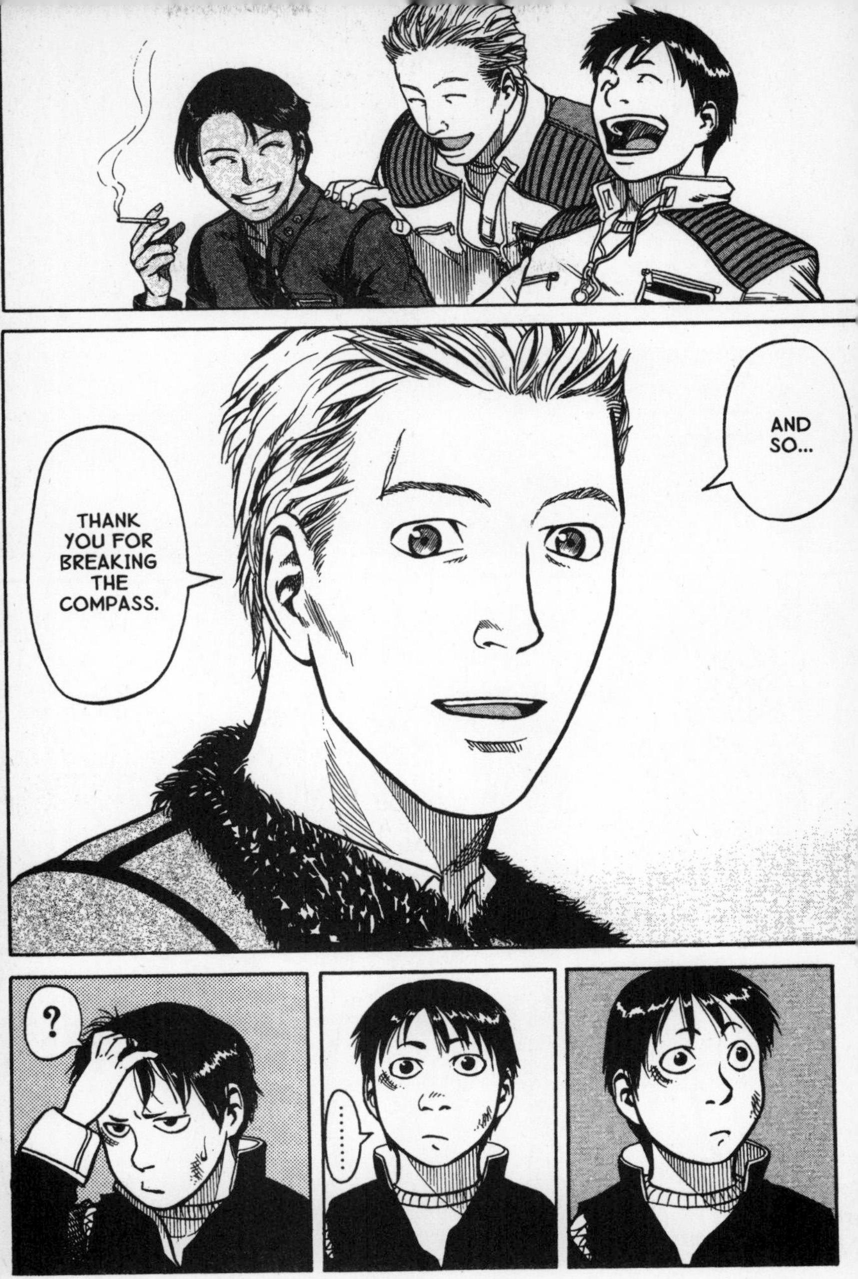
AND SO...
THANK YOU FOR BREAKING THE COMPASS.
......
?

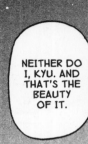

はははは

I DON'T REALLY GET IT.

NEITHER DO I, KYU. AND THAT'S THE BEAUTY OF IT.

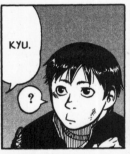

KYU.

?

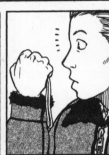

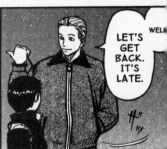

WELM

LET'S GET BACK. IT'S LATE.

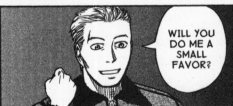

WILL YOU DO ME A SMALL FAVOR?

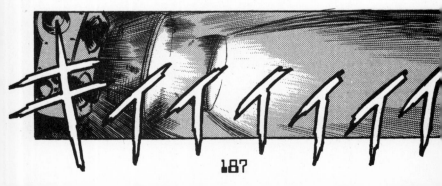

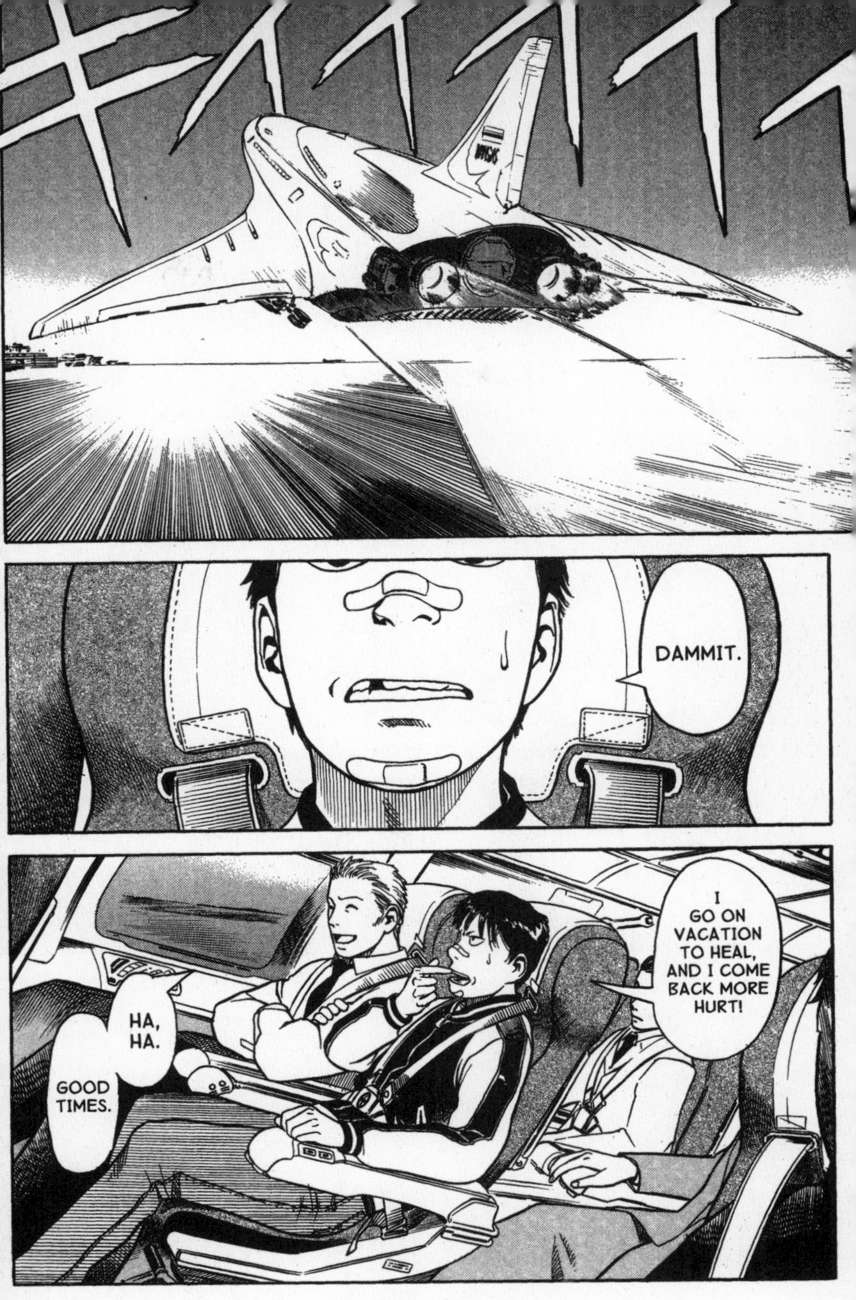
DAMMIT.
I GO ON VACATION TO HEAL, AND I COME BACK MORE HURT!
HA, HA.
GOOD TIMES.

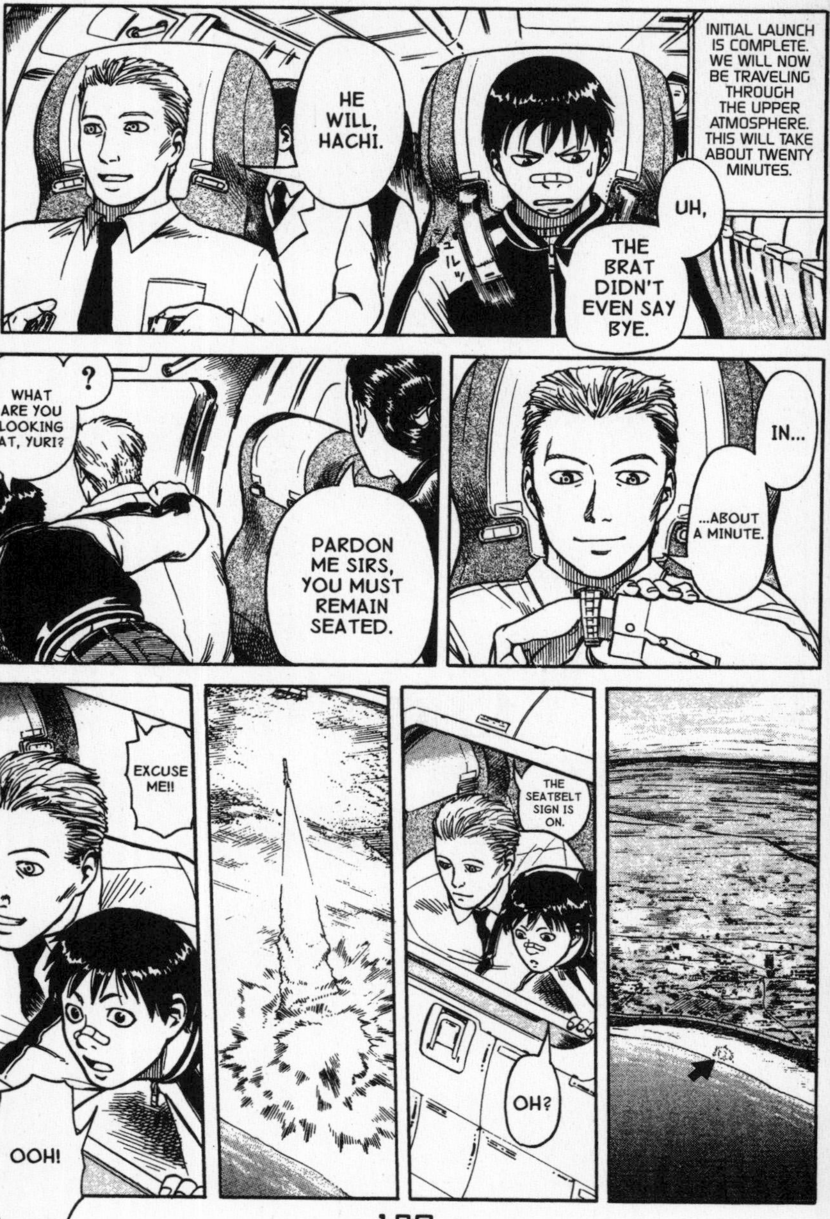
INITIAL LAUNCH IS COMPLETE. WE WILL NOW BE TRAVELING THROUGH THE UPPER ATMOSPHERE. THIS WILL TAKE ABOUT TWENTY MINUTES.
UH,
THE BRAT DIDN'T EVEN SAY BYE.
HE WILL, HACHI.
IN...
...ABOUT A MINUTE.
?
WHAT ARE YOU LOOKING AT, YURI?
PARDON ME SIRS, YOU MUST REMAIN SEATED.
THE SEATBELT SIGN IS ON.
OH?
EXCUSE ME!!
OOH!

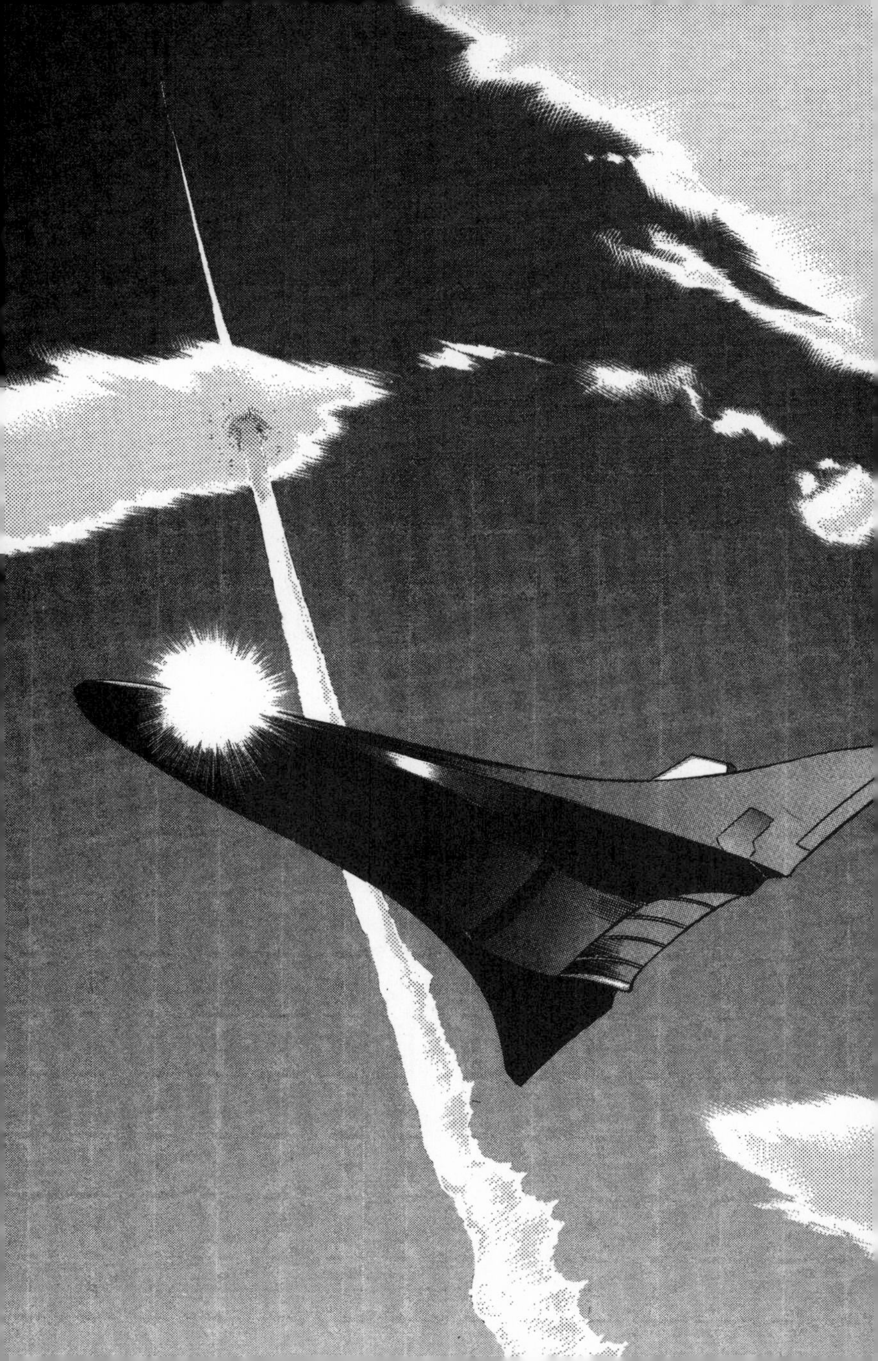

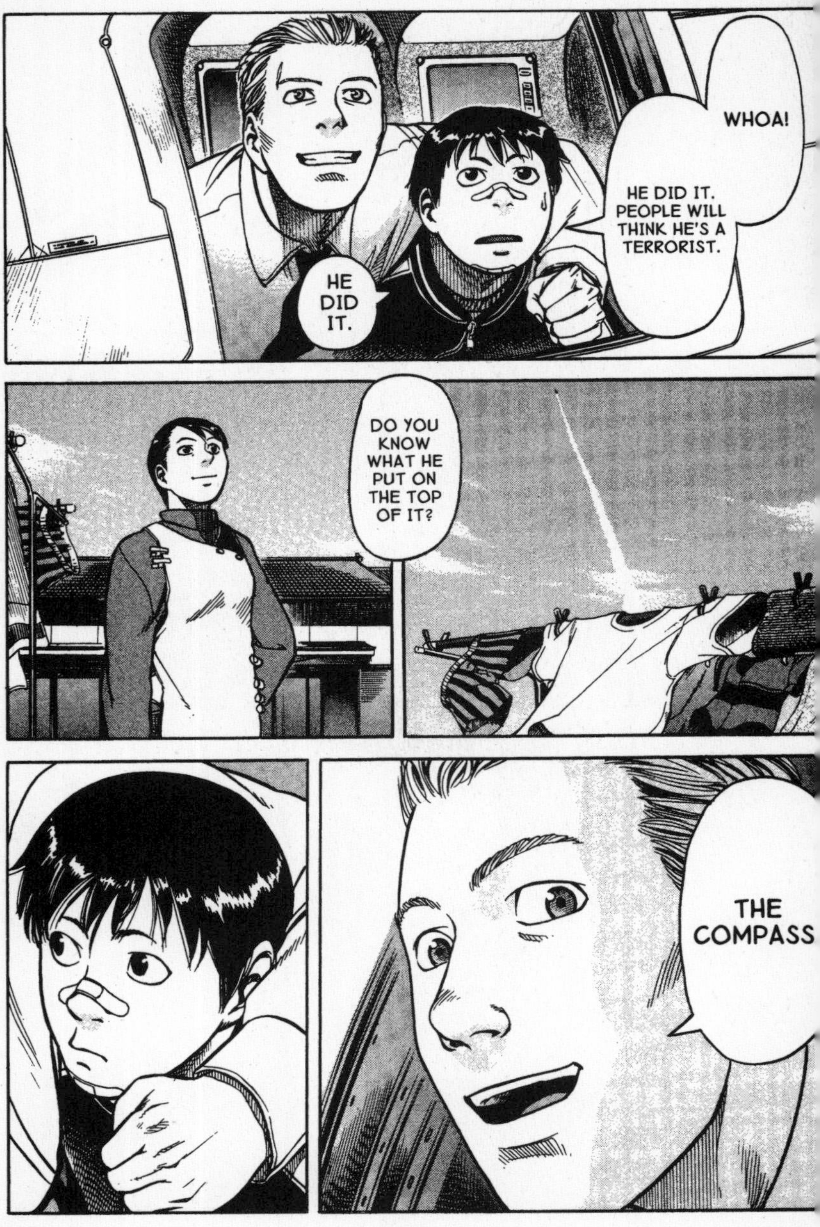
WHOA!
HE DID IT. PEOPLE WILL THINK HE'S A TERRORIST.
HE DID IT.
DO YOU KNOW WHAT HE PUT ON THE TOP OF IT?
THE COMPASS

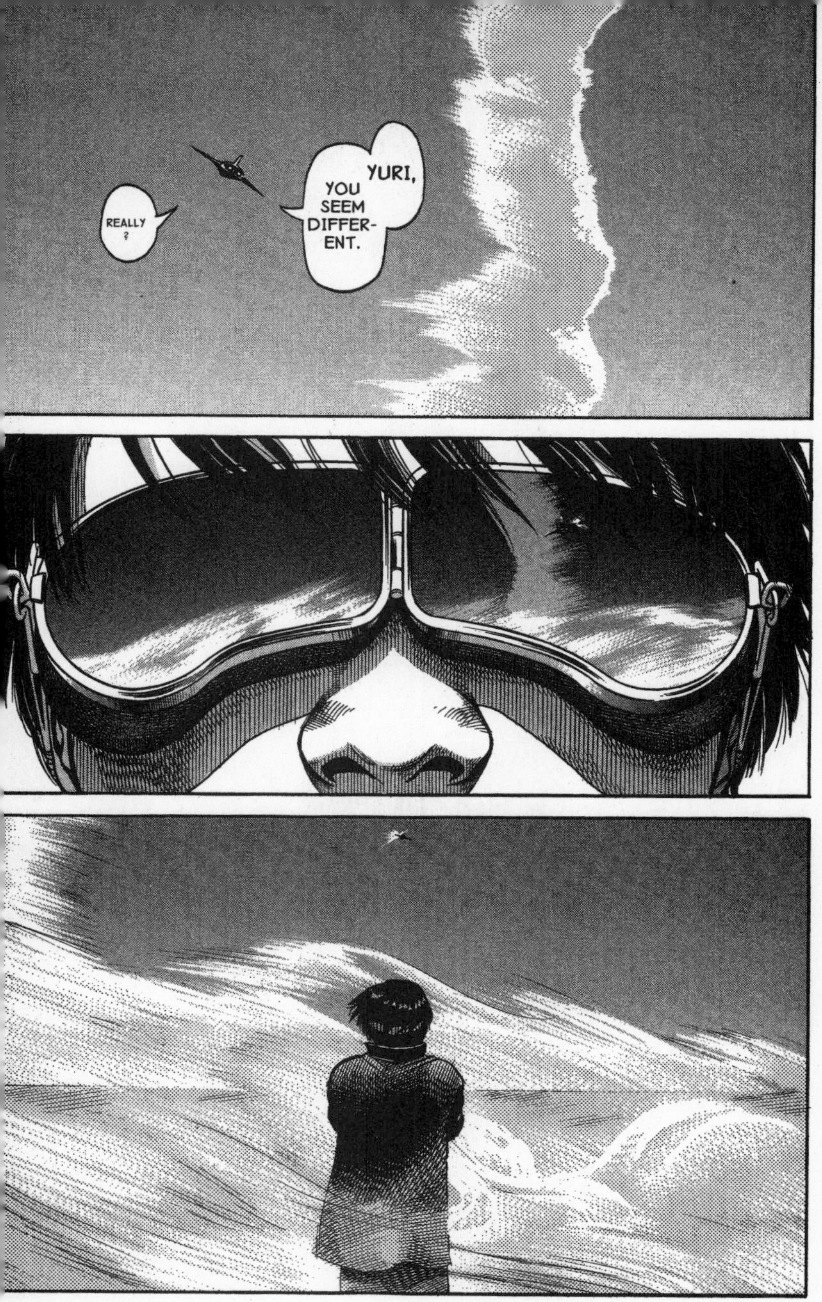
YURI, YOU SEEM DIFFERENT.
REALLY?

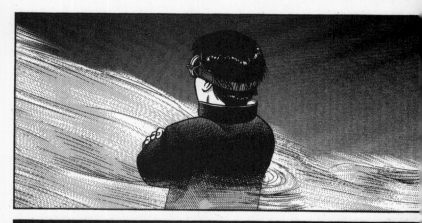

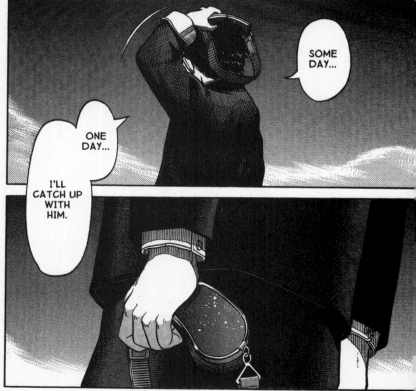

SOME DAY...

ONE DAY...

I'LL CATCH UP WITH HIM.

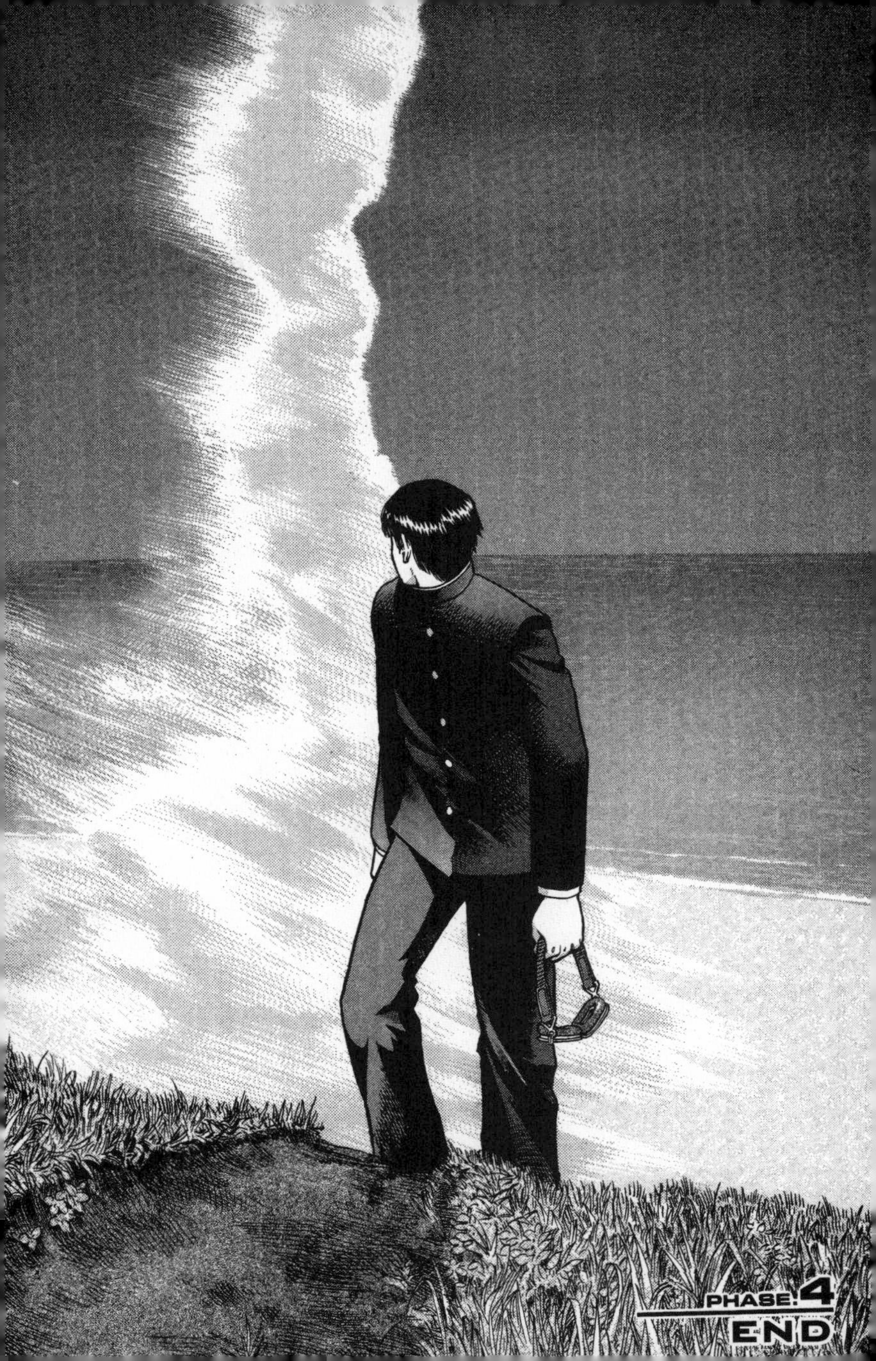
PHASE 4
END

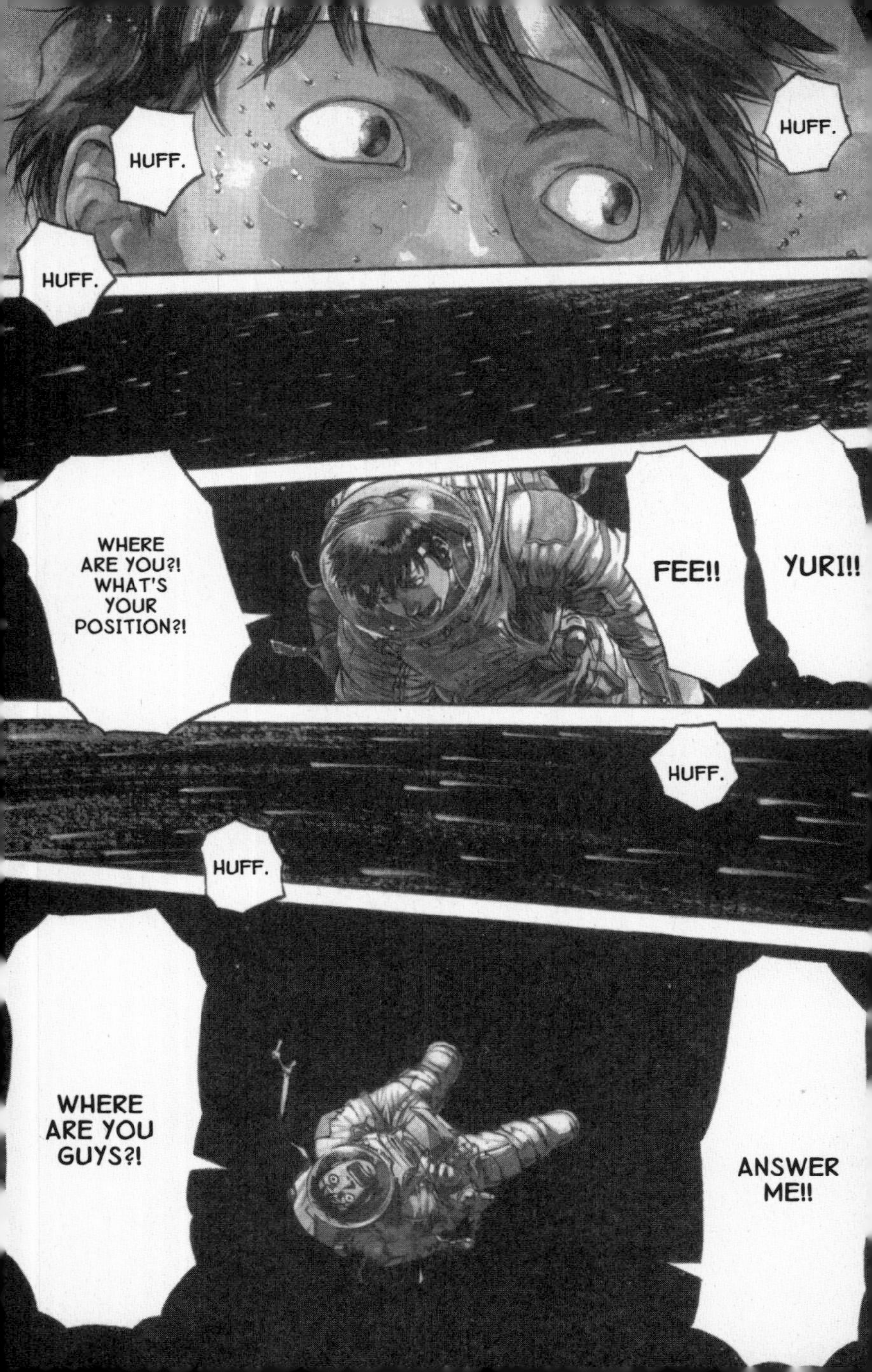
HUFF.
HUFF.
HUFF.
YURI!!!
FEE!!
WHERE ARE YOU?! WHAT'S YOUR POSITION?!
HUFF.
HUFF.
ANSWER ME!!
WHERE ARE YOU GUYS?!

PHASE. 5 IGNITION

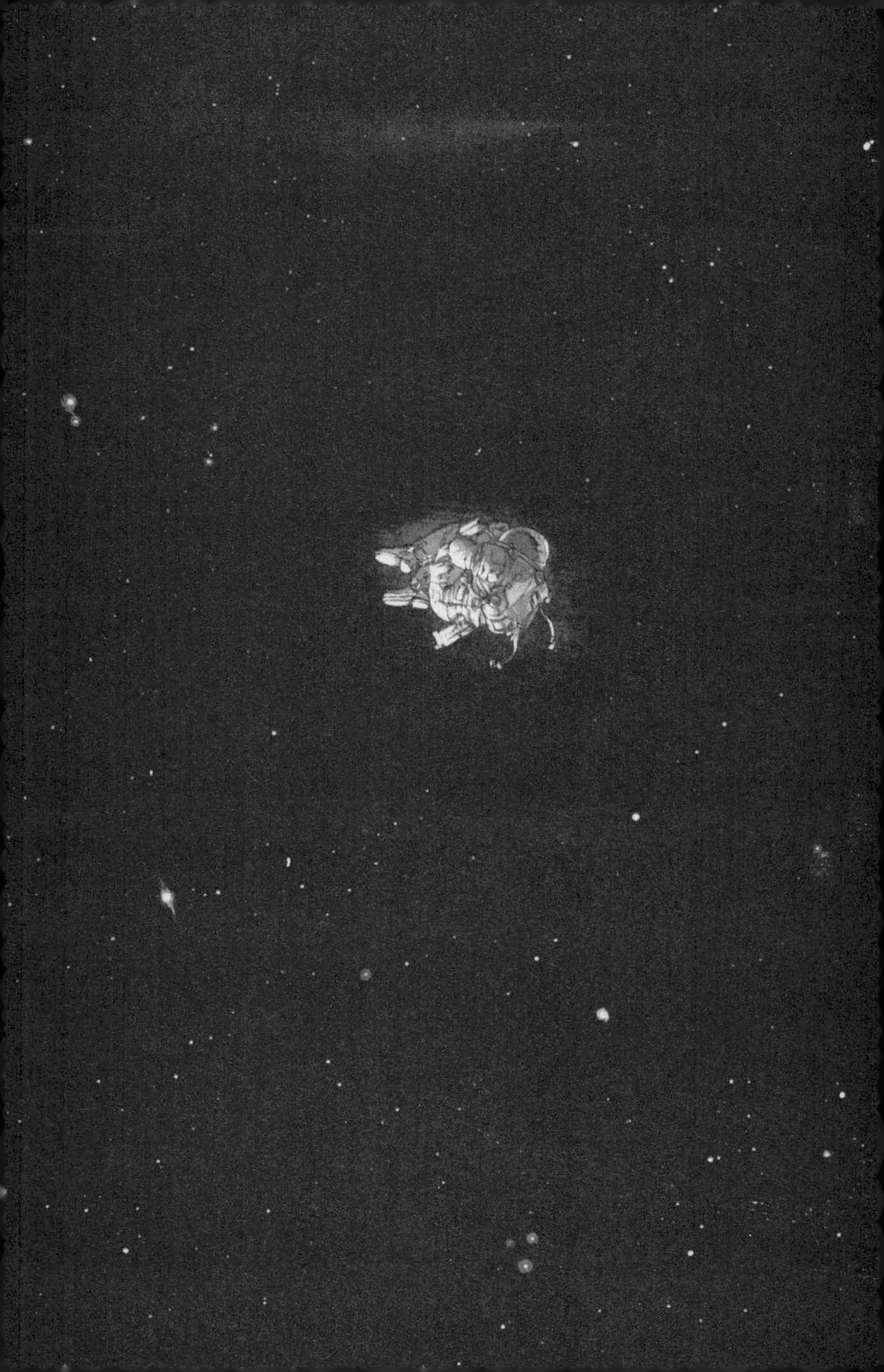

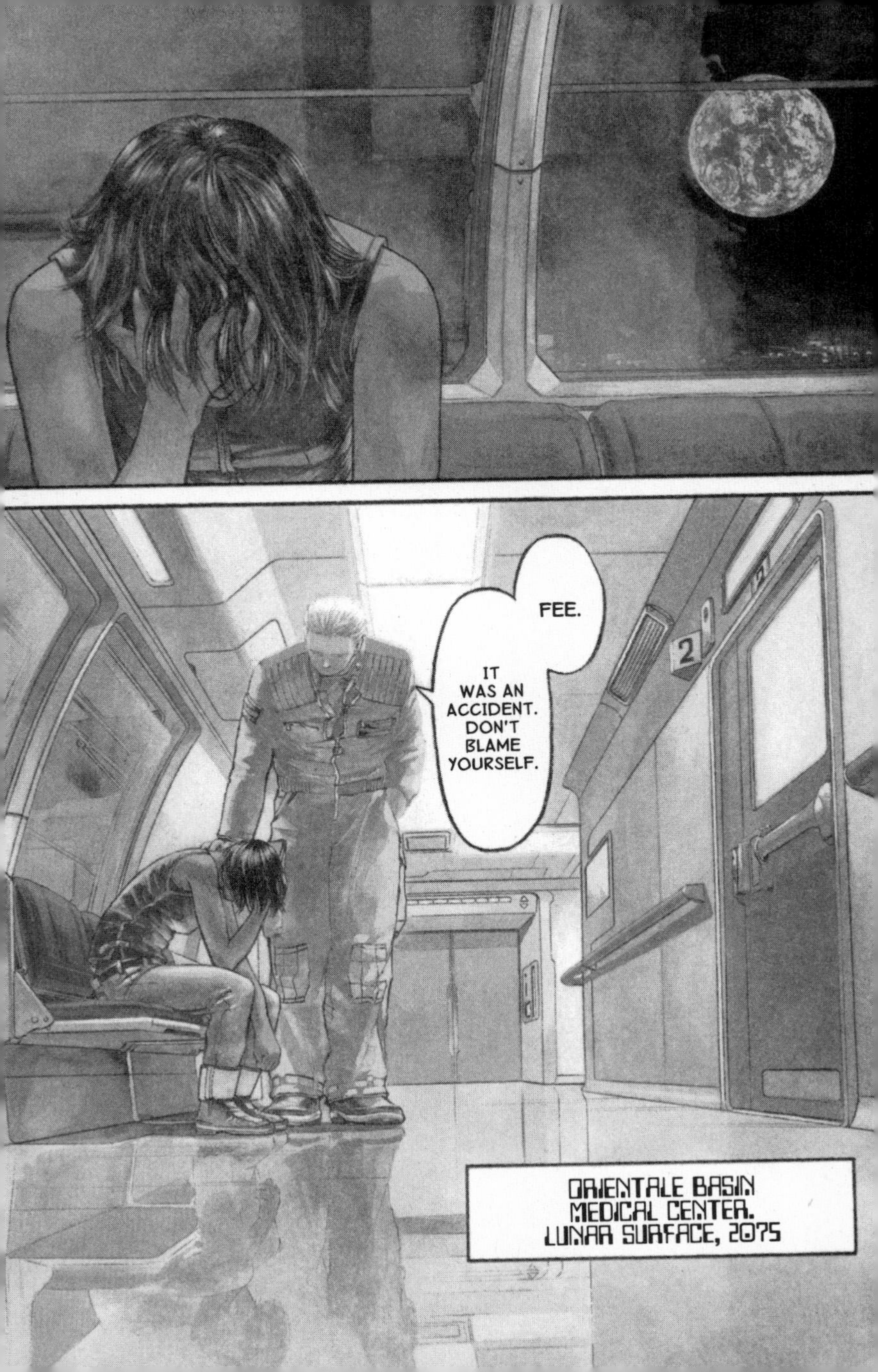
FEE.
IT WAS AN ACCIDENT. DON'T BLAME YOURSELF.
ORIENTALE BASIN MEDICAL CENTER. LUNAR SURFACE, 2075

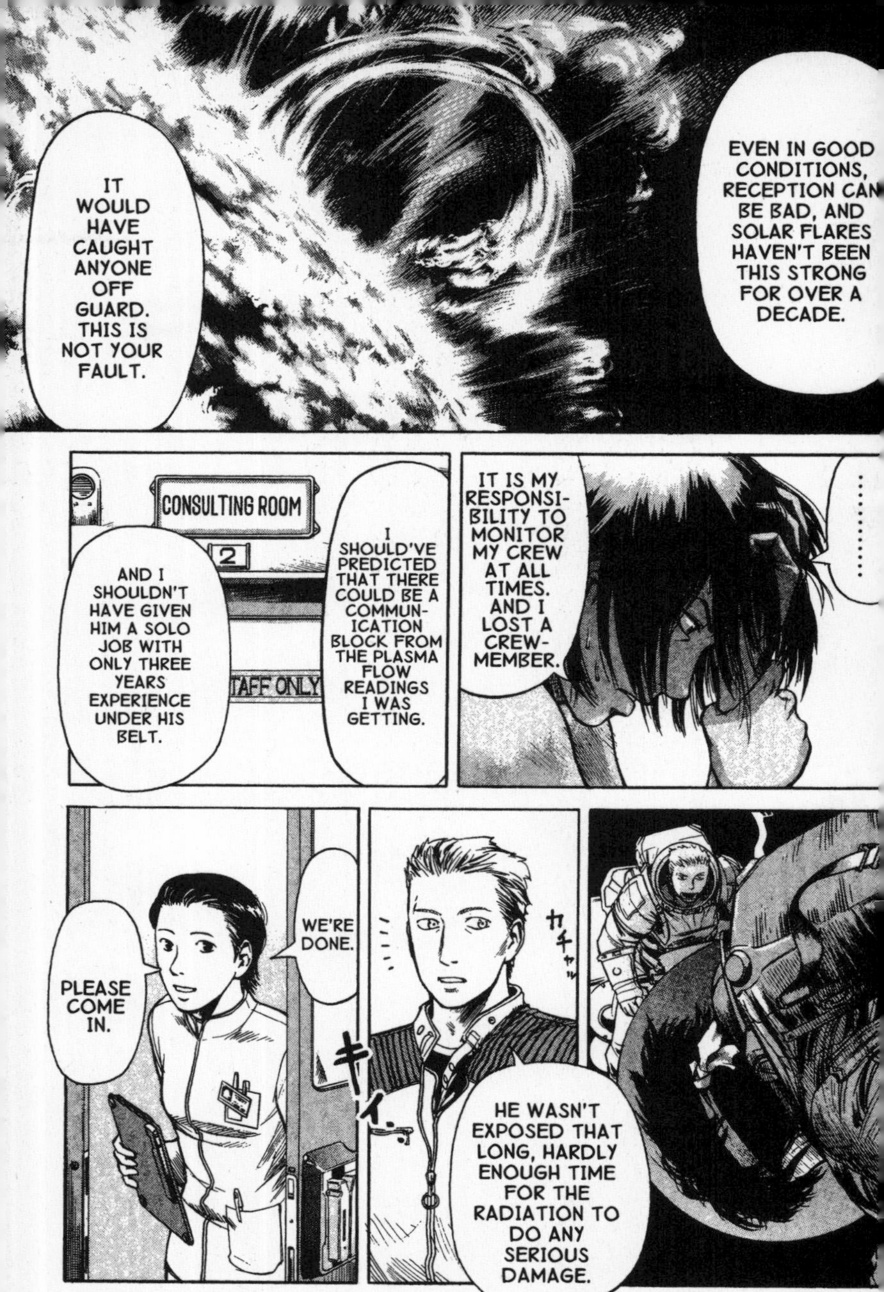
EVEN IN GOOD CONDITIONS, RECEPTION CAN BE BAD, AND SOLAR FLARES HAVEN'T BEEN THIS STRONG FOR OVER A DECADE.
IT WOULD HAVE CAUGHT ANYONE OFF GUARD. THIS IS NOT YOUR FAULT.
....
IT IS MY RESPONSIBILITY TO MONITOR MY CREW AT ALL TIMES. AND I LOST A CREW-MEMBER.
CONSULTING ROOM
2
TAFF ONLY
I SHOULD'VE PREDICTED THAT THERE COULD BE A COMMUNICATION BLOCK FROM THE PLASMA FLOW READINGS I WAS GETTING.
AND I SHOULDN'T HAVE GIVEN HIM A SOLO JOB WITH ONLY THREE YEARS EXPERIENCE UNDER HIS BELT.
カチャッ
HE WASN'T EXPOSED THAT LONG, HARDLY ENOUGH TIME FOR THE RADIATION TO DO ANY SERIOUS DAMAGE.
WE'RE DONE.
キィ
PLEASE COME IN.

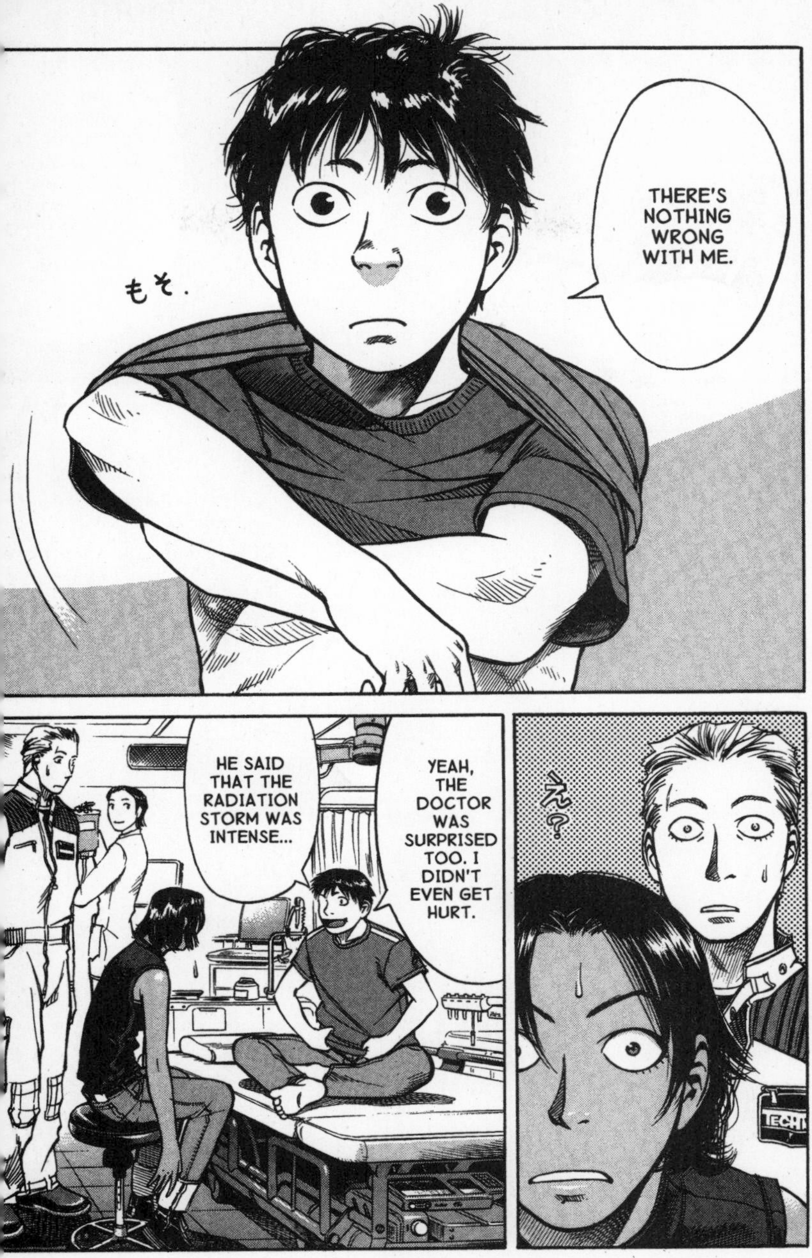
THERE'S NOTHING WRONG WITH ME.
もそ.
え?
YEAH, THE DOCTOR WAS SURPRISED TOO. I DIDN'T EVEN GET HURT.
HE SAID THAT THE RADIATION STORM WAS INTENSE...

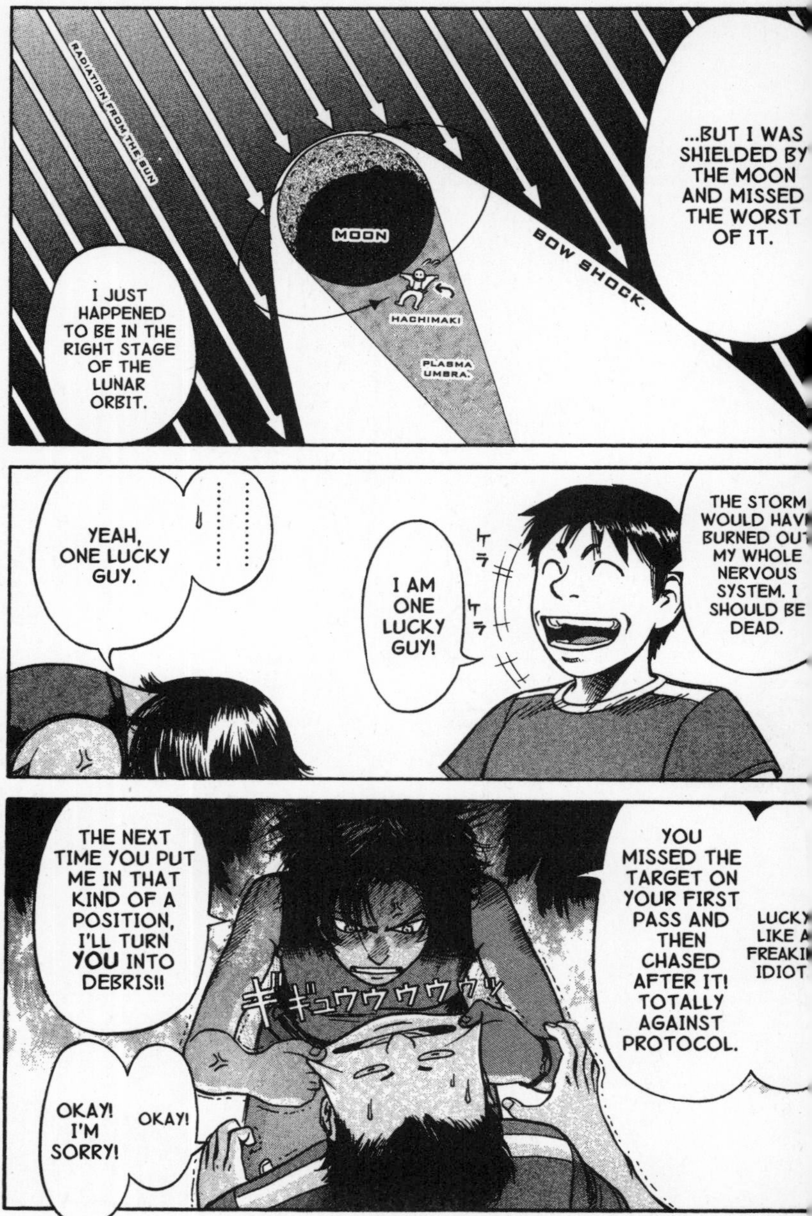
...BUT I WAS SHIELDED BY THE MOON AND MISSED THE WORST OF IT.
RADIATION FROM THE SUN
BOW SHOCK.
MOON
HACHIMAKI
PLASMA UMBRA.
I JUST HAPPENED TO BE IN THE RIGHT STAGE OF THE LUNAR ORBIT.
THE STORM WOULD HAV BURNED OUT MY WHOLE NERVOUS SYSTEM. I SHOULD BE DEAD.
ケラ
ケラ
I AM ONE LUCKY GUY!
......
YEAH, ONE LUCKY GUY.
YOU MISSED THE TARGET ON YOUR FIRST PASS AND THEN CHASED AFTER IT! TOTALLY AGAINST PROTOCOL.
LUCKY LIKE A FREAKI IDIOT
THE NEXT TIME YOU PUT ME IN THAT KIND OF A POSITION, I'LL TURN **YOU** INTO DEBRIS!!
ギュウウウウウッ
OKAY!
OKAY! I'M SORRY!

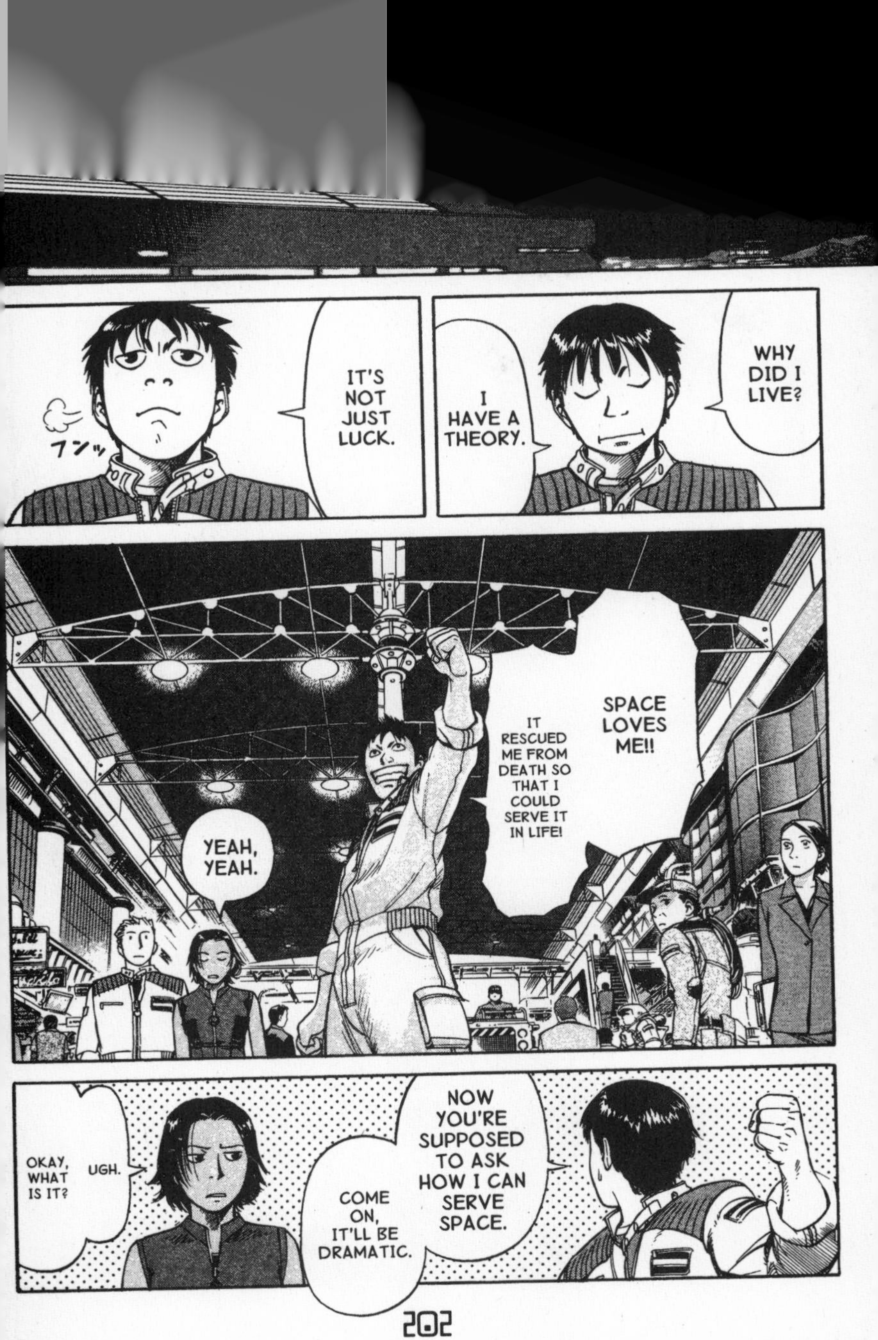
WHY DID I LIVE?
I HAVE A THEORY.
IT'S NOT JUST LUCK.
フンッ
SPACE LOVES ME!!
IT RESCUED ME FROM DEATH SO THAT I COULD SERVE IT IN LIFE!
YEAH, YEAH.
NOW YOU'RE SUPPOSED TO ASK HOW I CAN SERVE SPACE.
COME ON, IT'LL BE DRAMATIC.
UGH.
OKAY, WHAT IS IT?

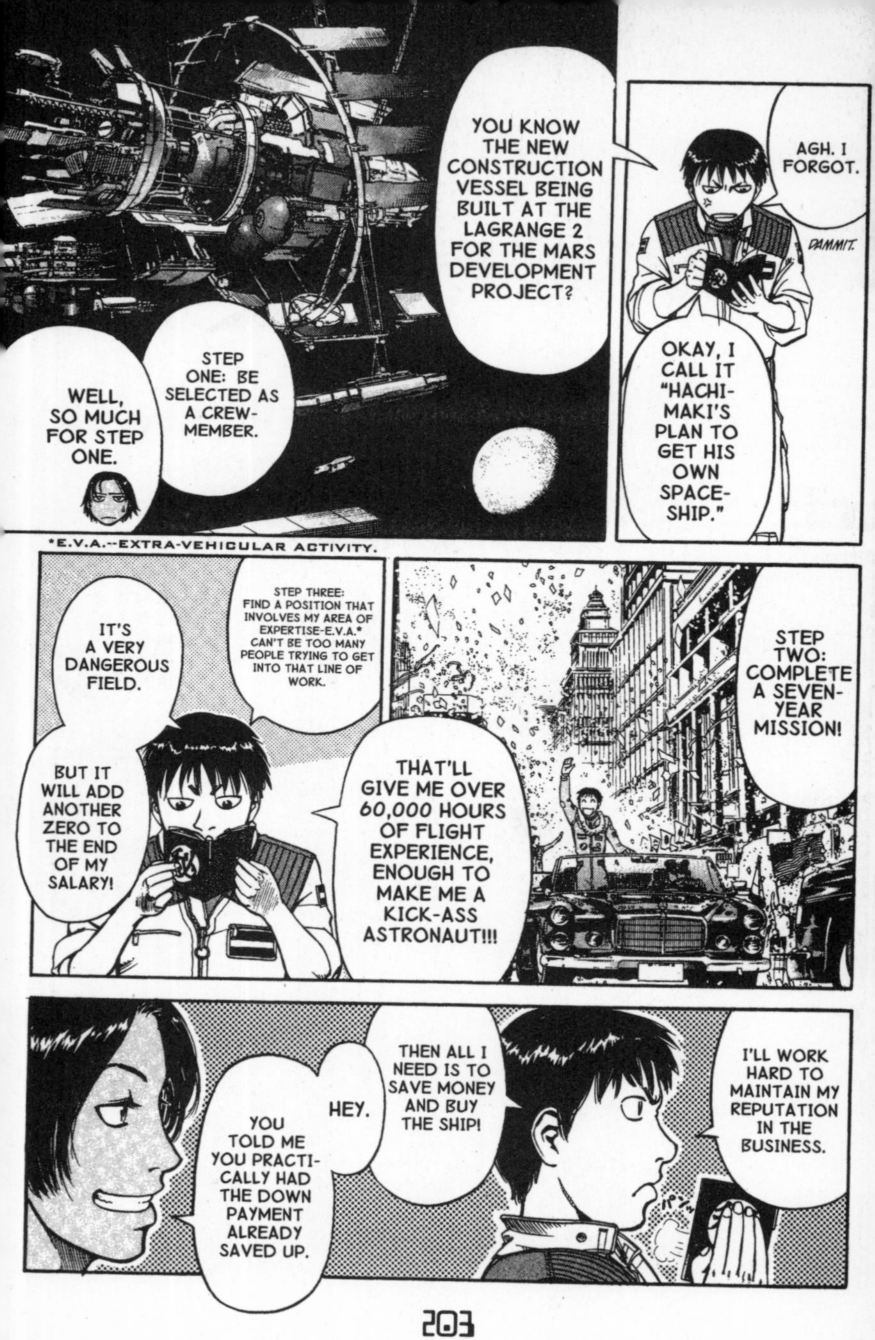
AGH. I FORGOT.
DAMMIT.
OKAY, I CALL IT "HACHI-MAKI'S PLAN TO GET HIS OWN SPACE-SHIP."
YOU KNOW THE NEW CONSTRUCTION VESSEL BEING BUILT AT THE LAGRANGE 2 FOR THE MARS DEVELOPMENT PROJECT?
STEP ONE: BE SELECTED AS A CREW-MEMBER.
WELL, SO MUCH FOR STEP ONE.
*E.V.A.--EXTRA-VEHICULAR ACTIVITY.
STEP TWO: COMPLETE A SEVEN-YEAR MISSION!
STEP THREE: FIND A POSITION THAT INVOLVES MY AREA OF EXPERTISE-E.V.A.* CAN'T BE TOO MANY PEOPLE TRYING TO GET INTO THAT LINE OF WORK.
IT'S A VERY DANGEROUS FIELD.
THAT'LL GIVE ME OVER 60,000 HOURS OF FLIGHT EXPERIENCE, ENOUGH TO MAKE ME A KICK-ASS ASTRONAUT!!!
BUT IT WILL ADD ANOTHER ZERO TO THE END OF MY SALARY!
I'LL WORK HARD TO MAINTAIN MY REPUTATION IN THE BUSINESS.
THEN ALL I NEED IS TO SAVE MONEY AND BUY THE SHIP!
HEY.
YOU TOLD ME YOU PRACTI-CALLY HAD THE DOWN PAYMENT ALREADY SAVED UP.

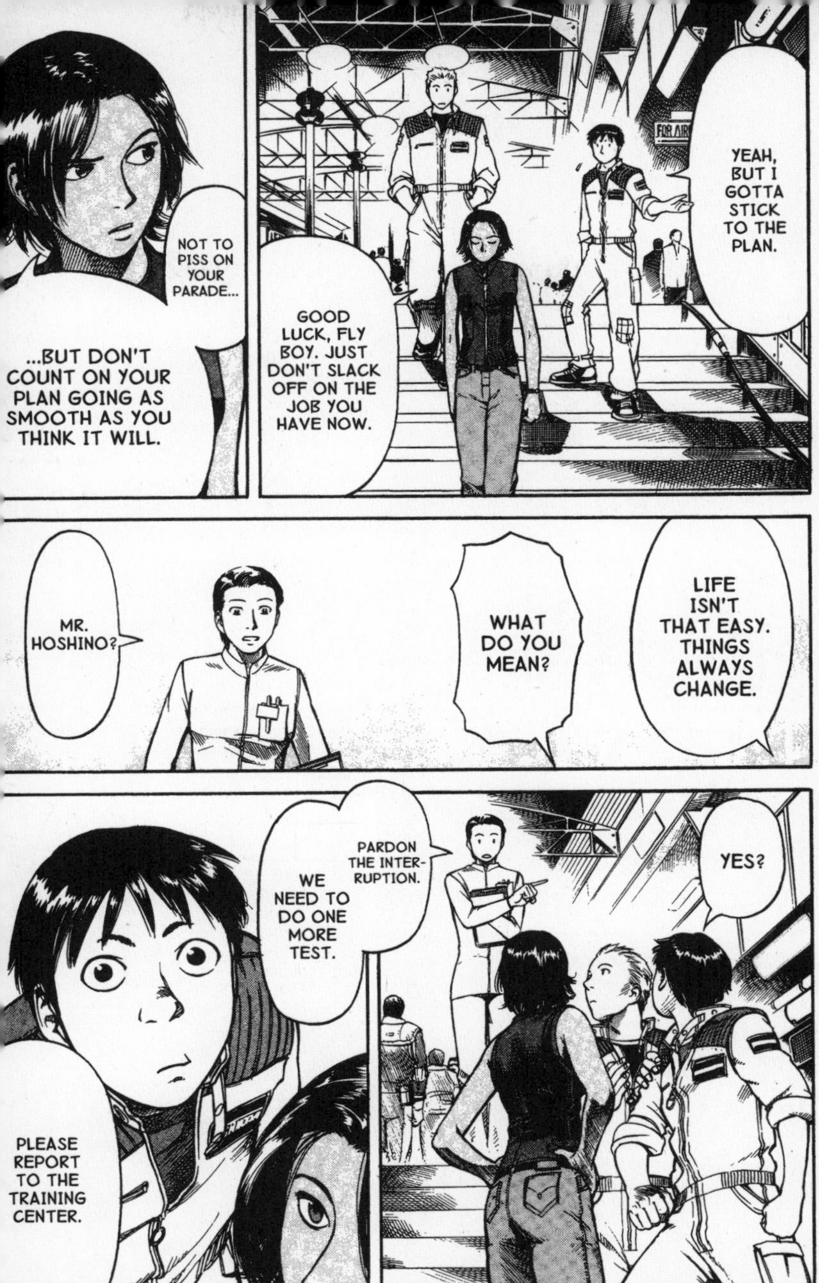
YEAH, BUT I GOTTA STICK TO THE PLAN.
GOOD LUCK, FLY BOY. JUST DON'T SLACK OFF ON THE JOB YOU HAVE NOW.
NOT TO PISS ON YOUR PARADE...
...BUT DON'T COUNT ON YOUR PLAN GOING AS SMOOTH AS YOU THINK IT WILL.
LIFE ISN'T THAT EASY. THINGS ALWAYS CHANGE.
WHAT DO YOU MEAN?
MR. HOSHINO?
YES?
PARDON THE INTERRUPTION.
WE NEED TO DO ONE MORE TEST.
PLEASE REPORT TO THE TRAINING CENTER.

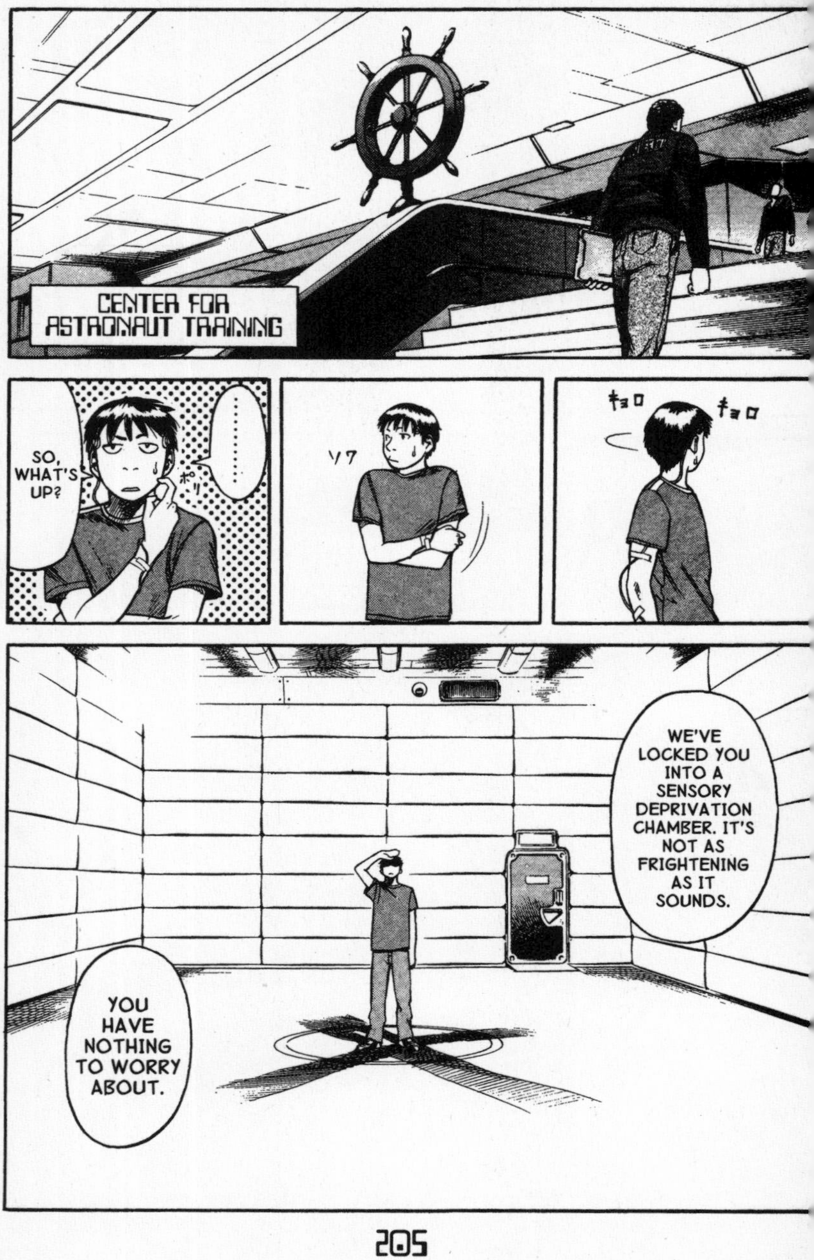

CENTER FOR ASTRONAUT TRAINING
キョロ
キョロ
ソワ
......
ポリ
SO, WHAT'S UP?
WE'VE LOCKED YOU INTO A SENSORY DEPRIVATION CHAMBER. IT'S NOT AS FRIGHTENING AS IT SOUNDS.
YOU HAVE NOTHING TO WORRY ABOUT.

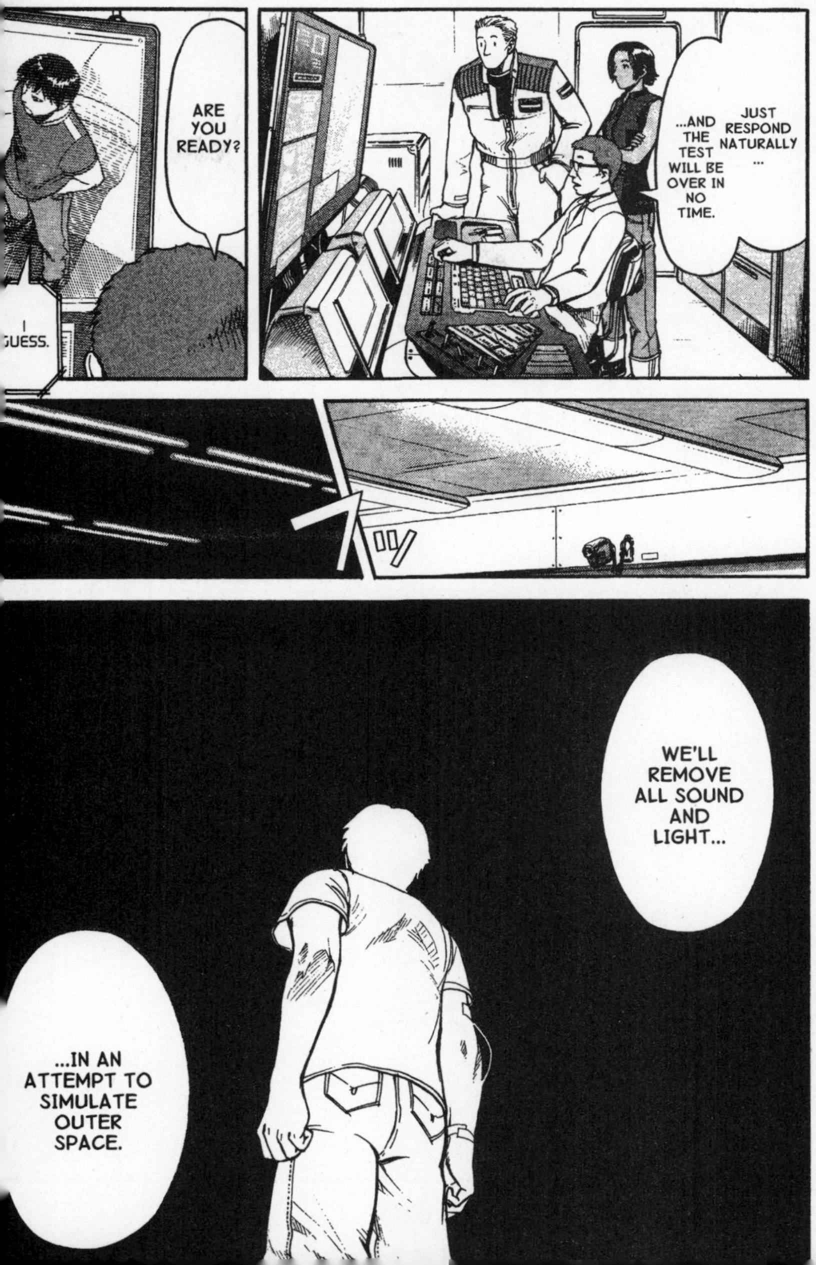
JUST RESPOND NATURALLY...
...AND THE TEST WILL BE OVER IN NO TIME.
ARE YOU READY?
I GUESS.
WE'LL REMOVE ALL SOUND AND LIGHT...
...IN AN ATTEMPT TO SIMULATE OUTER SPACE.

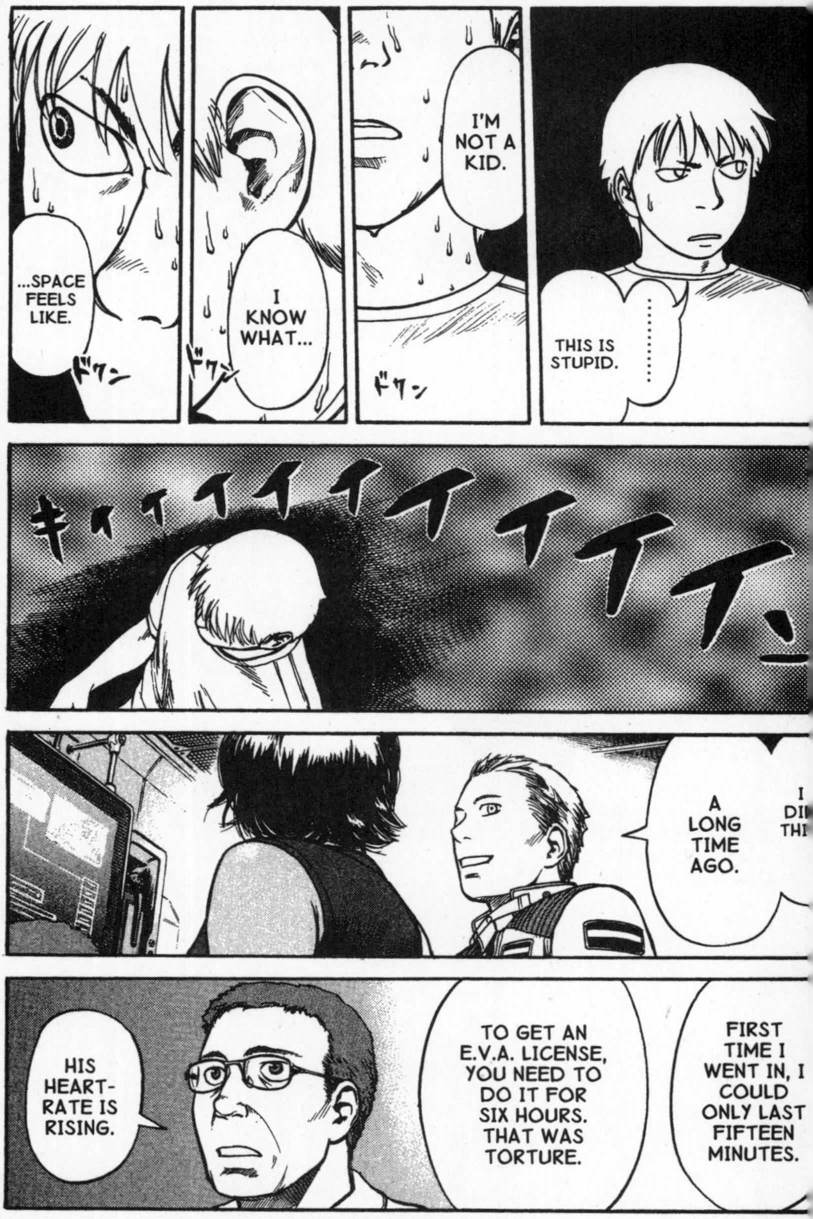
......
THIS IS STUPID.
I'M NOT A KID.
ドクン
I KNOW WHAT...
ドクン
...SPACE FEELS LIKE.
ドクン
キィイイイイイイン
A LONG TIME AGO.
FIRST TIME I WENT IN, I COULD ONLY LAST FIFTEEN MINUTES.
TO GET AN E.V.A. LICENSE, YOU NEED TO DO IT FOR SIX HOURS. THAT WAS TORTURE.
HIS HEART-RATE IS RISING.

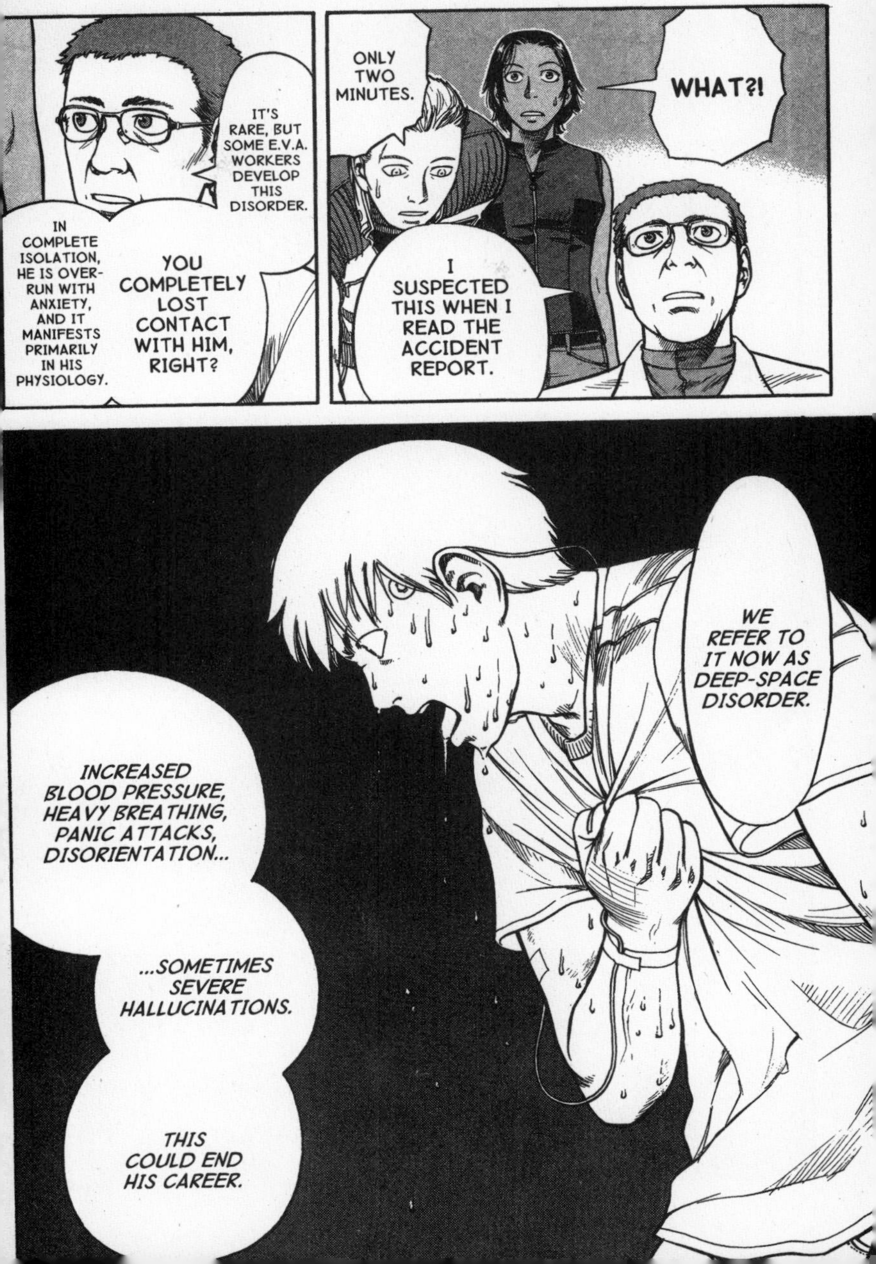
WHAT?!
ONLY TWO MINUTES.
I SUSPECTED THIS WHEN I READ THE ACCIDENT REPORT.
IT'S RARE, BUT SOME E.V.A. WORKERS DEVELOP THIS DISORDER.
YOU COMPLETELY LOST CONTACT WITH HIM, RIGHT?
IN COMPLETE ISOLATION, HE IS OVER-RUN WITH ANXIETY, AND IT MANIFESTS PRIMARILY IN HIS PHYSIOLOGY.
WE REFER TO IT NOW AS DEEP-SPACE DISORDER.
INCREASED BLOOD PRESSURE, HEAVY BREATHING, PANIC ATTACKS, DISORIENTATION...
...SOMETIMES SEVERE HALLUCINATIONS.
THIS COULD END HIS CAREER.

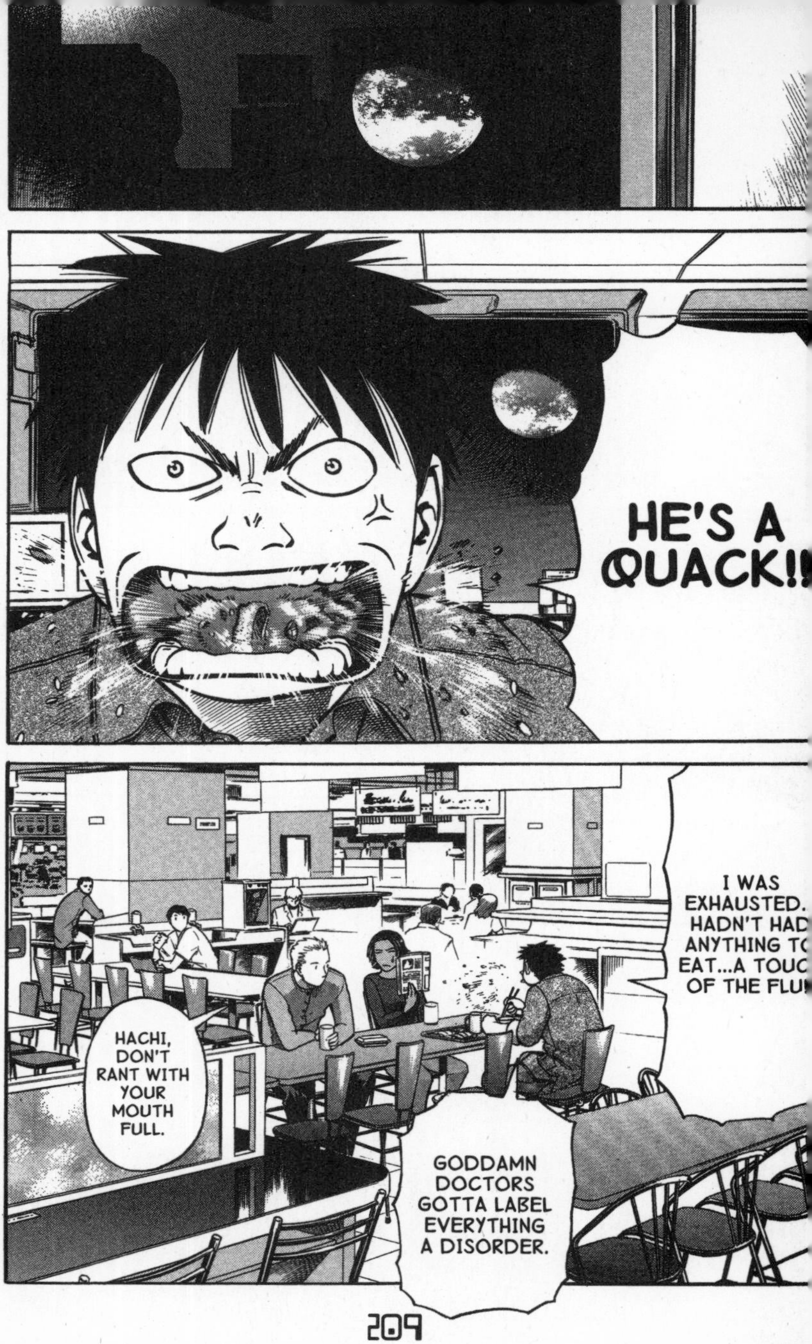
HE'S A QUACK!!
I WAS EXHAUSTED. HADN'T HAD ANYTHING TO EAT...A TOUC OF THE FLU
GODDAMN DOCTORS GOTTA LABEL EVERYTHING A DISORDER.
HACHI, DON'T RANT WITH YOUR MOUTH FULL.

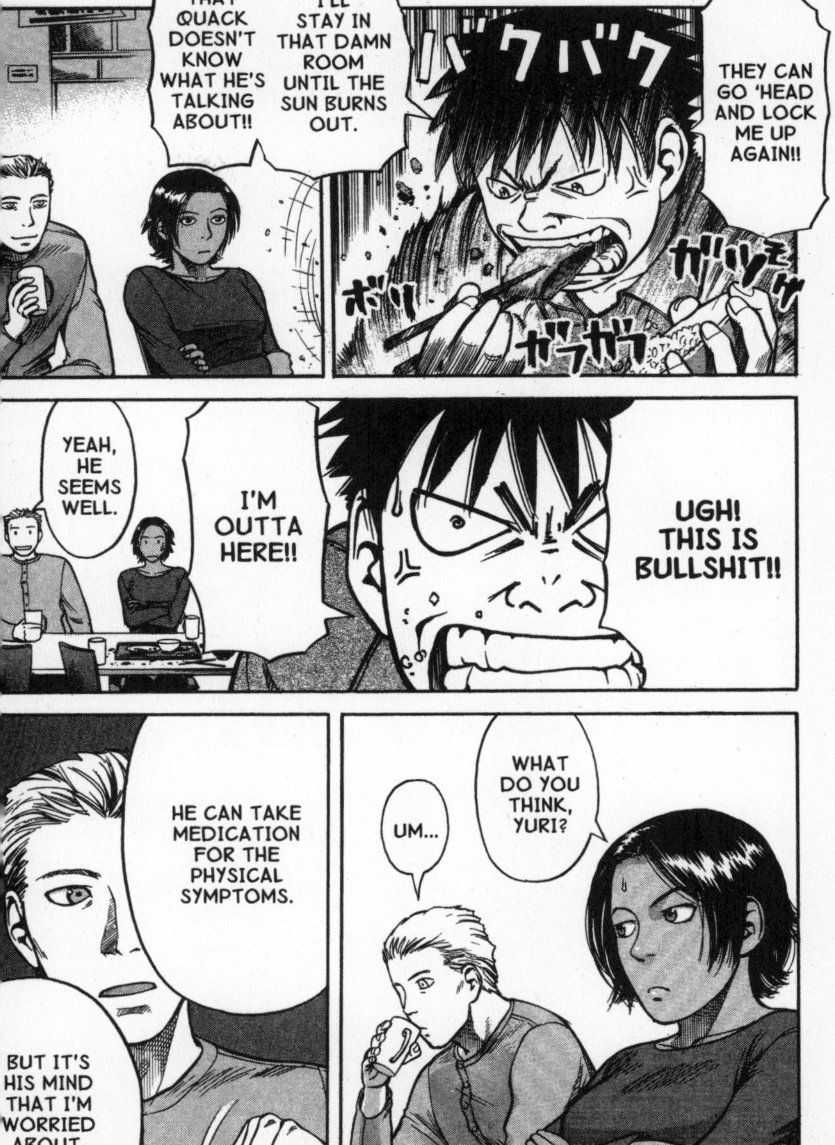

THEY CAN GO 'HEAD AND LOCK ME UP AGAIN!!
バクバク
I'LL STAY IN THAT DAMN ROOM UNTIL THE SUN BURNS OUT.
THAT QUACK DOESN'T KNOW WHAT HE'S TALKING ABOUT!!
UGH! THIS IS BULLSHIT!!
I'M OUTTA HERE!!
YEAH, HE SEEMS WELL.
WHAT DO YOU THINK, YURI?
UM...
HE CAN TAKE MEDICATION FOR THE PHYSICAL SYMPTOMS.
BUT IT'S HIS MIND THAT I'M WORRIED ABOUT.

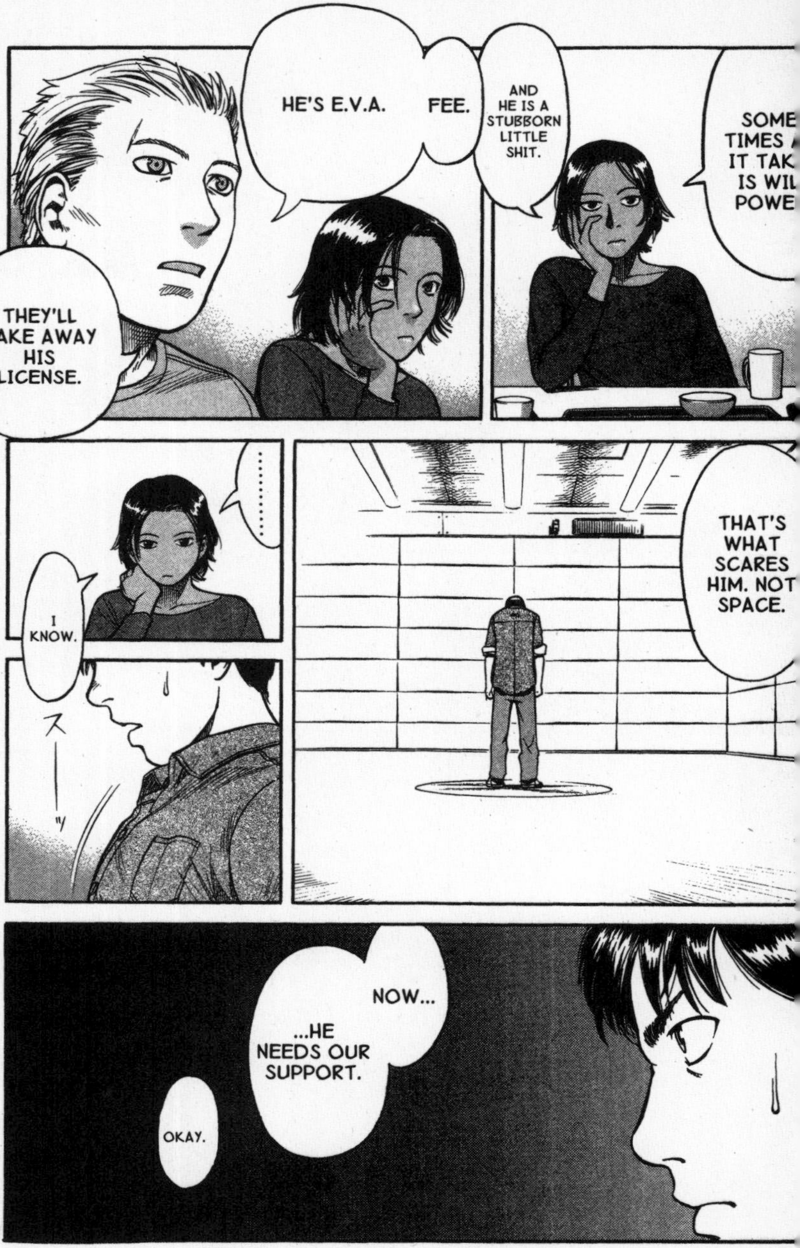
SOME TIMES
IT TAK
IS WIL
POWE
AND HE IS A STUBBORN LITTLE SHIT.
HE'S E.V.A. FEE.
THEY'LL TAKE AWAY HIS LICENSE.
THAT'S WHAT SCARES HIM. NOT SPACE.
......
I KNOW.
スーーッ
NOW...
...HE NEEDS OUR SUPPORT.
OKAY.

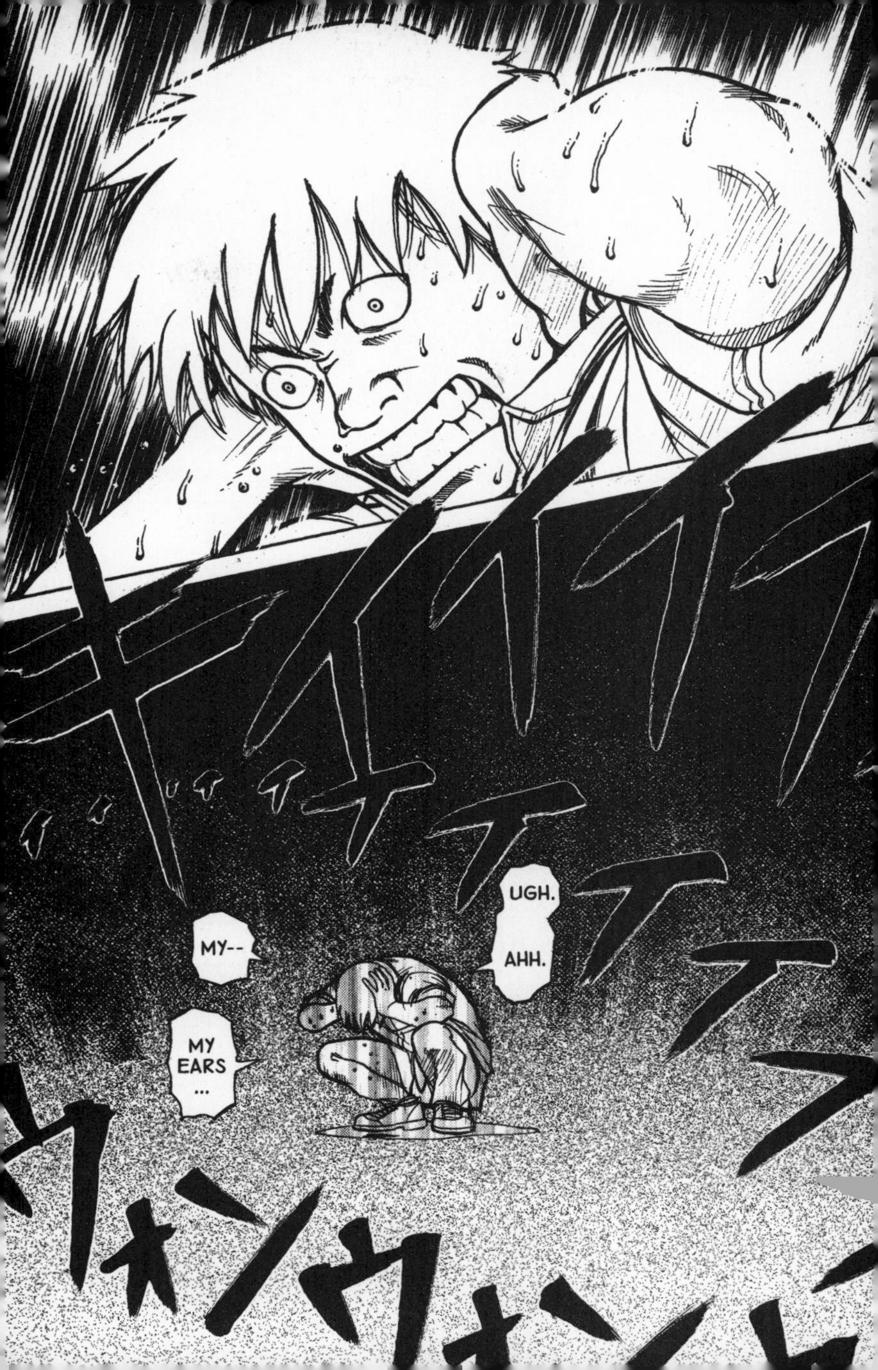
UGH.
AHH.
MY--
MY EARS ...

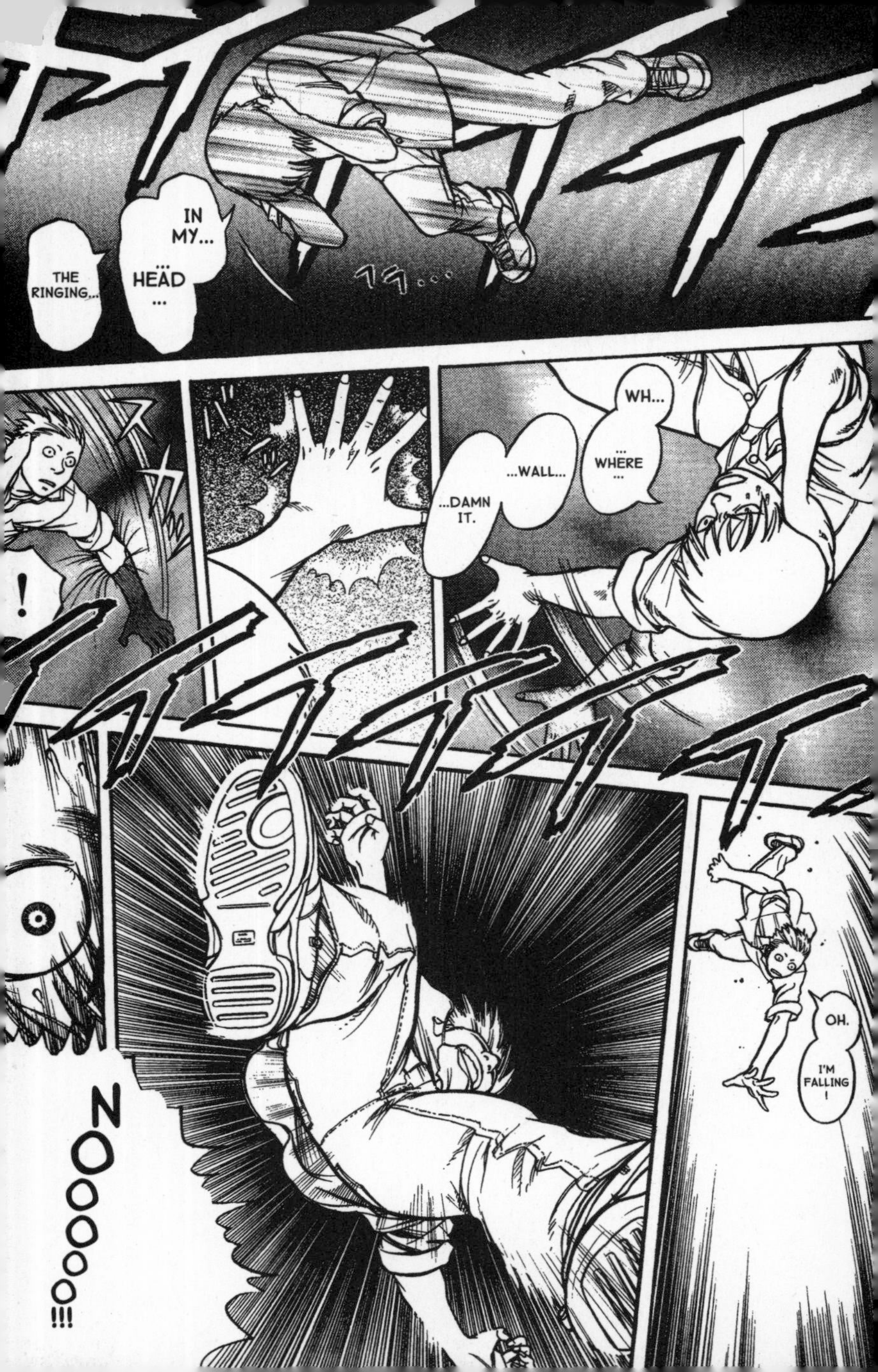

IN MY... ...HEAD ...
THE RINGING...
WH...
...WHERE...
...WALL...
...DAMN IT.
!
OH.
I'M FALLING!
NOOOOOOO!!!

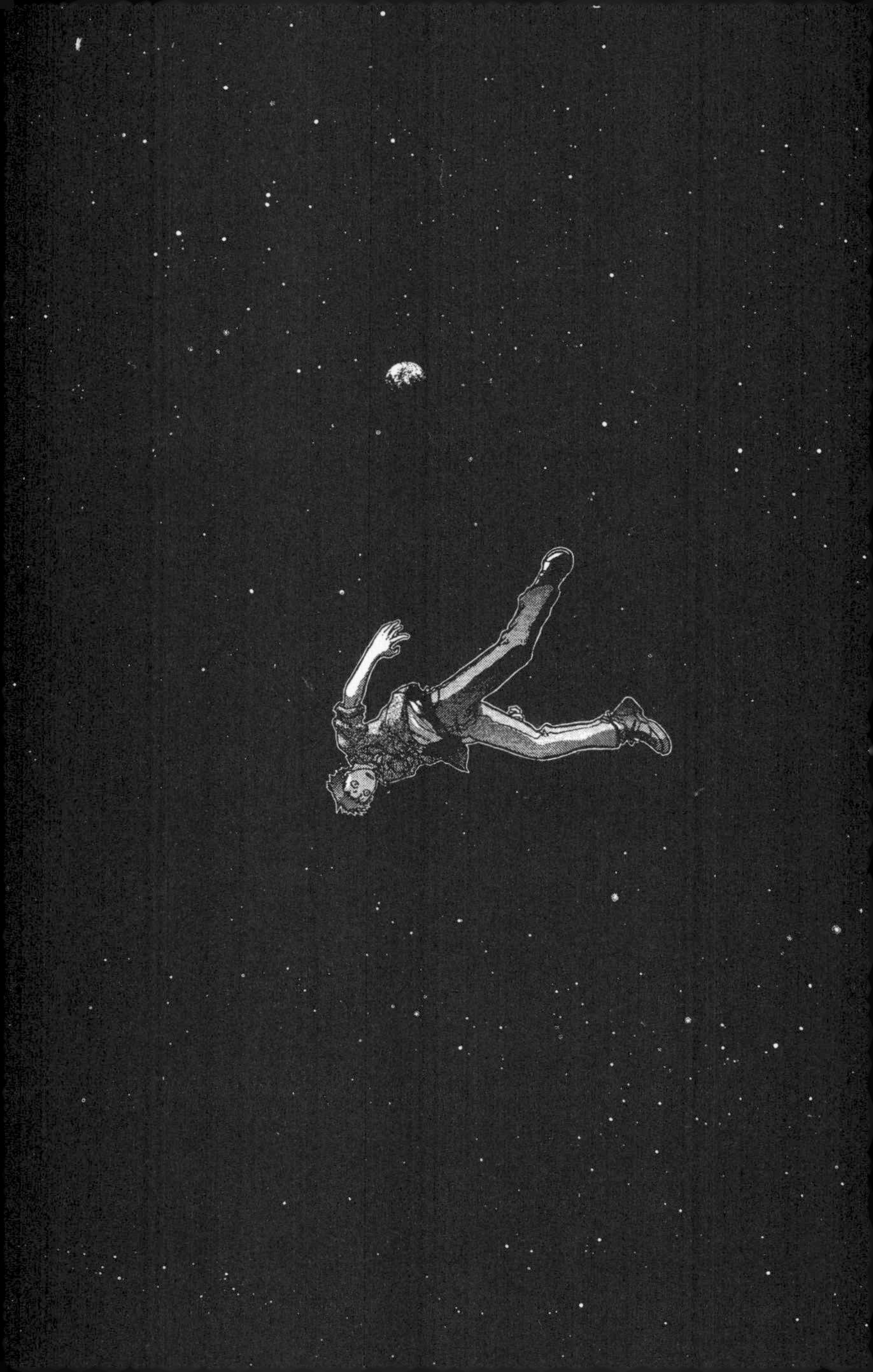

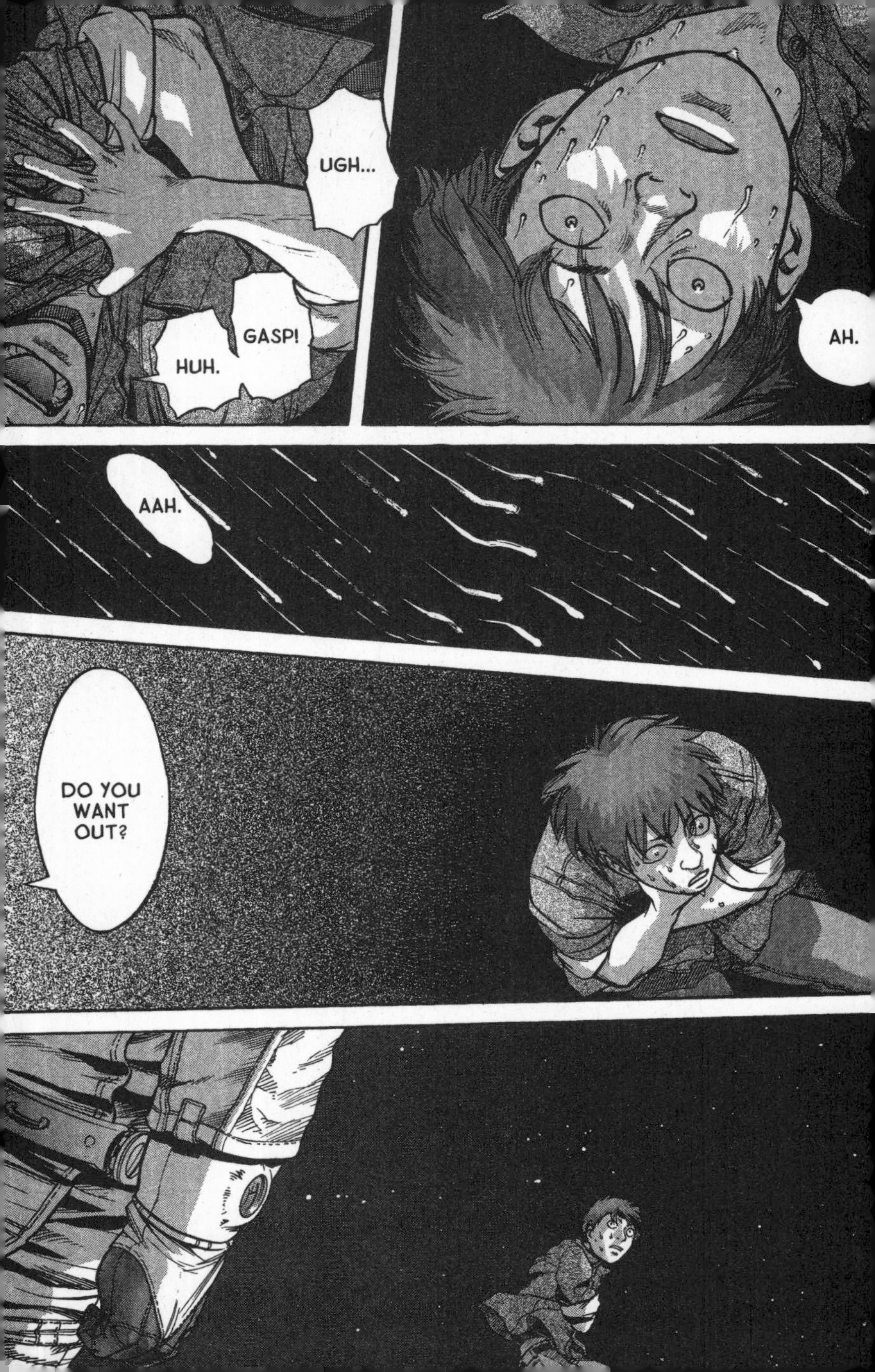
AH.
UGH...
GASP!
HUH.
AAH.
DO YOU WANT OUT?

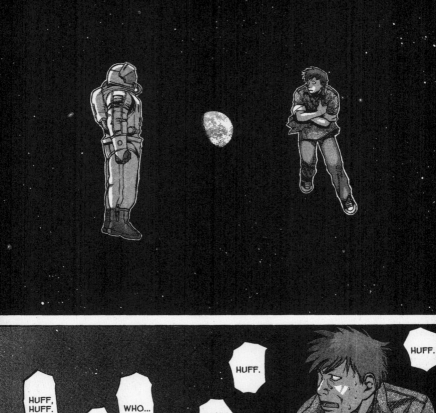

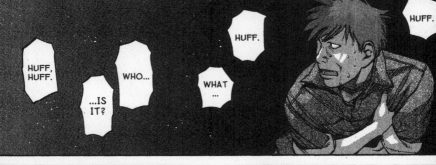

HUFF, HUFF.

...IS IT?

WHO...

HUFF.

WHAT...

HUFF.

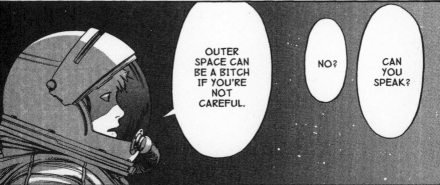

OUTER SPACE CAN BE A BITCH IF YOU'RE NOT CAREFUL.

NO?

CAN YOU SPEAK?

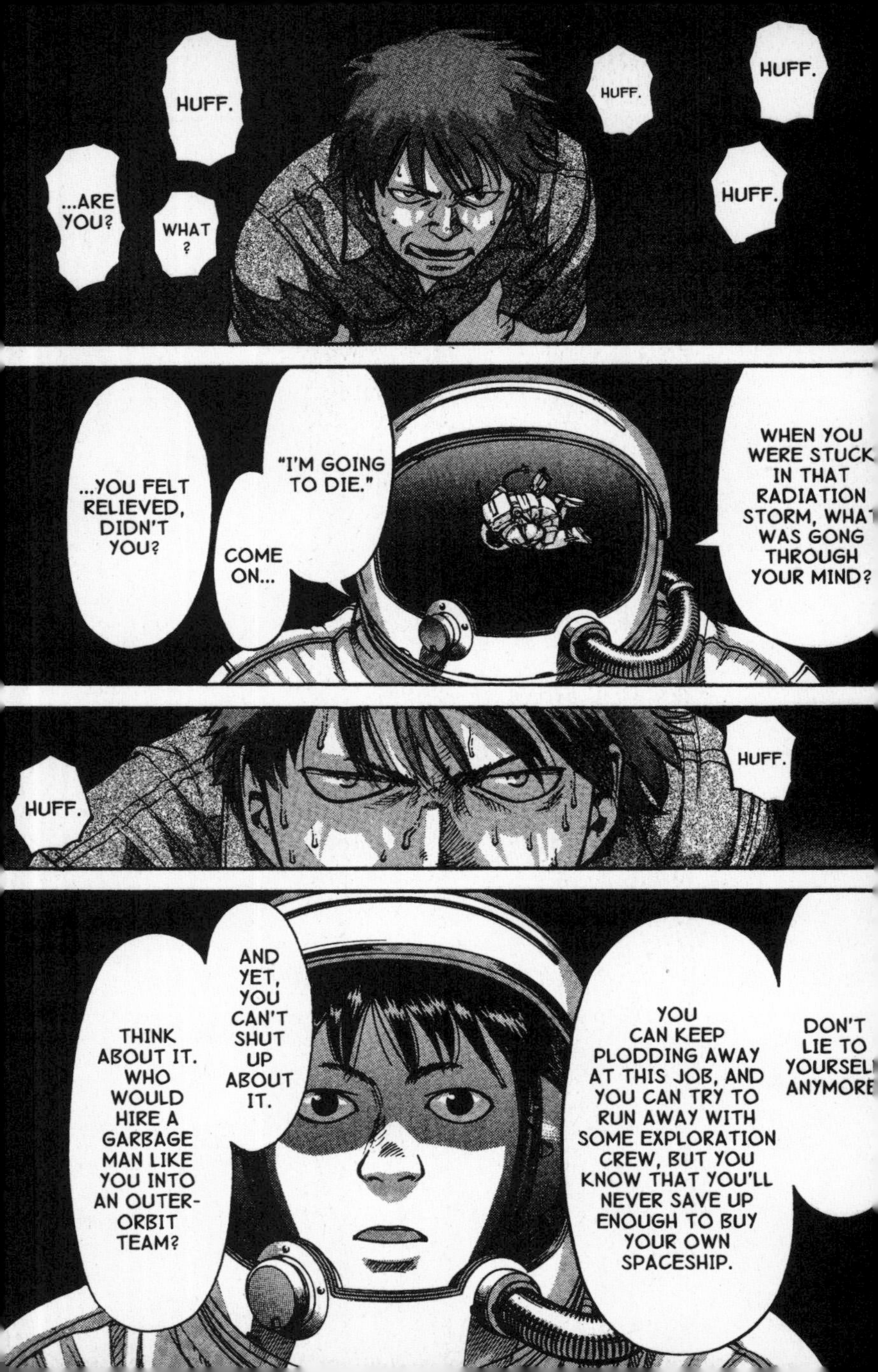
HUFF.
HUFF.
HUFF.
HUFF.
WHAT?
...ARE YOU?
WHEN YOU WERE STUCK IN THAT RADIATION STORM, WHAT WAS GONG THROUGH YOUR MIND?
"I'M GOING TO DIE." COME ON...
...YOU FELT RELIEVED, DIDN'T YOU?
HUFF.
HUFF.
DON'T LIE TO YOURSEL ANYMORE
YOU CAN KEEP PLODDING AWAY AT THIS JOB, AND YOU CAN TRY TO RUN AWAY WITH SOME EXPLORATION CREW, BUT YOU KNOW THAT YOU'LL NEVER SAVE UP ENOUGH TO BUY YOUR OWN SPACESHIP.
AND YET, YOU CAN'T SHUT UP ABOUT IT.
THINK ABOUT IT. WHO WOULD HIRE A GARBAGE MAN LIKE YOU INTO AN OUTER-ORBIT TEAM?

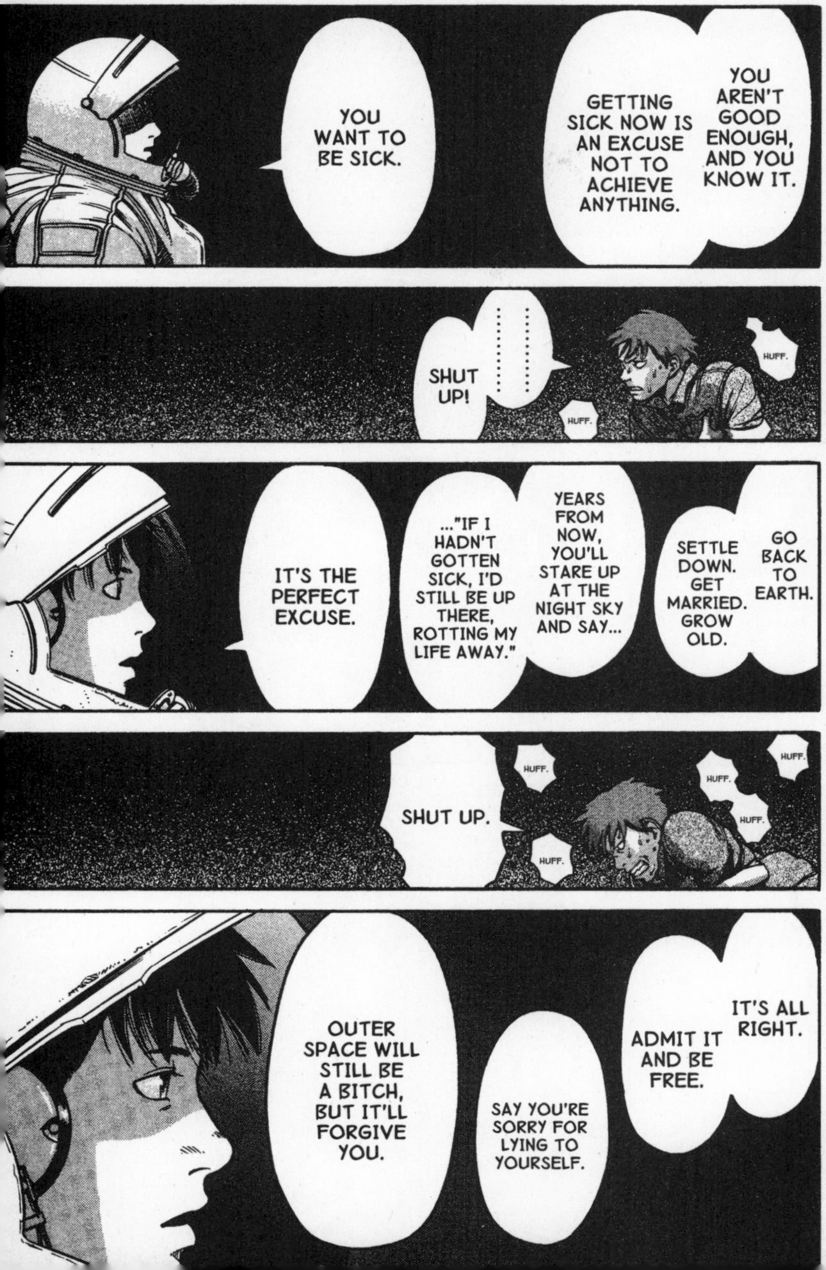
YOU AREN'T GOOD ENOUGH, AND YOU KNOW IT.
GETTING SICK NOW IS AN EXCUSE NOT TO ACHIEVE ANYTHING.
YOU WANT TO BE SICK.
HUFF.
......
HUFF.
SHUT UP!
GO BACK TO EARTH.
SETTLE DOWN. GET MARRIED. GROW OLD.
YEARS FROM NOW, YOU'LL STARE UP AT THE NIGHT SKY AND SAY...
..."IF I HADN'T GOTTEN SICK, I'D STILL BE UP THERE, ROTTING MY LIFE AWAY."
IT'S THE PERFECT EXCUSE.
HUFF.
HUFF.
HUFF.
HUFF.
HUFF.
SHUT UP.
IT'S ALL RIGHT.
ADMIT IT AND BE FREE.
SAY YOU'RE SORRY FOR LYING TO YOURSELF.
OUTER SPACE WILL STILL BE A BITCH, BUT IT'LL FORGIVE YOU.

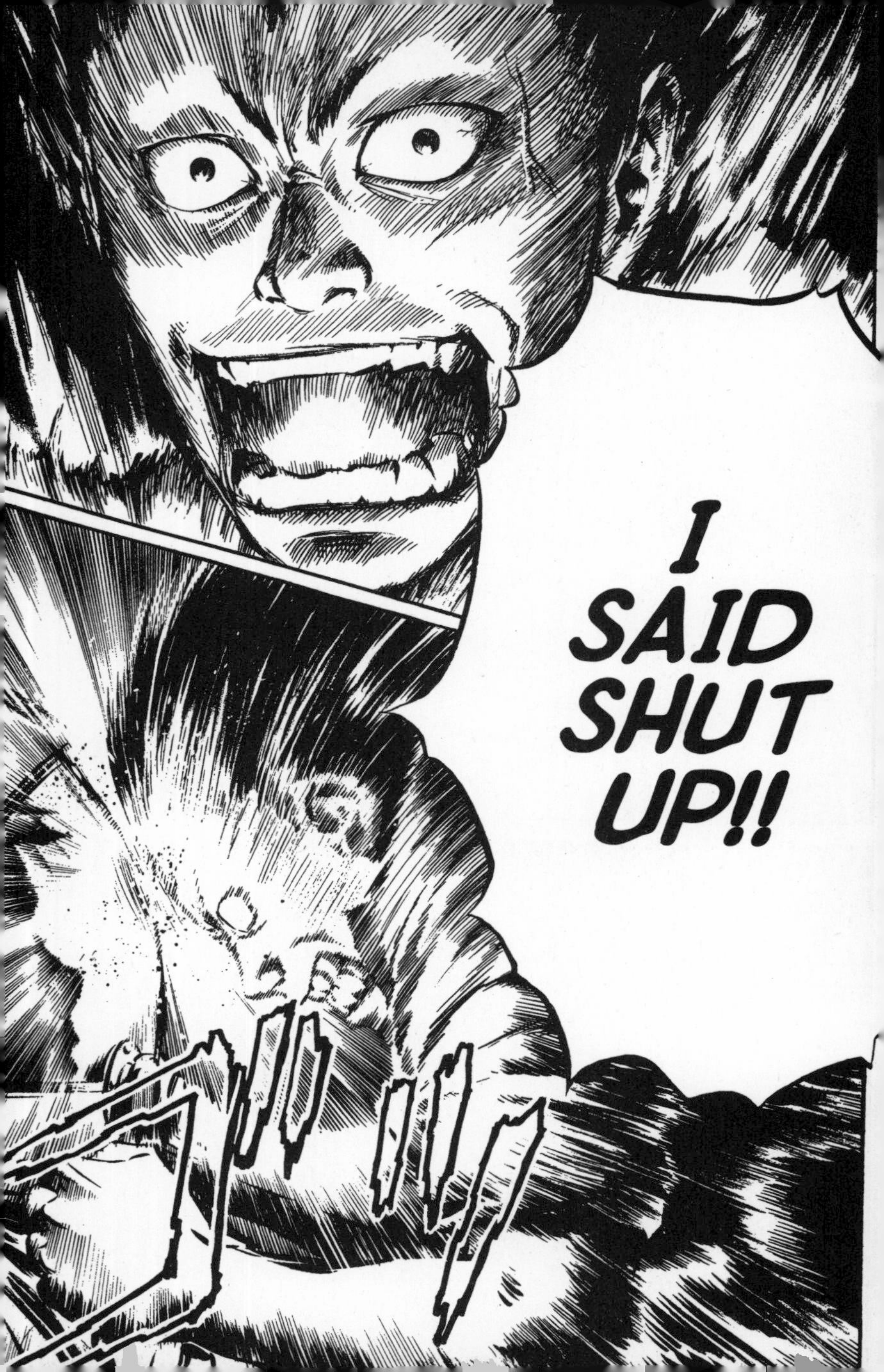
I SAID SHUT UP!!

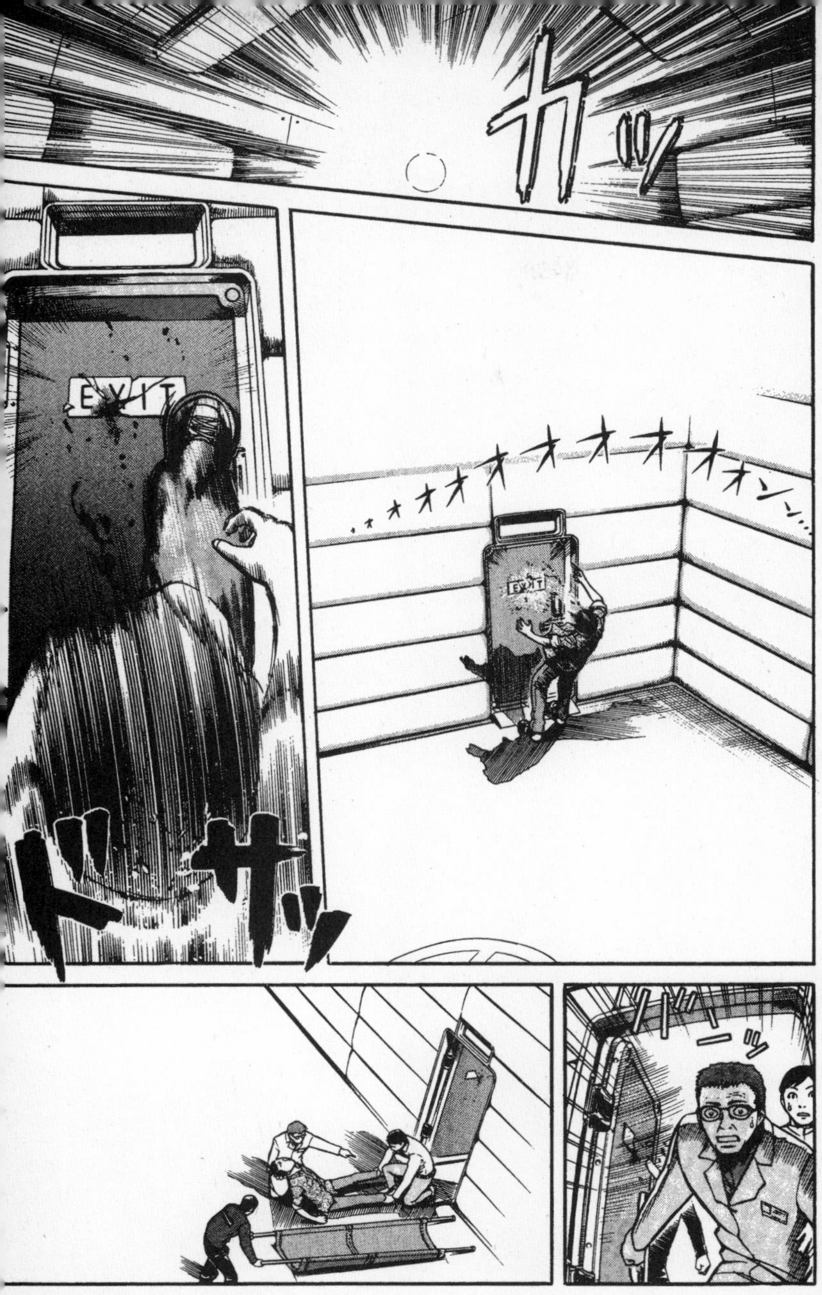
カッ
‥ォォオオオオオオオオオン…
ドサッ

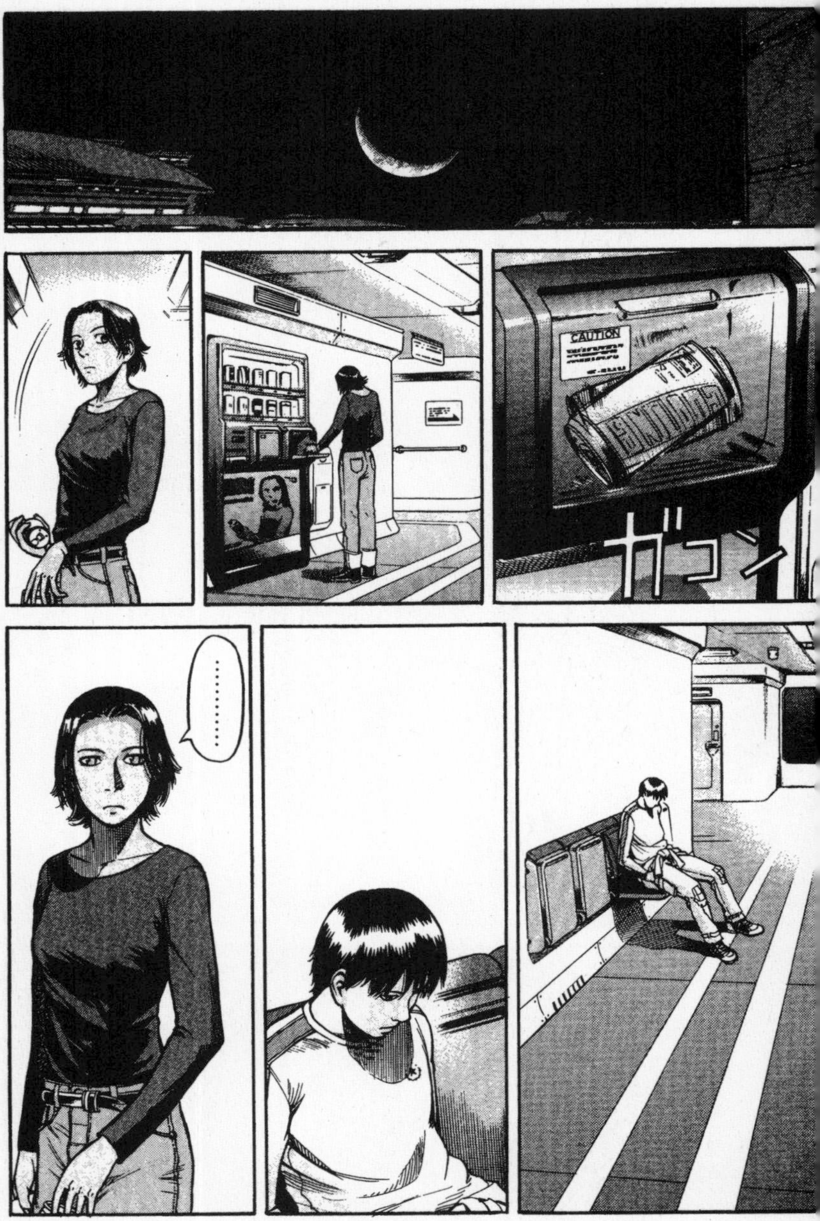
CAUTION
ガコン
……

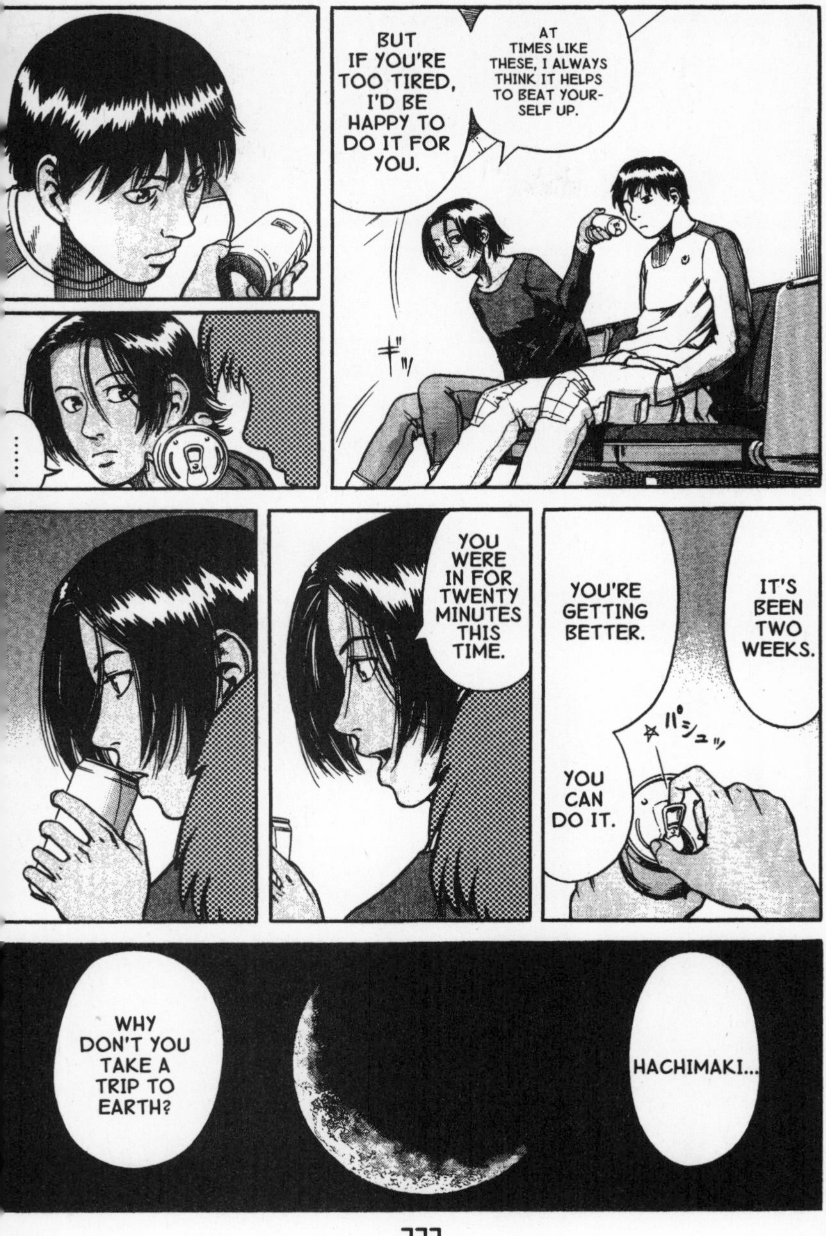
AT TIMES LIKE THESE, I ALWAYS THINK IT HELPS TO BEAT YOURSELF UP.
BUT IF YOU'RE TOO TIRED, I'D BE HAPPY TO DO IT FOR YOU.
ギッ
......
IT'S BEEN TWO WEEKS.
YOU'RE GETTING BETTER.
パシュッ
YOU CAN DO IT.
YOU WERE IN FOR TWENTY MINUTES THIS TIME.
HACHIMAKI...
WHY DON'T YOU TAKE A TRIP TO EARTH?

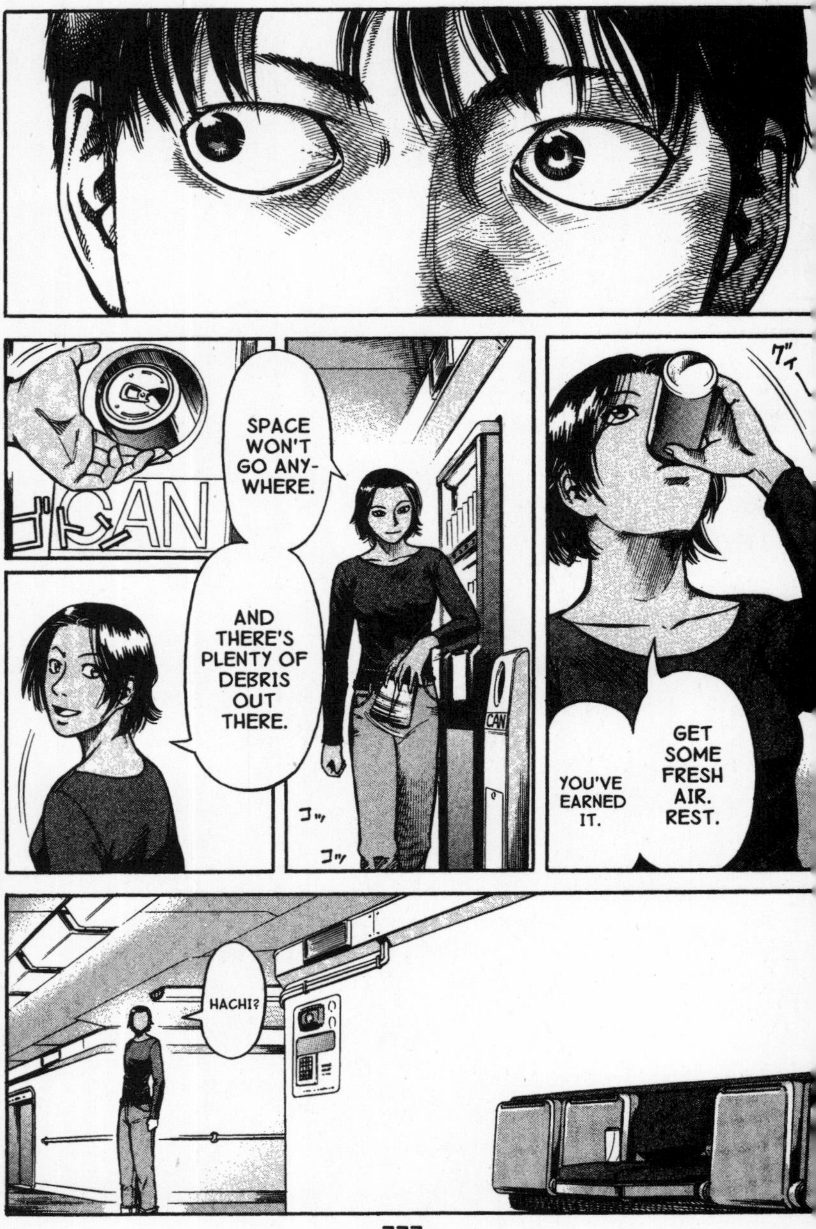
GET SOME FRESH AIR. REST.
YOU'VE EARNED IT.
SPACE WON'T GO ANYWHERE.
AND THERE'S PLENTY OF DEBRIS OUT THERE.
コッ
コッ
CAN
HACHI?

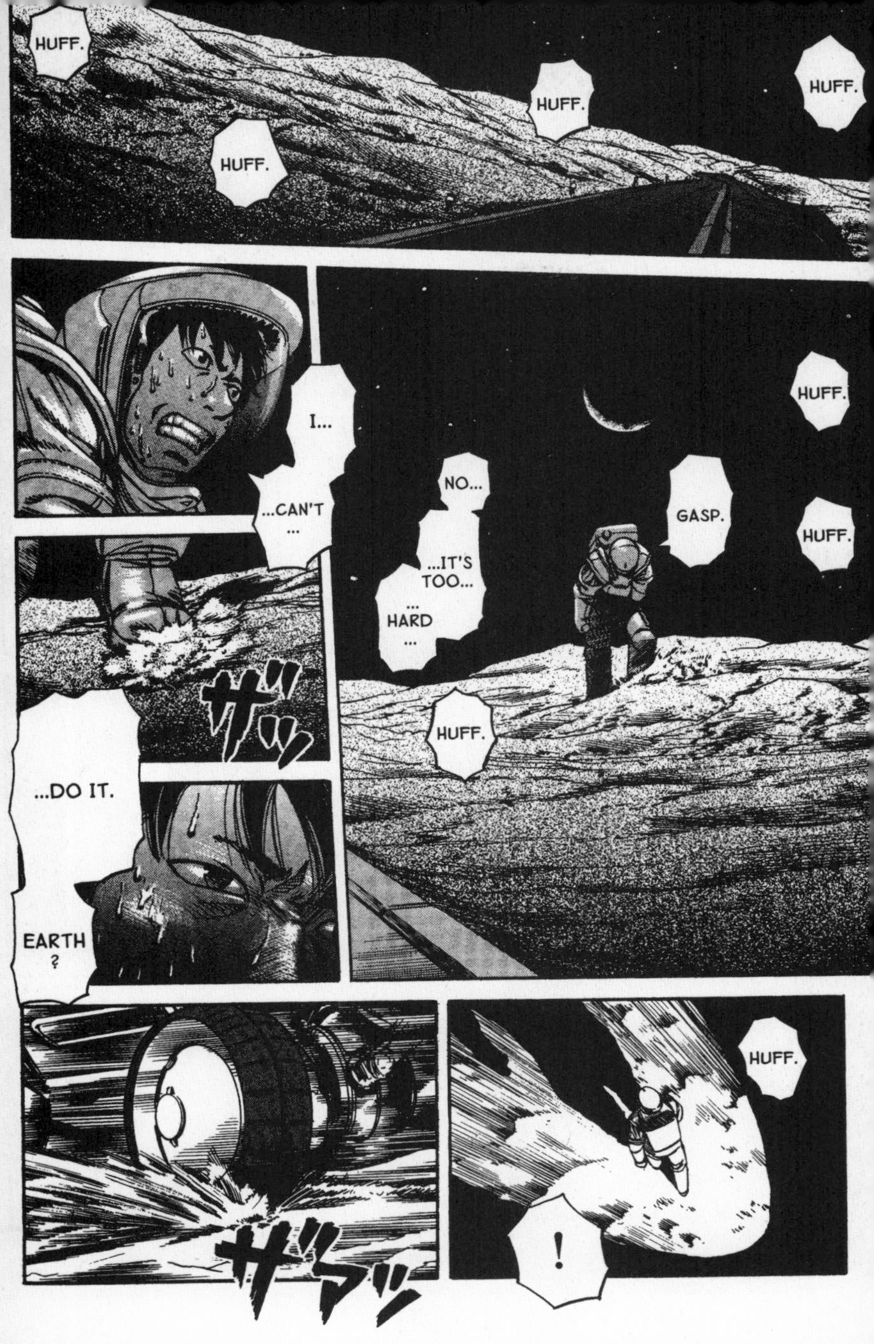
HUFF.
HUFF.
HUFF.
HUFF.
HUFF.
GASP.
HUFF.
NO...
...IT'S TOO...
... HARD ...
HUFF.
I...
...CAN'T ...
ザッ
...DO IT.
EARTH ?
HUFF.
!
ザラッ

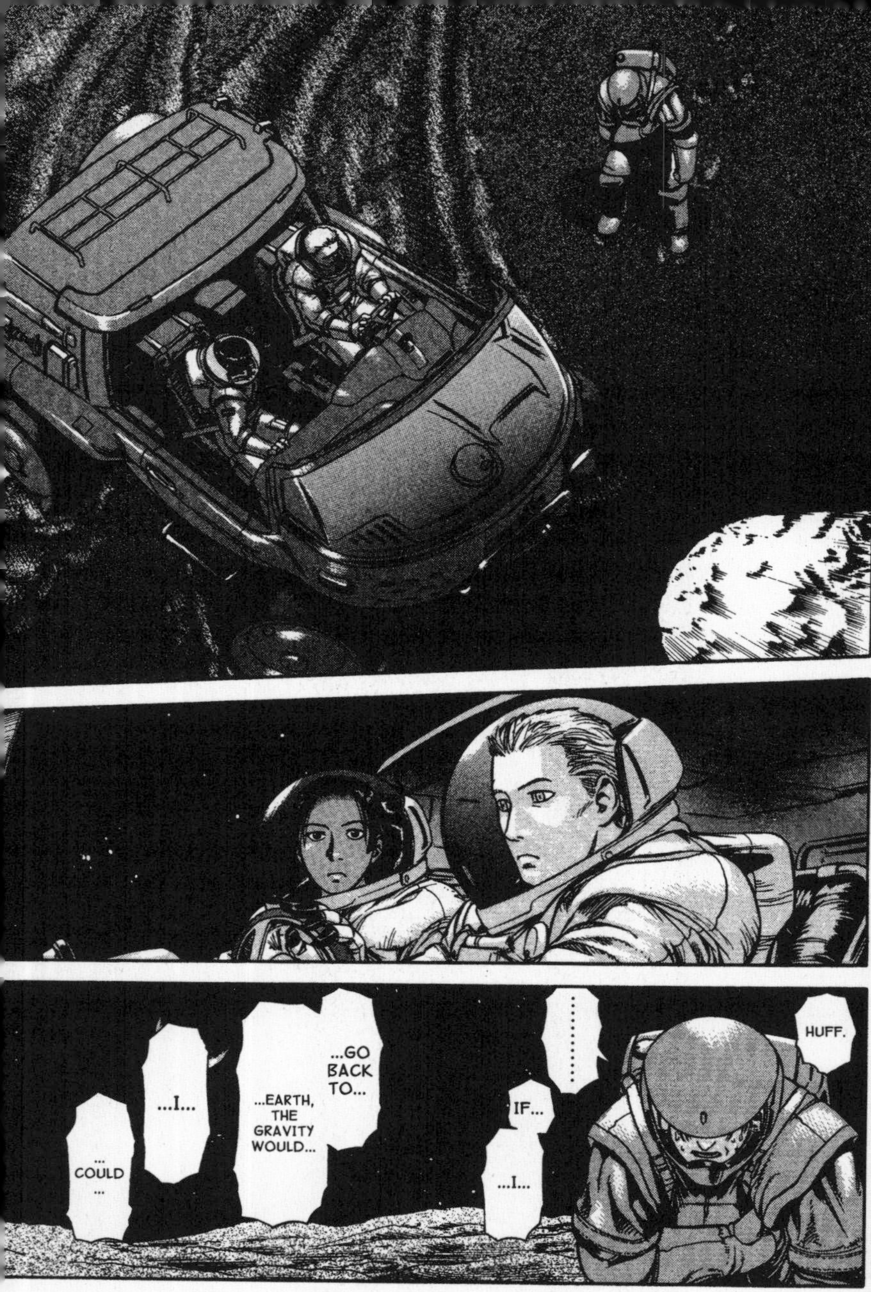
HUFF.
......
IF...
...I...
...GO BACK TO...
...EARTH, THE GRAVITY WOULD...
...I...
... COULD ...

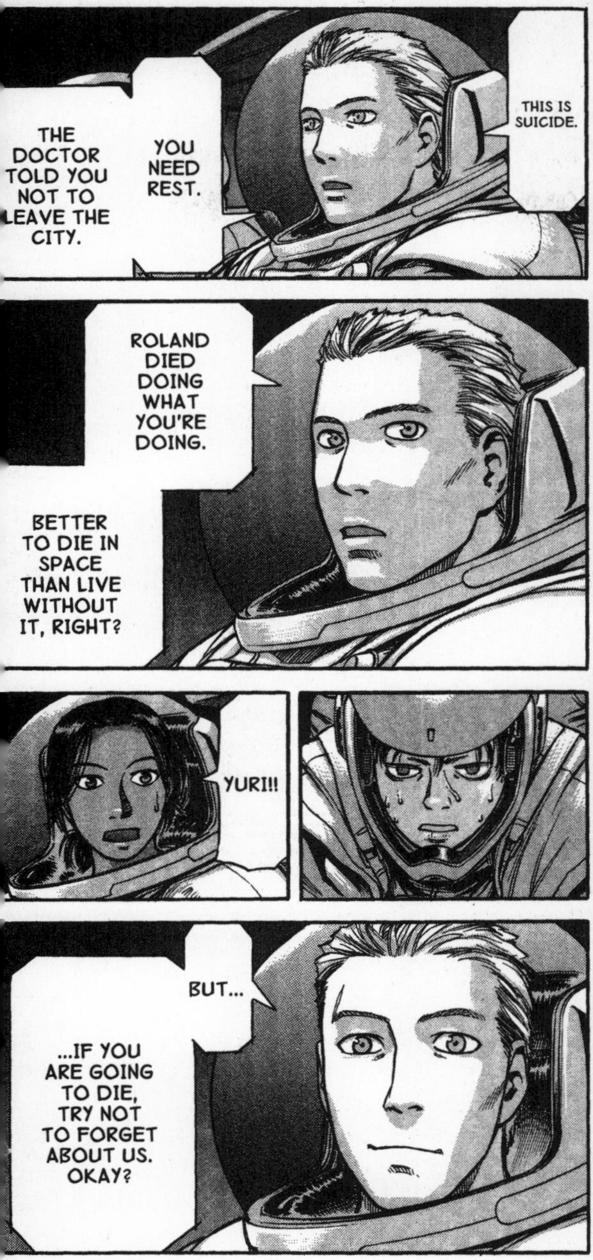

THIS IS SUICIDE.
YOU NEED REST.
THE DOCTOR TOLD YOU NOT TO LEAVE THE CITY.
ROLAND DIED DOING WHAT YOU'RE DOING.
BETTER TO DIE IN SPACE THAN LIVE WITHOUT IT, RIGHT?
YURI!!
BUT...
...IF YOU ARE GOING TO DIE, TRY NOT TO FORGET ABOUT US. OKAY?

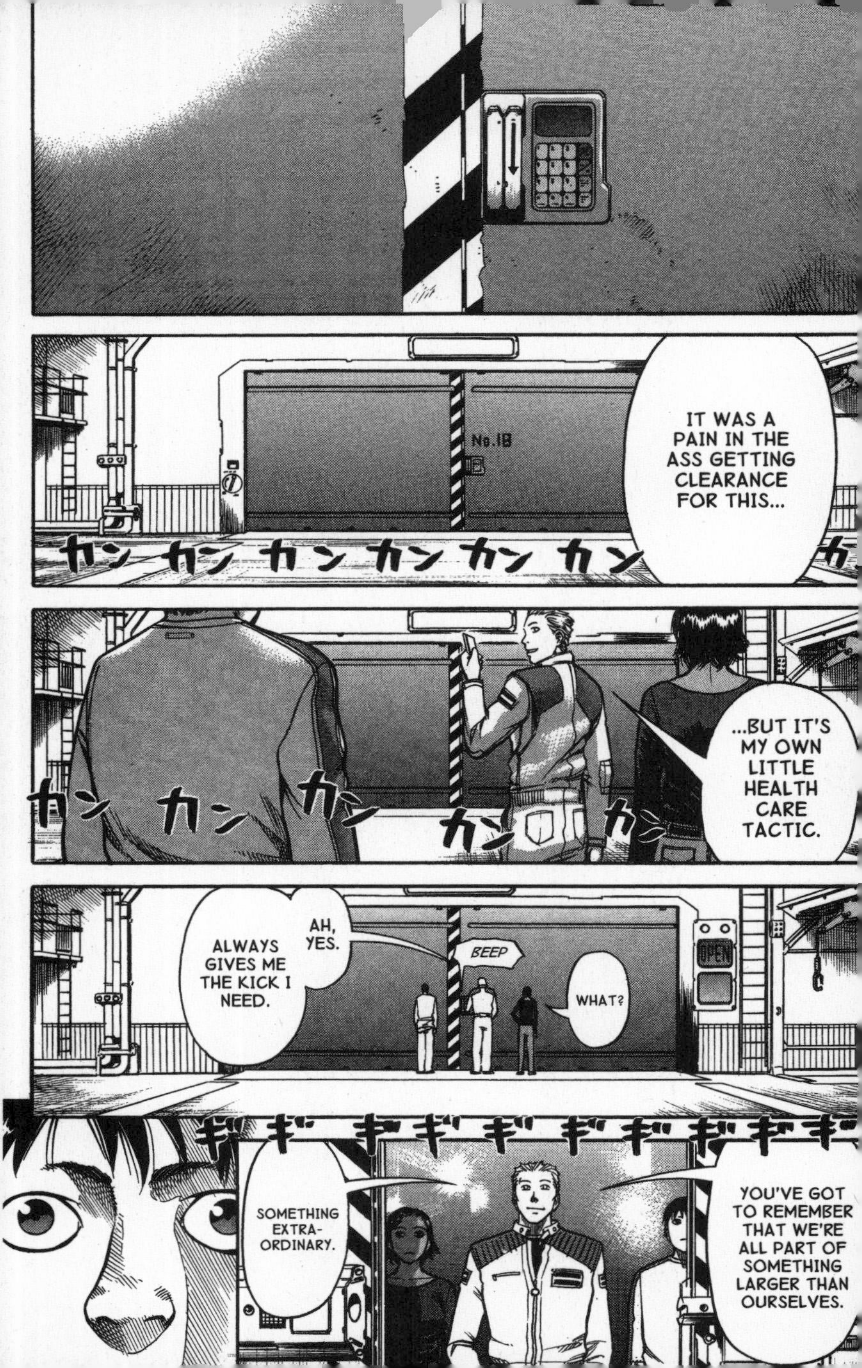
IT WAS A PAIN IN THE ASS GETTING CLEARANCE FOR THIS...
カン カン カン カン カン カン カン
No.18
...BUT IT'S MY OWN LITTLE HEALTH CARE TACTIC.
カン カン カン カン カン
OPEN
WHAT?
BEEP
AH, YES.
ALWAYS GIVES ME THE KICK I NEED.
ギギギギギギギギギ
YOU'VE GOT TO REMEMBER THAT WE'RE ALL PART OF SOMETHING LARGER THAN OURSELVES.
SOMETHING EXTRA-ORDINARY.

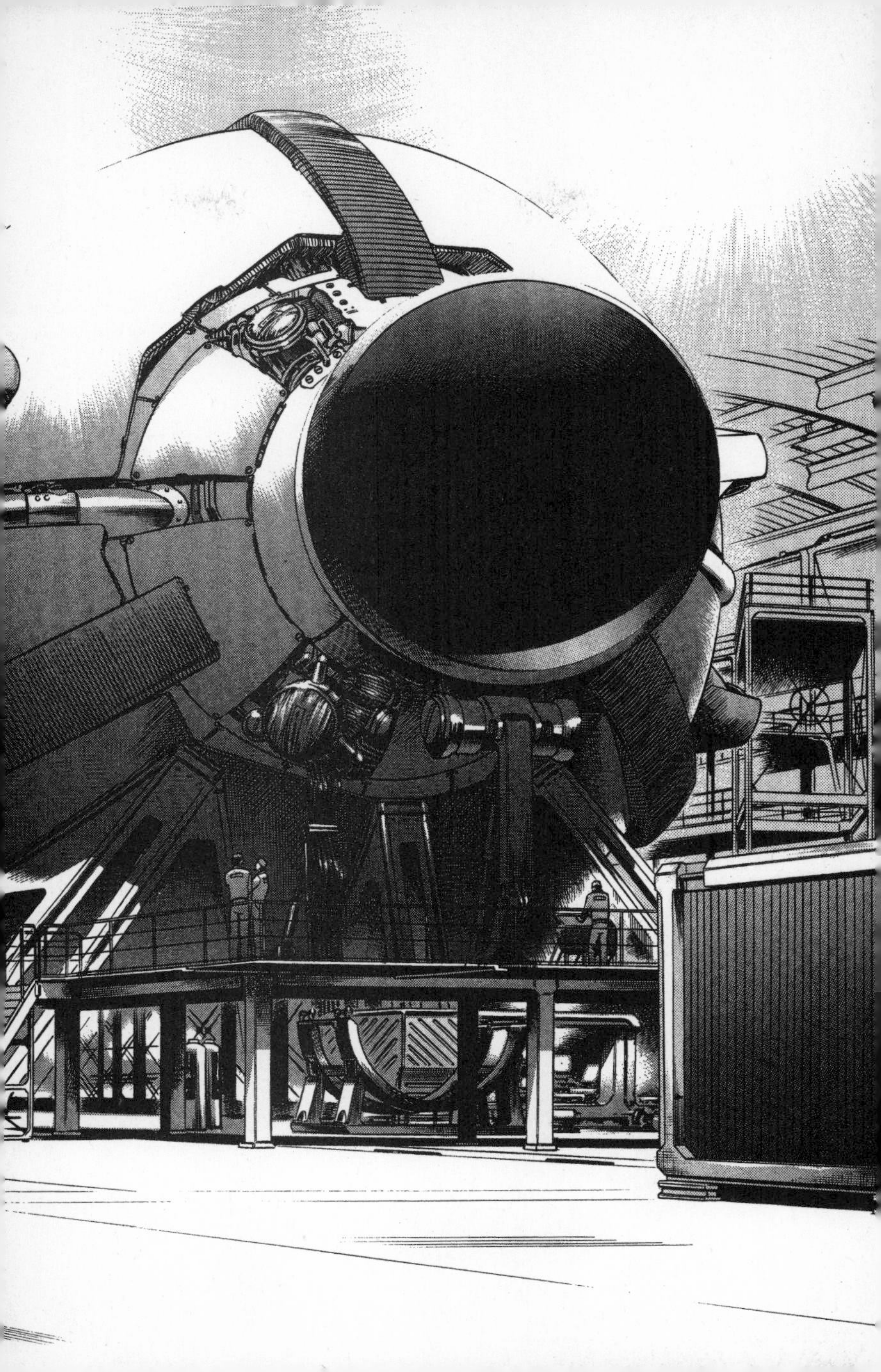

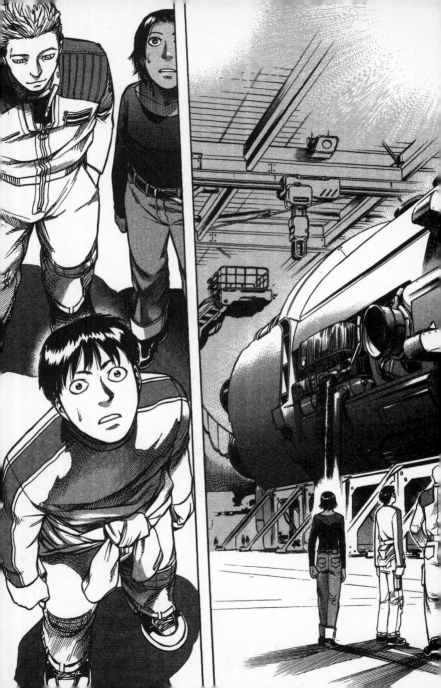

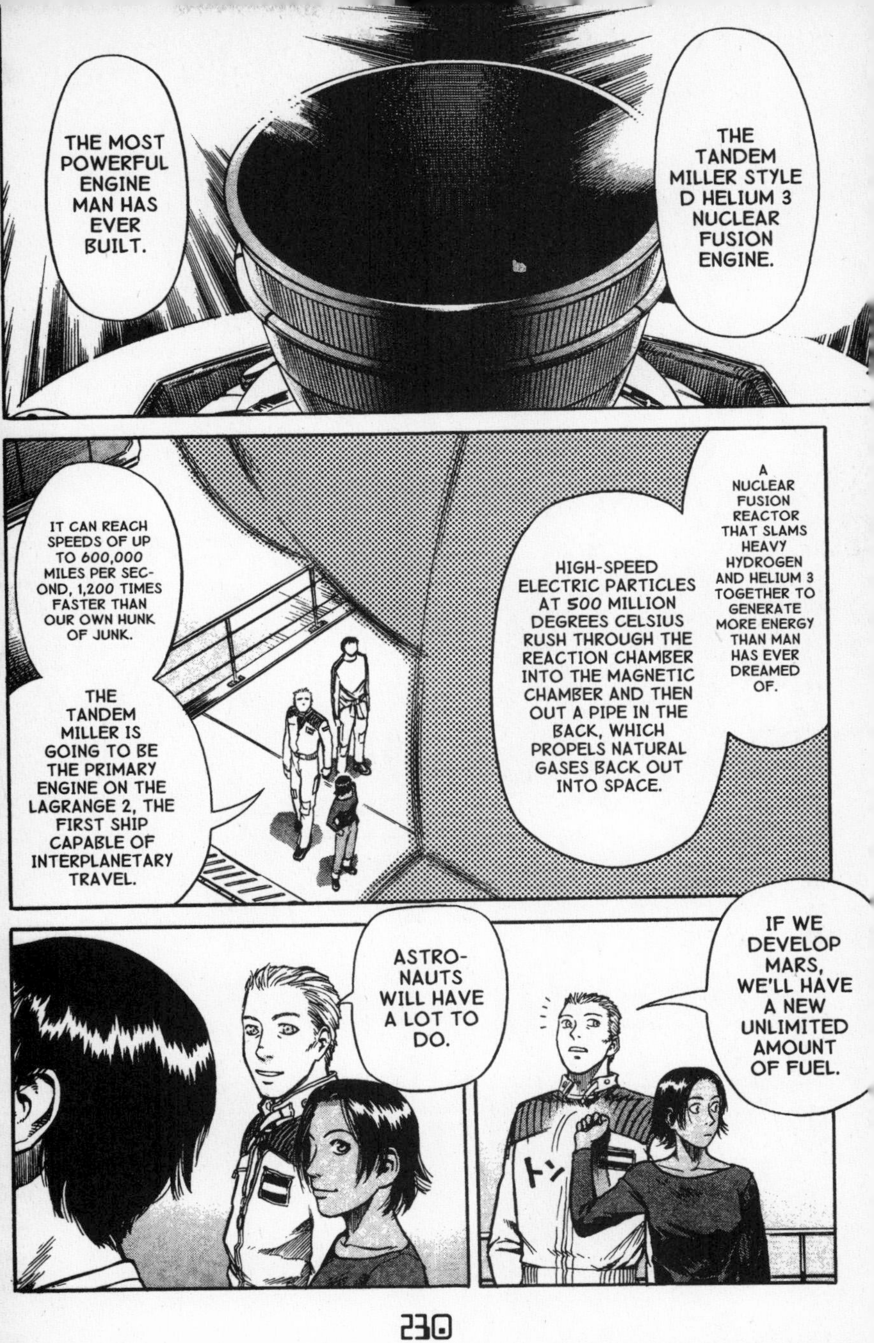
THE TANDEM MILLER STYLE D HELIUM 3 NUCLEAR FUSION ENGINE.
THE MOST POWERFUL ENGINE MAN HAS EVER BUILT.
A NUCLEAR FUSION REACTOR THAT SLAMS HEAVY HYDROGEN AND HELIUM 3 TOGETHER TO GENERATE MORE ENERGY THAN MAN HAS EVER DREAMED OF.
HIGH-SPEED ELECTRIC PARTICLES AT 500 MILLION DEGREES CELSIUS RUSH THROUGH THE REACTION CHAMBER INTO THE MAGNETIC CHAMBER AND THEN OUT A PIPE IN THE BACK, WHICH PROPELS NATURAL GASES BACK OUT INTO SPACE.
IT CAN REACH SPEEDS OF UP TO 600,000 MILES PER SEC-OND, 1,200 TIMES FASTER THAN OUR OWN HUNK OF JUNK.
THE TANDEM MILLER IS GOING TO BE THE PRIMARY ENGINE ON THE LAGRANGE 2, THE FIRST SHIP CAPABLE OF INTERPLANETARY TRAVEL.
IF WE DEVELOP MARS, WE'LL HAVE A NEW UNLIMITED AMOUNT OF FUEL.
トン
ASTRO-NAUTS WILL HAVE A LOT TO DO.

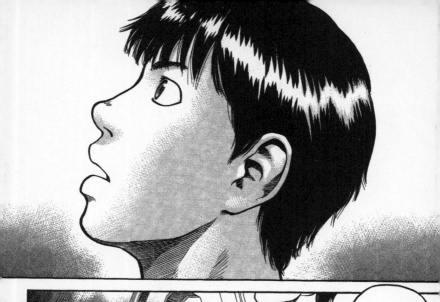

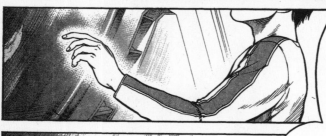

OUR VISION OF THE SOLAR SYSTEM WILL CHANGE RADICALLY.

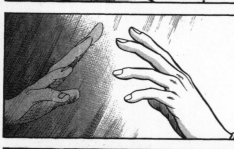

WE'LL NEED AMBITIOUS AND ENERGETIC ASTRONAUTS TO HELP USHER IN THIS FUTURE, HACHI.

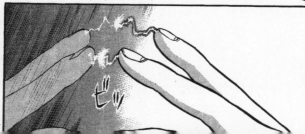

GUYS LIKE YOU.

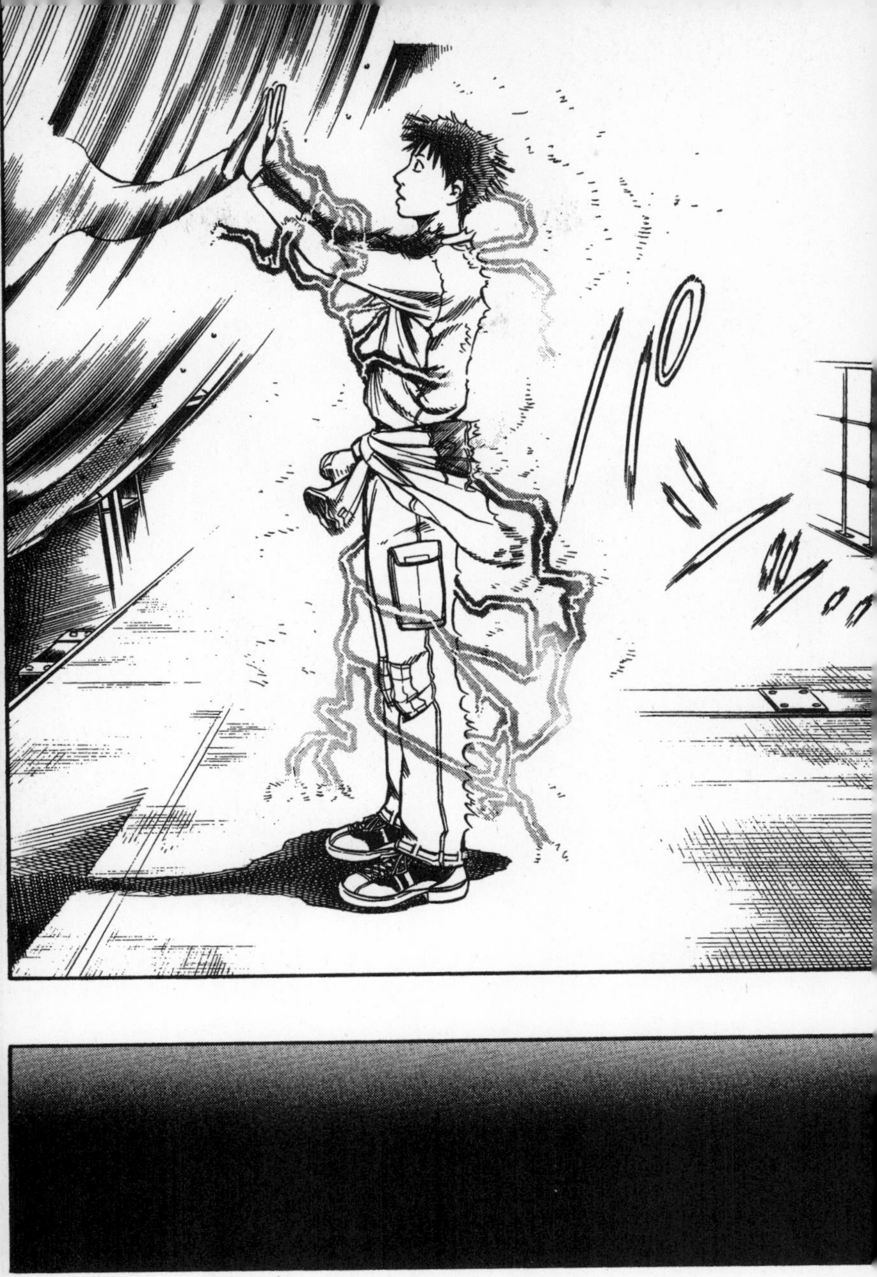

YOU SEEM RELAXED.
TELL ME.
WHAT'S ON YOUR MIND?

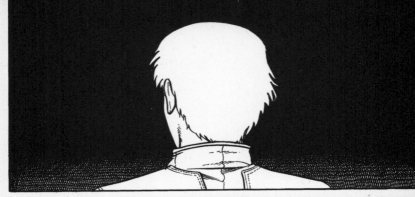

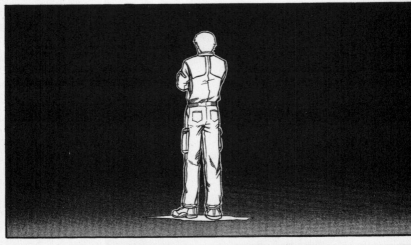

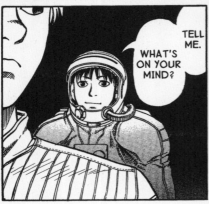

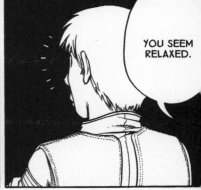

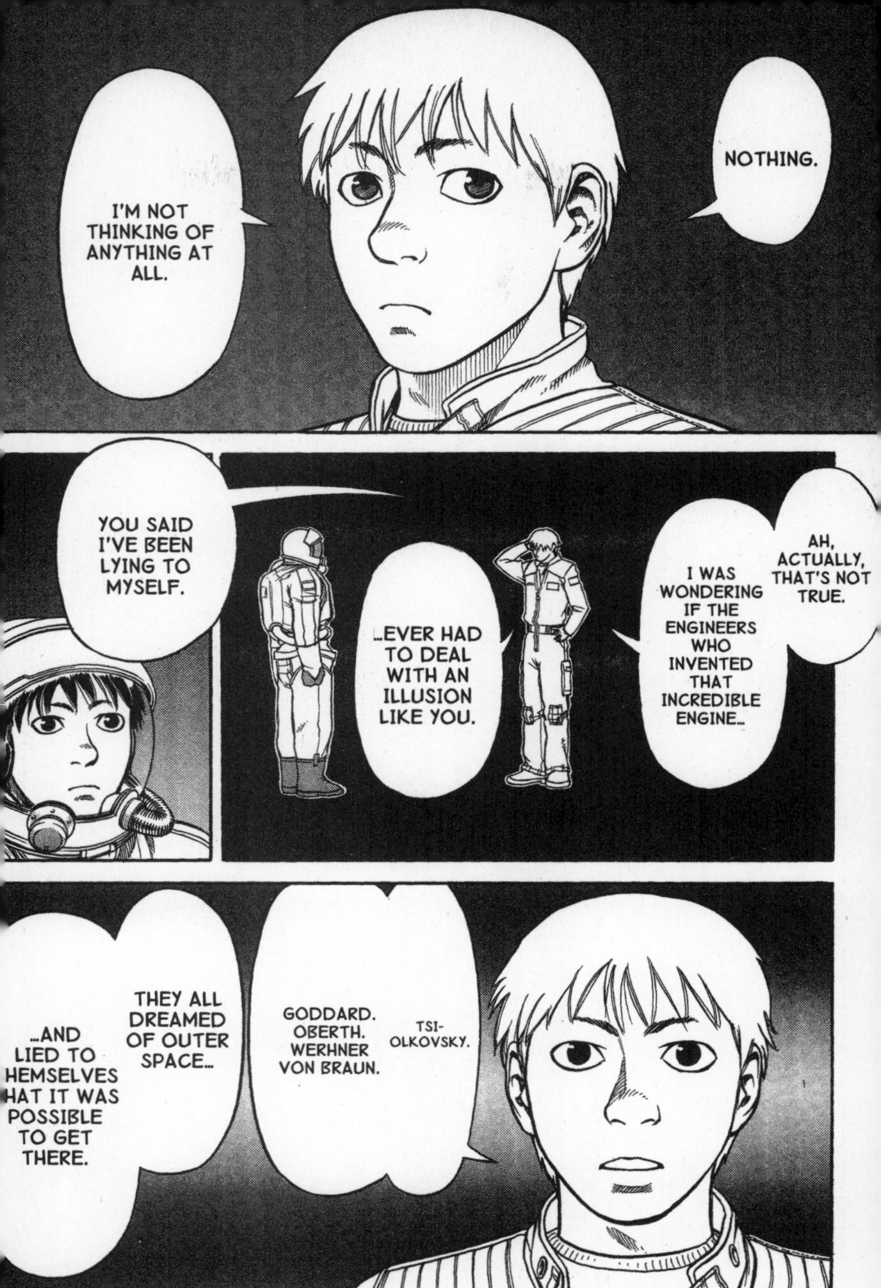

NOTHING.
I'M NOT THINKING OF ANYTHING AT ALL.
AH, ACTUALLY, THAT'S NOT TRUE.
I WAS WONDERING IF THE ENGINEERS WHO INVENTED THAT INCREDIBLE ENGINE...
...EVER HAD TO DEAL WITH AN ILLUSION LIKE YOU.
YOU SAID I'VE BEEN LYING TO MYSELF.
TSI-OLKOVSKY.
GODDARD. OBERTH. WERHNER VON BRAUN.
THEY ALL DREAMED OF OUTER SPACE...
...AND LIED TO HEMSELVES HAT IT WAS POSSIBLE TO GET THERE.

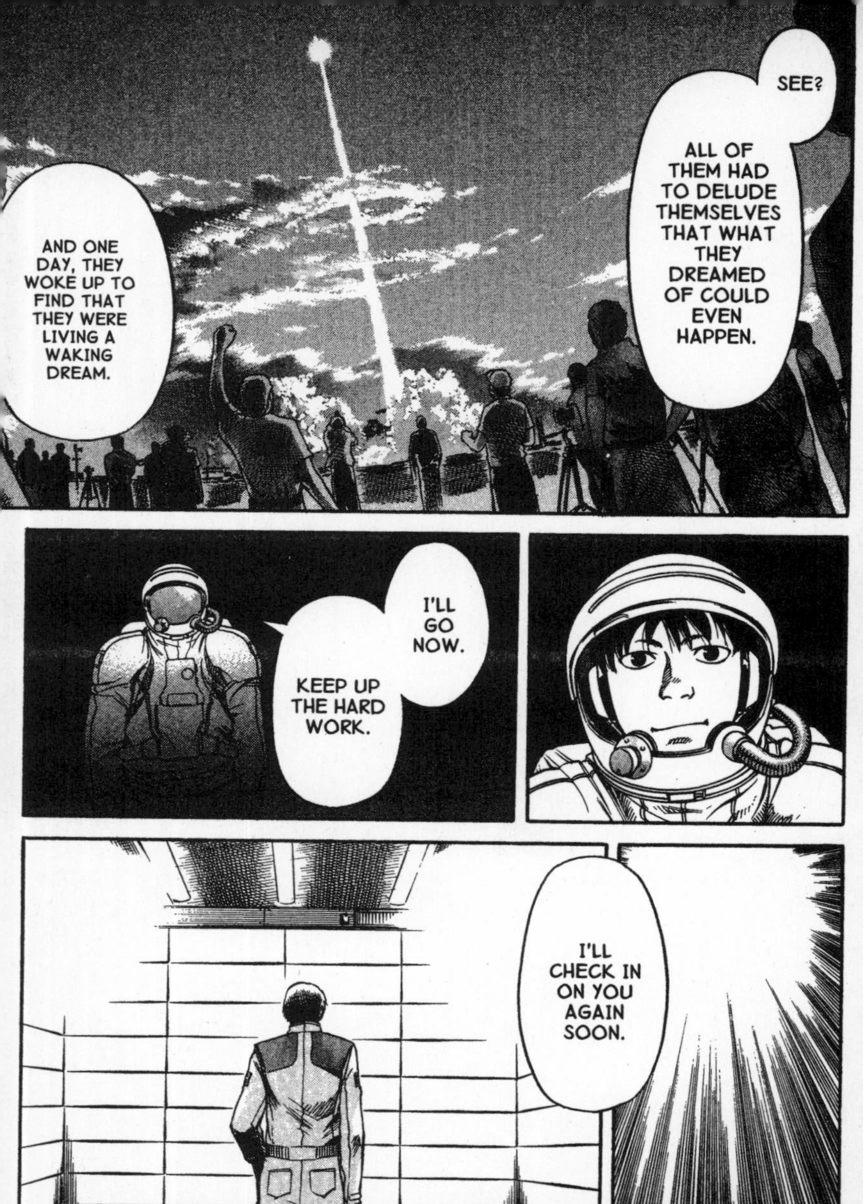
SEE?
ALL OF THEM HAD TO DELUDE THEMSELVES THAT WHAT THEY DREAMED OF COULD EVEN HAPPEN.
AND ONE DAY, THEY WOKE UP TO FIND THAT THEY WERE LIVING A WAKING DREAM.
I'LL GO NOW.
KEEP UP THE HARD WORK.
I'LL CHECK IN ON YOU AGAIN SOON.

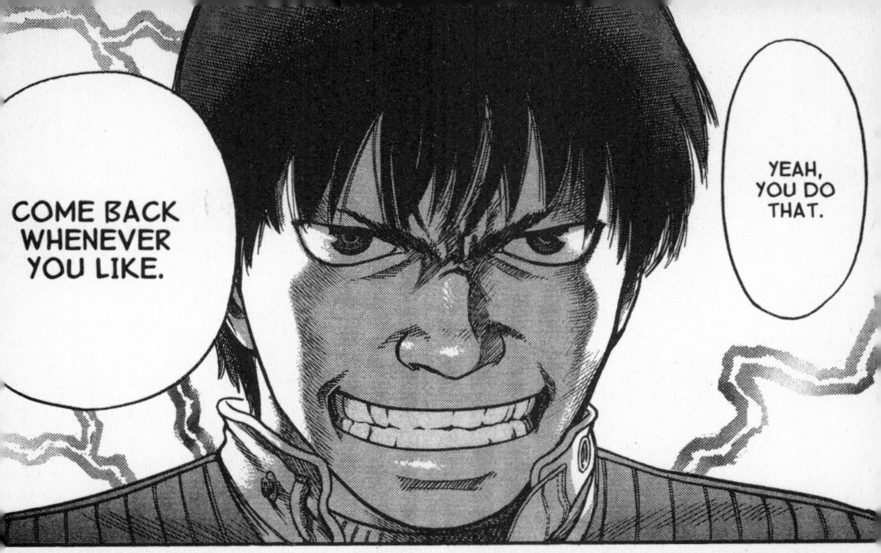
YEAH, YOU DO THAT.
COME BACK WHENEVER YOU LIKE.

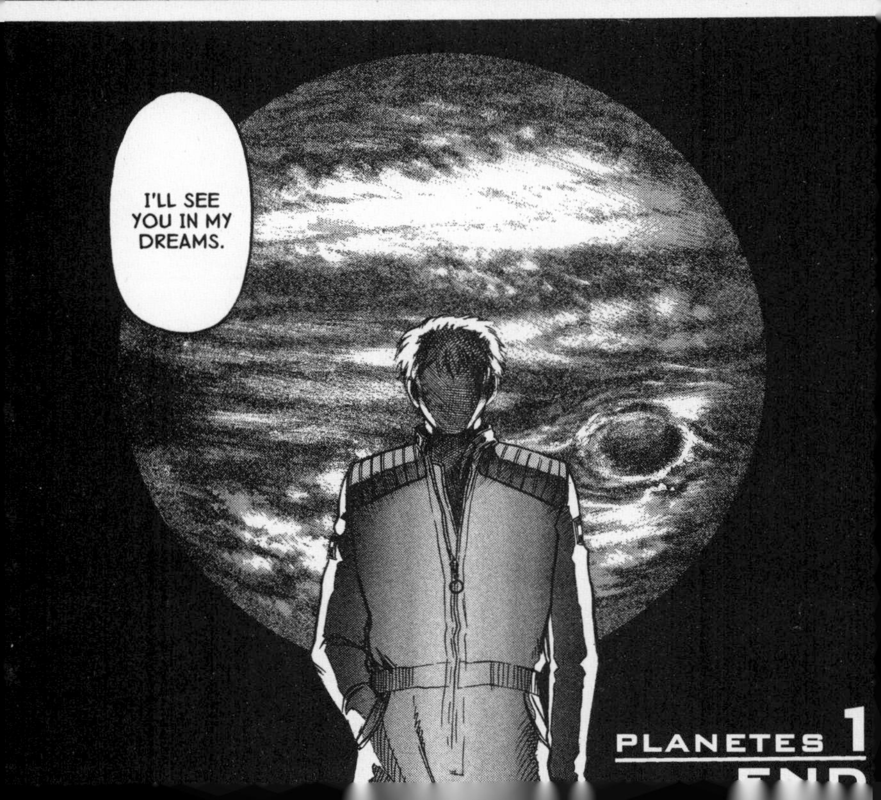
I'LL SEE YOU IN MY DREAMS.
PLANETES 1
END

PLANETES

NEXT VOLUME...

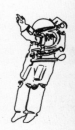

Hachimaki Hoshino's life collecting
space debris in orbit around Earth
doesn't satisfy the engine of his ambi-
tion. So the young rookie jumps when
the Earth Development Community
begins to look for a crew to man a new
Jupiter mission, which involves traveling
to the gas giant on the brand new
space ship Von Braun. Hachi's father,
Goro Hoshino, is the high-ranking
astronaut already assigned to be the
mission commander. But Hachi getting
selected for the mission will mean
proving the wealth of his knowledge in
space, demonstrating his capacity for
teamwork, and embracing love and
friendship as guiding principles for his
life.

A Brief History of Modern Rocket Science

Constantin Eduardovich Tsiolkovsky (1857-1935) — Russian scientist who created a logical proof for the possibility of space travel in a rocket. Noted as being the father of rocket technology and space flight, this Russian scientist penned *Free Space* (1883), a speculative work on life in space replete with a description of the effects of zero gravity and drawing of a spacecraft that could orient itself with reactive jets and change its position with propulsive jets, a concept that would later shape the design for spacecraft in the later half of the 20th century. In 1903, he first published the basic equation to reach space by rocket, an equation known to this day as the Tsiolkovsky Equation. Most influential in the future of space travel was Tsiolkovsky's idea that rockets needed to be built with liquid engines consisting of two components, a fuel and an oxidizer. However, he also posited that eventually space vessels could be outfitted with nuclear engines.

Dr. Robert H. Goddard (1882-1945) — A New England physicist who on March 16, 1926 became the first scientist to achieve flight with a liquid-fueled rocket. Unfortunately, his achievement impressed very little upon the US government, and Dr. Goddard was able to sustain his lifetime study of rocket technology only through various university and foundation grants. However, the world would certainly feel the impact of Dr. Goddard's work when the German's rained down V2 rockets on an unsuspecting England during World War II.

Hermann Julius Oberth (1894-1989) - Romanian-born German citizen whose thesis *The Rocket into Planetary Space* took the scientific world by storm in the early 20th Century, though the original draft was rejected by his doctoral committee, precluding him from acquiring the title doctor, a title that he was never anxious to embrace throughout the rest of his life. Oberth's biggest contribution to rocket propulsion was the concept of rocket sections. As the rocket burns its fuel, the mass of the rocket would remain the same, thereby making the rocket cylinder itself heavier in relation to the engine's ability to provide thrust. The solution: eject the parts of the rocket cylinder that were no longer needed.

Werhner von Braun (1912-1977) - German rocket science engineer who worked under Oberth, and, with his mentor, worked on the V2 rocket for the German Army during World War II. As the collapse of Nazi Germany became imminent, von Braun proved instrumental in shepherding his fellow scientists right into the hands of the Americans. Once in the US, and after a few years of indulging the military with his expertise in rocket technology, von Braun was able to steer away from developing rockets of destruction and concentrate on his true passion-space travel. In 1950, his team was transferred to Huntsville, Alabama where he eventually came to lead NASA's Marshall Space Flight Center.

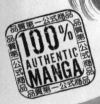

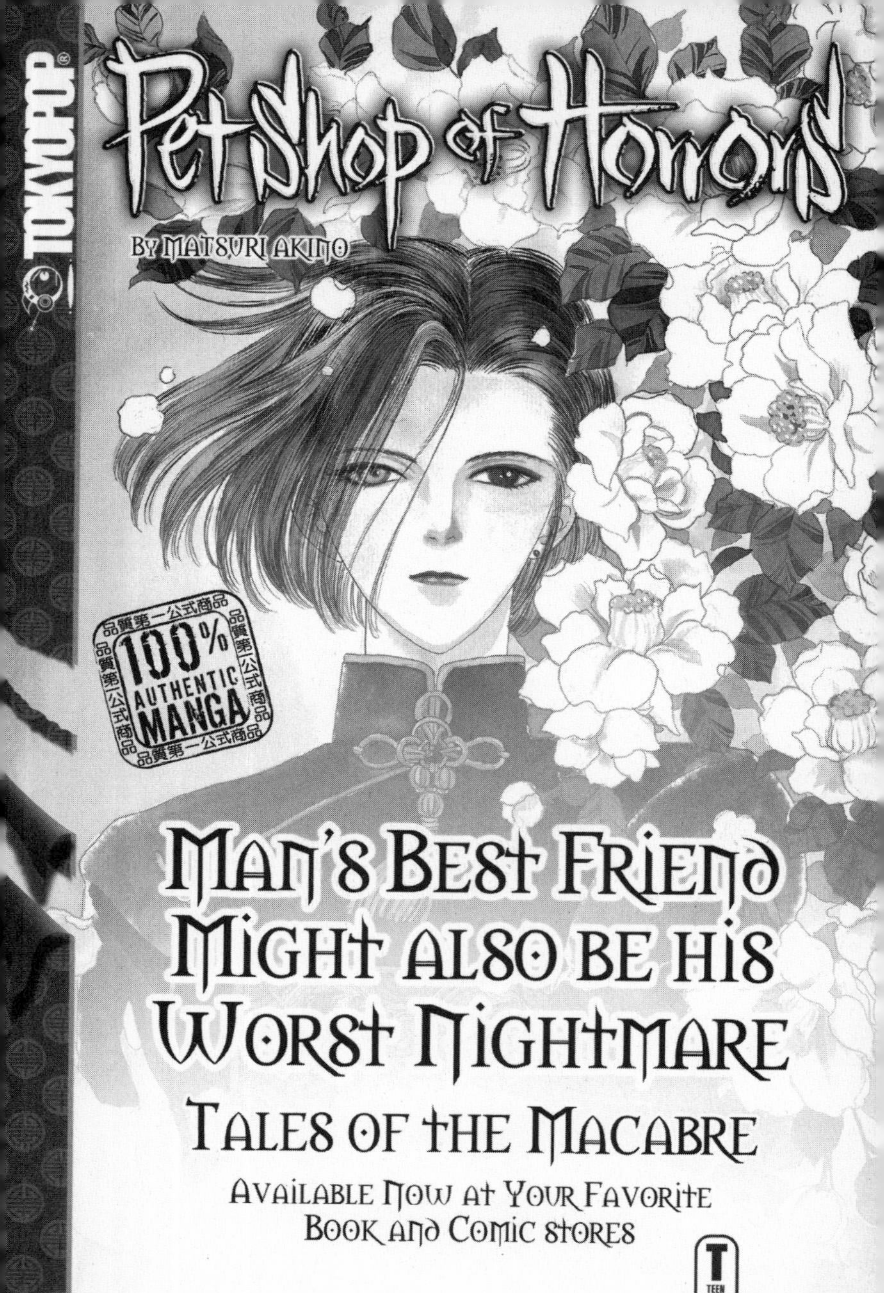

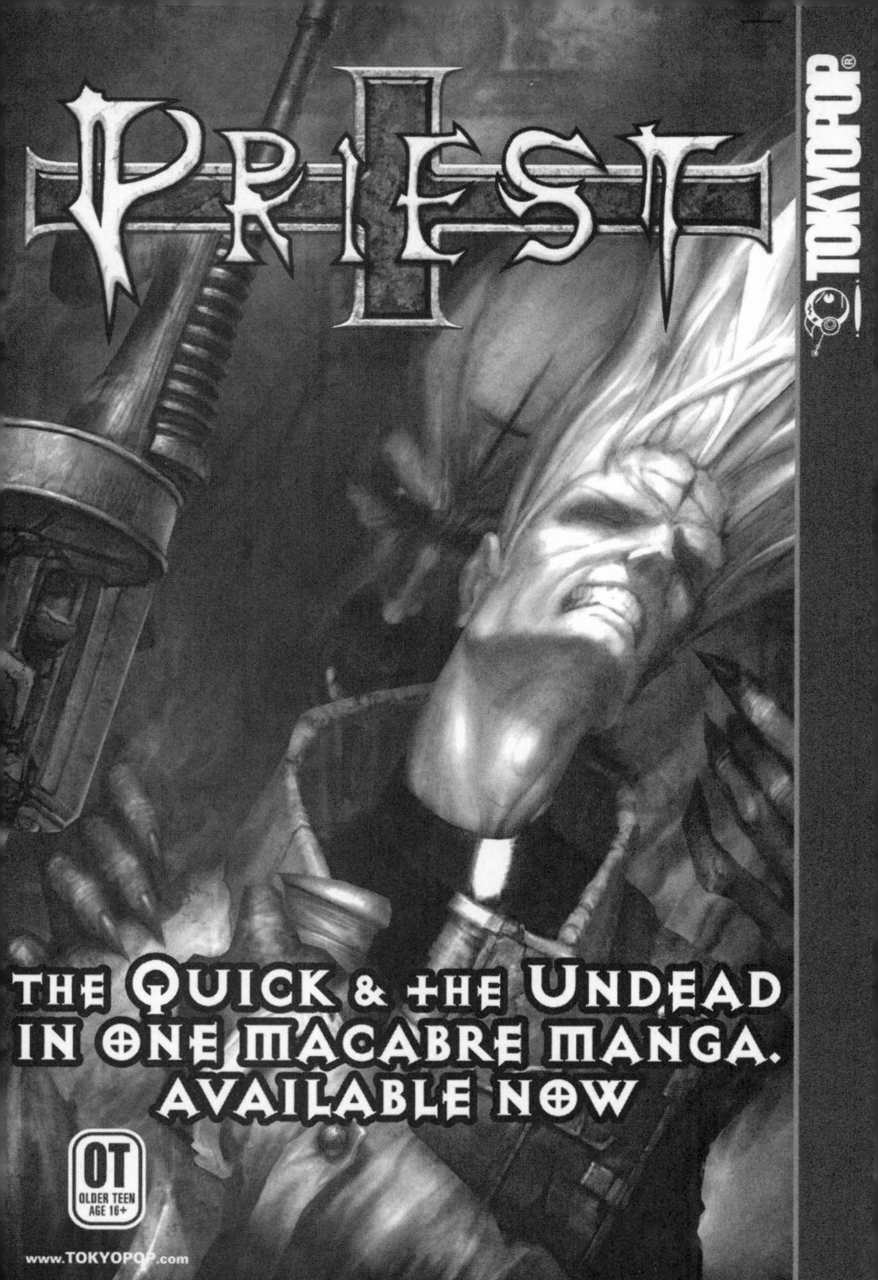
PRIEST
TOKYOPOP®
THE QUICK & THE UNDEAD
IN ONE MACABRE MANGA.
AVAILABLE NOW
OT
OLDER TEEN
AGE 16+
www.TOKYOPOP.com
PRIEST © MIN-WOO HYUNG. TOKYOPOP is a registered trademark of Mixx Entertainment Inc.

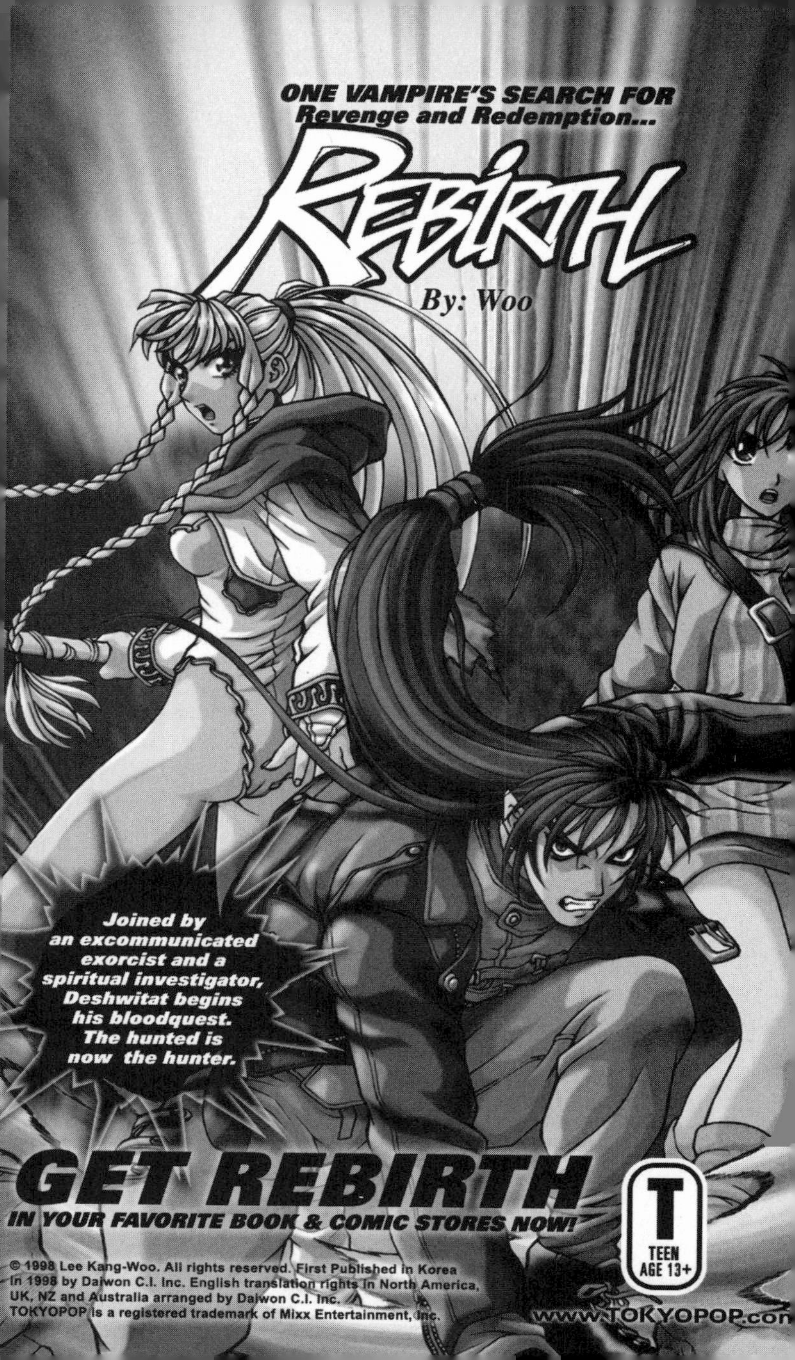

ONE VAMPIRE'S SEARCH FOR
Revenge and Redemption...

REBIRTH

By: Woo

Joined by
an excommunicated
exorcist and a
spiritual investigator,
Deshwitat begins
his bloodquest.
The hunted is
now the hunter.

GET REBIRTH
IN YOUR FAVORITE BOOK & COMIC STORES NOW!

T
TEEN
AGE 13+

www.TOKYOPOP.com

THE ORIGINAL INTERNATIONAL MAN OF MYSTERY

HE KEEPS HIS ENEMIES CLOSE . . . AND THE GIRLS CLOSER!

LUPIN III

BY MONKEY PUNCH

"...this is fun fantastic stuff...
Put on some club music, knock back
this baby with a chaser ...and see where
Kenichi Sonoda and *Cowboy Bebop*
got their cool."
— Animerica (December 2002)

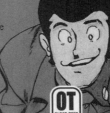

AMERICA'S MOST WANTED GRAPHIC NOVEL IN YOUR FAVORITE BOOK & COMIC STORES NOW . . . CHUM!

OT
OLDER TEEN
AGE 16+

www.TOKYOPOP.com

TOKYOPOP

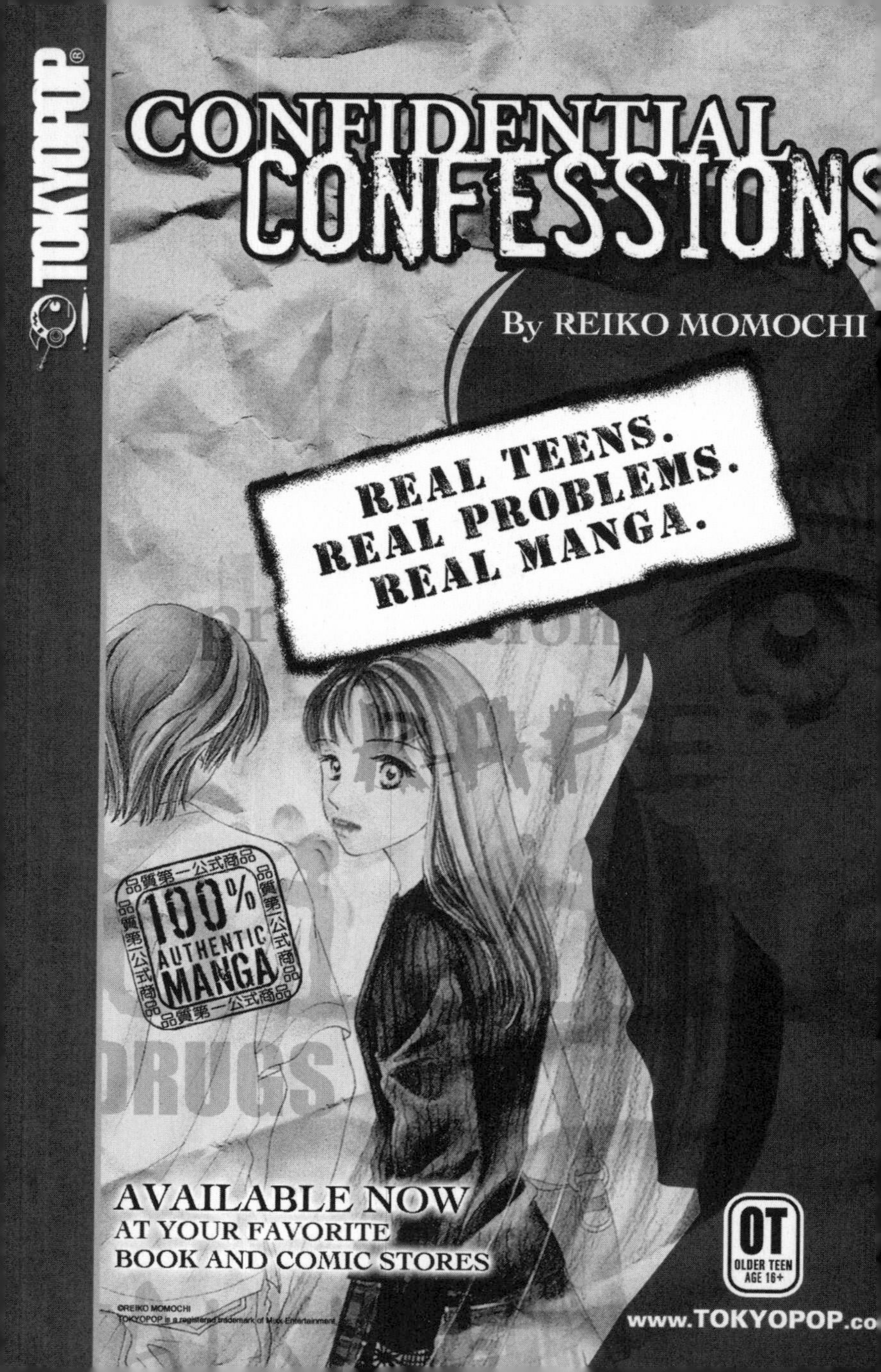
TOKYOPOP®
CONFIDENTIAL CONFESSIONS
By REIKO MOMOCHI
REAL TEENS.
REAL PROBLEMS.
REAL MANGA.
100% AUTHENTIC MANGA
品質第一公式商品
DRUGS
AVAILABLE NOW
AT YOUR FAVORITE
BOOK AND COMIC STORES
OT
OLDER TEEN AGE 16+
©REIKO MOMOCHI
TOKYOPOP is a registered trademark of Mixx Entertainment
www.TOKYOPOP.co

STOP!

This is the back of the book.
You wouldn't want to spoil a great ending!

This book is printed "manga-style," in the authentic Japanese right-to-left format. Since none of the artwork has been flipped or altered, readers get to experience the story just as the creator intended. You've been asking for it, so TOKYOPOP® delivered: authentic, hot-off-the-press, and far more fun!

DIRECTIONS

1
2
3
4
5
6
7
8
9
10

If this is your first time reading manga-style, here's a quick guide to help you understand how it works.

It's easy... just start in the top right panel and follow the numbers. Have fun, and look for more 100% authentic manga from TOKYOPOP®!

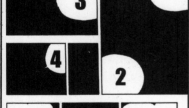

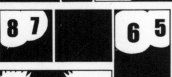

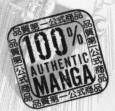